AF352279

POLITICAL THOUGHT AND THE
TUDOR COMMONWEALTH

POLITICAL THOUGHT AND THE TUDOR COMMONWEALTH

Deep structure, discourse and disguise

Edited by
Paul A. Fideler
and
T. F. Mayer

London and New York

First published 1992
by Routledge
11 New Fetter Lane, London, EC4P 4EE.

Simultaneously published in the USA and Canada
by Routledge
29 West 35th Street, New York, NY 10001

Phototypeset in 10 on 12 point Garamond by
Intype, London
Printed in Great Britain by
T. J. Press (Padstow) Ltd,
Padstow, Cornwall

British Library Cataloguing in Publication Data
A catalogue record for this
book is available from the
British Library.

Library of Congress Cataloging in Publication Data
Fideler, Paul A.
Political thought and the Tudor Commonwealth : deep structure,
discourse, and disguise / Paul A. Fideler and T. F. Mayer.
p. cm.
Includes bibliographical references and index.
1. Great Britain—Politics and government—1485–1603. 2. Great
Britain—History—Tudors, 1485–1603. 3. Political science—Great
Britain—History. 4. Great Britain—Economic policy. 5. Great
Britain—Social policy. I. Mayer, Thomas F. (Thomas Frederick),
1951– II. Title.
JN181.F53   1993
320.942—dc20   92–4645

ISBN 0–415–06672–7

Contents

Notes on contributors

Fred Conrad has taught at Washington University in St Louis, Missouri, and Augustana College in Rock Island, Illinois. He is completing *A Preservative Against Tyranny: The Public Career and Political Theology of Sir Thomas Elyot.*

Paul A. Fideler, Professor of History and Humanities at Lesley College in Cambridge, Massachusetts, is President of the North-east Conference on British Studies and, in 1992–3, is an ACLS Fellow in Humanities Curriculum Development at Harvard University. He is currently at work on *Policy Thought in Early Modern Britain: The Old Poor Law Tradition.*

Norman L. Jones is Professor of History and Associate Director of Liberal Arts and Sciences at Utah State University. He is author of *Faith by Statute, God and the Moneylenders,* and *The Parliaments of Elizabethan England,* as well as many articles on Elizabethan politics and religion.

Ben Lowe is Assistant Professor of History at Barry University in Miami, Florida. He has published articles on medieval and early modern political discourse, and is currently researching a book on the emergence of an English peace ethic, *The Problem of War and Ideas of Peace in England, 1337–1558.*

T. F. Mayer teaches history at Augustana College in Rock Island, Illinois, and is the author of *Thomas Starkey and the Commonweal* and numerous articles on Renaissance and Tudor intellectual history. He has an I. Tatti fellowship for the academic year 1992–3, and is completing *Reginald Pole, Prince and Prophet.*

A. J. Slavin, Justus Bier Distinguished Professor of the Humanities at the University of Louisville in Kentucky, is author of *Politics and Profit, The Precarious Balance,* and *The Tudor Age and Beyond.* He is at work on a study of Lord Chancellor Sir Thomas Wriosthesley: *Politics and Power.*

Neal Wood, Professor Emeritus of Political Science at York University in

Toronto, Ontario, is the author of numerous books including *The Politics of Locke's Philosophy* and *Cicero's Social and Political Thought*. He is completing *Foundations of Political Economy: Some Early Tudor Views on State and Society*.

D. R. Woolf, a member of the Department of History at Dalhousie University in Halifax, Nova Scotia, is the author of *The Idea of History in Early Stuart England*, and articles on the representation of the past in early modern England. He is currently at work on *Origins of Modern Historical Culture: Studies in the Perception of the Past in Early Modern England*.

Acknowledgements

This volume owes much to the good offices of Patricia Tatspaugh, acting executive director of the Folger Institute in 1990, and the staff of the Folger Shakespeare Library, where all but one of the contributors assembled in May of that year for a highly productive two-day conference devoted to the volume. Three of the authors benefited especially from the opportunity to present their work at the Late Medieval and Early Modern Colloquium at Dalhousie University. Finally, we could not have asked for more encouragement, patience and efficiency than we received from our editors at Routledge, Claire L'Enfant and Louise Snell, and from editorial manager Sarah Pearsall and desk editor Sarah-Jane Woolley.

Abbreviations

AHR	*American Historical Review*
APC	*Acts of the Privy Council*
BIHR	*Bulletin of the Institute of Historical Research*
Bodl.	Bodleian Library, Oxford
BL	British Library
C4S	Camden Fourth Series, London, Royal Historical Society
CSPSp	Pascual de Gazangos et al. (eds) *Calendar of State Papers, Spanish*, London, HMSO, 1862–1954
CSPV	R. Brown (ed.) *Calendar of State Papers and Manuscripts . . . in . . . Venice*, London, Longman, 1864–98
EcHR	*Economic History Review*
EETS	Early English Text Society
EHR	*English Historical Review*
Erasmus, *Education*	Desiderius Erasmus, *The Education of a Christian Prince*, trans. Lester K. Born, New York, Columbia University Press, 1936
HJ	*Historical Journal*
JBS	*Journal of British Studies*
JEccH	*Journal of Ecclesiastical History*
JHI	*Journal of the History of Ideas*
L&P	J. S. Brewer et al. (eds) *Letters and Papers, Foreign and Domestic of the Reign of Henry VIII*, London, Longman, Green, 1862–1932
P&P	*Past and Present*
PRO	Public Record Office, London
PS	Parker Society, London, Cambridge University Press
SCJ	*Sixteenth Century Journal*
SP	State Papers (in the PRO)
STC	*A Short-title Catalogue of Books printed in England, Scotland and Ireland . . . 1475–1640*, A. W. Pollard and G. R. Redgrave (eds), London, Bibliographical Society, 1926

STC²	*A Short-title Catalogue* . . . , 2nd edn rev. and enl., W. A. Jackson, F. J. Ferguson and K. F. Pantzer (eds), London, Bibliographical Society, 1976–91
StPhil	*Studies in Philology*
TRHS	*Transactions of the Royal Historical Society*

Introduction: the study of Tudor political thought

A pervasive sense of something amiss in the commonwealth characterized the Tudor years. Combined with the state's expanding pretensions in social and religious matters, this brought the government up against a variety of practical problems and challenges to its authority. In the process, confusions that inhered in the very notion of commonwealth became apparent. Was the commonwealth a moral community nourished by mutual regard, custom and traditional religion, or was it a civil body delimited by dynastic and constitutional claims and shaped by government initiatives? How was the commonwealth's proper order affected by greed and over-reaching or by laziness and lack of deference? How was it endangered by injustice and imperial claims or by heresy and insurrection? These questions and their like required fresh thinking under the broad rubric of 'political thought'. Nevertheless, Tudor political ideas and culture have received relatively little scrutiny for almost four decades.

The chapters in this volume begin to redress that deficiency, as well as to illustrate an array of methods and theoretical perspectives that can benefit the study of early modern intellectual history. They address nodal points in Tudor political thinking close to the praxis end of the theory–praxis continuum: political uses of the past, approaches to resistance, the changing role of counsel, the formulation of political economy, and the shifting policy debates and proposals surrounding war and peace, poverty, usury and bankruptcy. While the chapters differ a good deal in method, they all share to a greater or lesser degree in the orientations of the 'new' history of political thought, political anthropology and sociology, and literary historicism.[1]

In 1953 Christopher Morris declared that there had been little or no 'political' thought in the Tudor years, and that little had put society, not the state, in the priority position. Sir Geoffrey Elton, who endorsed Morris's views, affirmed far more strikingly the relative insignificance of Tudor political thought in *The Tudor Revolution in Government*, which appeared in the same year.[2] 'Whigs', the champions of 'decentralized and popular freedom', had written too much English history, according to Elton. Their bias blinded them to the other root of England's 'exceptional' history, its 'strong, efficient, and centralized administration'. Historians also had gone 'too far' in emphasizing the continuity of 'medieval' political and social structures well into the sixteenth century. Elton, attempting to revive interest in Tudor politics, if not political thought, insisted that the sixteenth century had produced 'something quite new in England'. In making his case that in the 1530s Thomas Cromwell transformed England's medieval Household government into a modern bureaucratic state, Elton called for renewed attention to the study of administration.

As he saw it, this revolution 'coincided' with changing social and political structures and 'accompanied, resulted from, and in a manner assisted in' the making of the early modern 'monarchical nation state'. At the same time, he played down the significance of ideas. The 'general intellectual and spiritual' consequences of the Revolution 'came later – as effects not causes', and 'noticeable changes in mental atmosphere' did not accompany the fundamental administrative developments. In England, at least, political events are 'commonly the result of physical forces and personalities', and they precede 'mental reorientation'.[3] While he concedes the historian's concern with 'all those human sayings, thoughts, deeds, and sufferings which occurred in the past and have left present deposit', his own predilection has been for the workings of government as revealed in its archival records. These and Cromwell's abundant extant correspondence permitted Elton to glimpse 'the inwardness of events' in the 1530s.[4]

Elton's compelling and carefully buttressed view of Tudor politics and his confident articulation of an uncomplicated, positivist historical method would dominate Tudor studies for a full generation. As one commentator on his influence puts it, Elton not only told us 'what happened and why . . . but also taught us what history is and how to practise it'.[5]

Earlier historians assumed that ideas had played an important role in Tudor statecraft, although they disagreed about how distinct Tudor government and policy were from their medieval counterparts. J. W. Allen, for instance, believed that the heritage of Ockham, Wyclif and Marsiglio presaged the requisite 'psychological' changes supporting the imposition of secular authority over the church; Henry VIII merely adapted them to a religiously grounded doctrine of obedience. Later, S. B. Chrimes held that Tudor monarchy rested on medieval constitutional foundations. Franklin L. Baumer, on the other hand, concluded that the Tudor 'theory of kingship' departed so 'radically' from the theory and 'political psychology' of the fifteenth century as to create the most 'striking contrast' in English history.[6] Elton weighed in on the Baumer side but with much different effect. The contrast, as Elton saw it, was not merely one from fifteenth- to sixteenth-century styles of government but from 'medieval' to 'modern'. Cromwell, the first 'modern minister' in England, in the manner of a Renaissance artist, put his personal stamp on the entire process, from archives to statutes. His crafting of the royal supremacy and elevation of the importance of statutory law 'destroyed the foundations of medieval polity and society and put something new in their place'.[7]

In his subsequent books, Elton turned to narrative and retold first the 'tragic' and then the 'comic' story of the Tudor struggle for constitutional reconciliation. In *Reform and Reformation: England, 1509–1558* (1977), the last of his important narrative studies, Elton 'reconsiders' somewhat his estimate of Cromwell's particular genius and success, but neither 'recants nor denounces' his original story. His later Cromwell is more an evangelical Protestant, influenced a bit by humanist ideas, and takes advantage of some movement away from Household government that had already begun in the fifteenth century.[8] But as brilliant and ground-breaking work always does, Elton's eventually provoked a fresh look at many of the pieties about Cromwell, Protestantism and the nature of the 1530s 'revolution' that his work had done so much to establish.

Revisions of Elton's thesis have developed generally along two lines. The first, following his lead, draws on archival and documentary research for the most part and focuses on Parliament, the Privy Council, the larger Court, the common law, the Court of Star Chamber, and royal and government finances. This scholarship has transformed Elton's precise moment of administrative modernization in the 1530s into a far more chaotic process of indeterminate beginning and end. For example, Jennifer Loach finds that Parliament became a more 'exciting' arena and the composition of both the Lords and the Commons changed during the 1530s. However, these developments were well under way in the fifteenth century, extended into the 1580s, and reflected throughout medieval 'patrimonial' values.[9] John Guy maintains that Cromwell's reconstruction of the Council simply carried forward Wolsey's 1526 Eltham Ordinance and the Council's permanent secretariat was established only in 1540. Furthermore, the Courts of Star Chamber and Requests continued through the 1530s as before and were not adjusted to the new-style Council until 1544.[10] David Starkey, analysing the Household, sees the formation of the Privy Chamber between 1490 and 1519 as the most significant new departure. Because of its susceptibility to factionalization, the Chamber was implacably opposed by Wolsey, the Court outsider, and later by Cromwell until, after 1536, he could use its capabilities to extend his own power. The Household, then, became stronger not weaker under Cromwell. Furthermore, Starkey finds that in both Wolsey and Cromwell expedient manoeuvring for power took precedence over the development of any particular model or form of government.[11]

The other challenge is a reaction to Elton's insistent privileging of Cromwell's outlook on policy initiatives in the 1530s. Most often the argument has centred on the relative importance of humanism and

Protestantism in the climate of thought within which Cromwell operated, but historians have also disagreed about just when policy thought aimed at enhancing the commonwealth began and who initiated it. These questions, like those about the role of ideas in Tudor government, antedated Elton's thesis. In the earlier histories, Tudor attempts to achieve social reforms and expanded civil freedoms were usually seen as the foundations or anticipations of the modern, liberal British state. A. F. Pollard at the turn of the century had given the nod to Protector Somerset – a 'seer', 'born before his time', Protestantism, the Commonwealth 'Party', and the brief years of Edward VI. The Lord Protector's repeal of heresy and treason laws, support for the Reformation, and 'sympathy' for the poor greatly appealed to Pollard.[12] In the 1940s W. Gordon Zeeveld made the case for the importance of humanism and its continuity as a force for reform from the late fifteenth century well into Elizabeth's reign. The post-Reformation 'propagandist humanists', figures as different as Thomas Starkey, Thomas Wilson and John Ponet, used their scholarly skills to find 'an anchor for expediency in tradition'. However, the 'new and more liberal context' they brought to this meant that they made an 'extraordinarily germinal' contribution to the history of political ideas.[13]

Elton accounted for whatever influence humanism had on his evangelical Protestant Cromwell by declaring that humanist values had already become pervasive by the 1530s and thus had no special significance in accounting for a sharp change of direction in those years.[14] Nevertheless, a number of scholars have continued to stress the importance of humanism before, during, and after the 1530s. James K. McConica argued that Erasmian humanism remained intact, and the Yale edition of Thomas More's *Utopia* deepened interest in More and Christian humanism. Subsequently, J. J. Scarisbrick claimed that Wolsey actually set humanistic goals for the Henrician government.[15] Margo Todd has traced the half-life of Christian humanism into the early seventeenth century in the 'Oxbridge' curricula and the lesson books of their students.[16]

Recently, John B. Gleason has reopened the question of 'Christian humanism' in his provocative study of one of its supposed founders, John Colet.[17] A similar approach to Tudor political thought has raised many of the same questions about the nature of humanism. Loosely called 'intellectual biography', this important lens on the 1530s appears in T. F. Mayer's careful analysis of Thomas Starkey.[18] Mayer provides us with a figure less influential in actual policy-making than heretofore assumed by Elton. On the other hand, in Starkey we see more clearly the presence of Italian humanism and evangelism, as well as precise plans for a revival of aristocratic government, which he may have shared with his patron, Reginald Pole.

Arthur B. Ferguson and David Starkey have each challenged Elton's emphasis on the new and unique policy climate in the 1530s, and placed the beginning of serious policy deliberations in the fifteenth century. Ferguson finds it as early as the 'Libell of Englische Policye' (1436); the commitment was taken up later in the century by Fortescue and again in the sixteenth century, first by humanists and then in the 1540s and 1550s by Protestant reformers. Although none of the policy advocates denied the moral nature of society, they extolled 'realism' in social analysis and advocated the application of law and government initiative to improve that which was malleable. In the 1530s Starkey provided perhaps the most insightful contemporary description of 'policy' and Richard Morison defended upward mobility into policy-making roles for the bright and learned. Nevertheless, Ferguson viewed both as transition figures rather than 'medieval' or 'modern' ones.[19]

Drawing largely on David Morgan's unpublished work, David Starkey holds that a new political language of 'commonwealth' was emerging in the mid-fifteenth century from the tumultuous events of Cade's Rebellion and the deepening struggle between Yorkists and Lancastrians. Fortescue may have laid its groundwork as early as the 1440s with his notion of a *regnum politicum et regale* in which the king co-operated with his Council to rule the realm, by contrast with the arbitrary monarchy of France. Discourse about the 'commonwealth' centred on a revived royal Council that would protect the king's prerogatives at the same time that it provided him with disinterested advice and helped him plan for the public welfare.[20] Another revision which detracts from Cromwell's role as commonwealth policy designer is John Guy's view that Christopher St German, soon to be Protestant but not employed by Cromwell, sketched the 'reform by statute' agenda perhaps as early as 1530.[21]

Recent scholarship yields an uncertain estimate of the importance of the Edwardian years for policy ideas and initiatives. Whitney R. D. Jones anatomized commonwealth thought into a spectrum from the Catholics More, Pole and Thomas Lupset to the Protestants William Tyndale, Hugh Latimer and Robert Crowley and from the politically conservative Thomas Elyot to the liberal and reform-minded Duke of Somerset. All agreed that the state should assume responsibility for the moral condition of the commonwealth that had previously resided with the church. W. K. Jordan claimed the most for Somerset; his portrait revealed a committed, if ineffectual, reformer and avid supporter of the Commonwealthmen. M. L. Bush revised the estimate substantially, constructing a Somerset much less interested in social reform than Jordan's and more concerned with his personal wealth and pursuing war with Scotland. Professor Elton has characteristically offered the boldest reassessment of the Edwardian policy climate and its importance in the larger setting of Tudor reform. He considers the Commonwealth Party a figment of Pollard's imagination, which since has become a platitude of Edwardian historiography. Furthermore, of all the social thinkers of the Edwardian years only Sir Thomas

Smith had anything of insight and use to offer his contemporaries. Elton finds Smith to be centrally important also as an actual link between the policy environment of Cromwell in the 1530s and William Cecil's in the 1560s.[22]

The Elizabethan years are as heavily contested historiographical turf as are those of Henry VIII. Recent scholarship leaves uncertain whether Calvinist militance or Catholic resistance was the more significant church issue. We have been learning about the nature of the Reformation – to what degree it was a top-down or a bottom-up phenomenon – and its political importance, both at the centre and in the Puritan 'citadels', from the work of Patrick Collinson and Peter Lake. An examination of William Harrison's mental world by J. G. R. Parry reveals the importance that he and perhaps other like-minded provincial Puritans placed in their quest to restore the 'True Church' drawn from their reading of ecclesiastical history. This explains their concerns not only with Elizabethan church polity, but also with 'commonwealth' issues of a political and social nature. At the same time, Christopher Haigh claims that Catholicism's presence at the grass roots persisted well into the Elizabethan years.[23]

Opinion remains divided on the degree to which Elizabethan politics should be seen as part of the 'causal sequence' that culminated in the Civil War.[24] It is beginning to appear that we may best think of two Elizabethan reigns, with the divide coming sometime in the 1580s. Certainly, government policy activity clusters in two distinct periods, the 1560s and early 1570s and the mid-1590s to 1603. The methodological priorities of the 'new social history' have largely shaped Elizabethan policy studies since the mid-1960s. Peter Clark, Paul Slack, A. L. Beier and Keith Wrightson have provided ingenious local, demographic and institutional studies of a range of Elizabethan social problems and local policy initiatives, from responses to vagrancy to implementing the Reformation. Only recently, however, have Elizabethan policy historians begun to call for greater attention to the ideas and ideologies that were informing policy at both the centre and in the localities.[25] Several of the authors in this volume respond to that call.

Without saying so, Morris, Elton and their followers graphically demonstrated the truth of Peter Laslett's memorable assessment in the 1950s that a crisis of confidence in contemporary political philosophy rendered it 'for the present, at least . . . dead'.[26] In the study of the seventeenth and eighteenth centuries, unlike that of the sixteenth, this situation triggered a more resourceful pursuit of the history of political theory. Over the next two decades Laslett, Michael Oakeshott, Quentin Skinner and J. G. A. Pocock developed the methodological foundations for a new contextual history of political thought that they hoped would eschew the old history's anachronistic treatment of texts for ideological, teleological, and canonical purposes. This 'new' history of political thought has now begun to revive interest in Tudor intellectual history and is one of the major theoretical orientations behind this volume.

Laslett provided the first fruit of this effort in his 1960 edition of Locke's *Two Treatises*. His searching Introduction to the texts emphasized the local and immediate concerns that shaped Locke's writing. In effect, Laslett sought to remove the *Two Treatises* from the ahistorical canon and reinsert them into the contingencies, pressures and linguistic options of their historical context.[27] Oakeshott brought Humean and Burkean predispositions to his effort to reclaim 'tradition' from its 'abridgement' by ideology, which reduced a tradition's 'full dimensions' and extracted behaviour and thought from their setting. Far from having an a priori 'destination' political activity is instead like 'sailing on a boundless sea'. Politics is ever-new, concrete activity and its accretion over time into a tradition. And one's earliest encounter with the present surface of a tradition is similar to exposure to a language; it is accepted and used before its grammar is understood. Since people's reflections about what has happened are as important as their behaviour itself, a tradition is 'nothing but a history of the problems philosophers have detected and the manner of solutions they have proposed'. Thus an important aspect of political education is a 'historical investigation' into the 'legend of [a society's] fortunes' which reveals the 'intimations', 'sympathies' or 'tendencies which are afoot' in its tradition.[28]

Skinner was convinced that the inclination of historians of political thought to be too concerned with 'perennial problems' and 'universal truths' had led to the reification of doctrines, the imposition of 'preconceived paradigms', histories of 'abstractions', and undue preoccupation with 'inner coherence', 'anticipations' and 'influences'. Skinner's antidote was to accept the 'logical and empirical criteria' that 'apply to the whole enterprise of making and understanding statements'. The 'history of an idea' is more usefully approached as a history of the 'various statements made with [a] given expression'. The historian is a decoder of the authorial intentions of specific utterances within their wider *linguistic* and social contexts, with 'context' understood to be a 'framework' rather than a 'determinant' for what an author said. But, why study the history of political thought if it can no longer be seen as a grand march to the present? For one thing, a 'dialogue between philosophical discussion and historical evidence' can be developed by studying the conditions under which languages change. For another, historical studies are the 'key to our self-awareness'; they help us to overcome the 'unrecognized constraints' placed on us by our own society and to appreciate the 'essential variety of viable moral assumptions and political commitments'.[29]

In his indispensable *The Foundations of Modern Political Thought* (1978), Skinner affirmed that 'political life itself sets the main problem for the political theorist'. In every era, a particular range of issues and questions are unsettling and become the heart of its 'ideological super-structures'. By approaching even great texts as works of ideology responding to local and immediate contextual issues and linguistic constraints, we can add to our understanding of the works themselves and to our broader knowledge of political life itself.[30]

Pocock's departure point in this revival of historical studies was the deleterious results of the canonical approach to texts: the 'coherence' of a work as 'political philosophy or as political theory' was 'mistakenly identified with its character as a historical phenomenon'.[31] He hoped to disentangle the confusion between philosophy and history. Pocock gave 'tradition' and political 'language' more subtle dimensions than did Oakeshott, and he differed with Skinner in urging that 'language paradigms' should take precedence over 'intentions' or 'illocutionary force' in historical studies. According to Pocock, since languages themselves have histories, those histories can be studied and commented upon.

Thomas Kuhn's historical insights into the 'linguistic and political' dimensions of scientific thought helped Pocock to see that the historian can draw 'connections' between language systems and political systems or view the conceptual and the social worlds as contexts for one another. Thus, the study of the history of political thought – actually, political languages – is at the same time the study of the history of political society, although the relation between language and experience is 'diachronous, ambivalent, and problematic' rather than simple and direct.

Nor is political language 'single disciplined'; it addresses 'all the purposes' and uses 'all the ways' human beings articulate and communicate their political activity and culture. Complex societies will manifest a 'plurality' of languages (*langues*) each with its own 'biases' on the 'definition and distribution of authority'. This convergence in the political life of a society produces not only speech acts (*paroles*) and debate, but also the 'migration' of concepts from one paradigm to another, changes within languages, and the efforts of intellectuals to form theories about the political activity surrounding them. Therein lies the 'richness of texture' to be found in the history of political thought and the reason for studying it.[32]

Dramatic 'moments' of revolution in paradigms and their appropriation in other periods and contexts particularly interest Pocock. The intellectual historian develops carefully contextualized encounters or dialogues across time with political thinkers ('historical actors') and their writings ('historical events'). But, the bourn of the historian's province is reached at the gate to the actor's consciousness. Even though political discourses provide 'scaffolding' for the 'individual ego's identity as a political being', their study does not reveal 'the nakedness of existential freedom or dereliction'. The paradigms actually exist to provide 'an exit' from this condition.

Often attacked from the Left because his method is not suited to study inarticulate 'romantic' revolutionary activity, Pocock has conceded the 'liberal' bias of the history of discourse. It presupposes a society in which 'one can utter and another utter in reply, made from a standpoint not that of the first performer'.[33]

In the very years of Skinner's and Pocock's innovative methodological work, Michel Foucault developed a theory of history which called into question the explanatory power of 'intellectual biographies' and the 'history of theories, concepts, and themes'. Foucault distinguished the conscious 'epistemological level of knowledge' from the unconscious 'archeological' one. He maintained that the a priori unconscious layer or *episteme*, 'never formulated' but pervasive, provided similar 'codes' to theories and concepts in different fields of endeavour contemporary to one another. As a result, they will have more in common among themselves than any one would have with its like across time. The *episteme* provides the rules for theory formulation, which the conscious actors conform to, even if unwittingly.[34] Against this background of 'open site' as opposed to tunnel, organic or dialogic history, the phenomenological privilege of the actor – to say nothing of his or her motives or intentions – seems to become less important.

In this vein, but with explicit attention to social, economic and political structures are Max Weber's subtle, historically-rooted characterizations of styles of rule. Weber was interested in how fundamental institutional contexts change, and his wide-ranging curiosity touched on early modern England among many other settings. Weber distinguished between 'patrimonial' and 'bureaucratic' officialdom, and the differences between them are hardly institutional at all. Patrimonial government is often 'bureaucratized' through increased 'functional division and rationalization', especially in 'clerical tasks' and the multiplication of levels through which 'official business' must be channelled. Nevertheless, unlike purely bureaucratic regimes, patrimonial office lacks the separation of the 'private' and the 'official' spheres. Although patrimonial power eventually must emanate from the ruler's 'table', 'supplies' and 'household' to designated beneficiaries, it remains a 'purely personal affair of the ruler'. But the patrimonial state is not a feudal state: it requires officials, not military retainers, and depends on the 'subject's good will'. The 'good king' is the mark of a patrimonial regime, which legitimizes itself as 'guardian of the subject's welfare in its own and in their eyes'.[35] Clearly, Weberian analyses of underlying political structures can provide important insight into the realities beneath the appearances of Tudor state formation, policy initiatives and their attendant political discourses.

Furthermore, if Pocock had to assume a more or less free exchange of utterances to insure the validity of language paradigms, what about historical settings that did not allow them? What do we make of utterances that may have been posed, acted or disguised? In those instances, what do we learn from the study of discourse? Richard A. Lanham has argued that 'rhetorical man' had different motives in language use from the 'clarity' that historians might hope for. His is a 'premeditated' use to 'master the rules the current game enforces'. Playful rather than 'sincere', rhetorical man approaches reality as a dramatic actor prepares for a role; the 'self', if it exists at all, remains both disguised and protean. Nevertheless, until we expand our historical sensitivity from discourses of the 'scientific' type to include those driven by 'literary' values, we stand to miss a great deal about the nature of politics and political thought.[36]

Since the early 1980s, probably the most resourceful purchase on the 'political', broadly and deeply conceived, in the Tudor and early Stuart years has been provided by 'literary historicism'. Following the lead of Foucault, Hayden White and Jonathan Dollimore among many others, new historicism adopts a sceptical position on the historian's ability to understand the past on its own terms. Interpretation becomes a matter of 'intervention' not 'dialogue'. Although the past does not anticipate our 'postmodern' world, the two can 'resonate' with one another in their preoccupations and lack of paradigms, if approached with the proper spirit of restricted expectations. Stephen J. Greenblatt, an early crafter of literary historicism, suggests that a revealing vibration between the present and the English Renaissance is the difficulty posed by self-definition within a context of fundamental structural-historical change. His 'anthropological criticism' draws on Clifford Geertz, Foucault and Jürgen Habermas, as well as Marx, Nietzsche and Freud to sketch a 'poetics of culture' that would investigate both the 'social presence to the world of the literary text and the social presence of the world in the literary text'. This allows Greenblatt to find in several English Renaissance writers revealing displays of 'self-fashioning' within the momentous shift in deep context from the '*consensus fidelium* embodied in the universal catholic church to the absolutist claims of the Book and the King'.[37]

Work of this type demonstrates the advantages to both historians of political thought and literature in not defining 'politics' too narrowly. For instance, F. J. Levy is able to see in *The Essayes* (1597 edn) the culmination of Francis Bacon's attempt 'to refashion' political thinking away from the ideals of humanism and toward the skills of self-advancement. And Louis Adrian Montrose and Annabel Patterson are convincing in pointing out the degree to which Elizabethan pastorals appropriated the benignity of the form to assuage or confirm discontentment with societal disharmony and authoritarianism at Court.[38]

Dominick LaCapra has done perhaps the most to alert intellectual historians to important developments in the 'neighbouring fields' of literary criticism and philosophy. LaCapra approaches as 'texts' materials as different as novels and archival records and, like Pocock, sees their creation as events in the history of language. He cautions strongly against the dangers of 'over-contextualization', however, which can reduce texts to 'mere documents' or conveyers of the literal or factual dimensions of reality. Equally important in all texts are their 'worklike' qualities through which they add to and subtract from that reality and speak directly to the historian as a reader. But the antidote to excessive contextualism is not 'free-floating' presentism. The challenge to historians is to balance the 'demand for documentation' against the 'responsive interpretations' to the materials they study. LaCapra would have historians seek a 'process of inquiry' that acknowledges a relationship with the past that is 'dialogical and historical' but that avoids both "'historicist' or 'presentish'" excesses.[39]

Our chapters constitute a brief for neither a new history nor an old, and we certainly have no agenda of 'historical correctness' to push. Quite to the contrary, we wish only to reinvigorate interest in Tudor political thought by beginning to clear fresh paths into its languages and debates. Through the adaptation of methods and perspectives from other times and disciplines, we offer new resources for the study of Tudor history which complement both the old and the new orthodoxies, the Eltonian and the anti-Eltonian. These approaches allow us to come to grips with vexing problems in Tudor intellectual history, especially its structures, its discourses and even its disguises. Virtually all the chapters are strongly interdisciplinary and tack between intellectual and cultural history. They may therefore contribute to '*détente*' between social and intellectual historians, as both rediscover the importance of culture and language. We also hope that the volume will encourage conversation among Tudor specialists and political scientists, policy analysts, anthropologists and students of literature. Equally important, many of the chapters demonstrate that developments in Tudor England can be understood only when set in a longer than usual span of time. Most of them also maintain that English ideas make more sense when placed in the context of continental thinking, whether Italian historiography, the German and Swiss Reformations, or the Court of Renaissance Venice.

Innovative as these chapters are, they remain works of history in a solidly traditional sense. They rest on a wide variety of sources, including state papers both domestic and foreign, many other manuscripts, parliamentary records, chronicles, literature, works of high-level political reflection (the usual focus of attention), moral and religious treatises, social commentary and letters. We agree with Elton, as all historians must, that 'questions for whose answer no material exists are strictly non-questions'.[40] But rather than taking this credo in the positivist sense Elton intended, we believe that questions may safely be sought outside the documents. We cannot limit our questions to what the materials literally will allow or to the search only for 'links between books and laws', as important as these are.[41] We hold that a broader view of political thought and culture, together with distinctions among 'policy thought', 'policy plans' and 'policy' (orders, proclamations, statutes, etc.) will enhance our understanding of the Tudor commonwealth. To privilege archival evidence and the end results of the policy-making process is a form of historical reductionism that squeezes too much out of an era.[42]

D. R. Woolf in Chapter 1 examines one of the important ways that the emerging Tudor monarchy sought to bolster its hold on the present – the appropriation of images of power from the past. Woolf seeks to understand how these typically ad hoc and reactive attempts to control the past and censure unacceptable views contributed to the generation and propagation of an 'ideology' of power in the Tudor years. The questions Woolf raises are close to those most typically associated with 'political anthropology', and the theoretical perspectives of Geertz and Victor Turner figure prominently in his methodology. Woolf ranges beyond the formal histories in his concern rather with state rituals, myths and recorded utterances by means of which the Tudors (in similar fashion to other Renaissance princes) sought to control, manipulate, reshape and sometimes repress community memory.

T. F. Mayer in Chapter 2 shares some of the same premises as Woolf's about power and its effects. Focusing on Reginald Pole and both his English and his Italian satellites, Mayer explores resistances to new 'absolutist' demands in the first half of the sixteenth century. These range from designs for conciliar government to displace imperial monarchy, through the creation of numerous personae to conceal and forward objections to political developments, to the writing of poems which rejected prevailing conventions of literary form intimately connected to the rise of 'new' monarchies. Mayer suggests that all these forms of rhetorical 'playing' ought to be taken much more seriously as ways of subverting absolutist pressures toward uniformity and conformity.

In Chapter 3 F. W. Conrad establishes two new dimensions of Sir Thomas Elyot's contribution to sixteenth-century theories of counsel. First, Conrad attends to the actual institutional context of Elyot's thinking about counsel and ties him much more closely to actual political and administrative responsibilities and their attendant risks than has been previously acknowledged. Thereby, Conrad challenges the usual verdict that Elyot's writings were abstract and remote from the realities of Henrician Court life. Second, his subtle reading of Elyot's corpus reveals that Elyot deployed Erasmian humanist appeals to the example of Roman *amici principis* and to the Greek ideal of *philoi* and combined them with medieval chivalric notions of informal, but deep, bonds between a lord and his affinity. Elyot emerges as an architect of the 'counsel of manners' paradigm, an important but often overlooked rival to the 'counsel of business' in the sixteenth century.

Ben Lowe finds a sustained resistance to war during the last three decades of Henry VIII's reign in Chapter 4. Similarly to developments toward the end of the Hundred Years War, the Tudor attraction to peace began as a moral imperative that eventually gave way to a deepening interest in the tangible benefits that peace could bring in and of itself to the commonwealth. Shifts in social and political contexts were matched in discourse. Writers and policy-makers incorporated speech acts of peace advocacy into several important political languages, including classical humanism, political economy, Protestantism and 'secular' humanitarianism. Thus chivalric notions of just war declined in their influence, and the 'imperfect shadow' of peace was pursued both inside and outside of government.

Neal Wood in Chapter 5 offers an important corrective to the usual reading of Sir Thomas Smith's *A Discourse of the Commonweal of This Realm of England* (1549). Wood shows it to have been more than a 'conventional' display of 'moral philosophy' and rather an early, and perhaps the first, example in England of an essay in political economy. Wood bases his assessment partially on the unique style and form that Smith gave to the work – a dialogue of ordinary contemporaries analysing high policy questions – and partially on important contextual matters. These include the work's relation to *De Republica Anglorum*, the view of human nature and economic activity that Smith appropriated from classical, humanist and Protestant discourses, and his keen insight into the mechanics of his immediate economic environment.

In Chapter 6 Norman L. Jones combines Eltonian archival postivism with a searching treatment of William Cecil's perspicacity. Jones rests his case on a substantial manuscript fragment in Cecil's hand, which may have been notes for a speech in the House of Lords. We learn much from it about Cecil's analysis of the commonwealth's ills and the assumptions that he used to drive the government's policy goals, especially but not exclusively as they applied to the Statute Against Usury (1571). Cecil carefully evaluated and blended scholastic, Protestant and contemporary secular estimates of usury into a cautious, pragmatic 'compromise' which was acceptable to Parliament and remained in place until 1624.

The Tudor preoccupation with poverty continues to be well studied by social, economic and administrative historians. Paul A. Fideler in Chapter 7 attempts a comprehensive characterization of the policy thought that informed sixteenth-century analyses of poverty and formulations of poor relief and anti-vagrancy policy. He locates important policy 'frames' and 'languages' in Christian humanism, Lutheranism, Calvinism and inchoate political economy. Fideler finds that policy thought in the first half of the century was dominated by abstract humanist assumptions which promoted ambitious government plans for poverty's remediation. By contrast, the paradigms of Calvinist congregationalism and political economy, which emerged as most influential in the Elizabethan years, seem to have been both more empirical and local in their attention.

Finally in Chapter 8, A. J. Slavin offers a reconceptualization of Tudor politics and culture which integrates political ideas into the processes of a 'patrimonial' state.[43] Slavin finds the frequent claim that Tudor government had modern, prescriptive authority incompatible with what we know about the 'deeply laid social bases' of Tudor political behaviour. Rights, duties and obligations depended on religious belief and what Weber called 'irrational' traditions of kinship, property and customary law. As such they would have been anathema to the 'impersonal and privileged rational-legal and constitutional order' that the 'modernists' posit. Drawing on theory from Weber, Emile Durkheim and S. N. Eisenstadt, Slavin develops a model of the Tudor state flexible enough to accommodate linkage between institutions and traditional belief systems in a dynamic political environment.

The questions raised in these chapters are essentially 'humanities' questions, the kind that either make room for *differing* assumptions about human agency, intentionality and values, or make no sense. Just as we hope to stretch the ground historians might cover, so we believe that method – and its discontents – lie near the heart of the way in which historians gallop across their territory. But, we hold, disputes over how to do history should issue in a realization that the most interesting questions do not have cut-and-dried answers. This awareness in turn may lead both to a greater tolerance for diversity, and to better tools with which to judge what is worth while and what not.

As John Dewey put it, the sciences and the humanities work better in *rapprochement* than confrontation. Scientists (including the historical kind) must openly acknowledge the inherent ethical and political dimensions of nearly all human undertaking, and scholars given to the perspectives of the humanities must concede the importance of thought engaged with the possibilities and problems of the world close at hand.[44] If historians continue to react to the historiographical ideas of others as Dr Johnson did to Bishop Berkeley's idealism, we put not only our feet at risk, but the rock, too. Once shattered, it may well prove impossible to tell it back together. We have chipped away at it, but not in order to demand more minute historical research. That would only further reduce whatever small utility professional historians have left. Then again, maybe we merely need some new stories in order to make sense of the detail.

We hope that the reader will find a few herein. However, we are in danger of running on too long, of proclaiming too loudly the 'whys' and the 'hows' of our venture; it is time we moved to the 'what'. As Professor Elton would remind us, 'There is work to be done rather than to be called for'.

P. A. F.
T. F. M.

NOTES

1 This Introduction cannot pretend to provide a comprehensive overview of the historiography of Tudor political thought or the methods by which it has been approached. Instead, we offer a general orientation to problems and in the Critical Bibliography a large number of suggestions for further reading. In addition, the *Journal of British Studies*, *The Historical Journal*, *History* and *Albion* (among others) regularly publish bibliographical essays on Tudor England. See also the annual *Literature Review* of the *Archiv für Reformationsgeschichte*.

2 C. Morris, *Political Thought in England: Tyndale to Hooker*, London, Oxford University Press, 1953, pp. 2, 3; G. R. Elton, *The Tudor Revolution in Government*, Cambridge, Cambridge University Press, 1953. Elton found Morris's volume to be a 'brilliant summary with many original and interesting suggestions to make'; see Elton, *England under the Tudors*, London, Methuen, 1955, p. 481.

3 Elton, 1953, op. cit., pp. 1–7, 425–7.

4 G. R. Elton, *The Practice of History*, New York, Thomas Y. Crowell, 1967, p. 12 (we have not yet seen Elton's *Return to Essentials: Some Reflections on the Present State of Historical Study*, Cambridge, Cambridge University Press, 1991); *Policy and Police*, Cambridge, Cambridge University Press, 1972, p. viii. Elton was never quite as dismissive of ideas as some of his programmatic statements seem to suggest. See his *Reform and Renewal: Thomas Cromwell and the Commonweal*, Cambridge, Cambridge University Press, 1973; 'The political creed of Thomas Cromwell', in his *Studies in Tudor and Stuart Politics and Government*, vol. II: *Parliament/Political Thought*, Cambridge, Cambridge University Press, 1974, pp. 215–35; and 'Reform by statute: Thomas Starkey's *Dialogue* and Thomas Cromwell's policy', *Proceedings of the British Academy*, LIV (1968), pp. 165–88.

5 C. Coleman, 'Professor Elton's "revolution"', in C. Coleman and D. Starkey (eds) *Revolution Reassessed*, Oxford, Clarendon Press, 1986, p. 1; Coleman offers an incisive discussion of how Elton's views on the 1530s have changed and how they have stayed the same over the years.

6 J. W. Allen, *A History of Political Thought in the Sixteenth Century*, London, Methuen, 1928, pt II, chs 1, 2; S. B. Chrimes, *English Constitutional History*, 2nd edn, London, Oxford University Press, 1953, ch. 2; F. L. Baumer, *The Early Tudor Theory of Kingship*, New York, Russell & Russell, 1966 (1940), pp. 2, 3, 210.

7 Elton, 1953, op. cit., pp. 5, 426.

8 G. R. Elton, *Reform and Reformation: England, 1509–1558*, Cambridge, Mass., Harvard University Press, 1977, Preface. For a very perceptive reading of Elton's work and his self-conceived mission as a historian, see A. J. Slavin, 'Telling the story: G. R. Elton and the Tudor age', *SCJ*, 1990, vol. 21, pp. 151–9.

9 J. Loach, 'Parliament: a "new air"?', in Coleman and Starkey, op. cit., pp. 117–34.

10 J. Guy, 'The privy council: revolution or evolution?', ibid., pp. 59–85.

11 D. Starkey, 'Court and government', ibid., pp. 29–58. See also in the same collection D. Hoak, 'Two revolutions in Tudor government: the formation and organization of Mary I's privy council', pp. 87–115; J. D. Alsop, 'The structure of early Tudor finance, c. 1509–1558', pp. 135–62; and C. Coleman, 'Artifice or accident? The reorganization of the exchequer of receipt, c. 1554–1572', pp. 163–98.

12 A. F. Pollard, *England under Protector Somerset*, London, K. Paul, Trench, Trubner, 1900, pp. 59–68, 93–5, 106, 120, 200, 215–16.

13 W. G. Zeeveld, *Foundations of Tudor Policy*, Cambridge, Mass., Harvard University Press, 1948, pp. iv, 3, 6, 10–12, 16, 36, 39, 224–5, 269–70; for a sign of further revision in Elton's attitude to ideas, see his recent positive assessment of Zeeveld's work in 'Humanism in England', in A. Goodman and A. Mackay (eds) *The Impact of Humanism on Western Europe*, London, Longman, 1990, pp. 259–78.

14 Elton, 1973, op. cit., pp. 5, 36, 99.

15 J. K. McConica, *English Humanists and Reformation Politics*, Oxford, Clarendon Press, 1965; T. More, *Utopia, The Complete Works of St. Thomas More*, vol. 4, New Haven, Conn., Yale University Press, 1965; J. J. Scarisbrick, 'Cardinal Wolsey and the common weal', in E. W. Ives, R. J. Knecht and J. J. Scarisbrick (eds) *Wealth and Power in Tudor England*, London, Athlone Press, 1978, pp. 47, 52.

16 M. Todd, *Christian Humanism and the Puritan Social Order*, Cambridge, Cambridge University Press, 1987.

17 J. B. Gleason, *John Colet*, Berkeley, Calif., University of California Press, 1989.

18 T. F. Mayer, *Thomas Starkey and the Commonweal*, Cambridge, Cambridge University Press, 1989.

19 A.B. Ferguson, 'Renaissance realism in the "commonwealth" literature of early Tudor England', *JHI*, 1955, vol. 16, no. 3, pp. 287, 288, 291–2, 302, 304–5; and *The Articulate Citizen and the English Renaissance*, Durham, NC, Duke University Press, 1965, pp. xvi, 17–106, 207, 247–8. For Starkey on policy, see *T. Starkey: 'A Dialogue between Pole and Lupset'*, T. F. Mayer (ed.), C4S, vol. 37, 1989, pp. 34, 113–17; Mayer, op. cit., pp. 205–7; Zeeveld, op.cit., p. 144.

20 D. Starkey, 'Which age of reform?', in Coleman and Starkey, op. cit., pp. 15, 21–22.

21 J. Guy, 'The Tudor commonwealth: revising Thomas Cromwell', *HJ*, 1980, vol. 23, no. 3, p. 684.

22 W. R. D. Jones, *The Tudor Commonwealth: 1529–1559*, London, Athlone Press, 1970, pp. 24–6; W. K. Jordan, *Edward VI: The Young King*, Cambridge, Mass., Belknap Press of Harvard University Press, 1968, pp. 305, 416–18, 505; G. R. Elton, 'Reformation and the "commonwealth-men" of Edward VI's reign', in P. Clark, A. G. R. Smith and N. Tyacke (eds) *The English Commonwealth 1547–1640*, Leicester, Leicester University Press, 1979, pp. 23–38.

23 P. Collinson, *The Religion of Protestants: The Church in English Society, 1559–1625*, Oxford, Clarendon Press, 1982; *The Elizabethan Puritan Movement*, Oxford, Clarendon Press, 1987; and *The Birthpangs of Protestantism*, New York, St Martin's Press, 1988; P. Lake, *Moderate Puritans and the Elizabethan Church*, New York, Cambridge University Press, 1982, and *Anglicans and Puritans? Presbyterianism and English Conformist Thought from Whitgift to Hooker*, London, Unwin Hyman, 1988. G. J. R. Parry, *A Protestant Vision: William Harrison and the Reformation of Elizabethan England*, New York, Cambridge University Press, 1987. C. Haigh (ed.) *The English Reformation Revised*, Cambridge, Cambridge University Press, 1987, Introduction.

24 A valuable overview of these debates is C. Haigh (ed.) *The Reign of Elizabeth I*, Basingstoke, Macmillan, 1984, Introduction.

25 See the Critical Bibliography (pp. 268–9) for a discussion of this historiography.

26 P. Laslett (ed.) *Philosophy, Politics and Society*, Oxford, Basil Blackwell, 1956, p. vii; sixteen years later, with the revival of contemporary and historical

interest in political theory well under way, Laslett, W. G. Runciman and Q. Skinner declared the earlier judgement to have been 'premature' and no longer operative (*Philosophy, Politics and Society*, 4th ser., Oxford, Basil Blackwell, 1972, p. 1).

27 J. Locke, *Two Treatises of Government*, P. Laslett (ed.), Cambridge, Cambridge University Press, 1960, Introduction.

28 M. Oakeshott, 'Political education', *Philosophy, Politics and Society*, 1st ser., pp. 1–20.

29 Q. Skinner, 'Meaning and understanding in the history of ideas' [*History and Theory*, 1969, vol. 8, pp. 3–53], in J. Tully (ed.) *Meaning and Context: Quentin Skinner and his Critics*, Princeton, NJ, Princeton University Press, 1988, pp. 32–46, 48–9, 63–7.

30 Q. Skinner, *The Foundations of Modern Political Thought*, 2 vols, Cambridge, Cambridge University Press, 1978, I, Preface.

31 J. G. A. Pocock, 'Languages and their implications: the transformation of the study of political thought', in *Politics, Language and Time*, New York, Atheneum, 1971, p. 4.

32 Ibid., pp. 5–7, 12–19, 21–3.

33 Pocock, 'On the non-revolutionary character of paradigms: a self-criticism and afterpiece', op. cit., pp. 276–7, 283; and 'Introduction: The state of the art', *Virtue, Commerce and History*, Cambridge, Cambridge University Press, 1985, pp. 18, 34.

34 M. Foucault, *The Order of Things*, New York, Random House, 1970 (1966), pp. ix–xxiv, 367–73; see also the Critical Bibliography (pp. 259–62).

35 M. Weber, *Economy and Society*, G. Roth and C. Wittich (eds), 3 vols, New York, Bedminster Press, 1968 (1951, 1956, 1958, 1964), III, pt II, chs XII, XIII, pp. 1,028, 1,031, 1,106–9.

36 R. A. Lanham, *The Motives of Eloquence: Literary Rhetoric in the Renaissance*, New Haven, Conn., Yale University Press, 1976, ch. 1; recall Pocock's dependence on Kuhn's model analysis of scientific discourse; see R. Barthes, 'Science v. literature', *Times Literary Supplement*, 28 September 1967, pp. 410–16.

37 S. J. Greenblatt, *Renaissance Self-Fashioning, from More to Shakespeare*, Chicago, Ill., University of Chicago Press, 1980.

38 All three essays are in A. Kinney and D. S. Collins (eds) *Renaissance Historicism*, Amherst, Mass., University of Massachusetts Press, 1987: F. J. Levy, 'Francis Bacon and the style of politics', pp. 146–67; L. A. Montrose, ' "Eliza, queene of shepheardes", and the pastoral of power', pp. 34–63; and A. Patterson, 'Re-opening the green cabinet: Clement Marot and Edmund Spenser', pp. 64–92; see also H. Dubrow and R. Strier (eds) *The Historical Renaissance*, Chicago, Ill., University of Chicago Press, 1988.

39 D. LaCapra, *Rethinking Intellectual History: Texts, Contexts, Language*, Ithaca, NY, Cornell University Press, 1983, pp. 14, 29–31, 63–5.

40 Elton, 1967, op. cit., p. 9.

41 For the central place of these links in his approach to policy studies see Elton, 1973, op. cit., p. 8.

42 D. Starkey has alluded to these issues in his 'Tudor government: the facts?', *HJ*, 1988, vol. 31, no. 4, p. 929.

43 Slavin's approach resembles Cynthia Herrup's recommendation that we treat the constitution of early modern England as a process; see C. Herrup, 'Beyond personality and pomp: recent works on early modern monarchies', *JBS*, 1989, vol. 28, p. 176.

44 J. Dewey, *Reconstruction in Philosophy*, Boston, Mass., Little, Brown, 1948 (repr. of 1920 edn), ch. 7.

1

The power of the past:
history, ritual and political authority in Tudor England

D. R. Woolf

The Tudor regime matched its hold on present events with a firm grip on the understanding and interpretation of the past. It has long been recognized that history was a genre of growing importance in sixteenth-century England, one which could be used either to support or to subvert official policy. Most studies of Tudor and Stuart historical writing have touched on this topic in the course of discussing contemporary attitudes to history and the social, religious or political benefits to be gained from its study.[1] The purpose of this chapter is not to repeat these treatments of history-writing as such; rather, it is to explore various types of connections between authority and history in the sixteenth century – between power and the past. 'Power' can be taken in this context to mean not merely the administrative and legal instruments through which a government (local or national) enforces its wishes, but the very image of potency that authority projects upon the governed. As one recent study puts it, power is 'a symbolic medium whose functioning does not depend primarily upon its intrinsic effectiveness but upon the expectations that its employment arouses in those who comply with it'.[2] Power thus embraces the narrower term 'ideology'; it is ideology which both provides power-relationships with their intellectual foundations, and rules the production of their governing symbols and texts, which include but are not confined to what is commonly called 'propaganda'.[3]

The past provided the sixteenth century with raw material for many of its linguistic and graphic expressions of power. These expressions are to be found not only in formal writings on history (chronicles, history plays and the like) but also in the much, much wider set of perceptions of past events, recorded as informal 'utterances' in virtually any writing from the period; these have been much less thoroughly explored, for the simple reason that they are not conveyed in any neat, easily searched package,

19

but lie scattered about in letters, diaries and government records, as well as in such visual forms as spectacle and drama.

Most Renaissance regimes realized the importance of controlling, manipulating, reshaping and sometimes suppressing the community memory.[4] There were many precedents for this in England alone: medieval kings had always been wary of saintly cults which occasionally sprang up around the graves of dead opponents. Various Anglo-Saxon kings and princes were turned into saints in the early Middle Ages.[5] Thomas of Lancaster was linked by his supporters with the murdered Archbishop of Canterbury, St Thomas Becket, in the fourteenth century. Edward II, Richard II and Archbishop Scrope all developed quasi-sacral political cults after their deaths, as did the hapless Henry VI.[6] In 1479 an ecclesiastical injunction in the northern province forbade excessive reverence toward a statue of Henry. This had been part of a series of images adorning the rood screen at York Minster (which, ironically, had a few decades earlier been the centre of the anti-Lancastrian cult of Scrope). The figure of Henry VI had been completed only in the late 1450s, and upon the king's murder after Tewkesbury it almost immediately became the focus of rumoured miracles, which resulted in its removal.[7] Even more dangerous was the status that figures such as Henry could assume as 'prophets' of future events. Throughout the sixteenth and seventeenth centuries political prophecy presented both a tool and a threat to various regimes, as figures from the past such as Henry, the British king Cadwallader and the wizard Merlin were resurrected to foretell the great events of the present.[8]

Tudor intervention in the perception of the past followed in this tradition but also extended it with the aid of a more efficient central government which had the new medium of print at its disposal. Much of this intervention tended to be ad hoc and reactive rather than the product of a positive programme, except in certain instances. The crown did occasionally make a more deliberate attempt to manipulate history for its own ends, but only sporadically, and mainly during periods of crisis, such as the 1530s and the 1590s. It used to be believed that the Tudors, and Henry VII in particular, had based a large part of their historical claim to power on their descent from the ancient British kings depicted in Geoffrey of Monmouth's *Historia regum Britanniae* and in a host of chronicles, poems and legends derived therefrom; Henry had even named his son and heir Arthur further to tighten this family tie to distant antiquity. Sydney Anglo demonstrated in 1961 that 'Arthurianism' was nothing new: Yorkist kings had used the same tactics in support of their claims to sovereignty.[9] The Tudors were heirs to, rather than creators of, a British mystique which was projected even before Henry's climactic confrontation with Richard III at Bosworth, and they deserve no special credit for the encouragement of the family of legends associated with Arthur and his even murkier ancestor, Brutus the Trojan. It is also true that their propagandists made frequent appeals to Anglo-Saxon as well as British forebears.[10] The ex-monk turned propagandist, Thomas Gardiner of Westminster, would present Henry VIII in 1542 with a pedigree showing his descent from Cadwallader ('the laste kynge of that blode from whome by trew and lynyall descensse' came the Tudor line), Alfred the Great, William the Conqueror and Hugh Capet. Finally, it can be added that the first concerted attack on these legends was made by the court-supported historian Polydore Vergil, though he delayed publication of his work for two decades and even then had it printed outside England.[11]

One should not, of course, mistake a lack of either novelty or of a systematic programme of Arthurian imagery for its unimportance, since Henry VII's panegyrists and image-makers did in fact make much of British mythology.[12] Pietro Carmeliano's verses on the birth of Prince Arthur refer specifically to Brutus' division of Britain and play up the name of the infant prince, though failing to make the connection between Arthur's name and the British descent of the Tudors. Henry himself may have appointed a commission of Welsh scholars and clergy to trace the royal genealogy back to Brutus, the results of which were still being used in the reign of Edward VI.[13] But the Tudors did not need to go out of their way to stress the British/Arthurian heritage. The legends were reasonably familiar among the aristocracy and upper gentry, and so widely accepted even by those few critics (Polydore Vergil excepted) who might doubt details of the Galfridean account, that throughout the century there would be an abundance of poets, antiquaries and historians who were prepared to make the obvious connection between ancient Britons and Welsh Tudors, and to defend the historicity of this part of the national heritage. Furthermore, the British connection could never be of more than secondary importance to royal image-makers: the past that the early Tudors really had to control was the recent past, the fifteenth century. Henry VII, who faced some half-dozen rebellions by disgruntled ex-Ricardians and would-be pretenders in the first fifteen years of his reign, stressed both his relationship by marriage to Edward IV and his direct descent, via the Lancastrian line, from Edward III. The Tudors, according to this view, became bona fide Plantagenets like their predecessors. They were thus ancestrally the equals of, but in many ways preferable to, their Yorkist and Lancastrian forebears, since Henry Tudor, through his marriage to Elizabeth of York, had united the two roses and restored the royal monarchy to that perceived unity and stability it had possessed before Henry Bolingbroke's rebellion in 1399.

The blackening of Richard III's reputation is well known though the chronology of its development remains obscure. As with the British myth, the Tudors found anti-Ricardians without having to look too hard. Thomas More, whose own unfinished *History of King Richard III*, as taken up by later chroniclers and by Shakespeare, really fixed the public image of the evil usurper, did not write that book for the love of Henry VII, who had not dealt kindly with his family. Rumours of Richard's nefarious crimes were quickly elevated from mere propaganda into resilient, durable myth. The stain would remain on Richard's name long after it had ceased to be politically necessary to nurture a belief in his villainy.[14] Although in England, unlike France, no official Historiographer Royal was appointed until the Restoration, certain historians occasionally enjoyed special favour at Court. A strong Yorkist historical tradition endured into Henry VII's reign.[15] The king, not surprisingly, saw the need for a dynastic revision of recent English history, and employed a number of second-rank humanist émigrés, including the blind poet, Bernard André, who panegyrized the new monarchy in verse and prose, leaving behind him the first history of the reign.[16] But it is in Pietro Carmeliano, erstwhile Yorkist camp-follower, that one can most readily see the pressure to revise the past in the light of shifting political winds. Carmeliano, a poet of indifferent ability whose literary talents were scorned by Erasmus, had as recently as 1484 heaped praise on Richard III. The accession of Henry VII and the birth of his heir a year later, however, saw Carmeliano writing a lengthy set of Latin verses on the civil wars in which the 'tyrant' Richard is charged with the murders of his nephews and of Henry VI.[17] More capable than Carmeliano, but clearly performing a similar function, was Polydore Vergil, whose *Anglica Historia* was almost certainly commissioned by Henry VII about 1506 to provide an account of national history which would lead up to the accession of his own line and, by making that accession seem inevitable and providential, enhance its legitimacy.

The anti-Yorkist tone of early Tudor historical writing was not, as is often mistakenly assumed, a *cantus firmus* sounded constantly throughout the century; rather, it reappeared at certain points as the political situation changed. After the preoccupation with the union of the houses and the condemnation of Richard that marks Henry VII's reign, other themes occupied centre stage in the 1510s and 1520s, such as the Hundred Years War. In the 1530s and 1540s, with the dynasty relatively secure and most possible pretenders extinct, establishing the imperial status of England and a Rome-free past for the church assumed far greater importance than further recitations of the fifteenth-century struggles. When Eustace Chapuys, the imperial ambassador, suggested to Thomas Cromwell that the king of England could dispense with the laws of the realm whenever he wished, citing the example of Richard III, Cromwell agreed but observed, matter-of-factly, that Richard had been a tyrant and a bad man, and that he had been punished for his crimes. The parchment pedigree drawn up in 1542–3 by the former monk, Thomas Gardiner, dwells on Henry VII's inherent virtues rather than contrasting the king with his tyrannical rival; the murder of the princes is mentioned, but there is none of the vitriol of Carmeliano's or More's accounts, nor any foretaste of the stage Machia-vellianism that would develop later in the century. The restoration of real interest in the disasters of the fifteenth century awaited the later years of the childless Elizabeth, and then the regime would assume a much more defensive posture.[18]

Properly motivated, Henry VIII could take as keen a personal interest in the past as his father had, and in many ways his reign set the tone for later Tudor reaction to alternative interpretations of history by defining dissent on the past as being equivalent to subversion in the present. The king was remarkably touchy about invasions of his prerogative, even when these were purely symbolic. At the very end of the reign, the earl of Surrey's quartering of the royal arms, including the putative arms of Edward the Confessor, proved to be the last of several acts of youthful folly which led the earl to the scaffold: to lay claim to the arms of a king, even one dead five centuries, was equivalent in the early Tudor mind to a treasonable invasion of royal rights. But Henry's attentiveness to history went beyond mere reactive paranoia to acquire, especially at critical junctures in the reign, a ritualistic, even superstitious fervour. Prior to his first French campaign Henry authorized a life of Henry V drawn largely from Tito Livio Frulovisi's seventy-year-old *Vita Henrici Quinti*. The work of an anonymous writer, this served as a reminder of earlier English successes across the Channel and presented an image of the heroic, conquering king in whose shoes he trod. Always preoccupied with honour and a sense of living up to (or exceeding) his forebears, Henry made emulation of the great Lancastrian warrior king a central part of the chivalric ethos at his Court, just as his father had played upon a link with the saintly Henry VI.[19]

This was more than mere opportunistic image-making. In confronting the meaning of the past, the Renaissance mind was less interested in cause and effect than in analogy and similarity, in patterns from history that could be emulated in the present. As one scholar has recently pointed out, the whole anti-French tenor of Henrician foreign policy was in large measure dictated by Henry's sense of keeping up with history: 'To equal or outdo his ancestors, Henry had to fight France'. Urged on by the poets and courtiers around him, Henry fashioned himself into a latter-day Henry V, an English champion who would restore to his subjects their empire in France. As Henry V, in a famous incident, had convinced the hostile preacher Vincent of Ferrer of the justice of his war, so did Henry VIII persuade the pacific humanist Colet of the Christian virtue of his own campaign. Just as the second Lancastrian had executed the earl of Cambridge and his co-conspirators in 1415, before the Agincourt campaign, so did the second Tudor put to death the long-imprisoned dynastic rival Edmund de la Pole, a little less than a century later, as he, too, prepared to embark for France.[20]

The break with Rome in the 1530s marked a new and particularly active phase in the Tudor manipulation of history, partly because of the association of a number of humanist writers under the banner of reformation, and partly because the king's claim to supremacy in matters concerning the English church was grounded in the language of history and custom as much as that of theology.[21] The reference to 'divers sundrey old authentic histories and chronicles' in the Act of Appeals (1533) is well known, as is the tactic taken in that statute of arguing that England was an independent, sovereign 'empire' because such records showed that she had always been understood as such. More recently the government's compilation of historical evidence to support its claims has been thoroughly investigated.[22] The Donation of Constantine, the authenticity of which had been challenged in the previous century by Lorenzo Valla and Reginald Pecock, was finally now exposed as a fraud, while the evangelical divine Robert Barnes turned his knowledge of continental historical writing towards a recounting of the sins of the popes.[23]

The saints were next, and above all the offensive Thomas Becket who, according to one Reformation tale, was put on trial for treason and condemned *in absentia*.[24] Whether or not this judicial action against the long-dead archbishop took place, Becket's memory was unquestionably obnoxious to the regime. In 1535 one of Cromwell's correspondents, Robert Ward, saw at St Thomas of Acres church in London 'certain windows wherein was pictured the life of St Thomas, especially a superstitious and popish remembrance in the absolution of the king that was in that time'. The image had portrayed several monks smiting the naked, kneeling Henry II. Before his execution in May 1538, Friar John Forest declared that St Thomas of Canterbury had suffered for the rights of the church, 'as many holy fathers have suffered now of late, as that holy father the bishop of Rochester'.[25] The government had soon had enough. In August, Thomas Cranmer was organizing the exposure of Becket's blood at Christ Church, Canterbury, as 'but a ffayned thinge and made of some Redde okere or such like mater'; and within a few weeks Cromwell had opened a serious campaign to despoil shrines, under the direction of his associate Sir Thomas Wriothesley.[26] Becket's remains at Canterbury were exhumed for treason and his bones burnt, a canonical procedure previously reserved for notorious heretics such as Wyclif.[27] Becket's image at the high altar in St Thomas of Acres was taken down. So were the stained glass windows which had vexed Robert Ward three years earlier, together 'with the image of his puttinge to death that was at the aulter, where the sayinge was, that he was borne allso', according to Wriothesley's cousin Charles, the chronicler, 'so that there shall no more mention be made of him never'.[28] On 22 November a proclamation declared that Becket not be 'esteemed, named, reputed, nor called a sainct, but Bishop Beckett'. Throughout the land his images were to be removed, his festival days ignored, the long-standing prayers to him unspoken.[29] To remove any possible doubt as to the government's attitude toward the recalcitrant prelate, a circular to the Justices of the Peace explicitly rewrote the history of Becket's martyrdom in favour of the crown. Harpsfield, the biographer of another victim of the Reformation, Thomas More, derided the crown's cynical attempt to revise the inherited version of events:

> Albeit we have of late . . . unshryned him, and burned his holye bones; and not onely unshryned and unsancted him, but have made him also, after so manye hundred yeares, a traitour to the king that murdered him.[30]

As times and regimes changed, so did official attitudes to the past; public attitudes were expected to follow suit. Under Mary, Becket's image was erected again over the gate of Mercer's chapel, and the exiled reformer Thomas Sampson gloomily passed on to Heinrich Bullinger the news from London that 'Thomas à Becket is publicly set up as a saint'.[31] The Marian regime proved short-lived, but recent reassessments of the endurance of saint-worship and other elements of Catholicism in the countryside suggest that, at least for a few decades, the queen's attitude toward Becket may have been less at odds with popular perceptions of the past than were the views of her father, brother and sister. Indeed, the very attention lavished on Becket's reputation may only have enhanced it in some quarters, as he joined Merlin, Cadwallader and Henry VI among the ranks of ancient prophets, resurrected to 'foretell' current events by astrologers such as William Lilly in the seventeenth century.[32]

Tudor and early Stuart control over perceptions of the past had a positive and a negative side. The first, which depended on the participation of artists, poets and performers both within and outside the immediate circle of the court, lay in the deliberate creation of an image for the monarchy that could be expressed and reinforced in a variety of aural and visual media: in public ritual and ceremonial events, in painting and sculpture, in woodcuts and the printed word.[33] The negative side consisted in the crown's disciplinary potential to react to any instance of speaking, writing and especially printing of dangerous matter from the past with punitive measures. Government control, exercised through treason statutes and proclamations and enforced in prerogative courts such as the Star Chamber and High Commission, relied more on an author's fear of punishment and public embarrassment than on the crown's actual capacity to enforce its will through a censorship that was both limited and unsystematic.

Historiographical dissent can never be completely silenced under any regime. In the sixteenth century, it was at best submerged, waiting to reappear in an extremely politicized form after the collapse of the censorship and the outbreak of civil war in the 1640s. By and large, however, Tudor and early Stuart historians were among the most conservative students of the past. They were conscious of the punishment of Aulus Cremutius Cordus, the Roman historian executed by Tiberius for his favourable comments about the assassins of Julius Caesar. Cordus' fate, as recounted by Tacitus, became a topos during the later sixteenth century, most famously in Ben Jonson's play of 1605, *Sejanus his Fall*, in which one character, with reference to Cordus' history, makes a statement which could apply equally well to many episodes in the English past: 'Those times are somewhat queasie to be toucht'.[34] As in other literary arenas, the mere prospect of punishment usually proved sufficient to enforce a degree of self-censorship.[35] When combined with the active cultivation of historical images, and the overpowering tyranny of certain beliefs about the past, even this very limited form of censorship proved sufficient to ensure the crystallization and durability, from about the middle of the sixteenth century till the 1630s, of what on the surface was a relatively monochromatic and rarely challenged interpretation of English history.

Examples of Tudor and early Stuart monarchs playing symbolic games with history are easy to find. From about the middle of her reign, Elizabeth I successfully captured and annually recaptured the national feeling of relief at her accession in a national holiday, 17 November, which continued to be celebrated long after her death.[36] The Accession Day tilts combined this celebration with a chivalric nostalgia and created one of the most effective sets of political images in early modern Europe: Elizabeth became Astraea, Cynthia, Belphoebe, her courtiers knights out of a world which seemed increasingly remote, an allegorical world of chivalry, honour, military prowess and romance, presided over by a female symbol in robes and crown.[37] Celebration of accession days was made a matter of national ritual by Elizabeth and her successors, who periodically issued official Forms of Prayer to mark Elizabeth's accession on 17 November, James's on 24 March and Charles I's on 27 March. Sermons for such occasions carried strong political messages, and those who gave them frequently appealed to English, classical or scriptural history. Lancelot Andrewes preached just such a sermon on Accession Day, 1607, on the text Judges xvii.6: 'In those dayes there was no king in Israel, but every man did that which was good in his owne eyes'.[38] Local communities joined in the celebrations from time to time, incorporating national days of rejoicing into civic calendars. Thus sixteenth-century Norwich on various occasions employed town waits to mark Armada Day (often observed as late as 18 November to follow Accession Day), and the locally significant anniversary of Kett's 1549 rebellion. Some of these customs did not survive the reigning monarch: in Norwich, Armada Day was last kept in 1603, though it lived on elsewhere in England; the celebration of the Spanish victory at St Quentin in 1557 died with Queen Mary after only one anniversary.[39]

Virtually all royal ceremonial had a historical or even commemorative element: the important variations occur in the type of content and the degree of sophistication with which it was expressed.[40] As a continuous theme, few connections were more firmly suggested than that with the last Anglo-Saxon king, the saintly Edward the Confessor. A tableau vivant laid on by the citizens of Coventry in 1456 in honour of the visit of Queen Margaret and her son Edward, prince of Wales, featured the nine worthies, augmented by the figure of the Confessor, who greeted the royal visitors:

> Moder of mekenes dame Margarete princes most excellent
> I kyng Edward wekum you with affeccion right cordiall.[41]

The Tudors continued the practice of laying their dead to rest in St Edward's chapel; an anonymous chronicler records the burial of Henry VII's youngest daughter in 1495 'upon the lyfte hand of Seynt Edwardes Awter'; four years later she was joined by the king's youngest son, Edmund.[42] But the Confessor's most important role was to be played out, again and again, in that most central of all medieval and Renaissance political rituals, the public coronation.[43]

The ancient coronation ceremony was repeated, with occasional modifications, by every early modern king or queen from Edward IV to the Hanoverians, and it provides a particularly strong (and well-documented) instance of the political connections between past and present, and between time and space.[44] Richard III began his short reign by donning Edward the Confessor's robes and making the mandatory visit to his shrine, where the king exchanged Edward's crown, 'with many other Relyques', for his own.[45] The festivities for the making of a new queen allowed a restatement of this link to the Anglo-Saxon past. The celebrations for Anne Boleyn took place over several days at the end of May 1533, and included pageants of mythical and religious figures such as St Anne, but not many historical personae. The conduit in Cheapside was 'newly painted with armes of devises', while the nearby Standard was 'richely painted with ymages of kynges and quenes and hanged with banners of armes', or, as one observer put it, 'garnished wth gold and azure, with arms and stories'. Most of the pageants, however, lacked even this heraldic element. The formal coronation on 1 June, a more austere affair, concluded with the ritual bestowal of the Confessor's crown, shortly followed by its removal ('beyng hevy') and replacement by her own, and concluding with the queen's strolling to St Edward's shrine to make an offering.[46]

One must take into account the structure as well as the content of public celebrations if one is to understand their political function. In the case of the coronation ceremony and of the pageants which invariably preceded and followed it, as also in the cases of certain civic rituals such as mayoralty processions, one is repeatedly struck by the emphasis on *motion*, movement on foot, horse or vehicle, across land or water, from one designated point to another, across a pre-set route; these ceremonies exhibit the transitional quality noted by Van Gennep in his classic study of rites of passage.[47] Processions, progresses and triumphal entries, like the smaller ceremonies of going in to dinner or dressing and undressing, all involve the transfer of real and symbolic persons from one location to another, room to room, street to street, or town to town.

'The crucial test of any political order', writes Edward Muir, 'comes when power or authority is transferred'.[48] The Tudor era ended not with the death of Elizabeth on 24 March 1603, nor with her burial five weeks later, but with the coronation of her successor in late July, which brought a period of mourning to a symbolic close. The crowning of James in a 'wonderful' year otherwise marked by a disastrous round of plague provides a particularly good example of the spatial aspect of political festivals, since it marked not simply the regular succession of one prince to another, but the admission of a foreign monarch to the territory possessed by his new English subjects and by his royal predecessors.[49] While the new king proceeded slowly from Edinburgh to London in the early spring of 1603, he and his family existed in an extended 'liminal phase' between his old kingdom and his new one.[50] A few months later, that progress was acted out anew, along much more formal lines and within a confined space. This time, James stood on a threshold between his previous condition as a foreign prince and his future one as an English monarch. But not all the motion within that ceremony, nor the liminality which it enfolds, is spatial. Rather, the movement took place in a dimension of 'space/time', inhabited not just by real, living and present subjects, but by a gallery of figures from the past who welcomed the new prince to their fold and passed their authority on to him 'in person'.[51] Thus the Scot, and with him a foreign realm, entered the ceremonial space/time of his Tudor, Plantagenet and Norman predecessors, ironically inverting the traditional belief in the feudal overlordship of England over Scotland. James's passage into the space/time of England was thus achieved both allegorically *within* the ceremony (by the explicit harking back to earlier monarchs through verse, speech and play) and literally *through* the ceremony, by the king's active participation in the proceedings.

When James received the crown of his new realm, he was careful to adhere to the long-standing ceremonial form, according to which he was invested with the regalia not just of English kingship, but of a *particular* king, St Edward the Confessor.[52] Following James's anointment (itself a sacralization with historical roots reaching back via the Anglo-Saxons to the Old Testament) and the communion, both king and queen walked to the Confessor's chapel. There Edward's robe and crown were removed, restoring the king's identity as a distinct individual, and as a flesh-and-blood, not merely symbolic and semi-divine, monarch; the royal couple then received their own robes at the hands of the Great Chamberlain of England while the Archbishop of Canterbury placed the imperial crowns of England on their heads. But the king, his individuality displayed in his own garments, now re-established his connection with the past by taking the Confessor's sceptre in hand. This last rite had been repeated by most of England's kings over the centuries, but James's Scottishness, his obvious difference in speech and manner from the social body surrounding him, made this particular instance all the more striking. Through it, a prince who was not simply young or new, but alien, accepted responsibility for and the allegiance of his new subjects; as he acquired the symbols of royal power that had belonged to the last Anglo-Saxon monarch, so he swore at the same time to uphold the 'laws' which, tradition asserted, that king had codified.

The ceremony did not stop, however, with this 'formal' and internal segment. It was then opened to a wider public, and to the intrusion of additional informal ceremonies and performances whose substance was of an historical nature even if their form varied from event to event.[53] Now that the prince was a part of English space/time, all of English history lay within his domain, and events and personae from the past could present themselves, like so many vassals doing homage to their new lord. In a pageant following the coronation, the two roses of England, a reminder of the unity and peace that Henry VII had brought to his realm, were offered the king as garlands. Another planned 'device' (which, it turned out, could not be performed after the order of procession was unexpectedly changed), involved two knights, representing the two national patron saints, St George and St Andrew, greeting each other, and riding toward the king where they would be welcomed by the 'Genius of the Place'. Two national symbols of chivalry and honour, each with the sacred sheen provided by sainthood, would be tracked visually by king and spectators, coming together forever at a designated symbolic point in space/time; the change of route which prevented that set course being followed thus made the entire pageant unworkable. More successful was a pageant, this time involving the king as participant rather than spectator, sponsored by the Italians resident in London. This produced echoes of a more recent past, and centred on the issue of dynastic succession rather than the meeting of nations. In it the king rode toward the figure of Henry VII, at whose hands he received a sceptre, thereby having his authority from the Confessor 'overlaid' with that of his more recent Tudor forebear. The whole line of kings stretching back to the Conquest (a subtle shift in emphasis and implication, since it did not involve any direct link to the pre-Conquest regime of St Edward) became the subject of a speech to the king later in the coronation festivities, when the Recorder of London, Sir Henry

Montagu, pledged the loyalty of the city while boasting of the 'Twentie and more . . . soveraigns we have served since our Conquest'. This picked up on the theme articulated earlier by William Hubbock upon James's first entrance into the Tower, when the king was welcomed on the 'first step of your investiture into a kingdome, determined unto you by divine decree before you were borne'. That brief ceremony had been followed by a lecture on the history of the 'Bloody' Tower, including the murder of the princes by Richard III.[54]

Public ceremonies added to the lustre of public monarchy, and they emphasized the roots of newly acquired powers in old traditions. As Richard Hooker would point out in his defence of ceremonies at the end of the sixteenth century, such rituals were a natural part of the order of things:

> No nation under heaven either doth or ever did suffer publique actions which are of waight whether they be civil and temporall or els spiritual and sacred, to passe without some visible solemnitie; the very strangenes whereof and difference from that which is common, doth cause popular eyes to observe and to marke the same.

In order to have their legitimizing effect, rituals in any society must be re-enacted according to certain accepted principles or rules.[55] Almost all Tudor and Stuart public ceremonial took place according to long formalized customs, but as in the case of James's coronation, changes were sometimes forced, reluctantly, by physical constraints. On 24 October 1549 the mayor's feast took place in London as usual, but with only one dish, in recognition of the general dearth which three months earlier had sparked Kett's rebellion. In the afternoon the mayor, 'ryding to Pawles after the ould custome', was obliged to proceed in a 'newe order' to the 'Bishop's stone' where he said the psalm *De profundis* 'which they of ould tyme used to say about the stone'. The minor change of route, sufficiently important to merit contemporary comment, was necessitated by the tearing down, earlier that year, of the cloister known as Pardon Churchyard, the traditional passage for Lord Mayors, to clear space for the 'protectors' place'.[56] The most carefully planned procession could be subverted by something as innocent as a tactless decoration or device. In August 1554 the conduit in Gracechurch Street was 'newe paynted and gilded' for the entrance of Philip and Mary. On its turrets were painted the nine worthies and Kings Henry VIII and Edward VI; each of these figures bore maces, swords or pole-axes except for Henry, who was depicted with a sceptre in one hand and a book 'whereon was wrytten *Verbum Dei*' in the other, clearly inspired by the title page of the 1539 English Bible. Bishop Gardiner summoned the painter and threatened him with imprisonment until he repainted Henry 'in the sted of the booke of *Verbum Dei*, to have in his handes a newe payre of gloves'.[57]

In most instances, pageants mixed historical or pseudo-historical elements with allegorical ones derived from the Bible or from classical mythology: it is worth remembering that modern notions of the division between 'real' historical figures or events and mythical or biblical ones do not apply to the early modern mind. On his progress into York in 1486, Henry VII was greeted by 'the begynner' of the city, Ebrauk, who presented him with its keys, as well as by Solomon (representing wisdom) and David (representing imperial power); further along, by the Council chamber at Ouse Bridge, stood 'sex kinges Crouned betokining the sex henries'.[58] An elaborate series of tableaux vivants for the entry of Katharine of Aragon into London in November 1501 and her marriage to Arthur, perhaps the most sumptuous of all early Tudor spectacles, included two figures on London Bridge representing St Ursula and St Katherine. After playing on the names of two stars, 'Ursus Minor' and 'Arcturus', and thereby investing the match with cosmic rather than merely historical significance, Ursula declares:

> As Arthure your Spouse, than the second now
> Succedeth the first Arthure in dignite,
> So in like Wise, Madame Kateryn, you
> As second Ursula shall succede me.[59]

But most of the figures who address Katharine are not of British origin. In fact, with the sole exception of 'Alfonso', her distant Spanish ancestor, they are not really historical at all. Job, Boethius, 'Pollicy' (dressed as the early Tudor idea of a Roman senator, in Renaissance clothing) and the archangel Raphael do not derive from national legends or even dynastic myths; they inhabit a boundless and fluid allegorical domain which has room alike for biblical characters, angels and personified virtues. The palace constructed by Henry VIII in 1520 for his meeting with Francis I at the Field of Cloth of Gold would, in similar fashion, feature a gate 'set with compassed Images of ancient Princes, as Hercules, Alexander and other by entrayled worke', and masquers dressed as the nine worthies danced in celebration of the concord of two great princes. Hercules was mythical; Alexander, though like the rest of the nine worthies a real person, might just as well have been mythical given the enormous distortion in his biography wrought by centuries of romances in which he figured as a quasi-Christian crusading knight – a Greek St George. Together, these figures assisted Henry's own fashioning of himself as a latter-day champion.[60]

Pageant-makers for Elizabeth I proved no less adept at mixing myth and history into the imagery of power, but their past-references become more 'realistic' and specific, and draw on themes from relatively recent history. Under the first two Tudors the Wars of the Roses were a recent agony, to be recalled in carefully controlled ways as a reminder of the blessings of peace, and I have suggested that the regime's interest in them declined after 1530. Under Elizabeth, echoes of the calamitous fifteenth century were to sound anew. On Elizabeth's passage from the Tower to Whitehall in 1559, one of several pageants featured figures of Henry VII with a red rose, Elizabeth of York with a white and Henry VIII in his imperial crown, accompanied by music. At the queen's coronation any suppression of her father and brother's memory that may have occurred under Mary was sharply reversed:

> and at Grasyus [Gracechurch] strett a goodly pagantt of kyng [Henry] the viij and quen Ane ys wyff and of ther lenege, and in Cornelle [Cornhill] a-nodur goodly pagantt of kyng Henry and kyng Edward the vjth.[61]

London spectators were thus reminded of the early days of the Reformation, now revived by the providential accession of Henry's younger daughter, and they were simultaneously cast back to a more remote, mythical past, represented at Temple Bar by 'ij grett gyanttes, the one name was Goot-magott a Albaon and thodur Corineus'.[62]

Perhaps even more effective a medium for the use of history was the history play. It reached a smaller number of people at any time than the pageant, but unlike the pageant it could be staged repeatedly; and, unlike the noisy confusion of a procession, the drama's messages, represented in a confined space through dialogue as well as image, left less to the imagination. From Bale's early prototype *King Johan*, through Sackville and Norton's *Gorboduc* in 1561 and on to Ford's *Perkin Warbeck* in the 1630s, the plays re-enacted key moments in British history from mythical times to the reign of Elizabeth: in Lily Campbell's famous phrase, they served as mirrors of Elizabethan policy.[63] They also reveal the ready acquiescence in dynastic myth and the acceptance of official teaching on subjects like rebellion, obedience and power that made the Tudor and early Stuart interpretation of the national past no mere propaganda but an expression of deep convictions about the order of things, albeit an order open to sporadic and muted challenges.[64] To defend the drama against its puritan critics at the start of the seventeenth century, Thomas Heywood appealed specifically to its generally didactic and specifically political functions, which in his view were most effective in histories:

> Plays are writ with this ayme, and carryed with this methode, to teache the subjects obedience to their King, to shew the people the untimely ends such as have moved tumults, commotions and insurrections, to present them with the flourishing estate of such as live in obedience, exhorting them to allegeance, dehorting them from all trayterous and felloneous strategems.[65]

So long as plays continued to express a shared view of the past, and so long as their performance was controlled through the various companies of actors dependent on royal or aristocratic patronage, they offered a more immediate and effective means to harness history than any printed book. The danger lay in their potential to present, equally effectively, messages antithetical to immediate policy. The notorious example of the staging of *Richard II* on the eve of Essex's rebellion brought down the wrath of Elizabeth, and it has recently been shown that criticism of specific policies, such as the Spanish match in the 1620s, would be incorporated in drama by dramatists in the patronage of aristocrats such as the third earl of Pembroke.[66] From 1581, plays were screened by the Revels Office for potentially subversive material which was excised to ensure orthodoxy. Whole scenes were removed from the anonymous play book *Sir Thomas More* by the Master of the Revels, Edmund Tilney, in the early 1590s. In Tilney's view, the opening scene in which the commons are urged to unite and seek redress of grievances, along with other episodes portraying popular unrest, were not mere literary effects but instances of past disorders too dangerous to re-enact on a public stage.[67]

As the sixteenth century wore on, the number of new chronicles, prose histories, historical poems and plays increased, peaking in the period between 1580 and 1620. Yet Tudor and early Stuart governments that were otherwise quick to employ printed propaganda in other contexts did little to turn this to positive advantage. When Courts and civic oligarchies all across Europe either boasted an official historiographer or sponsored semi-official histories through the patronage network, English examples of royal encouragement of historical research and writing are conspicuous only because they are rare. Henry VII and Henry VIII's limited ventures in this regard have already been mentioned, and between 1548 and 1551 Edward VI supported the historical writing of the continental reformer Johannes Sleidan.[68] As for Elizabeth, whatever love she may have felt for history did not match her fear of it. She ignored a suggestion by John Dee at the start of her reign that a national library be established for the preservation of historical documents and books; a similar petition near the end of the reign, from Sir Robert Cotton and two fellow members of the first Society of Antiquaries, would also go unanswered.

Royal control of the interpretation and representation of the past seemed strongest precisely when it was being threatened or subverted. A number of famous incidents of government suppression or censorship of history and historians have survived. Following Thomas Cromwell's execution the Council was forced to issue an order restricting the flow of ballads in his praise. Ballads, letters and rhymes on the persecution of Protestants such as Anne Askew and the duchess of Suffolk appeared throughout Mary's reign, inspiring the *Act against seditious words and rumours*, which made the printers as well as the authors of 'heynous, sedicious and sclanderous writinges, rimes, ballads, letters, papers and bookes' liable to prosecution.[69] Every incident, personality or image from the past instantly conjured up a constellation of associated facts from elsewhere in time. A history favourable to Richard III, such as that written (but not published) by Sir George Buck early in the 1610s, implicitly suggested the illegitimacy of the king that had deposed him.[70] One favourable to Henry IV's rebellion in 1399 would be equally unacceptable because it implied that rebellion against an anointed prince could prosper. Works on foreign history, generally safe territory, might be censored or suppressed – the *Historie of Italie* by William Thomas, the Protestant humanist and politician who was executed in 1554 for complicity in Wyatt's rebellion, was burnt by the hangman in 1549 but reprinted in 1561. Translators might also eliminate or gloss rough or offensive passages in their texts, as Geffray Fenton did with his *Guicciardini*, or as Richard Knolles did in 1606 by rendering Jean Bodin's *République* as the less sinister 'common weal'.[71] In such cases, loyalty to one's text placed a poor second to allegiance to the crown. The Tudor inclination to restrict the range of possible interpretations of history is most evident, however, in its treatment of works on the English past. Hall's chronicle was suppressed in 1555, the year of the royal marriage.[72] The same year saw the suppression of the first edition of the *Mirror for Magistrates*, which would nevertheless survive to become one of the most popular of Elizabethan works on English history, with its cautionary tales told by the ghosts of ill-fated princes and nobles. Both its contents and subject, long part of *de casibus* literature, would have escaped suspicion but for its appearance in the year following Wyatt's rebellion.[73]

Elizabeth's actions in this respect are famous, and during her reign words like 'York', 'Lancaster', 'Bolingbroke' and 'Richard II' became code words for obedience, red flags trotted out by queen and Council at the first sign of trouble from a factious Commons, a troublesome noble or an indiscreet author. When John Stubbs published his *Discovery of a Gaping Gulf* in 1579 to dissuade the queen from her prospective French match, he provided many historical examples of unsuccessful royal marriages (that of Mary being still painfully fresh). The Council responded swiftly and terribly. Author and printer both lost their right hands; a proclamation of 27 September protested indignantly that the queen was hurt and offended by the contents of the book, all the more so since her Commons had persistently badgered her to marry as the only remedy to precisely the horrors named in the objectionable book, 'and namely to avoid all such or greater civil wars and bloodsheds as betwixt the houses of York and Lancaster are lamentably recorded for the crown'.[74]

The Elizabethan regime responded in like fashion to any form of historical reference that smacked of potential sedition.[75] An order of the archbishop and of the bishop of London in 1599 forbade the publication of unlicensed books, chronicles or plays on English history, along with satires and epigrams. As all good Shakespearean scholars know, several pages from the second edition of Holinshed's *Chronicle* were expunged by the Council in 1587. Most famous of all is Elizabeth's fury over John Hayward's incomplete life of Henry IV, which was dedicated to Essex. A relatively harmless book in itself, it appeared to make a case for the deposition of Richard II. Hayward was examined twice by the Council and his book was recalled (a particularly ineffective form of Tudor censorship resembling the barn door through which the horse has already escaped). After Essex's men mounted their impromptu version of *Richard II*, Hayward found himself in the Tower; he perhaps only narrowly escaped joining his patron on the scaffold.[76]

Richard II did indeed strike a raw nerve where Elizabeth was concerned, though precise parallels between the reigns, aside from both monarchs' lack of an evident successor, are actually rather scarce. When the queen granted William Lambarde an audience in August 1601, she welcomed the presentation copy of his pandects of the Tower records with enthusiasm before suddenly falling on the reign of Richard II. 'I am Richard II. Know ye not that?' Lambarde nervously mumbled a critical comment against the 'most unkind gentleman' who had so recently risen, like Bolingbroke, in rebellion against his prince, to which the queen replied 'He that will forget God, will also forget his benefactors; this tragedie was played 40tie times in open streets and houses'. Elizabeth had recently been presented with a portrait of Richard II by Lord Lumley, which she had put 'in order with the ancestors and successors'; as a special privilege, she commanded the keeper of her private gallery at Westminster to show it to the antiquary.[77]

Yet when all is said, explicit instances of the suppression or enforced revision of history are surprisingly few in relation to the growing quantity of historical research and writing; as a result they stand out all the more and can mislead liberal-minded modern scholars into blowing them out of proportion. Although the constraints of writing historical prose (even the epigrammatic Tacitean prose of the late sixteenth century) allowed less room for the sort of moral and political reflection and questioning which is so apparent in historical verse and drama, historical writers did have some freedom of movement; they knew where the vague boundaries between speakable and unspeakable lay, and generally did not venture beyond them. Two excellent recent studies have, in different ways, demonstrated that both in the interpretation and the depiction of historical characters there was an accepted 'safe zone' within which the historian or biographer was more or less at liberty to say what he liked.[78] The boundaries were rarely drawn out, because they were generally acknowledged and tacitly accepted both by the government and by writers. A historian could point out the faults of past princes, but he must use restraint and choose his words carefully. As an epitaph on James I put it,

> Princes are gods. (O!) do not then
> Rake in their graves to prove them men.[79]

No one argued this principle more clearly than George Puttenham, putative author of *The Arte of English Poesie*, according to whom,

> in speaking or writing of a Princes affaires & fortunes there is a certaine decorum, that we may not use the same termes in their busines, as we might very well doe in a meaner persons, the case being all one, such reverence is due to their estates. As for example, if an Historiographer shal write of an Emperor or King, how such a day hee joyned battel with his enemies, and being over-laide ranne out of the fielde, and tooke his heeles, or put spurre to his horse, and fled as fast as he could: the termes be not decent.[80]

The state of historical knowledge was simply not clear enough to tie historians down to a rigid, crown-sponsored 'party line' and because Elizabethan and Jacobean chronicles and histories do so often seem to be saying the same things about the same kings we are apt to lose sight of the shadings, nuances and echoes that made them different works. Moreover, the writer of history was faced with a number of conflicting restrictions on interpretation which he had somehow to reconcile through understatement or ellipsis. Camden, reluctantly dragooned into writing his *Annales* by James and Salisbury, faced the daunting task of defending the reputation of Mary Stuart without detracting from that of Elizabeth. A perennial problem, dating from the time of Foxe's *Acts and Monuments*, was what to do about Henry VIII and Mary Tudor, two manifest persecutors of the godly. Like MPs reluctant to think ill of the monarch, historians generally opted for the convenient whipping-boy of the 'evil counsellor'. In this manner Mary could be tastefully drawn as a good, or at least noble queen, misled by her popish upbringing and by the wicked bishops, Gardiner and Bonner. Henry VIII became the godly reformer, temporarily duped by papists into executing his most faithful minister, Cromwell, and into assenting to the Act of Six Articles, and so on. Often it was easier simply to sidestep the issue altogether. Thus John Lyly's Euphues, reciting the recent history of England, skirts Mary's reign in a bland, inoffensive, three lines:

> The elder sister the Princes Marie, succeeded as next heire to the grave, touching whose life, I can say little bicause I was scarse borne, and what others say, of me shalbe forborne.

Francis Godwin, bishop of Llandaff and Hereford, offered a similarly noncommittal assessment of Mary, though the change of dynasties allowed him, and others, to treat Henry VIII as a mercurial despot.[81]

Earlier events and personalities posed similar problems: Henry V was a national hero, and his reputation peaked under Henry VIII and again under Elizabeth. Yet historians and playwrights were aware that he had become king only through his father's usurpation. Shakespeare resolves this tension in his *Henry V* with the famous 'expiation' speech (IV. i, 310–14) in which the young king acknowledges his father's fault while imploring the Almighty not to visit this sin upon him in battle:

> O not to-day, think not upon the fault
> My father made in compassing the crown.
> I Richard's body have interred new,
> And on it have bestowed more contrite tears,
> Than from it issued forced drops of blood.

Edward III proved less troublesome; although he had gained the throne through the deposition and murder of his own father, he could be described not as an accomplice to parricide but as a vengeful Orestes destroying his mother and her lover, Roger Mortimer, to avenge his father's death. Yet even here doubts remained, and many later Tudor and early Stuart historians mouthed Polydore Vergil's providential interpretation of English history whereby every successive line of English kings was snuffed out in the third descent.

Another route lay open, but it was an implicitly dangerous one which few historians cared to travel before the early seventeenth century. This consisted in acknowledging that the king of the day, the *de facto* ruler, ruled by the right of conquest, which also signified divine favour. Throughout the sixteenth century, historians and chroniclers were uneasy with this concept, and preferred to explain so-called 'conquests' in other ways: they declared William I the true heir of Edward the Confessor, and happily accepted the early Tudor claim that Henry VII had deposed not a king but a usurping tyrant and a monster. But by the end of the century, when widespread fear of a disputed succession (compounded by a dread of international Catholicism and by an acute awareness of the disasters which had for several decades torn France apart) had turned the memory of the civil wars into something very nearly approaching a national obsession, one begins to note an embryonic tendency toward 'de factoism'. This was doubtless aided by the growing influence among English historians and poets of 'politique' authors, both ancients such as Tacitus and Seneca and modern commentators like Bodin, Montaigne and the neo-stoics, particularly Justus Lipsius.[82] The traitor's fate which befalls Kent in Marlowe's *Edward II*, misled into rebellion on his deposed brother's behalf, provides one illustration. Samuel Daniel's *Civil Wars*, conceived in the 1590s amid fears of renewed dynastic conflict, refuses to bestow legitimacy on either the Yorkists or the Lancastrians, while his later prose history offers numerous examples of the overthrow or bypassing of rightful heirs, including Rufus and Henry I's of their elder brother, Robert of

Normandy, John's of his nephew Arthur of Brittany, and Edward III's of Edward II. The ordinary subject must acquiesce in such an event, not compound usurpation with rebellion, commented Daniel, citing as his authorities 'th'auncient fathers of the law', Thorpe and Fortescue.[83]

To men of such views, the justness of the Yorkist cause – never safe to espouse under the Tudors – lost even its technical validity. Henry IV might well have sinned in taking the crown, but had he not paid for that sin with fourteen miserable years of rebellions and an early grave? By the time his grandson reached his majority, the Lancastrian line had been sanctioned by God for forty years. The steady rule of a family with dubious title was infinitely preferable to the carnage that could be wrought by a Richard of York, however just his claim. The same could be said of Edward IV's reign. When he was on the throne, he ruled as king, and the good of the country was best served by obeying him whom providence had so favoured – at least until providence changed its mind. In his two-part play *Edward the Fourth* (first printed in 1599 and reprinted several times under James I), which he based on the popular ballad of Edward and the tanner of Tamworth, Thomas Heywood offers as bald a statement of the *de facto* theory as one can find before the civil war. The fugitive King Edward, on the run during the Lancastrian readeption, disguises himself as Ned, the king's butler, and meets John Hobs, a tanner, whom he discovers to be quite indifferent to the rights and wrongs of the dynastic dispute:

KING: Shall I say my conscience? I think Harry is the true king.
HOBS: Art advised of that? Henry's of the old house of Lancaster, and
    that progeny do I love.
KING: And thou doest not hate the house of York?
HOBS: Why, no; for I am just akin to Sutton Windmill; I can grind which
    way soe're the winde blow. If it be Harry, I can say well fare Lancaster.
    If it be Edward, I can sing Yorke, Yorke, for my money.[84]

The important thing to Heywood's tanner was not the legitimacy of any single monarch but the continuity of the succession: Lancastrians and Yorkists were all Plantagenets, as were their Tudor heirs. Heywood was a popularizer of history, not a political theorist, but the very unspeculative character of his thought suggests that technical questions of strict legitimacy were beginning to matter rather less by 1600 then they had fifty years earlier. James VI's own claim to the throne of a queen who had refused to name her successor was far from impeccable, and Henry VIII's will had also specifically excluded the Stuart line sixty years earlier. Yet almost everyone preferred to sweep any such objections under the carpet, except for Catholic polemicists such as Robert Parsons, who objected to any heretical succession, and the bungling conspirators in the Bye and Main plots.[85]

The attitude of early Stuart historians toward William the Conqueror provides another example. A few, like Sir John Hayward, continued to cling to the line that William had merely claimed what was rightfully his. Samuel Daniel, on the other hand, was convinced that the Norman had seized the throne by conquest from Harold, the rightful and duly elected English king. Yet according to Daniel's scheme of things, no less than Hayward's, William I, Rufus, Henry I and Stephen, each of whom had dubious titles, still merited obedience as the kings for the moment. Antiquaries such as Camden had no doubt that William and his progeny 'ruled like conquerors with their swords in their hands', while James I himself openly claimed that his distant ancestor, Fergus, had held the throne of Scotland by right of conquest.[86]

Only after 1640 did the issue of rule by conquest, and the legitimacy of a *de facto* regime, acquire more than a theoretical interest, becoming a central concern, for instance, of Hobbes and other participants in the Engagement Controversy following Charles I's execution. As it did, traditional shibboleths like the rule of primogeniture over succession (which, the antiquaries had by now realized, was a development of the high Middle Ages, not an immemorial practice) gradually yielded to more pragmatic attitudes. In the Exclusion Crisis of the early 1680s, it would be the crown and its apologists, as much as their opponents, who claimed to be upholding the 'fundamental laws' of the realm by refusing to abandon the principle of primogeniture.[87] By that time, of course, recent memories of a far more terrible conflict combined with long-standing anti-popery to lay the ghosts of Plantagenet kings once and for all, making further reference back to the fifteenth-century wars seem almost trivial.

Though the power of the past remained strong throughout the seventeenth century, power *over* the past was dissipated after 1640, redistributed and channelled into the expanded ideological spectrum stretching from leveller and republican to royalist, as the variety of histories written in the second half of the century amply demonstrate. Any attempt to reimpose a Court monopoly on historical interpretation was for that reason doomed before it began. Charles II, significantly, was the first English monarch since Henry VII to feel the need to appoint a Court historiographer, filling the position with the professional writer James Howell. A revival of censorship probably did something to muffle historical argument in the 1660s and 1670s. But it could never silence it. Historians had simply become accustomed to the cut and thrust of historical controversy, and so had their readers.[88] Like so much else, the civil war had redefined the ways in which contemporary political and religious issues played into and were in turn influenced by perceptions of the past. That peculiar dialogue with history which was so much a part of Tudor statesmanship, as it was for other Renaissance regimes, had disappeared, replaced by a chorus of discordant voices.

NOTES

1 F.S. Fussner, *The Historical Revolution*, London, Routledge & Kegan Paul, 1962; F. J. Levy, *Tudor Historical Thought*, San Marino, Calif., Huntington Library, 1967; M. McKisack, *Medieval History in the Tudor Age*, Oxford, Clarendon Press, 1971; A. B. Ferguson, *Clio Unbound: Perception of the Social and Cultural Past in Renaissance England*, Durham, NC, Duke University Press, 1979. Popular perceptions of the past remain largely unexplored territory, but in the mean time see K. Thomas, *The Perception of the Past in Early Modern England*, Creighton Lecture, London, 1983. Earlier drafts of this chapter were read and discussed at the Folger Shakespeare Library Symposium in May 1990 which resulted in the present volume; at the Halifax Medieval and Early Modern Studies Colloquium; and at Queen's University in Kingston, Ontario. I am grateful to the editors and to the participants at these sessions for their helpful comments, and in particular to Roy Martin Haines, Cynthia Neville, Adriana McCrea and A. J. Slavin.

2 M. J. Swartz, V. Turner and A. Tuden (eds) *Political Anthropology*, Chicago, Ill., Aldine, 1966, p. 14.

3 C. Geertz, 'Ideology as a cultural system', in *The Interpretation of Cultures*, New York, Basic Books, 1973, pp. 193–229.

4 G. Ianziti, *Humanistic Historiography under the Sforzas: Politics and Propaganda in Fifteenth-Century Milan*, Oxford, Clarendon Press, 1988, pp. 41–80; F. Gilbert, *Machiavelli and Guicciardini: Politics and History in Sixteenth-Century Florence*, Princeton, NJ, Princeton University Press, 1965; W. J. Bouwsma, *Venice and the Defence of Republican Liberty: Renaissance Values in the Age of the Counter-Reformation*, Berkeley and Los Angeles, Calif., University of California Press, 1968, pp.556–623, and his article, 'Three types of historiography in post-Renaissance Italy', *History and Theory*, 1965, vol. 4, pp. 303–14; E. Cochrane, *Historians and Historiography in the Italian Renaissance*, Chicago, Ill., University of Chicago Press, 1981, pp. 479–93; G. Spini, 'The art of history in the Italian Counter Reformation', in E. Cochrane (ed.) *The Late Italian Renaissance 1525–1630*, New York, Harper & Row, 1970, pp. 91–133.

5 D. W. Rollason, 'The cults of murdered royal saints in Anglo-Saxon England', *Anglo-Saxon England*, 1983, vol. 11, pp. 1–22; S. J. Ridyard, *The Royal Saints of Anglo-Saxon England*, Cambridge, Cambridge University Press, 1988.

6 J. W. McKenna, 'Piety and propaganda: the cult of King Henry VI', in B. Rowland (ed.) *Chaucer and Middle English Studies in Honour of Rossell Hope Robbins*, London, 1974, pp. 72–88; J. W. McKenna, 'Popular canonization as political propaganda: the cult of Archbishop Scrope', *Speculum*, 1970, vol. 45, pp. 605–23; J. M. Theilmann, 'Political canonization and political symbolism in Medieval England', *JBS*, 1990, vol. 29, pp. 241–66.

7 The cult of Henry VI received new support from Henry VII's regime, and the statue of Henry at York Minster was restored (or at least replaced) in 1516, only to be removed again at the Reformation as a source of idolatry – a very different reason from that motivating the earlier removal: G. E. Aylmer and R. Cant (eds) *A History of York Minster*, Oxford, Clarendon Press, 1977, pp. 182–7; McKenna, 1974, op. cit., p. 74.

8 Bodl. MS Rawl. D.1062, fos 92r–119v; PRO SP 9/47/1, fo. 5r. 'The prophecye of Sybyll & of Merlyn'; K. Thomas, *Religion and the Decline of Magic*, New York, Scribner, 1971 repr. Harmondsworth, Penguin, 1973, pp. 461–514; Sharon L. Jansen, *Political Protest and Prophecy under Henry VIII*, Woodbridge, Suffolk and Rochester, New York, Boydell Press, 1991.

9 S. Anglo, 'The British history in early Tudor propaganda', *Bulletin of the John Rylands Library*, 1961–2, vol. 54, pp. 17–48, and S. Anglo, *Spectacle, Pageantry, and Early Tudor Policy*, Oxford, Clarendon Press, 1969, pp. 44–5; R. F. Brinkley, *Arthurian Legend in the Seventeenth Century*, Baltimore, Md, Johns Hopkins University Press, 1932, is in need of revision; meanwhile, the best discussion of the legends remains T. D. Kendrick, *British Antiquity*, London, Methuen, 1950.

10 BL MS Cotton Julius B. XII, for instance, contains the ceremonials for Prince Arthur's christening (fo. 21v); various other ceremonies and armorial displays anchor the dynasty in the Norman, Anglo-Saxon, British and biblical past through references to, and in some instances addresses by, figures such as William the Conqueror, Ebraucus, Solomon, David, St George and Ethelbert (fos 10v–20v).

11 Bodl. MS Eng. hist. e. 193; D. Hay, *Polydore Vergil: Renaissance Historian and Man of Letters*, Oxford, Clarendon Press, 1952, pp. 79–81, 129–68 and appendices. The *Anglica Historia* was first printed at Basle in 1534: for translation, see H. Ellis (ed.) *Three Books of Polydore Vergil's English History*, London, Camden Society, old series (hereafter o.s.), vol. 29 (1844); H. Ellis (ed.) *Polydore Vergil's English History*, London, Camden Society, o.s., vol. 36 (1846); D. Hay (ed. and trans.) *The Anglica historia of Polydore Vergil, A.D. 1485–1537*, London, Camden Society, 3rd ser., vol. 74 (1950).

12 Anglo, 1969, op. cit., pp. 45–56; BL MS Add. 46354, fo. 30r; A. R. Wagner, *Catalogue of English Medieval Rolls of Arms*, Oxford, Oxford University Press, 1950, pp. 120–1.

13 BL MS Add. 33736, fos 3r, 10v; MS Arundel 26, fos 58r–63v; MS Royal 18 A. lxxv.

14 T. More, *The History of King Richard the Third*, R. S. Sylvester (ed.), *The English Works of St. Thomas More*, New Haven, Conn., Yale University Press, 1976; A. F. Pollard, 'The making of Sir Thomas More's *Richard III*', in J. G. Edwards, V. H. Galbraith and E. F. Jacob (eds) *Historical Essays in Honour of James Tait*, Manchester, privately printed, 1933, pp. 223–38; Levy, 1967, op. cit., pp. 69–73; A. Fox, *Politics and Literature in the Reigns of Henry VII and Henry VIII*, Oxford, Basil Blackwell, 1989, pp. 108–27.

15 Fox, op. cit., pp. 17–19. See, for instance, an anonymous pro-Yorkist tract in the papers of Thomas Wriothesley the herald (uncle of the more famous first earl of Southampton), concerning Edward IV's escape from 'many great and perilous daungers and dyficultes', together with a description of the earl of Warwick's revolt: BL MS Add. 46354, fos 32v–36r. I owe this reference to the kindness of A. J. Slavin.

16 B. André, *Bernardi Andreae Tholosatis de vita atque gestis Henrici Septimi historia*, in *Memorials of King Henry the Seventh*, J. Gairdner (ed.), Rolls series, vol. 10, 1858, pp. 9–130; André's *Les Douze triomphes de Henry VII*, written c. 1497, compares the king's deeds to the twelve labours of Hercules. For the account therein of the death of Richard III, see the presentation copy of the manuscript in BL MS Royal 16 E. xvii, fo. 8v, printed in Gairdner, *Memorials*, pp. 133–53.

17 Erasmus to Andrea Ammonio, 9 May 1512, P. S. Allen (ed.) *Opus Epistolarum*

Desiderii Erasmi Roterodami, 12 vols, Oxford, Clarendon Press, 1906–58, vol. 1, p. 513; M. Firpo, 'Carmeliano, Pietro', *Dizionario Biografico degli Italiani*, vol. 20, pp. 410–13; P. Carmeliano, *Petri Carmeliani Brixiensis poetae suasoria Laeticiae ad angliam pro sublatis bellis civilibus et Arthuro principe nato epistola* (written 1486), BL MS Add. 33736, fos 1–11v; Hay, 1952, op. cit., p. 79.

18 *CSPSp, 1534–35*, p. 468; Bodl. MS Eng. hist. e. 193, parch. 2; 'King Richards feilde' (an undated late Elizabethan poem), Bodl. MS Tanner 306, fos. 162r–172r.

19 C. L. Kingsford (ed.) *The First English Life of King Henry the Fifth*, Oxford, Oxford University Press, 1911; C. L. Kingsford, 'The early biographies of Henry V', *EHR*, 1910, vol. 25, pp. 58–92; A. B. Ferguson, *The Indian Summer of English Chivalry*, Durham, NC, Duke University Press, 1960, passim; G. Kipling, *The Triumph of Honour: Burgundian Origins of the Elizabethan Renaissance*, Leiden, Leiden University Press for the Sir Thomas Browne Institute, 1977, pp. 11–30.

20 S. Gunn, 'The French wars of Henry VIII', in J. Black (ed.) *The Origins of War in Early Modern Europe*, Edinburgh, John Donald, 1987, p. 40; Bodl. MS Eng. hist. c. 380, fos 1–13v, 18r, 25v is an undated early Tudor compilation, possibly assembled for the king's benefit, from chronicles by Walsingham, Higden and others; it concerns Edward III's claim to France and also lists notorious evil counsellors such as Piers Gaveston and Michael de la Pole:

21 J. K. McConica, *English Humanists and Reformation Politics under Henry VIII and Edward VI*, Oxford, Clarendon Press, 1965, pp. 150–99; for revisions to McConica's interpretation, see G. R. Elton, *Reform and Renewal: Thomas Cromwell and the Common Weal*, Cambridge, Cambridge University Press, 1973, pp. 38–65; M. Dowling, *Humanism in the Age of Henry VIII*, London, Croom Helm, 1986, pp. 55–68; T. F. Mayer, *Thomas Starkey and the Common Weal*, Cambridge, Cambridge University Press, 1989.

22 G. R. Elton, *The Tudor Constitution*, 2nd edn, Cambridge, Cambridge University Press, 1982, p. 353; G. D. Nicholson, 'The nature and function of historical argument in the Henrician Reformation', Cambridge University PhD thesis, 1977, passim; but cf. E. Surtz and V. Murphy (eds) *The Divorce Tracts of Henry VIII*, Angers, *Moreana*, 1988, Introduction; A. J. Slavin, 'Defining the Divorce: a review article', *SCJ*, 1989, vol. 20, pp. 105–11.

23 J. M. Levine, *Humanism and History: Origins of Modern English Historiography*, Ithaca, NY, Cornell University Press, 1987, pp. 54–72; R. Pineas, 'Robert Barnes's polemical use of history', *Bibliothèque d'Humanisme et Renaissance*, 1964, vol. 26, pp. 55-69.

24 *L&P* XIII, ii, 133, p. 49; D. Wilkins, *Concilia Magnae Britanniae et Hiberniae* (4 vols, 1737), iii, 835, reprinting documents from C. Henriquez, *Phoenix reviviscens* (Brussels, Joannis Meerbecii, 1626), pp. 199–212. Though the story of a mock trial seems too good to be true, there is in fact evidence to support the claim that some type of judicial procedure was brought into play. Thomas Knight's letter to Cromwell of 5 October 1538 refers to Thomas Wriothesley's involvement 'in that play', implying some kind of staged judicial process: *L&P* XIII, ii, 542. It is clear that Rome believed the saint to have been formally condemned, though apparently on 16 November, not 11 June as in Henriquez. In October 1538 Paul III appointed Cardinals Campeggio and Contarini, among others, to investigate the despoiling of Becket's and other shrines; but the papal bull of 17 December, in renewing the 1535 excommunication of Henry VIII, cites as justification the burning of Becket's bones *after* he had been called to judgment and declared a traitor: *L&P* XIII, ii, 1087. For argu-

ments for and against the historicity of the trial see J. H. Pollen, 'Henry VIII and St Thomas Becket', *The Month*, 1921, vol. 137, pp. 324–31, and J. F. Davis, 'Lollards, Reformers, and St Thomas of Canterbury', *University of Birmingham History Journal*, 1963, vol. 9, pp. 1–15; G. R. Elton, *Policy and Police: The Enforcement of the Reformation in the Age of Thomas Cromwell*, Cambridge, Cambridge University Press, 1972, pp. 16, 23, 257n.

25 Robert Ward to Cromwell, n.d. 1535, *L&P* VIII, 626, p. 237; confession of Friar John Forest (burnt 22 May 1538), *L&P* XIII, i, 1043, p. 385. According to Davis, op. cit., some headway had been made against the cult of Becket by Lollards and early reformers well before the campaign of 1538. Royal hostility to Becket, however, represented a significant new departure, not a continuation of medieval attitudes. Since Henry II's penance for his murder, English kings had been careful to acknowledge Becket's wrongful murder and to take advantage of his growing saintly reputation; many even conducted pilgrimages to the archbishop's shrine, and the last jubilee of Becket was observed at the Field of Cloth of Gold. I wish to thank my former colleague Roy Martin Haines for bringing this point to my attention.

26 Bodl. MS Tanner 343, fo. 18r–v, printed in H. Jenkyns (ed.) *Remains of Thomas Cranmer*, 4 vols, Oxford, Oxford University Press, 1833, vol. 1, p. 260; BL MS Arundel 97, fo. 34v (calendared in *L&P* XIII, ii, 1280, p. 534). For a good example of the despoiling of a shrine, see the inventory of gold and silver plate, crosses and chalices at St Swithin's, Winchester, in BL MS Harl. 358, fo. 17v.

27 Wriothesley to Cromwell, 27 September 1538, *State Papers Published under the Authority of his Majesty's Commission, King Henry VIII*, 11 vols, London, 1830–52, vol. 8, p. 51; also in *L&P* XIII, ii, 442; *L&P* XIII, ii, 401 and 430.

28 C. Wriothesley, *A Chronicle of England during the Reigns of the Tudors*, W. D. Hamilton (ed.) (hereafter cited as Wriothesley, *Chronicle*) vol. 1, p. 87, Camden Society, new ser., vols 11, 20, 1875–7; *L&P* XIII, ii, 741.

29 Wriothesley, *Chronicle*, vol. 1, p. 90. On 13 December 1538 Bishop Rowland Lee reported a case from his diocese of a simpleton who 'repined' against the royal injunctions, especially that concerning Becket: *L&P* XIII, ii, 1,037, p. 443; ibid., 1179, pp. 488–9.

30 *L&P* XIII, ii, 1,171, p. 485; N. Harpsfield, *The Life and Death of Sir Thomas Moore*, E. V. Hitchcock (ed.) EETS, old ser., vol. 186, 1932, p. 215. R. Pynson had printed *The Lyfe of the Blessed Martyr Saynte Thomas* about 1520 (*STC* 23954). Harpsfield noted with equal dismay that the bones of St Augustine of Canterbury, who had 'brought the fayth of Jesus Christe first into this Realme' (and introduced popery, from the reformers' point of view) had also been taken up and burned.

31 John Strype, *Ecclesiastical Memorials, Relating Chiefly to Religion*, 3 vols in 6, Oxford, Clarendon Press, 1822, vol. 3, pt one, p. 333; Sampson to Bullinger, 13 September 1556, in H. Robinson (ed.) *Original Letters Relative to the English Reformation* (hereafter *Original Letters*), PS, vol. 26, Cambridge, 1846–7, p. 177.

32 Bodl. MS Ashmole 241, fos 190–200v; for parallel shifts in attitudes toward King John, see C. Levin, *Propaganda in the English Reformation: Heroic and Villainous Images of King John*, Lewiston, NY, Edwin Mellen Press, 1988; A. R. Braunmuller (ed.) *King John, The Oxford Shakespeare*, Oxford, Clarendon Press, 1989, Introduction, pp. 38–72.

33 See the theoretical discussions in R. W. Cobb and C. D. Elder, *The Political Uses of Symbols*, New York, Longman, 1983, pp. 81–5, 118–23; D. I. Kirtzer,

Ritual, Politics, and Power, New Haven, Conn., Yale University Press, 1988, pp. 3–14, 174–84.

34 B. Jonson, *Sejanus his Fall* (1605), Acts I and III, in C. H. Herford, P. Simpson and E. Simpson (eds) *Ben Jonson*, 10 vols, Oxford, Clarendon Press, 1925–52, vol. IV. Natta's remark is in Act I, line 83.

35 A. Patterson, *Censorship and Interpretation: The Conditions of Reading and Writing in Early Modern England*, Madison, Wis., University of Wisconsin Press, 1984. The phenomenon Patterson describes may be largely an Elizabethan development, since the propaganda and political ballads by earlier Tudor authors such as Skelton do not show the same evidence of restraint: G. Walker, *John Skelton and the Politics of the 1520s*, Cambridge, Cambridge University Press, 1988, pp. 90–123, 188–217; Fox, 1989, op. cit., pp. 132–72. Even under Elizabeth, much evidence survives in manuscript of writers saying things they would likely not commit to print. A good example is provided by William Harrison's chronologies: G. J. R. Parry, *A Protestant Vision: William Harrison and the Reformation of Elizabethan England*, Cambridge, Cambridge University Press, 1987, pp. 270–3.

36 M. A. E. Green (ed.) *Diary of John Rous*, London, Camden Society, o.s., vol. 66 (1856), p. 98; J. E. Neale, 'November 17', in *Essays in Elizabethan History*, London, Jonathan Cape, 1958, pp. 9–20; R. Strong, *The Cult of Elizabeth: Elizabethan Portraiture and Pageantry*, London, Thames & Hudson, 1977, pp. 117–28.

37 F. Yates, *Astraea: The Imperial Theme in the Sixteenth Century*, London, Routledge & Kegan Paul, 1975, pp. 19–87; A. Young, *Tudor and Jacobean Tournaments*, New York, Sheridan House, 1987; J. N. King, *Tudor Royal Iconography: Literature and Art in an Age of Religious Crisis*, Princeton, NJ, Princeton University Press, 1989, pp. 221–66.

38 L. Andrewes, *XCVI Sermons*, in *The Works of Lancelot Andrewes*, 11 vols, Oxford, Library of Anglo-Catholic Theology, 1841–54, vol. 5, pp. 169–85; D. Cressy, *Bonfires and Bells: National Memory and the Protestant Calendar in Elizabethan and Stuart England*, Berkeley, Los Angeles and London, University of California Press, 1989, chs 8 to 10, passim. Other anniversaries, such as the Gowrie conspiracy (5 August) and the Gunpowder Plot (5 November) would also be assigned specific prayer forms.

39 D. Galloway (ed.) *Norwich 1540–1642*, Records of Early English Drama (hereafter *REED*), Toronto, University of Toronto Press, 1984, pp. 122, 155, 346–51; Cressy, op. cit., ch. 7.

40 P. Connerton, *How Societies Remember*, Cambridge, Cambridge University Press, 1989, pp. 41–72.

41 St Edward's Day was celebrated every 13 October: Wriothesley, *Chronicle*, vol. 1, pp. 46, 66–7; R. W. Ingram (ed.) *REED: Coventry*, Toronto, University of Toronto Press, 1981, pp. 31, 33.

42 BL MS Arundel 26; MS Harl. 3504, fos 252v–259r; Bodl. MS Eng. hist. b. 211, fos 1–3; BL MS Cotton Vitellius A XVI, cited in C. L. Kingsford, *English Historical Literature in the Fifteenth Century*, Oxford, Clarendon Press, 1913, p. 207.

43 R. Strong, *Art and Power*, London, Boydell Press, 1984; S. Orgel, *The Illusion of Power: Political Theatre in the English Renaissance*, Berkeley and Los Angeles, Calif., University of California Press, 1975; E. Muir, *Civic Ritual in Renaissance Venice*, Princeton, NJ, Princeton University Press, 1981, pp. 263–89 provides a useful comparison. For the early Stuarts, see G. Parry, *The Golden Age Restor'd: The Culture of the Early Stuart Court, 1603–1640*,

Manchester, Manchester University Press, 1981; R. M. Smuts, *Court Culture and the Origins of a Royalist Tradition in Early Stuart England*, Philadelphia, Pa, University of Pennsylvania Press, 1987.

44 For the coronation of Henry VII, see *Rutland Papers: Original Documents Illustrative of the Courts and Times of Henry VII and Henry VIII*, W. Jerdan (ed.), Camden Society, o.s., 21, 1842, pp. 1–24; for the crowning of Elizabeth of York in 1487, see BL MS Cotton Julius B. XII, fos 30r–45r. For a late Tudor collection of various late medieval and Tudor coronation *ordines*, including Henry VII's, see MS Harl. 3504, fos 241r–244r, 264v–265r: the famous coronation oath of Edward the Confessor is included at fo. 241v. For coronation rites in general, L. G. W. Legg, *English Coronation Records*, Westminster, A. Constable, 1901, pp. xxix–xxxi; P. E. Schramm, *A History of the English Coronation*, L. G. W. Legg (trans.), Oxford, Clarendon Press, 1937, pp. 96–140.

45 Bodl. MS Eng. hist. b. 211, fos 4v–5r; Anon., 'Gods motive to repentance', Bodl. MS Rawl. D. 13, fos 112v–113v.

46 H. Ellis (ed.) *Hall's Chronicle*, London, J. Johnson et al., 1809, repr. New York, AMS Press, 1965, pp. 798–803; W. de Worde, *The Noble Triumphant Coronation of Queen Anne, Wife unto the Noble King Henry the viiith*, London, 1533, reprinted in E. Arber (ed.) *An English Garner*, 8 vols, Westminster, Constable, 1895–6, vol. 2, pp. 41–60.

47 A. Van Gennep, *The Rites of Passage*, M. B. Vizedom and G. L. Caffee (trans), Chicago, Ill., University of Chicago Press, 1960.

48 Muir, op. cit., p. 263; E. Shils and M. Young, 'The meaning of the coronation', *Sociological Review*, 1953, new ser., vol. 1, no. 2, pp. 63–81; N. Birnbaum, 'Monarchies and sociologists: a reply to Professor Shils and Mr Young', *Sociological Review*, 1955, new ser., vol. 3, no. 1, pp. 5–23.

49 T. Dekker, *The Wonderfull Yeare. 1603*, London, T. Creede, 1603, *STC* 6535; G. P. V. Akrigg, *Jacobean Pageant*, Cambridge, Mass., Harvard University Press, 1962, pp. 29–33; C. Geertz, 'Centers, kings and charisma: reflections on the symbolics of power', in his *Local Knowledge: Further Essays in Interpretive Anthropology*, New York, Basic Books, 1983, pp. 121–46; V. Turner, *The Ritual Process: Structure and Anti-Structure*, Chicago, Ill., Aldine, 1969, esp. pp. 169–203; V. Turner, *From Ritual to Theatre*, New York, Performing Arts Journal Publications, 1982, pp. 61–88.

50 V. Turner, 'Liminality and the performative genres', in J. J. MacAloon (ed.) *Rite, Drama, Festival, Spectacle: Rehearsals toward a Theory of Cultural Performance*, Philadelphia, Pa, Institute for the Study of Human Issues, 1984, pp. 19–41.

51 J. W. Legg, *The Coronation Order of King James I*, London, F. E. Robinson, 1902; compare the French experience as documented in R. A. Jackson, *Vive le Roi: A History of the French Coronation from Charles V to Charles X*, Chapel Hill, NC, University of North Carolina Press, 1984, pp. 176–80.

52 J. Nichols (ed.) *The Progresses, Processions and Magnificent Festivities of King James the First* (hereafter Nichols, *Progresses of King James*), 4 vols, repr. New York, 1967, vol. 1, p. 231.

53 R. M. Smuts, 'Public ceremony and royal charisma: the English royal entry in London, 1485–1642', in A. L. Beier, D. Cannadine and J. M. Rosenheim (eds) *The First Modern Society: Essays in English History in Honour of Lawrence Stone*, Cambridge, Cambridge University Press, 1989, pp. 65–93.

54 B. Jonson, *Part of the Kings Entertainment in Passing to his Coronation* (1606), in *Ben Jonson*, vol. 7, pp. 81–109; T. Dekker, *The Magnificent Entertainment given to King James . . .*, in F. Bowers (ed.) *The Dramatic Works of Thomas*

Dekker, 4 vols, Cambridge, Cambridge University Press, 1964–70, vol. 2, pp. 253–303, especially p. 262. James was also reminded early on of the great qualities of his predecessor, which had, according to Henry Marten's oration on the king's entry into London, 'not beene read or heard of in our dayes, nor since the raigne of great Augustus': Bodl. MS Rawl. D. 859, fos 101r–102v; Nichols, *Progresses of King James*, vol. 1, pp. 128–32, 325–6, 360.

55 R. Hooker, *Of the Laws of Ecclesiastical Polity*, G. Edelen (ed.), Book IV, *Folger Library Edition of the Works of Richard Hooker*, W. S. Hill (gen.ed.), Cambridge, Mass., Harvard University Press, 1977–), vol. 1, p. 274; S. Lukes, 'Political ritual and social integration', *Sociology*, 1975, vol. 9, pp. 289–308, esp. p. 290.

56 J. G. Nichols (ed.) *Chronicle of the Grey Friars of London*, Camden Society, o.s., 53, 1852, p. 58; Wriothesley, *Chronicle*, vol. 2, p. 29; H. Wheatley (ed.) *Stow's Survey of London*, London, Dent, 1912, p. 293. Such alterations offer a warning against accepting at face value contemporary claims that such rituals always took place exactly according to ancient forms; as R. Giesey observed in the case of French funeral obsequies, minor changes necessitated by circumstances might often be retroactively justified and explained by those recording them, allowing the changes thereby to creep into the ceremony and gain a false air of antiquity: *The Royal Funeral Ceremony in Renaissance France*, Geneva, Droz, 1960, pp. 23ff.

57 BL MS Harl. 419, fo. 131; J. G. Nichols (ed.) *Chronicle of Queen Jane, and of Two Years of Queen Mary*, Camden society, o.s., vol. 48, 1849, pp. 78–9; J. Foxe, *Acts and Monuments*, 3 vols, London, Company of Stationers, 1641, vol. 3, p. 103. Foxe embroidered on this by adding that the painter accidentally wiped away the king's fingers during the repainting.

58 BL MS Cotton Julius B. XII, fos 8v–21r; A. F. Johnston and M. Rogerson (eds) *REED: York*, 2 vols, Toronto, University of Toronto Press, 1979, vol. 1, pp. 139–42, 146–50.

59 BL MS Royal Roll 14 B. 39 (wardrobe accounts), include a sum of £1,020 0s 8¾d for the marriage of Arthur and Katharine; C. L. Kingsford, *Chronicles of London*, Oxford, Clarendon Press, 1905, p. 236; Anglo, 1969, op. cit., pp. 52–97.

60 Kipling, op. cit., pp. 72–95; *Hall's Chronicle*, p. 619; H. Ellis (ed.) *Grafton's Chronicle*, 2 vols, London, J. Johnson et al., 1809, vol. 2, p. 303. Edward VI would follow his grandfather in choosing instead to cultivate the more suitable biblical figure of Solomon (as would James I six decades later); the triumph at Norwich for Edward's coronation featured a pageant devoted to the wise king of the Israelites: *REED: Norwich*, p. 20. On the development of a distinction between the historical and legendary or poetic, see W. Nelson, *Fact or Fiction: The Dilemma of the Renaissance Story-Teller*, Cambridge, Mass., Harvard University Press, 1973. The Renaissance and seventeenth-century contexts of this gradual loss of faith in the ancient legends can be found in R. H. Popkin, *The History of Scepticism, from Erasmus to Spinoza*, Berkeley and Los Angeles, Calif., University of California Press, 1979, pp. 66–109; B. J. Shapiro, *Probability and Certainty in Seventeenth-Century England*, Princeton, NJ, Princeton University Press, 1983, pp. 119–62.

61 Anonymous, *The Royall Passage of her Majesty from the Tower to White-Hall*, London, 1558, repr. London, S. Stafford, 1604, *STC*, 7592, sigs A3–A4; J. M. Osborn (ed.) *The Quenes Majesties Passage through the Citie of London to Westminster the Day before her Coronacion, Anno 1558*, New Haven, Conn., Yale University Press, 1960; J. G. Nichols (ed.) *The Diary of Henry Machyn*,

Camden Society, o.s., vol. 42, 1848, p. 186; J. Nichols (ed.) *The Progresses and Public Processions of Queen Elizabeth*, 3 vols, London, 1823, vol. 1, pp. 41, 43, 48–50, 55.

62 Restrictions of space have made a discussion of the historical elements in civic pageantry impossible here, but it is clear that provincial towns as well as London utilized such themes, for instance in mayoral processions: see C. Phythian-Adams, 'Ceremony and the citizen: the communal year at Coventry, 1450–1550', in P. Clark and P. Slack (eds) *Crisis and Order in English Towns 1500–1700*, London, Routledge & Kegan Paul, 1972, pp. 57–85; D. Bergeron, *English Civic Pageantry, 1558–1642*, London, Edward Arnold, 1971, pp. 140–62.

63 L. B. Campbell, 'The use of historical patterns in the reign of Elizabeth', *Huntington Library Quarterly* (hereafter *HLQ*), 1938, vol. 1, pp. 135–67, and her *Shakespeare's Histories: Mirrors of Elizabethan Policy*, San Marino, Calif., Huntington Library, 1947, passim; R. P. Adams, 'Despotism, censorship, and mirrors of power politics in late Elizabethan times', *SCJ*, 1979, vol. 10, pp. 5–16.

64 For a different view, intelligently argued, see M. D. Bristol, *Carnival and Theatre: Plebeian Culture and the Structure of Authority in Renaissance England*, New York and London, Routledge, 1985.

65 T. Heywood, *Apology for Actors*, London, N. Okes, 1612 *STC* 13309, sig. F3; Campbell, 1947, op. cit., p. 102.

66 M. Heinemann, *Puritanism and Theatre: Thomas Middleton and Opposition Drama under the Early Stuarts*, Cambridge, Cambridge University Press, 1980, pp. 151–71, 200–36; cf. the very different picture drawn by some recent works: T. Cogswell, 'Thomas Middleton and the Court, 1624: *A Game at Chess* in context', *HLQ*, 1984, vol. 48, pp. 273–8; M. Butler, *Theatre and Crisis, 1632–1642*, Cambridge, Cambridge University Press, 1984; J. Limon, *Dangerous Matter: English Drama and Politics in 1623–24*, Cambridge, Cambridge University Press, 1986.

67 J. Clare, ' "Grater themes for insurrection's arguing': political censorship of the Elizabethan and Jacobean stage', *Review of English Studies*, 1987, new ser., vol. 38, pp. 169–83.

68 The story that John Leland filled the office of 'king's antiquary' has no authority in contemporary documents: A. D. Momigliano, 'Ancient history and the antiquarian', in *Studies in Historiography*, New York, Harper & Row, 1966, pp. 1–39; W. H. Herendeen, 'William Camden: historian, herald and antiquary', *St. Phil.*, 1988, vol. 85, pp. 192–210; Bullinger to Hooper, 8 April 1549, *Original Letters*, p. 54; D. R. Kelley, 'Johann Sleidan and the origins of history as a profession', *Journal of Modern History*, 1980, vol. 52, pp. 573–98.

69 *Statutes of the Realm*, vol. 4, pp. 240–1; H. E. Rollins (ed.) *Old English Ballads 1553–1625*, Cambridge, Cambridge University Press, 1920, p. xvii.

70 Sir G. Buck, *The History of King Richard the Third*, A. N. Kincaid (ed.), Gloucester, Alan Sutton, 1979.

71 A passage concerning the secular power of the Roman church was expunged from Book IV of G. Fenton's *The Historie of Guicciardin*, London, T. Vautroullier for W. Norton, 1579, *STC* 12458, p. 235. A 'safe' version of this passage would eventually be translated by W. Jones as *Two Discourses*, London, P. Short, 1595, *STC* 12462. Something closer to the original, ascribing papal authority to Christ himself, survives in the manuscript 'Discourse of the Secolar Power of the Church and of her Pollitique Govrenement: a peece prohibited

& expunged from the vulgar coppies in the fourth booke of M. Francisco Guiccirdines History of Italie': Bodl. MS Tanner 301, fos 77r–89r.

72 A. F. Pollard, 'Edward Hall's will and chronicle', *BIHR*, 1931–2, vol. 9, pp. 171–7. G. Pollard, 'The bibliographical history of Hall's Chronicle', ibid., 1932–33, vol. 10, pp. 12–17.

73 W. Baldwin et al., *A Memorial of Suche Princes as since the Tyme of King Richard the Seconde have been Unfortunate in the Realme of England*, London, J. Wayland, 1555, *STC* 1246. For a complete list of historical poetry in the Tudor era, see N. A. Guttierez, *English Historical Poetry, 1476–1603: A Bibliography*, New York and London, Garland, 1983.

74 Proclamation of 27 September 1579: P. C. Hughes and J. F. Larkin (eds) *Tudor Royal Proclamations*, 3 vols, New Haven, Conn., and London, Yale University Press, 1964–9, vol. 2, p. 448; J. Stubbs, *The Discovery of a Gaping Gulf*, in L. E. Berry (ed.) *John Stubbs's Gaping Gulf with Letters and other Relevant Documents*, Charlottesville, Va, University Press of Virginia for Folger Shakespeare Library, 1968, app. I, pp. 150, 164–5; T. E. Hartley (ed.) *Proceedings in the Parliaments of Elizabeth I*, Leicester, 1981– , vol. 1, pp. 60–1; M. Levine, *The Early Elizabethan Succession Question 1558–1568*, Stanford, Calif., Stanford University Press, 1966, pp. 45–61.

75 Various pre-Elizabethan statutes against rumour, false news and sedition, culminating in 1 & 2 Philip and Mary c. 3, *An Acte against Sedityous Woordes and Rumours* (*Statutes of the Realm*, vol. 4, pp. 240–1) had laid down penalties ranging from pillory and loss of ears to imprisonment.

76 Bodl. MS Rawl D. 882 is an eighteenth-century copy of the suppressed pages of Holinshed; J. Hayward, *The First Part of the Life and Raigne of King Henrie the IIII*, London, J. Wolfe, 1599, *STC* 12996; F. J. Levy, 'Hayward, Daniel, and the beginnings of politic history in England', *HLQ*, 1987, vol. 50, pp. 1–34. Hayward never published the substantial second part of his *Henrie IIII*, a copy of which exists in Folger Shakespeare Library MS G.a. 12.

77 R. M. Warnicke, *William Lambarde, Elizabethan Antiquary*, London and Chichester, Phillimore, 1973, p. 136.

78 J. Anderson, *Biographical Truth: The Representation of Historical Persons in Tudor-Stuart Writing*, New Haven, Conn., Yale University Press, 1984; Patterson, op. cit., pp. 10–21. For a more traditional view of the authoritarian character of Stuart censorship, see C. Hill, 'Censorship and English literature', in his *Collected Essays, I: Writing and Revolution in Seventeenth-Century England*, Amherst, Mass., University of Massachusetts Press, 1985, pp. 32–71.

79 Anonymous (erroneously attributed to William Camden), 'On epitaphs', in T. Hearne, *A Collection of Curious Discourses*, J. Ayloffe (ed.), 2 vols, London, W. and J. Richardson, 1771, vol. 1, p. 351.

80 G. Puttenham *The Arte of English Poesie*, G. D. Willcock and A. Walker (eds), Cambridge, Cambridge University Press, 1936, p. 273; D. Norbrook, *Poetry and Politics in the English Renaissance*, London, Routledge & Kegan Paul, 1984, pp. 77–9, 126.

81 J. Lyly, *Euphues and his England*, London, 1580, in R. W. Bond (ed.) *Complete Works of John Lyly*, 3 vols, Oxford, Clarendon Press, 1902, vol. 2, p. 206; F. Godwin, *Rerum Anglicarum Henrico VIII, Edwardo VI et Maria regnantibus, annales*, London, J. Bill, 1616, *STC* 11945; trans. M. Godwin as *Annales of England*, London, A. Islip & W. Stansby, 1630, *STC* 11947. The bishop's own corrections may be seen in BL MS Add. 45140, fos 6–9, and the autograph MS of the Latin version is BL MS Cott. Titus C.XI. On evil counsel as the explanation for Mary's reign, see S. L. Collins, *From Divine Cosmos to Sover-*

eign State: An Intellectual History of Consciousness and the Idea of Order in Renaissance England, New York and Oxford, Clarendon Press, 1989, pp. 17–18.

82 J. Lipsius *Two Bookes of Constancie*, R. Stradling (trans.) (1595), *STC* 15695, I, iv, 8; Lipsius, *Six bookes of politickes or civil doctrine*, W. Jones (trans.), *STC* 15701, bk VI; J. L. Saunders, *Justus Lipsius: The Philosophy of Renaissance Stoicism*, New York, Liberal Arts Press, 1955; A. Grafton, 'Justus Lipsius', *American Scholar*, 1986–7, vol. 56, pp. 382–90; G. Oestreich, *Neostoicism and the Early Modern State*, B. Oestreich and H. G. Koenigsberger (eds), D. McLintock (trans.), Cambridge, Cambridge University Press, 1982, pp. 13–75.

83 S. Daniel, *The Civil Wars*, L. Michel (ed.), New Haven, Conn., 1958, VII, st. 77; *The Collection of the Historie of England*, London, Nicholas Okes, 1618, *STC* 6248, pp. 21–51, 67. Daniel appears to echo Montaigne's essay 'Of Physiognomy', *Complete Essays of Montaigne*, D. Frame (trans), 3rd edn, Stanford, Calif., Stanford University Press, 1965, III, 12, p. 797: 'But is there any disease in a government so bad that it is worth combating with so deadly a drug?'

84 T. Heywood, *Edward the Fourth*, pt one, in *Dramatic Works of Thomas Heywood*, 6 vols, London, J. Pearson, 1874, vol. 1, pp. 44–7.

85 R. Doleman (pseudonym for Robert Parsons, et al.), *A Conference about the Next Succession to the Crowne of England*, Antwerp, A. Conincx, 1594, pt one, p. 56; pt two, pp. 57, 67.

86 J. Hayward, *The Lives of the III. Normans, Kings of England*, London, R. Barker, 1613, *STC* 13000, pp. 43–5, 50, 122; Daniel, *Collection of the Historie of England*, pp. 21–4, 44, 51, 67; Q. Skinner, 'History and ideology in the English Revolution', *HJ*, 1965, vol. 8, pp. 155–78; J. P. Sommerville, 'History and theory: the Norman Conquest in early Stuart political thought', *Political Studies*, 1986, vol. 34, pp. 249–61; J. G. A. Pocock, *The Ancient Constitution and the Feudal Law*, 2nd edn, Cambridge, 1987, pp. 53–64, 281–2.

87 Q. Skinner, 'Conquest and consent: Thomas Hobbes and the engagement controversy', in G. E. Aylmer (ed.) *The Interregnum: The Quest for Settlement 1646–1660*, London, Macmillan, 1972, pp. 79–98; J. W. Gough, *Fundamental Law in English Constitutional History*, Oxford, Clarendon Press, 1955, pp. 147–56.

88 D. Hay, 'The Historiographers Royal in England and Scotland', *Scottish Historical Review*, 1951, vol. 30, pp. 15–29. This argument is developed more fully in my book, *The Idea of History in Early Stuart England: Erudition, Ideology and the 'Light of Truth' from the Accession of James I to the Civil War*, Toronto, University of Toronto Press, 1990.

2

Nursery of resistance:
Reginald Pole and his friends

T. F. Mayer

During the wait for the opening of the long-delayed first session of the council of Trent in 1545, one of the papal legates to the council sought relief from studies and the heat. Two of his emissaries arranged an outing to a suburban garden. They also proposed the topic of conversation: the republic and religion. The temporary lodger in the garden agreed, and ten years later he produced what purported to be a record of the day's disputes. Marco Gerolamo Vida, Christian epic poet, theorist of chess, sometime favourite of Leo X, and bishop of Cremona, published his *Dialogues on the dignity of the republic* in 1556.[1] By then its dedicatee, Reginald Pole, had become even more famous than he had been as legate at Trent. Cousin of Henry VIII, Pole had broken with the king and been made cardinal of England in reward, had been a nearly successful candidate for the papal tiara in the conclave of 1550 and five years later became papal legate for the reconciliation of England and, finally, Archibishop of Canterbury. His friends were Alvise Priuli, a Venetian noble, and the famous humanist Marcantonio Flaminio. The audience included the other two legates, Marcello Cervini and Giulio del Monte, both later popes.

Vida, under coercion, agreed to debate Flaminio, even though he conceded that Pole knew much more about the republic. (Vida also claimed to have discussed it with him at Maguzzano the day before Pole left for England in 1553.) Vida framed his dialogues by presenting Pole as an oracle of politics and then praising him as certain to bring splendour to 'our age by literary monuments'. This image may seem thoroughly eccentric in light of the hagiographical view of Pole, but it is crucial for the understanding of Vida's work, Pole's place in it, and their century.

The dialogue opened with a fairly standard Aristotelian disquisition on the commonwealth as natural but dependent on God for its felicity. Del Monte interrupted by asking Flaminio what the poets said about life before the republic. Vida assigned Flaminio, introduced as Pole's close friend and both a poet and rhetorician, a set of speeches defending the life of nature and bitterly opposed to civilized, urban existence. Among the first problems of cities which Flaminio pointed out were the crimes and frequent exiles they produced. There is no justice in cities, but even worse, no poverty, the only source of beatitude. Men in a state of nature, by contrast, had 'no empires, no domination, no magistracies, no public council, in short there could not have been such and so profound desire of commanding' as there is now. By comparison, the first humans lived in Arcadian bliss 'in their own families and households, offended by no communities'. Of course, they all lived in peace. Flaminio continued his paean to 'pristine liberty' for some fifteen pages.

Vida's rejoinder subtly regularized Flaminio's case by rooting it in Flaminio's poetic practice, according to which real poets could not compose on command (a position Flaminio himself insisted on in his letters). Vida, by contrast, had written his *Christiad* at Leo X's behest and was therefore not a real poet, but an orator. The character Pole strenuously praised Vida's success in writing decent, Christian epic, a stance which contrasts sharply with his silence when Flaminio was introduced. Having established a hierarchy of literary practices, Vida then refuted Flaminio's views one by one. The tone is equally strident, but much more personal. Bad man, bad ideas, declaimed Vida. Worst of all, Flaminio had behaved like a rhetorician.

Instead, Vida replied 'in the mode of a logician [dialectician]' interested solely in the truth. It eventually turned out to rest in the hands of Peter, the vicar of Christ, and to be found therefore in the heavenly city. Interestingly enough, within the shelter of their garden, Vida and Flaminio agreed about tyranny, although not about the role of consent in politics or about the necessity of law. Vida clinched his case with another literary attack, offering the testimony of historians to counter Flaminio's dependence on poets. After a catalogue of the benefits of civilization and a thoroughly Augustinian discussion of the necessity of sin and hence of the coexistence of good and evil, Vida first had Del Monte joke that the company should return to the city and leave Vida, the defender of civility, all alone, and then closed by throwing everything up in the air. Vida both violated the boundaries of his garden by leaving it and accompanying his guests *up to* the city gate (but not through it) and also partially subverted his quest for verisimilitude by turning a romance episode – Del Monte's jesting – into a mobile conversation with no conclusion: Priuli told Vida later that everyone had talked about him and Flaminio on the way back, trying without success to decide whose case had been stronger.

Thus ended an apparently eccentric pastime, designed to escape the tedium of hard work and bad weather, if, of course, this conversation ever took place. That question is much less important than establishing the cultural reality of the venue Vida chose and the events which took place therein. An aristocratic group composed of three princes of the church, one bishop, two (sometime) poets, a rhetorician and an orator engaged in debate about the fundamental principles of what those 'same' people were up to in the 'real' world of the council of Trent. In literary terms, within the topos of a *locus amoenus* (pleasant place), a garden, the site of romance, a battle more suited to epic was fought out between civilization and nature. By focusing on this event, its site and its principal occupant, Pole, we can unearth a wide range of resistances to new political, religious (and literary) developments in the sixteenth century. Often dismissed as frivolous, wildly unrealistic, or the product of aristocratic 'detachment', the pleasing pastimes in which Pole and his circles engaged deserve to be read more seriously.[2] Simultaneously political and literary, their play was more than escapism.

Just as Vida's garden 'resisted' the city and council of Trent by providing a protected place in which everything held dear by civilization, both civic and religious, could be called into question, so its romance episodes and open-ended dialogic structure 'resisted' the epic destruction of Flaminio which was probably high on Vida's list of motives for writing.[3] Since no one could decide who had won the debate, that left open the possibility that Flaminio not only continued to believe his Arcadian vision of reality, but might even have chosen to act on it outside Vida's garden. Likewise, Flaminio's own pastoral verse, written only in very small forms, refused the linearity and purposefulness of epic in the same way as his rhetorical speeches refused the corruption, domination and law of cities. So too did Pole's numerous dialogues – no matter how didactic some of them became – resist straightforward organization, closure and consequently interpretation. It is more than ironic that Vida chose the most ambiguous form of Renaissance literature simultaneously to exalt himself and Pole and to attempt to destroy Flaminio.

Vida's Pole, his Flaminio, and their friends offer an archetype of resistance on many fronts, especially through literature, beginning with Pole's own *De unitate* and ramifying into an enormous amount of writing. This is not a new idea, originating as it does with Pole. But the dynamics, the ramifications and the typicality of his responses have not been understood; the role of his circles in general and his household in particular as nurseries of resistance, a species of movable garden, has been largely missed in English language scholarship.[4] The list of Pole's intimates adjudged either then or later guilty of a wide range of resistances includes the Englishmen Thomas Starkey, Thomas Lupset, John Helyar, George Lily, Ellis Heywood, Nicholas Harpsfield and Nicholas Sander; Italians, beginning with Michelangelo, Giovanni Morone, Girolamo Seripando, Ludovico Beccadelli, Vittoria Colonna, Francesco Berni, Antonio Brucioli, Aonio Paleario, Donato Giannotti, Guido da Fano, Bartolomeo Spadafora, Trifone Benci, Donato Rullo, Pietro Carnesecchi and many others; Spaniards such as Bartolomé Carranza and Francisco de Navarra (both high-ranking bishops, Carranza perhaps the most celebrated victim of the Inquisition, in no small part because of his association with Pole in England); one Hungarian,

Andras Dudic; and at least two Flemings, Christophorus Longolius and Dominic Lampsonius. The mere geographical diffusion of Pole's circles suggests a major phenomenon.

Only some of these figures can be included here, and a great deal more subtle analysis will be needed to take full account of how their circumstances intersected in Pole's nursery. Nevertheless, it should already be clear that as in the case of the literary analogue to Pole's households/gardens, the 'pleasant places' of romance, it could be hard to predict what kinds of resistance might spring up there. Pole and his coteries exhibit some ten varieties. (1) As in the case of Vida's Flaminio or perhaps Pole in the early phases of his career, they might pledge ambivalent – and therefore always unstable – allegiance to the established order. (2) Contrariwise, as Pole and the Florentine exiles Giannotti and Brucioli often did, they might engage in subversion, whether in the form of supporting armed rebellion or more devious means of undermining a regime. (3) When that failed nearly all of Pole's circle tried resistance by exile, both internal and external.[5] (4) Less seriously but equally devastatingly, they might employ humour, even if much of it now seems of a gallows variety and very little of it as subtly ironic as the paradoxical encomia of Erasmus or the simultaneous praise and blame of Francesco Filelfo.[6] A witticism could be a devastating rejoinder to tyranny. (5) Knowing when to make a joke required some of the skills of a councillor, debates over whose function became one of the principal forms of sixteenth-century resistance, not merely for Pole and followers. Similarly, discussion of prudence functions as a locus of resistance, beginning with *De unitate*.[7] (6) Pole also developed a specific form of counsel, prayer, a not-so-covert appeal to a higher power which might well judge a prince's actions in ways other than he might wish, and (7) the closely related but more threatening resistance of prophecy. (8) These two came together in the sites of martyrs, idealized figures of resistance; Pole and many of his allies proved very adept at putting hagiography to work for their purposes. (9) Hagiographical or not, rewriting events turned out to be perhaps the most successful means of resistance. (10) Finally, a favourite strategy for Pole was wars of words, resistance by definition.

A number of difficulties, not unlike the diversions in the path of a romance hero, immediately arise in trying to redraw the map of Pole's resistances. Perhaps the most serious of these is the relation between Pole's life as lived the first time through and as reconstructed after the 'fact' into a different fact by Pole and his followers; one of the most curious reconstructions was the writing out of his life of his love for gardens.[8] A related problem concerns the relation between the 'Pole' in the texts, a *persona* (almost literally meaning mask), and the Pole outside them. The outside Pole must indeed have 'authored' some of the *personae* in the limited sense that a pen in Pole's hand wrote the first texts containing 'his' *personae*, but 'authorization' is at least equally likely to have run in the opposite direction. To say it bluntly, the Pole in the texts differs from the Pole outside them. These two Poles of course bore a family resemblance to one another. Yet their differences make it extremely difficult to follow custom and beg the question of action and its springs by collapsing the writings, *personae* and all, into a putative self, an identity, even a fractured one. Instead, treating life and *personae* as separate but equivalent types of behaviour opens the way to taking account of the instability, indeterminacy and randomness Renaissance writers notoriously felt. These all, of course, are excellent means of resisting the 'normal politics' (or literature or religion) imposed by despots of whatever kind. The gap between *persona* and self in particular offered one of the principal sites of resistance, one of the best places to hide in plain sight.

Certainly Pole succeeded in doing that. Just four years ago still another hagiographical life of him appeared in Italy.[9] Yet however saintly Pole might have been, this cannot obscure his political purposes. A function of both his station and his education, Pole's political prowess, often in the face of difficult conditions, is beginning to emerge.[10] At a not too metaphorical stretch, the action begins with the wilful trouble-making of Pole's maternal grandfather, George, duke of Clarence, brother of Edward IV. This august ancestry meant that in the eyes of a Yorkist, Reginald's elder brother Henry, Lord Montagu, had a better claim to the throne than Henry VIII. Still, even to a Yorkist partisan the relations of 'false, fleeting, perjured Clarence' needed watching. Despite Clarence's family's uncertain loyalties and very close connection to the monarchy, Henry VII and even more his son restored Clarence's daughter Margaret. Her son Pole from early manhood set out to become a successful royal servant. Whether or not Henry VIII originally conceived the idea of supporting his cousin's education in Padua, Pole begged Cardinal Wolsey for his stipend and offered to guarantee results in practical experience and glory for the king.[11]

Longolius, one of the first inmates of Pole's household, aptly summed up the brunt of his friend's studies when he noted that Pole eagerly scrutinized the governors of his native land, in search of 'that quality you would like to see in the majority of all responsible men these days – a talent perfectly suited to the running of affairs of state'.[12] Pole would appear to have derived this concern partly from his education. His principal tutor in Padua, Niccolò Leonico, has recently been made an example of the 'profound fusion of Aristotelian philosophy and Venetian political principles' created by Venetian and Paduan humanists.[13] The ardently anti-Medicean Giannotti both recommended Leonico's political expertise at the end of *Della repubblica de' Veneziani*, designed as a blueprint to save the Florentine oligarchy from the Medici, and also further intended to use him as the main speaker in a sequel on the general principles of republicanism.[14] Giannotti, who wrote *Della repubblica* in Padua, was further connected

to Pole through Pole's intimate Thomas Starkey, to judge from the dependence on Giannotti's work of Starkey's most important literary effort at
resistance.[15]

Pole behaved for quite a time as if he meant to capitalize on his
introduction to the theory of politics. In 1529–30 he dived energetically
into his first big assignment from the king and persuaded the theologians
of Paris to support Henry's divorce from Katharine of Aragon.[16] Nevertheless, immediately after Pole's return from Paris and despite high praise
from Henry, he went into seclusion in John Colet's retirement villa at
Sheen. According to Pole's later account, he honed his meterological skills
then by forecasting tempests over England. Perhaps he did; perhaps this
episode can be squared with the new account of Pole's behaviour in Paris
by labelling it the beginning of Pole's resistance to the direction of English
state-building. Some of Pole's companions in Sheen certainly did not much
favour withdrawal, even if their ideas of engagement might have reflected
more active resistance than Pole yet had in mind. Pole's chief secretary
Starkey, for one, spent his time composing much of his 'Dialogue between
Pole and Lupset' in which he simultaneously cast the character Pole as an
expert on the problems of the commonwealth and urged him to put his
knowledge to work as head of a revived nobility.[17] Starkey's hopes could
not have outstripped Pole's by too much, lest he lose Pole's patronage.[18]
Another member of Pole's household, Thomas Lupset, tried to further his
career in royal service at the same time; he wrote both stoic treatises on
dying well and libels against the direction of the king's policy, a combination of concerns which would prove very important to Pole a few years
later.[19]

Like Giannotti, Starkey pinned his hopes on the Venetian constitution
(which he discussed, as Giannotti claimed to have done, in a garden). This
implicated Starkey's work in yet another web of resistances, both inside
and outside Venice. Starkey's highly circumscribed image of the doge's
power reflected that in Gasparo Contarini's *De magistratibus*, but ignored
the real increase in his authority in the first several decades of the sixteenth
century.[20] Starkey's Venice was still more republican than oligarchical. At
the same time, the propagation of any image of Venice to the rest of
Europe may well have made Starkey a cog in the propaganda machine
responsible for the so-called 'age of Gritti', a cultural offensive launched
under doge Andrea Gritti to restore Venetian prestige after the humiliation
of the war of the league of Cambrai.[21] Starkey had close ties to one of
the principal architects of this campaign, Pietro Bembo, to whom he may
also have owed the decision to write about the serious subject of politics
in the vernacular.[22]

Starkey and Pole and other members of Pole's household danced a
complicated series of negotiations over the next five years, which resulted
in temporary success for Starkey in royal service, an equally temporary

breach with Pole, and a major swerve in Pole's itinerary, into open opposition. This came in the form of his massive broadside against Henry, *Pro ecclesiasticae unitatis defensione* (known as *De unitate*, *On the unity of the church*), written between September 1535 and March 1536. Like the rest of Pole's works, *De unitate* presents large textual problems.[23] Resistance by confusion had begun. So had resistance by prophecy, by insult, by martyrology (an especially fruitful mode for Pole), by fomenting rebellion and invasion (in two manuscripts and the first printed version of the text, not including the one Henry's advisory committee read), and by exile.

Pole claimed that *De unitate* repaid Henry for 'all the years I have spent in the labour of my studies [which] you supported'. Since these studies were overtly political and Pole treated this motive as distinct from 'the confession of Christ's name', he appears to have meant that *De unitate* was to be read as a political tract. Pole immediately claimed much skill in letters and their political use (IIIv, VIIr), and just as immediately made plain the intensity of his text's political resistance. Pole told Henry that he knew the king was not interested in the truth about 'the power of the Roman pontiff' and 'your new, and now first usurped honour, by which you have arrogated to yourself the right of the supreme headship of the English church'. Unable to agree with Henry's claim, Pole could see no option but to write and make himself guilty of treason and, worse, ingratitude. That would be the height of imprudence; the nature of true prudence becomes one of the major arguments of the work (Ir–v). Much of the strategy of *De unitate* turned on similar resistance by definition. This in turn depended on resistance by unmasking dissimulation, the highest form of political prudence.[24]

No matter how great Pole's political prudence, no matter how great the apparent contradiction between it and his strident denunciations of Henry, *De unitate* is anything but a straightforward text of resistance. For one thing, its superficial purpose – to bring the errant Henry back into the church by the shortest, epic path – frequently falls victim to romance interludes, including a meditation on the 'garden' of Henry's education and the golden age promised at the beginning of his reign, and at one of the climaxes of the work Pole's text wound up in a theatre watching a tragedy rather than in the streets of London demanding vengeance for the execution of Thomas More. Worse, while the shape of Pole's opposition to Henry may seem clear enough, the allegiance to the church he proposes as an alternative is anything but. Pole pursued resistance through various literary modes and on various fronts simultaneously. This creates a complicated web of a text.

Pole prescribed a simple remedy for Henry. The king must repent and do penance in order to re-enter the church, his mother. The meaning of this injunction is not so simple. Quite apart from the wildly spiralling family romances Pole constructed around Henry's 'mother', Pole defined the church differently from the way that his hagiographers have argued. True, he defended papal power, but as the mere title of his work must have reminded his learned readers, not necessarily at the expense of the rest of the hierarchy, particularly the bishops. The overtones were probably strong of Cyprian's most famous treatise, *De ecclesiae catholicae unitate*; although sometimes read as an unequivocally papalist statement, Cyprian actually defended a collective leadership of the church.[25] Pole, too, at several points implicitly defended episcopal authority. In his attack on Henry's argument from classical Christian precedent, Pole claimed that Constantine had intervened in the council of Nicaea only to shame the bishops into behaving themselves. That cleared the way for the council to gain the same authority as the apostles (XIXr). More importantly, when explaining Peter's primacy, Pole identified the church which never differed from Peter as the succession of the bishops 'the biggest thing the church contains' (XXXIIIv). Later Pole went so far as to define the church – along with Ockham – as 'the multitude of believers' (LXVIv).

The bishops, 'the successors of the apostles', might not individually always meet the apostolic standard, but that did not reduce the dignity of their office. Peter was important, but not singular even after he had undergone a metamorphosis produced by divine revelation of his new status. He was not even the only rock; Pole applied that label to all Christians. Peter did stand out in 'dignity and degree of excellence, nor did all get the same place of nobility in this building [of the church]' (XLVIIIv). Earlier Pole defended divine right episcopacy (XXr). Even in the heat of a protracted insistence on Peter's power, Pole both explicitly allowed that the other apostles might have had the same power, if not dignity, and he also pointed to the example of Moses and the seventy elders to illustrate that neither he nor the pope had their powers diminished by sharing them. A short and cryptic statement may tell most about Pole's attitude. Should the pope not feed Christ's sheep, he wrote, 'remedies are not lacking, by which the church can easily cure this evil' (CIr). Although Pole hurried on to talk of unity, he did so by turning to the council of Florence to refute Henry's claim that the Greeks did not recognize papal headship. Pole's mind easily turned from remedies to councils.

Pole rooted the present church in its primitive ancestor, as any humanist would. Not only did he stress its lowly social composition, but also he thought that not even the apostles collectively, much less Peter alone, had been its entire leadership – that included 'the others who [had] first fruits of the power of God's spirit' (XVr). Pole played the Augustinian card about the difference between Christ's 'doctrine' and the 'domination' of rulership to prove that Christ, and therefore, the church, did not claim coercive authority (XVIv). The clerical office, however, remained superior to the king's, since priests knew a higher form of wisdom than human prudence (XXIr). Their superiority and the entirety of their office consisted in prayer. That, like everything else the clergy did, was common to all priests (XXIIIIrff.). Likening praying priests to 'legates sent by everyone' to God was scarcely a hierocratic move, either (XXVr). (Later Pole added that priests 'stood above' kings who merely commanded, and could 'prescribe what ought to be done in the royal office'; XXVIr.) Eventually Pole came to describe the church in terms of a hierarchy of lower orders, priests, bishops, archbishops and 'he who bears the *persona* of God' (but no cardinals) (XXXVIIIr). In short, the leadership of the church was oligarchical (but not plutocratic), rather than monarchical, just as it was for Starkey and for Pole's friend and possible teacher in Padua, Marco Mantova.[26]

Ultimately Pole rested his case for the clergy on prophetic authority, which he set parallel to human prudence in secular government (XLIIv). Pole made his leanings crystal clear. He adopted a series of prophetic *personae* throughout, from David, to Moses (who also figured as a type of the secular ruler, giving rise to at least some peculiar overtones on what Pole thought of his own status), to Isaiah, probably the most frequent. Virtually the whole range of Old Testament prophets appeared. Pole frequently supported his points with one prophet or another speaking 'in the *persona* of God' (e.g. XXXVIr) and several times he made his own prophecies (e.g. XXXr). Immediately after his exhortation to Charles V to invade England, he effaced even the *persona* of prophet and claimed that the Old Testament prophets were speaking through him (CXIIIIv). The church's dependence on prophecy and revelation ran right to the very top. Peter owed his position to revelation and he alone knew precisely what it was because only he had direct, personal testimony from God (cf. XLIXr). This claim followed hard on a defence of ecclesiastical custom! Lest the point be missed, Pole quickly explained that such divine revelation had nothing to do with flesh and blood (XLVIr–v).

The principal requirement of the head of the church – elsewhere defined as nobility, although Pole never quite brought these two together – was lack of ambition. Christ had repressed 'contention over the principate [the papal office]' as 'most foreign to those who should rule the church of God, where humility, not ambition . . . should have the first place' (LIIIv). This statement posed a resistance of the first order, which Pole apparently really executed in the conclave of 1550.[27] Even stronger was Pole's claim that 'the house of God is ruled by charity' (quickly qualified as 'inflamed by the spirit of God'), which meant that no inferior should ever hesitate to correct an erring superior (LXXr). Pole maintained that the church knew God's will only thanks to 'the light of the Holy Spirit' (CIIv). Without necessarily adopting Max Weber's distinction between charismatic and routinized leadership, there is no doubt that Pole's view of the church was something less than fully hierocratic. Nor did his church require much institutional structure – it was not, after all, a physical building, even though composed of a multitude of men.[28]

The church did, however, need nobility, and Pole made a contest over Peter's true nobility the central point of his book.[29] As Pole thereby resisted both secular and ecclesiastical absolutism, so insisting on the status of the English nobility and of himself as one noble in particular furthered the same end. At first, it might have seemed that Pole was merely establishing another claim to be heard when he reminded Henry of how the king had singled him out, 'one out of all the English nobility' (IIIv; cf. CXXr). When he turned to how Henry had thrown the succession into doubt, Pole greatly magnified his own standing in a transparently threatening way (LXXXv) by justifying on grounds of scripture the innocence of his uncle, the earl of Warwick, whom Henry VII had quietly executed (LXXXIr). Pole also warned Henry that he would never get away with repudiating Mary; among 'such a number of most noble families' any disruption of the succession was certain to lead to sedition. That is, unless Henry did away with all the nobility (LXXXIv).

Thus when Pole shortly after this reminded Henry of his educational benefits to him by suggesting an analogy for what Henry had done to the church, he did not randomly choose a republic (*civitas*) undergoing a change from rule by the privileged classes (*populus*) to rule by one. 'Consult the histories of all republics, and you will find that those republics which were constituted by the rule of the people (*populus*) suffered no greater injury then when they were reduced under the power of one' (IIIIv). Only after this resoundingly aristocratic statement did Pole allow that rule by one was the 'best state' of a republic.

Even then, that 'one' could not behave as Henry had, as an 'emperor' who had conquered territory and could dispose of it as he wished. Henry might be a king and that might be the best form of rule, but a king was not absolute. Pole certainly knew Henry's more extreme claims. He reproduced the basic one that 'in a republic the cases of all citizens are referred to the king, as to the supreme head of the body politic' (XVIr). He obliquely referred to another when he applied language to Henry which echoed the famous legal maxim 'the king is an emperor in his own kingdom' (LXr). Henry had made similar noises, probably ventriloquizing his French predecessors, since early in his reign.[30] Later Pole compared Henry to the Great Turk, stressing the role of consent in England. The realm now had no more than 'a memory of its pristine liberty', despite the efforts of its best men (CIv). The king's office consisted in only two things: domestic justice and defence against foreign attack. (It will be noted that Pole allowed defensive war only.) 'Human prudence alone' could maintain civil concord (XXIr).

Pole caused himself most trouble by making it possible for 'the people' to reverse the decision by which they had constituted a single head for themselves (XIIr, XXIIr).[31] Arguing from origins Pole concluded that 'therefore on account of the people, the king, not the people on account of the king' (XXIIr). Many nations even got by entirely without kings, including the Jews. When they finally got theirs, God granted Saul 'not as a benefit, but rather for punishment' (XXIIIv, XXXVv). By talking about this transference of power in terms of the *lex regia*, Pole entered into the ongoing debate over the origins not only of royal but also of imperial power (LXr). The *lex regia* by which the Romans had allegedly transferred all their power to the emperor had been one of the proof texts medieval lawyers and political writers had used to resist various earlier moves in the direction of absolutism.[32] Pole's description of how secular society was modelled on the hierarchy of the universe further carefully made room for two layers of magistrates between the 'lowest common people' and 'the command [*imperium*] of one supreme [head]' (XXXIIr). This was the same argument German Lutherans had already begun to use to justify resistance by the lesser magistrates to the direction of Charles's religious policy, as Pole almost certainly knew.[33]

At the very least, a king had to listen to his councillors and friends, among whom Pole ranked himself very high (VIIr).[34] Bishop John Fisher and Sir Thomas More also should have been Henry's best friends; they certainly were Pole's, a point repeated often (e.g. XXXr). Henry, by contrast, was helpless, denuded of all his friends, and at the mercy of flatterers and self-servers among his advisers, Richard Sampson above all (CXVIIIv–CXIXr).

Pole engaged in one of the favourite forms of aristocratic behaviour in his confrontation with Sampson, casting most of the first two books of *De unitate* as literally a duel with Henry's champion. Sampson was like Goliath, pushing ahead of him an enormous spear and sword, the proem to his book. Then he was a gladiator, prematurely basking in the glory showered on him by the crowd. Sampson was mistaken not only in thinking he had won, but also in playing with a serious matter, or worse, deliberately deluding the English people (Xr).

Pole deserved to replace Sampson among Henry's councillors, in large part because of his pristine record of opposition to Henry's fatal politics. Here Pole offered resistance through autobiography, especially when rewriting the story of his role in Henry's consultation of the university of Paris about his divorce. As I have shown elsewhere, Pole's account may have saved his face, but it represented a much different kind of truth from that of what happened in the first place.[35] As in the case of his own life, Pole egregiously rewrote other kinds of history; one of the odder bits concerned the unwavering allegiance of the kings of France to the pope. Philip the Fair, to name only one of Francis's predecessors, had been erased (CVIIIv).

In both these cases, the play was the thing to Pole. He deployed a multitude of *personae* together with a great range of other literary devices, especially dramatic metaphors. One of Pole's best strategies was to offer a rhetorical criticism both of Sampson's book and of Henry's actions which became 'tragedies' in Pole's representation. A marginal note pithily summed up this line of attack: 'Sampson plays Goliath' (Xv). Near the beginning of book II, Pole replied at length to Sampson's rhetorical device of having Peter criticize his unworthy successors as pope. Dramatic metaphors litter this passage, above all *personae* in great plenty (XXXIIrff.). Shortly thereafter comes a long discussion of the dangers of rhetoric, but Pole objected most strongly to Sampson that he had violated verisimilitude in the characters he created, not that he had created characters at all. Sampson was a *bad* rhetorician who offended both against the 'laws of rhetors' and 'ordinary, vulgar prudence' (XXXIIIr). When explicating the equivalence of Peter and the rock on which Christ had founded his church, Pole offered a long lesson in how to read metaphors, a lesson in rhetoric (XLVIIrff.). Indeed, his entire case for Peter's superior nobility rested on what Pole explicitly termed a *similitudo*, a metaphor, that of the mystical body of the church (XLVIIIv).

At one of the climaxes of the book, Pole drew an extended theatrical analogy between the reaction of the Athenian *populus* to the death of Socrates and how Londoners had taken the execution of More. The Athenians had performed 'as if reciting words in a theatre', imitating 'some tragedy'; the Londoners, with juster cause for indignation, had not confined their rage to 'your [Henry's] theatre', but spread it wherever there were Christians. While the Athenians might have been playing, the Londoners were 'more than serious'. How could Henry have missed the implied sequel in the fate of Socrates's prosecutors, murdered by their enraged fellow citizens (XCIIIIv)?

Pole leaned very heavily on the deaths of Fisher and More in his attack on Henry.[36] Even an identification of More with Socrates was not enough; More would ultimately become a Christ-figure combating Henry's antichrist and sacrificing himself for the king (XCr, XCIIv).[37] Pole began by telling the king that 'your intelligence [*ingenio*], learning, prudence and finally experience' could never be compared to Fisher's and More's; this point later grew into several very long eulogies of More's prudence and political acumen (e.g. LXXXIXrff.).[38] Even if Henry's endowments had been superior, he still lacked the one thing needful, 'the spirit of Christ' which had made it possible for Fisher and More to understand the metaphors (*figurae*) of scripture (LXXIIv–LXXIIIr). Overtly political resistance had its place, but as in the case of the papacy, Pole found a charismatic defence much more appealing. But that did not mean that he neglected the brutally physical. Among the other uses to which Pole put Fisher and More, he dwelt at length on the ignominious manner of their deaths and the fate of their (and the other martyrs') bodies (LXXXIIIvff.). Even here, however, Pole could not resist several horrid puns on heads, including the rhetorical question 'can we doubt whose church's head [he means Satan's] cut off those heads' (LXXXIIIIr)? Pole repeatedly said he was crying while writing, but it seems that he must also have been laughing, however grimly.

Very shortly after this Pole swerved well out of the serious epic, even cosmic, path he had set himself. In order to remind Henry of how far he had already fallen, Pole recalled the high expectations for 'a golden age' early in Henry's reign. 'What did your outstanding virtues not promise, which shone in you especially in the first years of your reign?' Further, Henry's father had added to his education 'the care of letters, as streams pouring into a well-planted garden, by which, like waters, your virtues were irrigated, so that they might grow better and spread themselves more like the branches of a tree'. Making his favourite move, Pole then quoted the prophet Ezekiel to compare Henry to a tree in the Garden of Eden! This was true above all because Henry's tree had united in itself the contenders for the throne of England and thus brought the faction fights of the fifteenth century to an end. (Can Pole have been unconscious of the overlap between his garden metaphor, the genealogical one of a family tree, and the horticulturally labelled 'wars of the roses?') Henry himself had been part of a deliberately created garden, a pleasant place, but was fated to become twisted epic; quoting Isaiah this time, Pole warned that God had promised to destroy his vineyard, a proleptic move out of the idyll of Henry's early years into the current tragedy (LXXIXv).

Perhaps not by coincidence, Pole's ultimate move against Henry returned to a tragedy which began in a garden, a classic version of what Bakhtin called carnival.[39] 'The whole of this mystery is contained in Christ's passion', Pole told Henry. Only one who had 'eyes so illuminated by faith' could understand that Christ was 'the son of God, author of our felicity, and teacher of the same'.[40] Christ's bodily death set the pattern for all his 'members', who also had to suffer crucifixion of their bodies if they wished salvation. Such 'living books' revealed the will of God as no written books could, even those dictated by the Spirit. 'These books which were written in the blood of the martyrs are to be preferred to all others. These were archetypical books, in which the sole finger of God' – Pole naturally continued to think in terms of body parts – 'appears'. Pole pushed his anti-intellectual stance by continuing that any books, even divinely inspired ones, were subject to interpretation and therefore distortion, even deliberate invention, 'while those written in the blood of martyrs cannot be adulterated', a significantly physical term (XCVv–XCVIr).

Combining both martyrology and its original, Christ's passion, Pole developed the metaphor of legation which he had earlier applied to priests as emissaries to God. Before offering this (perhaps) metaphorical solution to Henry's problems, Pole assured the king that he was not 'playing seriously' in such a serious matter (XCVIIv). Metaphors had at least two edges. Pole tried to guard against being cut by one of them by a pre-emptive strike on his reader(s). Of course, the emissaries were to be Fisher, More and the monks, for all of whom Pole once more presented credentials in the form of capsule biographies. Pole quickly got back to carnival, however, via his argument against learned pretension and in favour of the ability of any 'simple Christian' to understand what he was talking about with the aid of revelation (CIIv). This Erasmian-sounding theme occurs frequently. Pole thoughtfully provided the *idiota*, the unlearned common person, with a long oration to Henry. Its point was simple: 'we do not listen to your words'. Pole's unlearned speaker concluded with Pole's own major point: 'we will not listen to words more, but now we will look at things written by the finger of God, that is, the holy martyrs' (CIIIr). As for Henry, all should pray not only that God would send him good councillors, but also that 'he might hear good councillors'. Having suggested a wide range of possible resistances, Pole left ordinary Christians only prayer (CVr).

That was not the only option. A prince and prophet like Pole could appeal to the bluntest strategy of resistance and call on Francis and Charles to attack England. Isaiah once more served to unmask 'your counsels', but Pole claimed that no one really needed a prophet to see what Henry was doing (CIXr–v). Charles above all could hardly miss it, given Henry's private injury to Charles's aunt Katharine, and the much more serious public one done to the church. Since Charles had just then scored a major victory over the church's external enemies in the battle of Tunis, he was fully prepared to deal with Henry (CXv). And if Charles somehow missed Henry's devilry, Pole told him about it. A long set oration followed, designed to shame Charles into dealing with a much more serious 'danger to the republic' (CXIr–CXIIIIr, continued on CXVIvf). Among the incentives he offered Charles, Pole included an English fifth column of 'whole legions, lurking [*latent*] in England' (CXIIv). In addition to military attack, Pole also returned to a proposal for economic warfare which he may have suggested in 1531; what would England do if its trade with the continent were cut off (CXVIIr–v)?

In the final book of *De unitate* Pole spelled out a dangerous implication he had raised earlier. He contrasted the early days 'in which the sons of the church abounded in the gifts of the holy spirit' with 'these same most corrupt times in which many judge that knowledge which is had through divine light to be almost extinct in men' (CXXVv). The same held true for secular history, whose countless examples could be understood only in the light of spiritual illumination. Since the test of successful illumination was consistency, both the church and secular power had to be in the same state as they had originally been. That was a tough standard, offering equally strong resistance on both ecclesiastical and secular fronts.

Pole then turned his back on both powers in favour of faith, sounding a note that he would strike consistently for at least the next decade. The only certain source of knowledge, faith was both the light and the fire 'through which light we believe and know [*cognovimus*] that Jesus is Christ'. 'The spirit . . . in that faith which is the gift of God . . . gives . . . firm and stable knowledge'. Pole then put forward a definition of faith as 'supernatural light' which gave form to unformed human belief (CXXXVIIr). 'True faith', as the marginal note had it, was 'the only way to be given entry to knowledge of the divine mysteries'. That meant, 'unless you believe, you will not understand'. Everything of any value in earthly bodies came from 'the image of faith', which Pole now called Henry to contemplate. The examples of Sennacherib and Sodom and Gomorrah sufficed to show what happens to people who trust in their own powers rather than faith (CXXXVIIv–CXXXVIIIr).

But that was not the sort of faith Pole had in mind. He meant faith which led to felicity 'and that kingdom with God which raises us an infinite distance above our nature'. Transcendence to the maximum degree became the final resistance. Again sounding a great deal like Erasmus, Pole offered this escape, as he had before, as especially appealing because 'it easily persuades [note the rhetorical emphasis] the wise both to hold in contempt their wisdom and to be least offended to take themselves as fools' (CXXXVIIIv).[41] Turning to Paul for an apostrophe of the transforming powers of divine light, Pole wound up back in the church, outside of which there could be no light of Christ (CXXIXr). Henry had no choice but to do penance and submit to ecclesiastical authority. Pole's belated introduction of the laws of the church, combined with a short argument that the scriptures owed their authority to the church may be a response to the difficulty raised by his demonstration of the power of unmediated faith (CXXXIv). In any case, Pole very shortly returned to the necessity and power of revelation, concluding his 'oration' with the words of Ezekiel 'and your iniquity will not be your ruin' (CXXXIIv–CXXXVIr).

Pole's later enemies within the church had trouble with his talk of faith. The usual story has them hounding him into withdrawal, just as Henry is supposed to have done before. Such a conclusion poses difficulties. Above all, Pole's retreat was always tactical, susceptible to reversal when the proper circumstances arose. This happened in 1537 when Pole undertook a lengthy legation designed to assist the Pilgrims of Grace to overthrow Henry. It happened in 1553 when he eagerly accepted another legation to reconcile England to the church. And it probably happened in any number of cases in between which are not well understood, for example, his pivotal role in brokering the deal by which the Farnese definitively gained the duchy of Parma.[42]

Pole would later try to squelch both dimensions of his early career, insisting that he was neither political nor a fideist. That was after he had lost several more rounds in his struggle with absolutism. Space precludes a complete discussion of this evolution, but suffice it to say that this was a long, drawn-out process, frequently much more responsive to short-term political demands than to those of ideology, whether Pole's (increasingly a powerful appeal for peace, at least unconsciously in part as a means of stunting the processes of state-building which depended, then as now, on aggression for their successful completion), Paul IV's (as much a Renaissance prince as Leo X, however their religious beliefs may have differed), Charles's or Mary Tudor's.[43] And Pole continued throughout to attract and nourish other resisters, on both religious and political grounds.[44]

The course of Pole's relations with Henry illustrates some of the complications in his resistance. Even after Pole entered into direct negotiations with the emperor in early 1535, sent *De unitate* in mid-1536, became a cardinal six months later, and manifested his hostility in 1537, neither Henry nor many of his supporters gave up on him, nor Pole on Henry (to read *De unitate* and its related correspondence at face – the safest – value).[45] Towards the end of Henry's reign, Pole at least gave his blessing to various efforts to regain the king, including propaganda and diplomacy, but excluding armed force.[46] Yet in the midst of the most epic moment in all these upheavals, his legation of 1537, while dodging assassins (some doubtless real) through France and the Low Countries, and retiring to another monastery – this time at Aulne – praying, reading the Bible and singing 'in the Theatine manner', Pole also scribbled a dialogue, an intellectual romance, 'On divine and human prudence'.[47]

In the context of the established view of Pole as paragon of posttridentine Catholic faith, this work looks weird. The character Pole held the balance between the *personae* of his friends Cosmo Gheri and Priuli. Gheri, supposedly another model of the virtues of pious withdrawal, played the Aristotelian proponent of human, civil prudence. Pole cast Priuli as the obscurantist defender of an extreme form of the contemplative and religious life. The action broke off before settling the dispute. Two years later, Pole apparently reversed his position in his famous condemnation of Machiavelli's argument in favour of dissimulation – what Pole again called human prudence – in political action.[48] Or did he? Pole's first biographer maintained that 'his purity was mixed with prudence, which allowed him to foresee many things' and then continued with the story of Pole's treason![49]

It strikes me as highly important that changing scholar's bonnet for cardinal's beret, and English royal service for a career in papal diplomacy did not permanently entrench Pole's resistances. Equally significant, the same uncertainty dominated Pole's circles in Italy. The case of four famous Venetian friends is well known – Contarini, one of Pole's closest allies; Gianbattista Egnazio, who tutored some of Pole's clients; Vincenzo Querini; and Paolo Giustinian.[50] This list could easily embrace Marco Mantova, perhaps Lazzaro Bonamico, close friend and Greek tutor of Pole, and Benedetto Lampridio, another of Pole's intimates.[51] For a decade and a half between 1509 and about 1524, this group tacked back and forth between withdrawal and political action. At one point Querini and Giustinian opted for the strict monastery of Camaldoli and only just failed to induce Egnazio to follow them. Contarini wavered. The rigorous life of a solitary hermit may have attracted Mantova.

Ultimately, most of these friends wound up in active service to the church, including Contarini whom Pope Paul III plucked out of a secular career in Venice in 1535. But like Contarini, Giustinian and Querini, none of them went quietly. These three continued deep resistance to the creation of papal absolutism in texts ranging from Giustinian and Querini's *Libellus ad Leonem X* (1514) to the *Consilium de emendanda ecclesia* (1537), the product of a reforming commission chaired by Contarini (and including Pole) which would have virtually dismantled the financial props of papal monarchy by using its own instruments against it.[52] Mantova kept alive conciliarist views of the ecclesiastical constitution as late as 1541, and arranged to have them widely disseminated.[53]

Another example of permanent uncertainty about resistance and withdrawal was Pole's household manager, Bartolomeo Stella. Even Stella's admiring biographer had to admit that the strength of Stella's religious vocation fluctuated constantly – it kept giving way to a curial life and to a penchant for writing obscene verse.[54] In this Stella behaved exactly like a large circle of Roman poets and sometime courtiers with close ties to Pole. They included the notorious Francesco Berni, author of some of the most outstanding obscene poetry of the early sixteenth century, off-again, on-again familiar of Pole's reforming ally Gian Matteo Giberti, sometime 'Lutheran', constantly reforming homosexual. (He was linked most closely to Pole through Priuli.)[55] Gianfrancesco Bini, a senior papal financial official, belonged to this coterie, as did Blosio Palladio; both loved gardens, Bini writing a poem of insults delivered by the speaking garden of its title (*L'orto*) and Palladio inheriting one of the most famous Roman gardens, the Corycius (which he also immortalized in the verse collection *Coryciana*).[56] Most of these were also friends of Michelangelo, whose transcendentally personal poetry took this kind of resistance to another plane, along with his overtly political and more subtle religious resistance.[57]

Far the most well known of Pole's resisting gardeners was Flaminio. Both of his recent biographers agree that the speeches Vida assigned to him probably reflect his ideas, as both of them struggle to make sense of Flaminio's errant career.[58] By his own testimony, it was held together by the desire for freedom from the constraints of a courtier's life, which Flaminio usually had to live. His chosen mode of expression was poetry, which he wrote in Latin and only in small forms, his specialties being pastoral odes and verse epistles (his late collection of these provides a directory of all the usual suspects). Then again, he also wrote several highly serious paraphrases of scripture, the Psalms above all, and co-authored the most famous product of the Italian reformation, *The Benefit of Christ's Death*. However this work is interpreted – whether as rooted in the possibly heterodox beliefs of Juan de Valdés, the certainly heretical ones of John Calvin, safely traditional Benedictine piety or something else – it most assuredly ignored institutional religion, stressing an almost mystical relation between God and the chosen few.[59]

Despite the best efforts of serious-minded historians, the fact remains that Flaminio did all these things *at the same time*. To take only one example from near the end of Flaminio's life, on 4 May 1549 he described a mystical experience of rejuvenation to Caterina Cibo.[60] In another letter of nearly the same date (and certainly before 27 May) Flaminio reported that he had decided to take the advice of Vincenzo Gheri (Cosmo's brother) and finish his collection of verse epistles, which included one to Pole in which Flaminio imagined himself Pole's lap-dog.[61] The balance of Flaminio's remaining letters concern his poetry, even if the very last surviving letter offered spiritual consolation to Lelio Torelli, an important councillor of Duke Cosimo I of Florence.[62] The habit of resistance through counsel was as deeply ingrained as resistance through poetry.

Flaminio, like Pole, has proved a difficult figure to understand. Since he always successfully escaped ecclesiastical office, it has been easier to dismiss him as a playful lightweight. This will not do, in either case. All of their resistances had a political root, whatever other sources of nourishment they may also have tapped. They responded in part to a profound change in their political circumstances. In both Pole's major venues, England and Italy, very similar developments in the direction of a new kind of monarchy were under way. The difference between the two places lay only in the direction of development. In Italy Courts and princes were a relatively new thing, proto-absolutism even newer.[63] In England, established Courts (above all the royal Court) took on new meanings and functions, but ones which had already been tried without much success a century and more earlier under Richard II. Venice, together with its dependent Padua, one of Pole's most constant Italian homes, underwent oligarchical contraction and a concomitant increase in the doge's power as a result of 'the crisis of the league of Cambrai' in the first two decades of the sixteenth century; this evolution was atypical only in its relative lateness.[64] And as Paolo Prodi brilliantly argues, Rome led the way, teaching the other European monarchs how to be absolutists.[65]

A wide range of experiments in opposition began simultaneously. Seeing life as a game was one of the best cultural resources of resistance. This was the choice of Richard Lanham's 'rhetorical man'. To rhetorical man, words counted for much more than ideas, and winning the game above all. Renaissance literature, says Lanham, was 'an attempt to keep man in the rich confusion of the mixed self' through a 'fruitful collision' or a 'self-corrective oscillation' between style or play and 'pure concept'.[66] Alternation between play and seriousness in an ongoing game describes politics especially well. It was a debating contest, which the players enjoyed for its own sake. A Renaissance politician 'as poet and critic' had to be adept at 'continually moving from purpose to game, serious to rhetorical coordinates, as circumstances require'.[67] His lack of a 'central self' also made it much easier to hide from those who demanded one.

Hence Pole's usual choice of literary, even playful, modes of resistance. But resistance these undoubtedly offered. Constructing gardens, real and 'imaginary', writing pastorals, orations and dialogues, all presented a serious challenge to the nascent order. Pole's lack of success by later standards cannot obscure the importance of his resistances for a more complete understanding of late Renaissance culture. Instead, they offer eloquent testimony about the power of absolutism to quash resistance and of playing to deflect absolutism.

NOTES

1 M. G. Vida, *Dialogi de rei publicae dignitate*, Cremona, V. Conte, 1556; truncated text in an appendix to G. Toffanin, *L'Umanesimo al Concilio di Trento*, Bologna, Zanichelli, 1955. My thanks to F. W. Conrad, Robert Hariman, Dean Hammer and Paul A. Fideler for their comments on a draft of this chapter.

2 E.g. G. Fragnito, *In museo e in villa: saggi sul Rinascimento perduto*, Venice, Arsenale, 1988, p. 12, and ch. 1 passim for detachment; A. Pastore, *Marcantonio Flaminio. Fortune e sfortune di un chierico nell'Italia del Cinquecento*, Bologna, Angeli, 1981, esp. p. 139.

3 Pastore, op. cit., pp. 138–9.

4 Much more attention needs to be given to Pole's closest circle, his household. I offer some suggestions here; for the most important previous work see W. G. Zeeveld, *Foundations of Tudor Policy*, Cambridge, Mass., Harvard University Press, 1948. Newer views will depend above all on the massive studies of M. Firpo, most recently *Fra alumbrados e 'spirituali': Studi su Juan de Valdés e il valdesianesimo nella crisi religiosa del '500 italiano*, Florence, Olschki, 1990; C. Mozzarelli (ed.) *'Familia' del principe e famiglia aristocratica*, Bologna, Bulzoni, 1988; and G. Fragnito, 'Cardinals and their households', paper given at the Sixteenth Century Studies Conference, St Louis, Mo., October 1990.

5 R. Starn, *Contrary Commonwealth: The Theme of Exile in Medieval and Renaissance Italy*, Berkeley, Calif., University of California Press, 1982.

6 D. Robin, *Filelfo in Milan*, Princeton, NJ, Princeton University Press, 1991.

7 R. Hariman, 'Prudence/Performance', *Rhetoric Society Quarterly*, 1991, vol. 21, no. 2, pp. 26–35, suggests an important new construction of the problem of prudence.

8 L. Beccadelli, 'Vita di Reginaldo Polo', in G. B. Morandi (ed.) *Monumenti di varia letteratura*, Bologna, Istituto per le Scienze, 1797–1804, vol. 2, p. 325, and Andras Dudic, *Vita Reginaldi Poli*, in A. M. Quirini (ed.) *Epistolarum Reginaldi Poli*, Brescia, 1744–57 (hereafter *ERP*), vol. 1, p. 55, both had Pole snub a Roman noble who wished that Pole could enjoy the noble's new garden

thirty years hence. For Pole's love of gardens, see his letter of condolence to Alessandro Farnese on the destruction of that prince's Roman gardens in *CSPV*, vol. 6, no. 614.

9 M. T. Dainotti, *La via media: Reginald Pole 1500–1558*, Bologna, EMI, 1987.

10 C. Höllger, 'Reginald Pole and the legations of 1537 and 1539; diplomatic and polemical responses to the break with Rome', Oxford University DPhil thesis, 1989, and my work cited below.

11 BL MS Vespasian F XIII, fos 283r–4r (not in *L&P*). The letter was dated Oxford, 6 October, and addressed to Wolsey as legate; the year must therefore be 1518 or 1519.

12 T. F. Mayer, *Thomas Starkey and the Commonweal: Humanist Politics and Religion in the Reign of Henry VIII*, Cambridge, Cambridge University Press, 1989, p. 49.

13 M. L. King, *Venetian Humanism in an Age of Patrician Dominance*, Princeton, NJ, Princeton University Press, 1986, p. 182.

14 Mayer, *Starkey*, p. 50.

15 Ibid., pp. 55–6, 67–71.

16 T. F. Mayer, 'A mission worse than death: Reginald Pole and the Parisian theologians', *EHR*, 1988, vol. 103, pp. 870–91.

17 Mayer, *Starkey*, chs 3–5, and *T. Starkey: 'A Dialogue between Pole and Lupset'*, T. F. Mayer (ed.), C4S, no. 37, pp. xiii, 1–2, 142–3.

18 Richard Lanham emphasizes that the best a courtier could hope to do was to 'become expert in drama, in stylistic manipulation, so that it will be convincing drama' which he plays before the prince, or in Starkey's case, his patron. R. A. Lanham, *The Motives of Eloquence: Literary Rhetoric in the Renaissance*, New Haven, Conn., Yale University Press, 1976, p. 153.

19 J. A. Gee, *The Life and Works of Thomas Lupset*, New Haven, Conn., Yale University Press, 1928, pp. 172–3, and Mayer, 'Mission worse than death', p. 872.

20 Mayer, *Starkey*, op. cit., pp. 59–61, and E. G. Gleason, 'Reading between the lines of Gasparo Contarini's treatise on the Venetian state', *Historical Reflections/Reflexions Historiques*, 1988, vol. 15, pp. 251–70.

21 M. Tafuri, '"Renovatio urbis Venetiarum": il problema storiografico', in M. Tafuri (ed.) *'Renovatio urbis': Venezia nell'età di Andrea Gritti (1523–1538)*, Rome, Officina, 1984, pp. 9–55.

22 Mayer, *Starkey*, p. 66.

23 T. F. Dunn, 'The development of the text of Pole's *De unitate ecclesiae*', *Papers of the Bibliographical Society of America*, 1976, vol. 70, pp. 455–68, to be used with care. The text cited is *Reginaldi Poli ad Henricum octavum Britanniae regem, pro ecclesiasticae unitatis defensione*, Rome, Antonio Blado, 1539. I have collated it roughly against the prooftext in Biblioteca apostolica vaticana [hereafter BAV], Vaticanus latinus 5970, fos 1–124r. Folio references in round brackets in the text. My translations. J. G. Dwyer (trans. and intro.) *Pole's Defense of the Unity of the Church*, Westminster, Md., Newman Press, 1965, contains many errors.

24 P. S. Donaldson, 'Machiavelli and Antichrist: prophetic typology in Reginald Pole's *De unitate* and *Apologia ad Carolum quintum*', in *Machiavelli and Mystery of State*, New York, Cambridge University Press, 1989, pp. 1–36. This piece is also very good on Pole's prophetic *personae*.

25 Pole relied heavily on Cyprian, putting him first in a list of interpreters of scripture (fo. XXXIr), for example, although he never cited his predecessor's *De unitate*. Pole did, however, use Cyprian's letter no. 59 to pope Cornelius

to defend obedience to divinely ordained priests, although the subject at issue was papal primacy alone. Pole claimed that Cyprian's whole letter made for his point, but quoted only (1) part of a sentence speaking of all the bishops as if it applied to the pope alone (LXIIv–LXIIIr; Wilhelm Hartel (ed.) *S. Thasci Caecili Cypriani Opera Omnia*, vol. 3:2, Wolfenbüttel, Herzog August Bibliothek, 1872, pp. 673–4; translated in *The Letters of St. Cyprian of Carthage*, vol. 3, trans. and notes by G. W. Clarke, New York, Newman Press, 1986, pp. 73–4); and (2) another part of a sentence calling 'the chair of Peter . . . the principal church whence arose priestly unity'. Cyprian's text continued by equating that see (if that was even certainly what Cyprian meant) with 'those Romans [not just the pope, again if that was what Cyprian meant by the 'chair of Peter'] whose faith was praised by the preaching apostle' (Hartel, p. 683; *Letters*, p. 82.) Was Pole deliberately distorting his source, or leaving it for his readers to fill in a blank? For Cyprian's text, see M. Bévenot (ed. and trans.) *De Lapsis & De Ecclesiae Catholicae Unitate*, Oxford, Clarendon Press, 1971, esp. pp. xivff. for his ecclesiology. P. O'Grady, *Henry VIII and the Conforming Catholics*, Collegeville, Minn., Liturgical Press, pp. 22 and 151 offers a start on Henrician interpretation.

26 T. F. Mayer, 'Marco Mantova, a Bronze Age conciliarist', *Annuarium historiae conciliorum*, 1984, vol. 14, pp. 385–408.

27 He spent much of his time writing another dialogue *De summo pontifice*, which argued that Christ-like humility was the principal requisite of a candidate for pope. For his acting of that role, see the detailed reports of the Venetian ambassador in *CSPV*, vol. 5, nos 595–6 and Beccadelli, 'Vita', p. 303.

28 *De unitate*, fo. XLIXv. See A. J. Slavin, Chapter 8 in this volume, for a demonstration of the utility of Weber's ideas about patrimonialism in analysing the Tudor state.

29 See Q. Skinner, *Foundations of Modern Political Thought*, vol. 1, *The Renaissance*, Cambridge, Cambridge University Press, 1978, pp. 45–6, 59–60, 81–2, 236–40 and 257–9 for an introduction to the debate on true nobility.

30 For some of these see T. F. Mayer, 'Tournai and tyranny: imperial kingship and critical humanism', *HJ*, 1991, vol. 34, pp. 257–77, and 'On the road to 1534: the occupation of Tournai and Henry VIII's theory of sovereignty', in D. Hoak (ed.) *Tudor Political Culture: Ideas, Images and Action*, Cambridge, Cambridge University Press, forthcoming.

31 At no time did Pole write about a 'pact' between king and people, as Dwyer, op. cit., p. 56, has it, translating '*quo pacto se Rex in suo munere gerat*' as 'the pact by which the king exercises his office' instead of simply 'how the king exercises his office' (XXIIIr).

32 H. Morel, 'La place de la *lex regia* dans l'histoire des idées politiques', in *Études offertes à J. Macqueron*, Aix-en-Provence, 1970, pp. 545–56.

33 See Skinner, op. cit., vol. 2, *The Reformation*, pp. 195–208, and L. D. Peterson, 'Melanchthon on resisting the emperor: the *Von der Notwehr Unterricht* of 1547', in J. Friedman (ed.) *Regnum, Religio et Ratio: Essays Presented to Robert M. Kingdon*, Kirksville, Mo., Sixteenth Century Journal Publishers, 1987, pp. 133–44, and 'Justus Mennius, Philipp Melanchthon, and the 1547 Treatise, *Von der Notwehr Unterricht*', *Archiv für Reformationsgeschichte*, 1990, vol. 81, pp. 138–57.

34 See F. W. Conrad's essay on Thomas Elyot and friendship, Chapter 3 in this volume.

35 Mayer, 'Mission worse than death'.

36 Josef Ratzinger takes Pole's major contribution to be a martyrological justifi-

cation of papal primacy. In light of Pole's attitude detailed here, Ratzinger's judgement about Pole's notion of the primacy may need modification, but there is no doubt that dead heroes meant a great deal to him: 'The papal primacy and the unity of the people of God', in J. Ratzinger, *Church, Ecumenism and Politics: New Essays in Ecclesiology*, New York, Crossroad, 1988, pp. 36–44.

37 Pole apparently also fostered this resistance by hagiographical transcendence when he returned to England twenty years later. His archdeacon of Canterbury, Nicholas Harpsfield, wrote the second life of More, and Ellis Heywood, allegedly one of Pole's secretaries, dedicated to Pole his *Il Moro*, significantly a dialogue which made More a Socratic saint. Nicholas Harpsfield, *The Life and Death of Sir Thomas More*, E. V. Hitchcock (ed.), EETS, o.s., vol. 186, 1932, pp. 4 and clxxxii–clxxxv, and R. L. Deakins (ed.) *Il Moro: Ellis Heywood's Dialogue in Memory of Thomas More*, Cambridge, Mass., Harvard University Press, 1972, p. 73. Pole's close collaborator Pedro de Soto also saved the holograph of More's *De Tristitia Christi*. T. More, *De Tristitia Christi*, C. H. Miller (ed. and trans.), New Haven, Conn., Yale University Press, 1976, vol. 2, p. 696. I am grateful to Prof. Miller for pointing this connection out to me.

38 This passage was among those cut on Contarini's advice; Dunn, op. cit., pp. 462–3.

39 M. M. Bakhtin, *Problems of Dostoevsky's Poetics*, C. Emerson (ed. and trans.) Minneapolis, Minn., University of Minnesota Press, 1984, esp. pp. 134ff.

40 This requirement excluded Henry, and may well refer to yet another mode of resistance, the belief in justification by faith to which Pole would tenaciously adhere until 1546 when Trent officially condemned it. Of another huge literature, see esp. E. G. Gleason, 'On the nature of sixteenth-century Italian evangelism: scholarship, 1953–1978', *SCJ*, 1978, vol. 9, pp. 3–25; P. Simoncelli, *Evangelismo italiano del Cinquecento. Questione religiosa e nicodemismo politico*, Rome, Istituto storico italiano per l'età moderna e contemporanea, 1979, and esp. the work of Firpo (see Note 4 above).

41 M. A. Screech, *Erasmus, Ecstasy and the Praise of Folly*, Harmondsworth, Penguin, 1988.

42 *CSPV*, vol. 5, nos 591 and 594. Pole's role was commemorated by his inclusion in the fresco of Ottavio receiving Parma from Julius III in the Farnese villa at Caprarola.

43 H. Lutz (ed.) *Friedenslegation des Reginald Pole zu Kaiser Karl V. und König Heinrich II. (1553–1556)*, *Nuntiaturberichte aus Deutschland*, 1. Abteilung 1533–1559, vol. 15, Tübingen, Niemeyer, 1981; for Paul IV see G. Fragnito, ' "Parenti" e "familiari" nelle corti cardinalizie del rinascimento', in Mozzarelli (ed.) op. cit., p. 572; A. Aubert, 'Alle origini della Controriforma: studi e problemi sul Paolo IV', *Rivista di storia e letteratura religiosa*, 1986, vol. 22, pp. 303–55; and R. De Maio, *Michelangelo e la Contrariforma*, Bari, Laterza, 1981; for Mary, D. Loades, *Mary Tudor*, Oxford, Basil Blackwell, 1989.

44 Guido da Fano makes one excellent example and Bartolomeo Spadafora another. A. Stella, 'Guido da Fano eretico del secolo XVI al servizio dei re d'Inghilterra', *Rivista di storia della chiesa in Italia*, 1959, vol. 13, pp. 196–238, and S. Caponetto, 'Origini e caratteri della riforma in Sicilia', *Rinascimento*, 1956, vol. 7, pp. 219–41, 281–325.

45 T. F. Mayer, 'If martyrs are exchanged with martyrs: the kidnappings of William Tyndale and Reginald Pole', *Archiv für Reformationsgeschichte*, 1990, vol. 81, pp. 305–27, and 'A diet for Henry VIII: the failure of Reginald Pole's 1537 legation', *JBS*, 1987, vol. 26, pp. 305–31. See also Höllger, op. cit. For

Pole's earlier treason, see *CSPSp*, 5:1, no. 172 (Contarini asking imperial protection for Pole); BL Add. MS 28,587, fos 7v–9v and *CSPSp*, 5:1, no. 109; Add. MS 28,590, fos 5v–6r (*CSPSp*, 5:2, no. 63); and *CSPSp*, 5:1, no. 133 (for the date, see Mayer, *Starkey*, p. 216, n. 64). Eustace Chapuys, the imperial ambassador in London, had talked up Pole's prospects already in 1532; *CSPSp*, 4:2, no. 888.

46 K. R. Bartlett, 'Papal policy and the English crown, 1563–1565: the Bertano correspondence', *SCJ*, forthcoming; J. Lestocquoy (ed.) *Correspondance des nonces en France Capodiferro, Dandino et Guidiccione 1541–1546, Acta nuntiaturae gallicae*, vol. 3, Rome, Presses de l'Université Grégorienne, 1963, nos 136ff; and T. F. Mayer, 'Reginald Pole in Paolo Giovio's *Descriptio*: a strategy for reconversion', *SCJ*, 1985, vol. 16, pp. 431–50.

47 I say scribbled because of the palaeographical problems posed by this work (BAV, Vaticanus latinus 5966, fos 3r–26r). The date is based mainly on the hand, which closely resembles that in other autograph documents stemming from this period.

48 'Apologia ad Carolum quintum caesarem', in *ERP*, vol. 1, pp. 136–8, 147–8. Pole's case against Machiavelli once more rested on martyrology, this time a defence of the power of Becket's body. Pole's identification with Becket became so complete that he had himself buried in Becket's by then empty tomb in Canterbury cathedral. He also owned a MS life of Becket by John de Grandison, now in the Bodleian (no. 2097, *Summary Catalogue of Western Manuscripts*), which bears Pole's name and the date 1539. A. Pastore, 'Due biblioteche umanistiche del Cinquecento. (I libri del cardinal Pole e di Marcantonio Flaminio)', *Rinascimento*, 1979, ser. 2, vol. 19, pp. 269–90, p. 273. S. J. Gunn helped greatly on this point.

49 Morandi (ed.) op. cit., vol. 2, p. 330, and in *ERP*, vol. 5, p. 389. I do not mean to say that Beccadelli's words accurately captured Pole's opinions, merely that the biographer thought they did. On him, see G. Fragnito, esp. *Memoria individuale e costruzione biografica*, Urbino, 1978, and *In museo e in villa*, op. cit.

50 H. Jedin, *Contarini und Camaldoli*, Rome, Edizioni di storia e letteratura, 1953; G. Alberigo, 'Vita attiva e vita contemplativa in un'esperienza cristiana del XVI secolo', *Studi veneziani*, 1974, vol. 16, pp. 177–225; G. Fragnito, 'Cultura umanistica e riforma religiosa: Il "De officio viri boni ac probi episcopi"', *Studi veneziani*, 1969, vol. 11, pp. 75–189; F. Gilbert, 'Religion and politics in the thought of Gasparo Contarini', in T. K. Rabb and J. E. Seigel (eds) *Action and Conviction in Early Modern Europe*, Princeton, NJ, Princeton University Press, 1969, pp. 90–116; J. B. Ross, 'Gasparo Contarini and his friends', *Studies in the Renaissance*, 1970, vol. 17, pp. 192–232, and 'Venetian schools and teachers fourteenth to early sixteenth century: a survey and a study of Giovanni Battista Egnazio', *Renaissance Quarterly*, 1976, vol. 29, pp. 521–66.

51 For Mantova, see T. F. Mayer, 'Marco Mantova and the Paduan religious crisis of the early sixteenth century', *Cristianesimo nella storia*, 1986, vol. 7, pp. 41–61; for Bonamico, Mayer, *Starkey*, pp. 51–3, 194, 196–7; and for Lampridio, ibid., pp. 194–6. Another of Pole's long-time friends and tutor in the ideas of Juan de Valdés, Marcantonio Flaminio, chose to use Lampridio as an example of competence in Greek in one of his religious tracts. Firpo, 'Valdesianesimo ed evangelismo: alle origini dell' "Ecclesia Viterbense" ', in *Tra alumbrados e spirituali*, op. cit., pp. 170–1.

52 W. F. Young, 'Reform ideology in the "Libellus ad Leonem X" ', paper read to the American Historical Association, New York, 1985. The text of the

Consilium is in E. G. Gleason (ed. and trans.) *Reform Thought in Sixteenth-Century Italy*, n.p., American Academy of Religion, 1981, pp. 81–100.

53 Mayer, 'Bronze Age conciliarist', pp. 407–8.

54 A. Cistellini, *Figure della Riforma pretridentina*, Brescia, Morcelliana, 1948, pp. 71, 79, 95 and passim.

55 Still the best life is A. Virgili, *Francesco Berni*, Florence, Le Monnier, 1881. Berni's link to Priuli is mentioned on p. 253 but see also Berni's letter to his Venetian friend in A. Virgili (ed.) *Rime, poesie latine e lettere edite e inedite*, Florence, Le Monnier, 1885, pp. 319–32. Anne Reynolds offers an important fresh start on Berni's poetry in 'Francesco Berni: the theory and practice of Italian satire in the sixteenth century', *Italian Quarterly*, 1983, vol. 24, no. 94, pp. 5–15.

56 On Bini's poetry and that of this circle see S. Longhi, *Lusus. Il capitolo burlesco nel Cinquecento*, Padua, Antenore, 1983 and the life in A. M. Ghisalberti (ed.) *Dizionario Biografico degli Italiani*, Rome, Istituto dell'enciclopedia italiana, 1960– . For Palladio's garden see esp. P. P. Bober, 'The *Coryciana* and the Nymph Corycia', *Journal of the Warburg and Courtauld Institutes*, 1977, vol. 40, pp. 223–39, and for his life G. Battelli, 'Un umanista romana del Cinquecento. Blosio Palladio', *La Bibliofilia*, 1941, vol. 43, pp. 16–23, and M.-H. Laurent, *Fabio Vigili et les bibliothèques de Bologne au début du XVIe siècle*, *Studi e testi*, vol. 105, Rome, Biblioteca apostolica vaticana, 1943, p. XI.

57 Both of Michelangelo's early biographers put Pole high on the list of his intimate friends. R. Beltarini and P. Barocchi (eds) Giorgio Vasari, *Le vite de' più eccellenti pittori scultori e archittetori*, Florence, Studio per edizioni scelte, 1966, vol. 1:1, p. 109, and Ascanio Condivi, *The Life of Michelangelo*, in C. Holroyd, *Michael Angelo Buonarroti . . . with Translations of the Life of the Master by his Scholar, Ascanio Condivi*, London, Duckworth, 1903, p. 84. For his poetry see most conveniently J. Saslow (ed. and trans.) *The Poetry of Michelangelo*, New Haven, Conn., Yale University Press, 1990. H. Hibbard, *Michelangelo*, New York, Harper & Row, 1974, offers the best short treatment in English. For Michelangelo's political art see esp. D. J. Gordon, 'Giannotti, Michelangelo and the cult of Brutus', in D. J. Gordon (ed.) *Fritz Saxl 1890–1948: A Volume of Memorial Essays*, London, Nelson, 1957, pp. 281–96 and S. Levine, 'The location of Michelangelo's *David*: the meeting of January 25, 1504', *Art Bulletin*, 1974, vol. 56, pp. 31–49, for the politics of that statue, and for Michelangelo's general political outlook G. Spini, 'Politicita di Michelangelo', *Rivista storica italiana*, 1964, vol. 76, pp. 557–600. For Michelangelo's artistic religious resistances, which come very close to some of Pole's ideas about papal primacy, see L. Steinberg, *Michelangelo's Last Paintings: The Conversion of St. Paul and the Crucifixion of St. Peter in the Cappella Paolina, Vatican Palace*, London, Phaidon, 1975 (the most detailed treatment, with fine illustrations) and above all W. Wallace, 'Narrative and religious expression in Michelangelo's Pauline Chapel', *Artibus et Historiae*, 1989, vol. 20, pp. 107–21.

58 C. Maddison, *Marcantonio Flaminio: Poet, Humanist and Reformer*, London, Routledge, 1965, pp. 154–8, and A. Pastore, op. cit., p. 139.

59 For an excellent summary of the state of the debate, see A. Aubert, 'Valdesianesimo ed evangelismo italiano: alcuni studi recenti', *Rivista di storia della chiesa in Italia*, 1987, vol. 41, pp. 152–75.

60 Marcantonio Flaminio, *Lettere*, A. Pastore (ed.), Rome, Ateneo & Bizzarri, 1978, no. 59.

61 Ibid., no. 60.

62 Ibid., no. 66.

63 L. Martines, *Power and Imagination: City-states in Renaissance Italy*, London, Allen Lane, 1980, esp. ch. 15.
64 Gilbert, 'Religion and politics', op. cit., and 'Venice in the crisis of the League of Cambrai', in *History: Choice and Commitment*, Cambridge, Mass., Harvard University Press, 1977, pp. 247–67; W. J. Bouwsma, *Venice and the Defense of Republican Liberty: Renaissance Values in the Age of the Counter-Reformation*, Berkeley, Calif., University of California Press, 1968; and R. Finlay, *Politics in Renaissance Venice*, New Brunswick, NJ, Rutgers University Press, 1980.
65 P. Prodi, *Il sovrano pontefice: Un corpo e due anime: la monarchia papale nella prima età moderna*, Bologna, Il Mulino, 1982.
66 *Motives of Eloquence*, op. cit., p. 32 and cf. p. 219.
67 Ibid., p. 155.

3

The problem of counsel reconsidered: the case of Sir Thomas Elyot

F. W. Conrad

When Ben Jonson wrote in his *Discoveries* that 'good councillors to princes are the best instruments of a good age' he was making a commonplace argument.[1] As the following brief catalogue testifies, the idea that good counsel was essential to successful government was articulated by a wide variety of medieval and early modern English authors. The lawyer Henry de Bracton argued that kings should rule by considered judgement rather than through their arbitrary will.[2] The poet Thomas Hoccleve advised the youthful Henry V never to undertake public activities without counsel, which 'may wele be likened to a bridelle/Which that an hors kepethe up from fallynge'.[3] Early Tudor humanists wrote works suggesting that it was incumbent upon wise men to benefit the commonwealth through service in the councils of kings.[4] Indeed, as late as 1642 the authors of the Nineteen Propositions implied a relationship between counsel and the public good when, echoing earlier writers, they suggested that the provision of counsel to an English monarch was too important to be limited to the king's private companions.[5]

Despite its obvious importance, good counsel has proved a difficult concept for scholars to define.[6] Just what counselling a prince entailed is a question too seldom put, and one whose answer is not immediately clear: what might Hythloday or Cardinal Pole be expected to effect in the service of a king, and how was this to be achieved? A contributing factor to our difficulty in readily answering such questions has been a propensity to investigate proposed remedies for perceived social and economic ills while downplaying the more frequent, but reputedly less realistic and less sophisticated, criticisms of kings' and counsellors' supposed moral failings. To appropriate a distinction made by Sir Francis Bacon, scholarly preference has been to study 'counsel concerning business' instead of 'counsel concerning manners'.[7] In continuing to exhibit such a preference, however, we threaten to skew the priorities of our subjects. More often than not, when medieval and renaissance Englishmen wrote about the importance of good counsel to good government, they had in mind the maintenance of their ruler's psychological well-being. While the flatterer

75

constituted an antitype, the ideal counsellor was envisaged as a friend of the prince, for, as Bacon put it, 'the best preservative to keep the mind in health is the faithful admonition of a friend'.

The following discussion seeks to elucidate this under-appreciated dimension of Renaissance Englishmen's understanding of counsel through an analysis of the writings of the early Tudor humanist Sir Thomas Elyot (*c.* 1490–1546), arguably England's foremost exponent of what Bacon termed 'counsel of manners'. The relations between kings and their counsellors are the chief subjects of Elyot's dialogues *Pasquil the Playne* and *Of the Knowledge Which Maketh a Wise Man*, both initially published in 1533, and are a complementary concern in several of his other compositions, the most celebrated being *The Boke named the Governour* (1531), which by 1580 had enjoyed eight separate editions. In addition to having the advantage of a wealth of source material on the subject of counsel, however, the selection of Elyot's political thought as a test case is propitious in that it affords an opportunity to assess the relevance of such views to the actualities of early Tudor politics. While it has often been claimed that Elyot's works treat political questions 'almost in the abstract, without reference to the controversies of the time' and are 'as remote from the realities of Tudor politics as it is possible to be', such contentions are far from self-evident.[8] During the 1520s and early 1530s Sir Thomas was a man intimately familiar with English political and administrative activity. From March 1526 to March 1530, the formative years of Henry VIII's divorce crisis, he enjoyed a privileged vantage point while serving as a clerk of the King's Council. Moreover, shortly after his dismissal from the Council clerkship, Elyot was appointed English ambassador to the Court of Charles V, and in that capacity was able to discuss the king's 'great matter' with both Katharine of Aragon's husband and nephew. Given this background, a distinct possibility exists that the relation of Elyot's thought to the problems of Henrician politics has yet to be fully discerned.

One of the most forceful and enduring classical precepts concerning the importance of political counsel was taken from the pages of Alexander Severus' biography in the *Scriptores Historiae Augustae*: '*meliorem esse rem publicam et prope tutiorem, in qua princeps malus est, ea, in qua sunt amici principis mali*'.[9] During the 1390s John Gower incorporated the maxim into Book Seven of his *Confessio Amantis*;[10] and two centuries later, the historian John Hayward narrated an account of Richard II's final years for the purpose of illustrating the moral: 'it is oftentimes as daungerous to a Prince, to have euil and odious adherents, as to be euil and odious himselfe'.[11] Indeed, the *Scriptores* precept was such an established part of sixteenth-century political thought that Innocent Gentillet availed himself of it when refuting what he took to be pernicious ideas contained in *Il Principe*'s chapter on flatterers.[12]

Evidence of Elyot's familiarity with the maxim is found in one of his lesser-known works, a collection of aphorisms entitled *The Bankette of Sapience*, the first known edition of which was published in 1539.[13] There, under the heading 'Counsayl and Counsayloures', he translates the sentence in question and correctly attributes it to Marius Maximus:

> That publyke weale is in better state, & in a maner more sure, where the prynce is not good, than where the kinges councellours and companions be yll.[14]

Sir Thomas's rendering of *amici principis* here as 'the kinges councellours and companions', instead of the more literal translation 'friends of the prince', is particularly noteworthy for two reasons. First, it is evidence of the thorough-going classicism one might expect from the compiler of the most comprehensive Latin–English *Dictionary* of his day;[15] and second, it is our first hint that ideals of friendship inform Elyot's conception of good counsel. Using Sir Thomas's translation from the *Scriptores* as a baseline, the present portion of my discussion aims to illuminate the general outlines of his political thought. As Elyot chose not to write as systematically as he thought, it will be necessary to refer to nearly all of his works.

The *amici principis*, as Elyot was well aware, were an artificial class of citizens in the Roman Empire. The designation, derived from the Hellenistic court title *philos* ('friend') and rooted in the practice of still earlier oriental rulers, referred not necessarily to personal friends of the emperor, but specifically to those who could pay him court. When referring to the immediate entourage of the emperor, wherever he might be, imperial Latin authors commonly employed the phrase '*cohors amicorum*'.[16] It is important to realize, however, that the *amici* were always greater in number than the emperor's present group of servants, sycophants and wits. Provincial governors and procurators, for example, are referred to in official documents by the epithet *amicus*, and this was by no means a vain title.[17] It served to indicate to the Empire's inhabitants the importance of those acting on behalf of Rome among them. Those designated *amici principis*, because of their intimacy with the emperor, were representatives of his authority.[18]

Moreover, within the *amici*, there was an important distinction between those of 'first' and those of 'second admission'; although it is uncertain whether this distinction rested on anything other than imperial favour, it is clear that a major function of the primary *amici* was advising the emperor – not merely on judicial decisions and military and administrative policies, but also on his public behaviour and personal life where these might adversely affect politics.[19] Although not a recognized constitutional body, the *consilium amicorum* ('council of friends') was a characteristic feature of every reign from Augustus to Constantine. Usually at daybreak, those *amici* in the emperor's proximity would gather at the vestibule door for the traditional *salutatio* before attending to other private or governmental duties. The primary *amici* present entered first and, after greeting the emperor, engaged him in discussion of current public business and judicial matters. Elyot reveals his awareness of this ancient practice when describing the daily routine of Alexander Severus in one of his last published works, *The Image of Governance* (1541; colophon 1540). Alexander's standard practice, according to Sir Thomas, was to receive all his 'friends' together in the afternoon after reading and signing letters.[20]

In fact, several years prior to the publication of *The Image of Governance*, Elyot had alluded to the *consilium amicorum* in a passage of *Pasquil the Playne*, his Lucianic dialogue regarding the merits of frank speech at Court. There the plain-speaking title figure Pasquil, a recently disinterred ancient Roman statue re-erected at Rome in 1501, reproves the modern schedule followed by two wayfaring councillors who are soon to attend upon their master after dinner:

> In olde tyme men vsed to occupie the mornynge in deepe & subtile studies and in counsailes concernynge the commune weale, and other matters of great importaunce. In like wise than to here controversies, and gyue iudgement. And if they had any causes of theyr owne/ than to treate of them. and that dydde they not without a great consyderation. procedynge bothe of naturall rayson, and also counsayle of phisike.[21]

The imperial Roman practice is here established by Elyot as an ideal standard from which the actions of these modern councillors and their unnamed master may be understood to deviate. What is important for our present purposes, however, is recognition of the fluid nature of Elyot's ideal. The *amici* did not participate in a formal institution with fixed membership and meeting times. Much like pre-1540 Henrician Councillors and Privy Chamber personnel, these men were not only counsellors, but also soldiers and local governors who spent much of their lives away from Rome on government service. When they were available or needed at Court, however, they were called in to give their counsel. The idea of a standing advisory body – men to spend years sitting in a council chamber – would have been entirely counter to the Roman system, whose essence was that a man must fit himself for high office by a variety of experience in all branches of the imperial service.[22]

Although we tend instinctively to assign a more prominent political role to the Roman Senate, few ancient Romans or Renaissance scholars would have made the same supposition. Indeed, the importance of the *amici* and their advice to the fortunes of government is attested numerous times in the literature of the Empire. In the pages of Tacitus, Helvidius Priscus claims: 'For a good government there is no greater instrument than the possession of *boni amici* [good friends]'.[23] According to Suetonius, the Emperor Titus 'chose as *amici* men whom succeeding emperors also retained as necessary to both themselves and the state'.[24] A bit later in the passage of the *Scriptores* translated by Elyot, Homullus is said to have reconciled Domitian's evil reputation and honest administration by the reflection, 'Domitian was a most evil man but he had *boni amici*'.[25] Hence Elyot's translation of *amici principis* as 'the kinges councellours and companions', although not literal, is entirely faithful to ancient usage. Moreover, his selection of the *Scriptores* passage for inclusion in the *Bankette* suggests a degree of sympathy for that strand of classical political thought which contended that friendship was essential to the preservation of monarchical government.

With this background we are now in a better position to perceive a relationship, often unacknowledged, between the opening chapters of *The Boke named the Governour* and the remainder of the volume. At the very outset of the work, after quickly dismissing social equality as an idea contrary to the natural order of the universe, Elyot staunchly asserts the superiority of monarchy to all other forms of government. Just as one sun rules over the day and one moon over the night, he writes, 'who can denie but that all thynge in heven and erthe is gouerned by one god, by one perpetuall ordre, by one prouidence?'[26] Consequently, a public weal ought to have only one sovereign governor. While this analogy is sometimes taken as implying unlimited royal power and anticipating the 1533 Act in Restraint of Appeals,[27] it must be remembered that Elyot was not engaged in discussing the relative authorities of church and state and nowhere seeks to justify the disreputable conduct of kings. As the historical examples which supply many of the work's opening pages indicate, Elyot was primarily concerned to demonstrate the inherent inferiority of all forms of divided sovereignty with respect to the maintenance of public order. Just as Sir Thomas would later praise the restoration of law and order which accompanied Henry VII's more recent reunification of the realm, here he notes the increased civility of the tenth century which followed the return of the monarch 'to his pristine estate and figure' by King Edgar.[28]

Having established that contention and confusion were inescapably linked to a plurality of sovereign governors, Elyot next argues for the necessity of magistrates in a public weal. Only a fool, he thought, would assert that one man might continually possess 'all virtues and good qualities'.[29] Moreover, reason, common experience and the *Politics* of Aristotle all plainly declare that in large and populous dominions it is 'convenient that a prince haue many inferiour gouernours, which be named of Aristotel his eien, eares, handes, and legges'.[30] These inferior governors, Elyot goes on to say, should whenever possible be chosen from the estate of 'worship-full' men.[31] Because of their financial status, such men were better equipped to resist corruption and attain a proper education towards the administration of the public weal. The sons of poor men, dependent on their unaided natural wit, were unlikely to rival the competence of the properly educated:

> the potter and tynker, only perfecte in theyr crafte, shall littell do in the ministration of iustice. A ploughman or carter shall make but a feble answere to an ambassadour. Also a wayuer or fuller shulde be an unmete capitaine of an armie, or in any other office of a governour.[32]

As obedience was best secured through virtuous example, Elyot thought only persons of superior understanding, 'excelling in knowlege wherby other be gouerned', should be rewarded with the responsibility of authority.[33] To this end, the remainder of the *Governour*'s first book, drawing largely upon Erasmus and Quintilian, outlines an educational regimen for the minds and manners of England's prospective governors.

These two dozen chapters describe the curriculum appropriate to successive age groups. Potential magistrates, nurtured from birth by virtuous nurses, should by the age of 7 have learned Latin.[34] During the next eight years, they were to become familiar with Greek, and further their competence in both languages through private tutoring in ancient didactic poetry.[35] From the age of 14, the students would successively be instructed in logic, rhetoric and history.[36] After three years of such preparation, the young men were deemed ready to begin studying the classic texts of moral philosophy.[37] Finally, at the age of 21, potential governors were allowed to undertake the study of jurisprudence.[38] While throughout this prodigious programme children were encouraged to engage in archery and other profitable forms of physical exercise, and those naturally inclined to painting or music might find suitable repose in such arts, 'the ende of all doctrine and studie', according to Elyot, was the provision of 'good counsayle'.[39] Governors brought up in accordance with this regimen, Sir Thomas hoped, would rival the ideal orators of Cicero and Quintilian in being able to speak wisely and effectively whenever and wherever required: whether in the capacity of courtier, councillor, diplomat, soldier or local official.[40]

Books Two and Three of the *Governour* deal almost exclusively with the conduct of the appointed governor, detailing the virtues he should embody and the vices he should shun. Under such headings as fortitude, ambition and deceit, Elyot first provides a careful definition of the quality under discussion before presenting a host of predominantly classical *exempla*, many previously unavailable in the vernacular. Since Elyot's emphasis on virtuous conduct throughout these books implies a desire to bridle the behaviour of kings as well as their servants, some critics who assert that the opening chapters of the *Governour* ascribe unlimited power to the sovereign have suggested that Sir Thomas, seeking to appeal to Henry VIII's growing belief in his imperial powers, may have added the initial chapters as an afterthought.[41] Not only do the verb tenses employed in these chapters seem indicative of a later insertion, but also Elyot's treatment of Tarquin the Proud in the opening pages appears strikingly different from the image of the last Roman king presented elsewhere in the book.[42] Indeed, the recent discovery of Elyot's late 1520s translation of Plutarch's essay concerning 'The Education of Children' might be taken as further support for the thesis that *The Boke named the Governour* was originally composed as an educational treatise and only awkwardly transformed into a political work shortly before its publication by the addition of three initial chapters in support of a strong monarchy.[43]

Despite this collection of circumstantial evidence, however, room for doubt persists. Many years ago Pearl Hogrefe demonstrated that the verb tenses of the opening chapters need not imply a later insertion, and the fact that Henry VIII developed and began to implement his theory of imperial kingship more than a decade before the *Governour*'s publication lends credence to her interpretation.[44] Moreover, the contention that Elyot's initial treatment of Tarquin the Proud contradicts later passages in the work also lacks foundation. According to the *Governour*'s most direct comment on the last Roman king, which occurs near the end of Book One, Tarquin was clearly a tyrant, the restoration of whose evil regime would likely have resulted in Rome's 'perpetuall servitude'.[45] Yet this passage should not be taken to infer that Elyot viewed ancient Roman history as demonstrating the inherent inferiority of strong monarchy to republican government. As Sir Thomas maintained in the *Governour*'s opening pages, only the extraordinary learning and wisdom of contemporary senators prevented the abolition of monarchical government which occurred upon Tarquin's expulsion from producing the tremendous internal discord one would have expected.[46] In the absence of more compelling arguments, it must be assumed that Elyot believed his first original composition in the vernacular to be an internally consistent work on the education and conduct of present and future English governors.

Indeed, it is possible to discern continuity between the *Governour*'s opening chapters and subsequent contents. In the final chapter of Book Two, Elyot returns to the same passage of Aristotle that he alluded to in the work's third chapter, this time with greater specificity:

Aristotell in his politykes exorteth gouernours to haue their *frendes* for a great numbre of eyen, earis, handes, and legges; considering that no one man may see or here all thinge that many men may see and here, ne can be in all places, or do as many thinges well, at one tyme, as many persons may do.[47]

The apparently casual repetition of allusion to Aristotle here should not be dismissed as coincidence. Sir Thomas later alluded to the same passage of Aristotle in a dedicatory epistle he wrote to Thomas Cromwell. He asked the then Lord Privy Seal to reflect on

> what commoditie, strength, and consolation it is to a realme, to have honourable, wyse, and circumspect counsaylours, attendynge on the person of the chiefe governour: Contrarywise in the lacke of them, what incommodytie, debilitie, and desolation, happeneth to the realme, where the prince lacketh suche counsaylours, whom Aristotle calle[th], his eies, his eares, his handes, and his fete. For admyt that he dothe excell all other in wysedom, yet beinge a man, and but one, lyke as he can not here or see al thinges, no more can he have at one tyme in his owne remembraunce all thynges necessarie, which many do thinke on. In this sort of treasure, wherof our most gracious soverain lorde, reignynge above all other princes in Sapience and most royall courage, is nobly adorned, your lordshyp may well be estemed a principall jewell, for the incomparable quyckenes of your lordshyps invencion, invincible eloquence, infatigable diligence, gravitie in judgement, incredible dexteritie, and many other vertues and qualities excellent.[48]

Clearly, for Elyot, Aristotle's teachings on monarchy were particularly relevant to the world of Henrician politics and administration.

Recognition of this fact is crucial to an appreciation of *The Boke named the Governour*. As we have seen, one of the aims of the *Governour* was to supply a training regimen for future English inferior governors, or, following Elyot's own verbal substitution in his Aristotelian allusions, 'friends' of the sovereign governor. In other words, the educational programme outlined in Book One was deliberately designed to produce contemporary English counterparts to the *philoi* of Hellenistic monarchs and the *amici principis* of imperial Rome. Stating the intention in this unusual fashion appears less startling when it is recalled that Elyot's eventual companion volume to the *Governour* on the practical workings of government, *The Image of Governance*, took the form of an historical account of the administration of the Roman Emperor Alexander Severus.[49] Large portions of the *Image* were translated directly from Alexander's *vita* in the *Scriptores Historiae Augustae*, the closing pages of which provided the sentence of Marius Maximus that Elyot translated in *The Bankette of Sapience*.[50]

It would be a mistake, however, to think of Elyot in the *Governour* as merely interested in educating more professional magistrates or 'friends' in name only. In chapter eleven of Book Two, entitled 'The true definition of amity and between what persons it happeneth', Sir Thomas noted that while contentious and overly serious studies tended to inhibit amity, similarity of education oftentimes promoted friendship, 'specially if the studies haue in them any delectable affection or motion'.[51] Not coincidentally, throughout Book One Elyot had stressed the need for education to be alluring, and in the very next chapter he pauses 'to recreate' his readers with the 'wonderfull', if appropriately mythic, history of the perfect friendship between Titus and Gisippus.[52] This *exemplum*, the work's lengthiest by far, expressed, he thought,

> the description of frendship engendred by the similitude of age and personage, augmented by the conformitie of maners and studies, and confirmed by the longe continuance of company.[53]

As Sir Thomas later told Thomas Cromwell in reference to their own friendship, similitude of studies was undoubtedly 'the moste perfeict fundacion of amitie'.[54] Elyot, it seems clear, hoped through the educational plan advocated in Book One of the *Governour*, to increase the likelihood of true friends among the ranks of England's inferior governors.

It is also clear that Elyot's vision in this regard was not naive. Such perfect amity, he realized, could not often be expected, if ever. Certainly it was seldom approached among the contemporary inferior governors Sir Thomas had served alongside:

> For where fyndest thou hym (saieth [Cicero]) that will nat preferre honoures, great offices, rule, autorite, and richesse before frendship? Therefore (sayeth he) it is very harde to fynde frendship in them that be occupied in acquirynge honour or about the affaires of the publike weale. Which sayenge is proued true by dayly experience.[55]

Why then, against the obstinacy of human nature, did Elyot wish to ensure the practice of friendship among those who occupied the station of 'friends'? As is often the case in Elyot's writings, the same predicament had been considered earlier by Erasmus, this time in the dedicatory epistle to Henry VIII of his Latin translation of Plutarch's essay 'How to Distinguish a Flatterer from a Friend' (1513). The opening portion of Erasmus' dedication helps to clarify Elyot's position:

> Although this world contains no more agreeable society than that of a true and genuinely candid friend and there is nothing a man needs more in the conduct of his affairs, at the same time nothing is harder to find than such a friend. . . . But, as Hiero ably maintains in the pages of Xenophon, none stand more sorely in need of this important constituent of happiness than princes . . . for a prince more than any other requires both many friends and right loyal ones too. Indeed

he needs to be clear-sighted who all by himself must see to the well-being of thousands. It is fitting therefore, that the prince be endowed with many eyes, or in other words with a multitude of friends.[56]

Almost paradoxically, friends faithful to the monarch were considered both essential and exceedingly rare. While human self-interest may render the second judgement understandable enough, the reasoning behind the former is not as obvious. Machiavelli, for instance, implied that certain principalities are more securely ruled through fear than friendship.

A clue to understanding Elyot's argument is to be found upon inspection of the passage of the *Politics* to which he so often had recourse. It occurs towards the end of Aristotle's discussion of absolute kingship:

It is by no means easy for one man to superintend many things . . . indeed, it is already the practice of kings to make to themselves many eyes and ears and hands and feet. For they make colleagues [*synarchoi*] of those who are their friends and the friends of their government. They must be friends of the monarch and of his government; if not his friends, they will not do what he wants; but friendship implies likeness and equality; and therefore, if he thinks that his friends ought to rule, he must think that those who are equal to himself and like himself ought to rule equally with himself.[57]

Two points here are worthy of notice. First, Aristotle's anatomical division of rule is as much descriptive as metaphorical, and ought not to be construed as a simple body politic formulation. In many ancient kingdoms those who made it their business to spy out what they could report to the monarch's advantage acquired the designation 'the king's eye' or 'the king's ear'. More important, however, is that Aristotle, perhaps with Alexander's recent successes in mind, has used the existence of the king's *philoi* – the collective advisory eyes and ears and the administrative hands and feet – to undermine the theoretical legitimacy of monarchy based solely on the sovereign's will. A truly absolute king, were he to exist, would have no need either to trust *archons* to represent his authority in remote regions of his domain or to base his judgement upon the advice of others. The fact that practical necessity forced even the most powerful ancient kings to rely on their 'friends' offered incontrovertible evidence that monarchical government should be considered a collegial rather than solitary enterprise, and Aristotle was not alone in this contention. As early as the fifth century BC Aeschylus voiced a corollary opinion when he remarked: 'it is a disease that somehow inheres in tyranny to have no faith in friends'.[58]

Elyot's decision to follow his defence of sovereign monarchy with an assertion of the necessity of inferior governors based upon this passage of Aristotle was deliberate: instead of simply promoting Henry's imperial style, the opening chapters of *The Governour* sought to explore its bounds. According to Sir Thomas, an authoritative monarch was required to maintain order and impede the development of faction, but his powers should never be considered without limit. The will of every sovereign was circumscribed to the extent he needed inferior governors or 'friends' to enact, enforce and help determine it. On the one hand, this limitation could prove unfortunate, as, for instance, was the case with Henry VIII's professed desire for the indifferent administration of justice throughout his realm. As Elyot learned first-hand during his tenure as a clerk of the Council, Cardinal Wolsey's efforts to ensure the diligent local execution of justice often met with little success. On the other hand, since Elyot refused to sanction civil disobedience, the king's necessary dependence on 'friends' offered to those in the royal entourage a crucial means of bridling a monarch's inclinations to cruelty or vice. As we shall see, Elyot viewed the continual presence of true friends and their counsel about the monarch as an inhibition to tyranny. To fully appreciate, however, the importance which the distinction between friend and seeming friend or flatterer held for Elyot, we must first examine his account of human psychology.

According to Elyot, man is a compound of body and soul. While the former constituent is sensual, mortal and beastly in nature, the latter is intellectual, immortal and godly. From this commonplace beginning, however, Elyot, following Aristotle's *De anima*, went on to divide the soul into three distinct parts: the vegetative, which is concerned with growth and common to all living things; the sensitive, which concerns feeling and is common to all animals; and the intellectual – termed by Elyot 'the understanding' – 'whiche is of all the other mooste noble, as whereby man is mooste lyke unto god and is preferred before all other creatures'.[59] In the *Governour* Elyot devoted an entire chapter to the understanding in which he defined its proper function:

> It is the principall parte of the soule which is occupied about the begynnynge or originall causes of thynges that may falle in to mannes knowlege, and his office is, before that any thynge is attempted, to thinke, consydre, and prepence, and, after often tossyng it up and downe in the mynde, then to exercise that powar.[60]

The final elements of the soul Elyot termed inclinations or 'affects', which he likened to the intention of a workman before he works. When a man exercises these inclinations with respect to his understanding, as is his duty, the result is a virtuous action.[61]

Yet men do not always act in accordance with their pre-eminence in the scale of nature. Not all inclinations are good. Some men are disposed to cruelty, others to avarice and deceitfulness, still others to sloth. When these or other base affections overrun the understanding and come to predominate in the soul, the result is an act of vice. In his 1533 dialogue

Of the Knowledge Which Maketh a Wise Man, an imaginary discussion between Plato and the Cyrenaic philosopher Aristippus concerning the former's experience of counselling Dionysius at Syracuse, Elyot set forth at considerable length the complex psychological mechanism by which the soul becomes corrupted.[62] According to Plato, pleasant sensations continually generate vicious inclinations which tempt the will. Whenever these sensual affections are left unbridled by human understanding, the soul 'loseth hir dignite, & becommith ministre vnto the sences/ which before were her slaues'. The subsequent loss of a man's proper disposition necessarily results in vicious or sinful conduct and a disorder in the chain of being: man becomes 'bireft of that portion/ wherein he was lyke vnto god' and is made 'equalle or rather inferior to brute beastes'.

Since Elyot considered governors of superior understanding essential to the welfare of the public weal, the political implications of this psychology were enormous. To every English governor, he asserted, there appertained a 'double gouernaunce':

> that is to saye, an interior or inwarde gouernaunce, and an exterior or outwarde gouernaunce. The firste is of his affectes and passions, which do inhabite within his soule, and be subiectes to reason. The seconde is of his children, his seruauntes, and other subiectes to his autoritie.[63]

From this dichotomy emerged what Elyot understood to be the fundamental predicament of early Tudor politics: the quality of Henry VIII's government, like that of all previous English monarchs, would always be conditional upon the self-governance of the fallible men who together ruled the country. Consequently, helping discern the ends and means of prudent policy, whether in the council chamber or in print, constituted only one type of political counsel, and not necessarily the most important.

Particularly telling with respect to Elyot's emphasis is his definition of tyranny in terms of psychological disposition. Following Plato's Socrates, Sir Thomas considered a tyrant anyone

> whose soule rulith not/ but excluding from hir, Knowlege and Raison, suffreth hir selfe to be gouerned bi the sensis/ and obeyeng to the folishe affectis, leteth them leade hir out of hir highe place in the lyne of Order, into a more base degree, and to be made equal or inferior to beastis.[64]

Hence flattery, by ancient definition speech appealing to the emotional or irrational elements in the soul, became, for Christians, a mortal pestilence leading men in positions of authority away from the path to salvation.[65] In the *Governour*, Elyot noted that 'by perverse instruction and flattery' the adulator 'slayeth both the soul and good renown of his master'.[66]

Fourteen years later, in his last published work, *A Preseruatiue Agaynste Deth*, he cited Origen and pseudo-Augustine to the same purpose:

> Flatery and Assentacion in the iudgemente of God, is wars than the sweorde of the murderer. For firste the flaterer kylleth his soule that he flatereth, if he receyue the stroke willyngly: and in kyllynge hym, he kylleth hym selfe.[67]

At one point Elyot went so far as to suggest that a law be made to torture flatterers openly, 'to the fearful example of others'.[68]

There was another remedy, however: namely the classical belief in the therapeutic power of conversation. In his popular medical handbook, *The Castel of Helthe*, Elyot noted that the cure for immoderate affections of the mind required 'the counsel of a man wise and well learned in moral philosophy'.[69] Here again, Erasmus had earlier written an adage on the subject entitled '*Animo Aegrotanti Medicus est Oratio*' in which he catalogued the relevant sayings of Plutarch, Isocrates, Solomon and others.[70] In fact, one of the passages cited by Erasmus, that from the *Prometheus Bound*, serves as a major subtext for Elyot's dialogue *Pasquil the Playne*.

Towards the middle of Aeschylus' drama, Oceanus, seeking Prometheus' sanction for his intended appeal of the captive's case to the tyrant Zeus, queries his reluctant comrade:

> OCEANUS: Do you not then, Prometheus, know this: that words are ailing temper's healers?
> PROMETHEUS: If at the proper time one soothes a heart and does not try by force to dry up a tumid spirit.[71]

Prometheus' wary and ironic retort, full of legitimate doubt concerning Oceanus' ability to 'dry up' anything, was widely known in antiquity. Both Cicero and Plutarch cite it.[72] Pasquil's explication of this passage and subsequent defence of his interpretation against the rival opinions of his interlocutors comprise virtually the whole of Elyot's dialogue. The kernel of Pasquil's rendering is that effective counsel is comprised of three constituents: proper occasion, appropriate content and soothing manner. Potentially profitable counsel, Elyot suggests, might sometimes legitimately be delayed in anticipation of a time and place when its delivery would prove more effective, but it should never be withheld entirely. As Sir Thomas would later tell readers of his Latin–English *Dictionary*:

> it is human to slip, to err, to be deceived; but to fail to assist one who slips, to fail to bring back on course one who errs, or to fail to help with advice and assistance one who is deceived when you are able, especially a friend, is thought to be not only wanting in humanity but even despicable in the eyes of all good men.[73]

To suggest, as does Starkey's Pole in the 'Dialogue Between Pole and

Lupset', that without a virtuous and receptive prince 'all counseyl is voyd and never can take place' would be to render counsel 'a vayne worde'.[74] Viciously disposed princes not desiring to hear any counsel might unknowingly persist in their errors.

Moreover, should these errors acquire the force of habit – the psychological point of no return tantamount to damnation – seasonable speech would be too late.[75] Elyot's dialogue *Of the Knowledge Which Maketh a Wise Man* dramatizes just such a situation. Plato counsels the increasingly tyrannical Dionysius in order that he might 'reuoke agayne vnderstandynge', subdue his affections, and quickly be restored to his proper dignity.[76] Because his knowledge and reason have been extinguished by affections, however, the Syracusan ruler fails to heed Plato's admonition. Instead of thanking Plato for his elucidation of the distinction between kingship and tyranny, the ungrateful Dionysius enslaves the man Elyot represents as *'perchaunce his mooste assured frende'*.[77] The momentous potential that Renaissance intellectuals like Elyot discerned in counsel is perhaps best summed up in the pointed reflection with which Erasmus concluded his adage on medicinal speech:

> In fact, just as speech is a swift and efficacious medicine when administered in friendly, healing and timely fashion, so talk that is unfriendly or inflammatory or untimely is a deadly poison.[78]

Because flattery was an everpresent danger, especially at royal courts, its antidote – seasonable, appropriate and friendly counsel – ought, ideally, always to be at hand. Unsurprisingly, the charge of maintaining the prince's proper psychological disposition rested upon those whose position afforded the greatest opportunity – those in his immediate entourage, his 'friends'.

Here then is why Elyot was so intent on ensuring the practice of friendship among those who occupied the station of 'friends'. Reproving vice in another was considered an act of friendship. When Elyot described Plato's counsel to Dionysius along these lines in *Of the Knowledge Which Maketh a Wise Man*, he could have been drawing on any number of classical authorities. Plutarch, for example, separated the soul into rational and emotional constituents; the friend, he wrote, 'is always found on the better side as counsel and advocate trying after the manner of a physician to foster the growth of what is sound and preserve it'.[79] Likewise, Cicero considered the ability both to give and receive frank admonition a distinguishing characteristic of friends; and Isocrates, in a work translated by Elyot, urged the Cyprian monarch Nicocles to consider most loyal those who 'do blame the thing wherein thou errest'.[80] The ancient text most closely resembling Elyot's phrasing, however, was Galen's treatise *On the Diagnosis and Cure of the Soul's Passions*, which identified 'the one who shows us our every fault as our deliverer and greatest friend'.[81] Finally, it should be noted that Elyot is sometimes credited with the authorship of an anonymous short treatise entitled 'The maner to chose and cherysshe a frende', whose conclusion translates a passage of Cicero's *De amicitia* which addresses precisely these issues:

> Frendes muste ofte be monisshed, and rebuked, and that muste be taken frendly/ whan hit is done of good wyll. But for so moche as Terence saythe, Trouthe bredeth hate/ whiche is as a poyson to frendshyppe/ we must take hede, that our monition be not sowre, and that the rebuke be without vile wordes.[82]

As demonstrated by the failure of Reginald Pole's *De unitate* (1536) to prompt reformation in his cousin Henry VIII, inflammatory rebukes often did more harm than good. The art of admonishing kings, whether in person or in print, required the skills of both a consummate orator and courtier, not only devotion but also tact.

For Elyot, then, like several ancient writers on politics, monarchy, in all but very small domains, was necessarily a collegial enterprise between the monarch and his 'friends'. The difference between good and bad rule was defined primarily as a function of the ruler's psychological disposition, and the latter as a function of his relations with his 'friends' at Court. Yet Elyot was unwilling to share the opinion of his Spanish contemporary Antonio de Guevara that 'the well-being of both king and realm is assured if the king surrounds himself with good men and banishes the wicked from his presence'.[83] He recognized that the ancient image of the ruler as benign if he ruled his passions and tyrannical if he was ruled by them was inescapably confined to wherever the royal Household might be. It explained well enough how the tyrant might develop as sensualist and homicide, and spend his time feasting, fornicating and killing, but because of the physical impossibility of an individual being in two places at the same time, it left wide open the problem of governing the provinces. Proverbially, however, a friend constituted a 'second self', and herein lay the theoretical underpinning behind the ancient Roman practice of *amici principis* acting as provincial governors, procurators and other representatives of imperial authority.

Perhaps now we may profitably re-examine Elyot's second allusion to Aristotle's *Politics* in *The Boke named the Governour*, the context here slightly enlarged:

> Aristotell in his politykes exorteth gouernours to haue their *frendes* for a great numbre of eyen, earis, handes, and legges; considering that no one man may see or here all thinge that many men may see and here, ne can be in all places, or do as many thinges well, at one tyme, as many persons may do. And often tymes a beholder or loker on espieth a defaulte that the doer forgetteth or skippeth over.

> Whiche caused the emperour Antonine to enquire of many what
> other men spake of him; correctinge thereby his defautes, whiche he
> perceyued to be iustly reproued.[84]

The reason a public weal with a bad prince could be considered 'in a
better state and in a manner more sure' than one with evil *amici* was
simply because – provided he was still curable – many good counsellors
and companions might well supply the want of wisdom in a prince like
Henry VIII, and moderate his unbridled appetites while their counterparts
in positions of authority in the provinces maintained an honest administration. A good prince alone, however, could not hope to hold in check
many evil men scattered throughout his realm. Elsewhere in the *Politics*
Aristotle put the relationship between friendship and good government in
terms of a slightly different opposition. History, he remarked, had shown
that 'whereas friends preserve kingship, it is a mark of a tyrant to be
extremely distrustful of his friends'.[85]

Before turning to consider the relevance of Elyot's political thought to
the realities of early Tudor politics, the place of Sir Thomas's ideas in the
larger context of the history of political thought needs to be clarified.
First, it should be recognized that ideals of friendly counsel persist in later
literature of Tudor England. Perhaps the most blatant example is Richard
Edwards's tragedy *Damon and Pithias*, performed before Queen Elizabeth
at Whitehall during the Christmas season of 1564, but seemingly not
published until 1571. The following stanza from the play's farewell song
is characteristic:

> The strongest garde that Kynges can have,
> Are constant friends their state to save:
> True friends are constant, both in word and deede,
> True friends are present, and help at each neede:
> True friends talke truly, they glose for no gayne,
> When treasure consumeth, true frindes wyll remayne,
> True frindes for their tru Prince, refuseth not their death:
> The Lorde graunt her such frindes most noble Queene Elizabeth.[86]

Although Edwards is a minor literary figure about whom little is known,
the same ideal informs works of more highly regarded writers. Sir Thomas
Wyatt's epistolary satire to Sir Francis Bryan (*c.* 1539), for instance, constitutes a meditation on the consequences of friendly conduct at Court;[87]
Christopher Marlowe's *Edward II* (1594) dramatizes a corrupt political
environment in which all friendships have been subverted by desires for
pleasure, power and profit.

Just as Elyot was not the last Renaissance author to interpret politics
in terms of friendship, so too he was not the first. Contemporary analogues

to Elyot's political thought are not hard to find. Ottaviano Fregoso in Castiglione's *Book of the Courtier*, for example, defined 'the aim of the perfect courtier' much as Elyot would later delineate the function of the prince's 'friend' when resident at Court; the courtier, he asserted, should strive to win his prince's mind and favour,

> that he may be able to tell him, and always will tell him, the truth about everything he needs to know, without fear or risk of displeasing him; and that when he sees the mind of his prince inclined to a wrong action, he may dare to oppose him and in a gentle manner avail himself of the favor acquired by his good accomplishments, so as to dissuade him of every evil intent and bring him back to the path of virtue.[88]

Similarly, Erasmus and Thomas More also granted an important role to 'confessors and counsellors' in bridling a monarch's affections.[89] Indeed, Antonio de Guevara is merely the best-known Spanish political theorist of the period who espoused ideals of monarchy similar to those of Elyot. Although the loss of Sir Thomas's library coupled with his frequent failure to acknowledge sources now makes it impossible to discern the degree of his familiarity with individual thinkers, his indebtedness to the work of continental humanists is beyond question. Elyot's forerunners not only discovered and published many new texts concerning the *amici principis* of imperial Rome and the *philoi* of Hellenistic Greece, but also attempted to reconcile the precepts and examples found in Plutarch, Isocrates and other pagan authors with those of Christian authorities.

Unfortunately, recognition of the correspondences between Elyot's political thought and that of earlier humanists too often has served to obscure the medieval English precedents for Sir Thomas's ideas. In considering monarchical government the collective responsibility of the king and his chosen companions, and designating those associates 'friends', Elyot stood firmly within English tradition. According to the anonymous legal treatise known as *Fleta*, composed *circa* 1300, 'Earls . . . are called *comites* from *comitiva*, companionship, and when they perceive the king to be unbridled, they are bound to bridle him'.[90] Moreover, Angevin royal servants and courtiers who had no feudal affinity with the king, along with specially designated magnates, were known as royal *amici*, and played an important role in English politics and administration under Henry II.[91] When the author of *Mum and the Sothsegger* advised Richard II that the young and low-born men he had elected to his Council were pushing aside 'all youre best frendis', his words should be interpreted in this context.[92]

Despite the considerable changes in English government between the twelfth and the sixteenth centuries, resonances of the institutional designation 'friend' persist well into the period of Elyot's clerkship of the Council. By that time, chivalric ideals of faithfulness, the disintegration of feudal ties, and the legal prohibition of contractual retaining, had all served to emphasize friendship as the bond cementing lordship and affinity.[93] What resulted was the frequent intermingling of the rhetoric of friendship with the rhetoric of service. Henry VIII, for example, considered Wolsey his 'best beloved servant and friend' and signed several of his letters to the Cardinal regarding government business as 'your loving sovereign lord and friend'. When, for some reason, Wolsey tried to appoint Isabel Jordan the new Abbess of Wilton Priory in July 1528 contrary to Henry's expressed wishes, he received a dignified and measured letter of rebuke from his 'master and friend' informing him that his conduct in the affair had not been what it should: namely, that of a 'trusty loving friend and servant'.[94]

What most distinguishes Elyot's political thought from that of his medieval predecessors is not any specific set of doctrines so much as the precision and range of his classical allusions, his greater interest in rhetoric, and his subordination of noble birth and land ownership to talent and moral rectitude as qualifications for royal service. If Thomas Starkey's 'Dialogue Between Pole and Lupset' appears to have been influenced by its author's knowledge of baronial opposition literature,[95] Elyot's political thought belonged to a separate tradition. Implicit in Aristotle's discussion of a monarch's *philoi* as his colleagues in the *Politics*, and made explicit by fourteenth-century commentators on the passage, was the contention that friends of the prince should be mindful of the public welfare. Writing about 1338 and following Peter of Auvergne's *Commentary on the Politics* verbatim, the Englishman Walter Burley, in his own *Commentary*, argued that friends of the prince owed allegiance not merely to the prince but to the principate:

> Princes make those co-rulers [*comprincipes*] who are their friends as well as those of the principate. For if they were not friends of both, but only of one, as for instance the principate, they would not care about the good of the Prince, but only about the principate. Contrariwise, if they would not love the principate, but only the Prince, they would not care for the good of the principate. Therefore the co-rulers have to take care of the good of both the Prince and the principate . . . only he that loves the prince as Prince, loves the principate. For he that rules may be considered in two ways: either according to his being Prince, or according to his being an individual man. If you love him according to his being Prince, you love the principate, and by obtaining the good of one, you obtain the good of the other. If, however, you love the Prince because he is this or that man, you do not necessarily love the principate: and then you obtain the good of this and that individual without obtaining the good of the principate.[96]

As long as the inclinations of the prince remained in concert with the good of the principate, the king's friends could concentrate on administration. Whenever the royal will happened to favour a measure harmful to the public good, however, as in a fallen world it inevitably must, friends of the king were morally obliged, while remaining loyal, to engage in political opposition. Like Starkey, Elyot considered Henry VIII's desire to divorce Katharine of Aragon a clear-cut instance of an English king pursuing a policy counter to the public good through the 'tyranny of hys owne heddy jugement'.[97] Unlike Starkey, though, Elyot did not consider legal or institutional modifications a constructive way to remedy a weakness in human character. Instead of promoting the establishment of rival councils, through the publication of his dialogue *Pasquil the Playne*, Elyot sought to persuade Henry VIII's current 'friends' that love and friendship for their master should not be construed as flattering capitulation to his every desire, but an obligation to admonish his errant ways. The following analysis of *Pasquil the Playne* will clarify Elyot's opposition stance.

Pasquil the Playne is the earliest English example of a pasquinade, and essential to its interpretation is an appreciation of the origins of the genre. At Rome in 1501 Cardinal Caraffa had the mutilated remains of a recently disinterred ancient statue erected at the corner of his palace near the Piazza Navona. Under his patronage, it became customary on St Mark's day for professors and students to dress the stone figure after the image of some ancient historical or mythological character and salute their new creation by affixing to it specially composed Latin verses. Soon, however, the statue, dubbed '*Pasquino*' by the public, became a repository for anonymous and unsolicited verse lampoons of prominent public figures, especially churchmen. Equally satirical replies to these *pasquinate* were often attached to another statue known as Marforio ('*a foro Martius*'), located in the Campus Martius. So fashionable became the practice that not only collections of actual *pasquinate*, but even mock verse dialogues between the two stone figures were published.[98] Although primarily an Italian phenomenon in Elyot's day, the custom was not unknown or unappreciated in English Court circles. Edmund Bonner's 1532 Christmas present to Thomas Cromwell was a copy of a recent imaginary dialogue between Pasquino and Marforio.[99]

This then was the tradition which Elyot drew upon to inform his 'mery treatise, wherein plainnes and flateri do come in trial'.[100] At base, *Pasquil the Playne* is little more than a schematic meditation on the merits of frank speech at Court. On a festival day in May when it is lawful to place on him taunts in verse or prose against any person regardless of their estate, the dialogue's title character Pasquil, the plain-speaking 'image of stone sitting in the city of Rome openly', engages two wayfaring flatterers from Court in a discussion about the responsibilities of a counsellor.[101] The first, a household servant named Gnatho after the sycophantic character in the *Eunuchus* of Terence, is an obsequious flatterer who believes in verbally affirming all his master's actions.[102] Indicative of his falseness and concern for appearances, he openly carries a New Testament while concealing beneath his gaudy attire a copy of *Troilus and Criseyde*. Pasquil's second opponent, Gnatho's cousin Harpocrates, is an acquiescent flatterer, named after the chief priest of the Temple of Isis and Serapis, 'whose image is made holdynge his fynger at his mouthe, betokeninge silence'.[103] A counsellor and confessor to the same unnamed 'master', he too believes in approving whatever his master does, but by means of tacit consent and a stern visage.

The substantive portion of the dialogue begins when Gnatho affirms that following the counsel of Aeschylus – 'holdyng thy tonge wher it behoueth the. And spekyng in tyme that whiche is conuenient' – is the surest way to promotion.[104] When Pasquil asks Gnatho to explain what he thinks Aeschylus meant by this sentence, he is told that the meaning is obvious:

> It behoveth a man to holde his tunge, whan he aforeseeth by any experience, that the thinge/ which he wolde purpose or speke of to his superior, shall nether be pleasantly herde nor thankefully taken. And in wordes opportunitie and tyme alwaye do depende on the affection and appetite of hym that hereth them.[105]

For Gnatho, the counsellor's primary objective is not to offend and thereby lose his place. His advice should always accord with his master's current inclinations.

To Pasquil, however, this interpretation fails to take into consideration the primary responsibility of a counsellor: namely, the maintenance of his master's virtuous disposition. Fear of lost preferment only enables the vicious conduct of those in high place to pass without reprimand. In opposition, the statue offers his own interpretation of Aeschylus' sentence. He too recognizes a time for refraining from rebuke:

> Where thou seest thy lorde or mayster in the presence of many/ resolved in to fury or wantonnesse/ thoughe thou hast all redy advertisementes/ how he shall refrayn it: yet holde thy tonge than, for troublynge that presence.[106]

Confrontational speaking which would promote wrath instead of understanding should be avoided. To increase its chances of being effective, corrective counsel should be withheld until more favourable circumstances of time and place present themselves:

> Whan thou perceiuest thy Maister to be resoled in to wrath or affections dishonest. Before wrathe be increased to fury, and affection

into beastly enormitie: As opportunitie serueth the, reuerently and with tokens of loue towarde hym, speke suche wordes as shalbe conuenient.

Oportunitie consisteth in place or tyme, where and whan the sayd affections or passion of wrath be some dele mitigate and out of extremitie. And wordes be called conueniente, whiche haue respecte to the nature and state of the person, vnto whom they be spoken, and also to the detriment, whiche mought ensue by the vice or lacke that thou has espied ... oportunitie and tyme for a counsayllour to speke/ do not depend of the affection and appetite of hym that is counsayled.[107]

Although impressed by Pasquil's ability to reason, Gnatho considers open rebuke of his master too threatening to his security ever actually to be attempted.

Having laid bare Gnatho's greater regard for his social standing than his master's spiritual health, Pasquil now turns to the recently arrived Harpocrates, who is promptly informed by his cousin of an impending council meeting after dinner. Under interrogation, Harpocrates modifies his advocacy of silence by admitting that in moments of imminent peril – when his master takes up a poisoned drink, or has a naked sword drawn at his back – it is appropriate for a counsellor to provide admonition. Before such time, counsel is unprofitable to the counsellor, who risks his master's displeasure. Afterwards, it is of no use to the hearer: 'For where may be no longer defence/ or resistence, speche nothing auaileth.'[108]

Pasquil's counter-argument is that while admonition is better late than never, it is best when presented well in advance. Unless one is 'well seen in predestination' or as subtle in discrimination as 'a good Duns man', he tells Harpocrates, it is often difficult to distinguish 'the instante whan it appereth/ that your frende shall be slayne' from 'the instante whan he is in sleyinge'.[109] Only partners to a conspiracy are likely to know the specific times and places danger will occur. The good servant should not merely inform his master of perils that have become obvious to all, but keep him apprised of potential future dangers as well. Moreover, silence is no guarantee of surety. The fortunes of master and attendant counsellor are inescapably linked by proximity, and even should both manage to escape being slain or poisoned, the servant would be vulnerable to the accusation of having failed to provide advance warning.

Yet if ye warned youre mayster at the begynyinge/ though he toke it not thankfully/ yet did you your duetie/ and can not lacke rewarde of god, who loueth truthe, for your fidelitie. And thoughe he, whom ye disappointed/ or his affinitie, shall seke howe to be auenged on you: either god wyll defende you, or if there fall to you thereby any aduersitie, finally falsehode longe kepte in/ wyll berste oute at

> the laste/ and than shal repentance cause your simplicite to be had
> in renome and perpetual memorie: whiche parte of honour to euery
> honest man passeth al other rewarde, that may be gyuen in this lyfe
> that is transitorie.[110]

Even though properly delivered admonitions would not always be favour-
ably received, in the mind of a good counsellor, considerations of honour
and *fama* should outweigh those of preferment.

Moreover, Pasquil continues, as his master's confessor, Harpocrates
should know that the consequences of the death of his master's soul –
'perpetuall infamie, the subuercion of the common weale, or vniversall
destruction of all the hoole countrey' – ought to be feared more than his
corporeal death.[111] Indeed, early warning of psychological dangers is crucial
since false opinions and vicious affections become more difficult to uproot
the longer they endure. If they persist unchecked too long, speech loses
its power to assist in effecting a cure, and recovery can be effected only
by God's grace.[112] Pasquil warns Harpocrates, however, not to presume
that grace will come to the aid of those who seek not to help themselves.
The confessor's advocacy of silence is only appropriate for a world in
which all men, like St Paul, are elected. Yet even the example of St Paul
attests to the importance of the provision of friendly counsel. Had Christ
remained silent on the road to Damascus, Saul 'wold by likelyhode haue
continued still in his errour'.[113] Harpocrates and Gnatho find themselves
defeated by reason but unchanged in motivation. As the dialogue reaches
its conclusion, the two return to court for a council meeting with their
master resolved to continue their respective styles of flattery.[114]

Of crucial importance in interpreting *Pasquil the Playne* is an appreciation of the disjunction between Pasquil's advocacy of friendly counsel
and his actual practice of counselling. As a statue – particularly one which
speaks but once a year – it would be difficult for him to heed his own
words even were that his desire. Given his fixed location and limited
opportunities, he babbles, as he himself admits.[115] No doubt his irritating
manner also contributes to his failure to prompt reformation in either
Gnatho or Harpocrates. When the latter suggests to Pasquil that his words
would be more likely to effect change if delivered in private, the statue
outlines a public stragety unworkable in the 'privie chambre or galeri'.[116]
His annual collection of taunts and rebukes, he claims, are delivered with

> thintent that men shall perceive, that theyr vices, which they thinke
> to be wonderfull secrete/ be known to all men. And that I hope
> alwaye/ that by moche clamoure/ and open repentance, whan they
> see the thing not succeede to theyr purpose/ they wyl be ashamed.[117]

Pasquil, therefore, is not interested in providing corrective counsel himself,
merely in making disclosures of public discontent.

Nevertheless, Pasquil's speech is a direct consequence of the negligent conduct of Gnatho and Harpocrates he reproaches. Through their flattery and dissimulation, the likes of Gnatho and Harpocrates have brought 'Popes, emperours, kinges/ and cardinalles' into 'the hate of god and the people'.[118] Eventually, the world became so far out of frame that complaints which should have been voiced at Court had to be uttered by stones. Had 'both spiritual and temporall governours' banished from their services all flatterers who refused to amend their condition instead of dismissing the statue's annual counsels as idle ranting:

> many thinges mought haue ben preuented, that were after lamented. Germany shulde not haue kicked agayne her mother: Emperours and princis shuld not haue ben in perpetual discorde/ & often tymes in peril/ prelates haue ben laughed at, as dissardes [fools]: saynctes blasphemed, and miracles reproued for iougglynges/ lawes and statutes contemned, and officers litell regarded.[119]

According to Pasquil, the irresponsiveness of the church to pleas for reform was the reason 'nowe a dayes mens deuocion waxeth even as colde, as the mounkes be in the quyer at midnyght'.[120] While Elyot was not a vigorous critic of abuses, his writings contain enough anti-clerical comment to suggest that this was probably his view too.[121] Belief that the spirituality had 'digged the diche that thei be now fallen in', he told John Hackett, English ambassador in the Low Countries, on the eve of the passage of the Act in Restraint of Appeals, 'causith many goode men the lass to pitie theim'.[122]

While unlikely, in the absence of more definitive evidence the possibility cannot be dismissed that Elyot's 'mery treatise', issued anonymously by the king's printer, Thomas Berthelet, sometime prior to 12 April 1533,[123] was published in the hopes that it might help consolidate anti-Roman sentiments on the eve of the fourth session of the Reformation Parliament.[124] If the king and Council did indeed expect *Pasquil the Playne* to serve as a minor contribution to their propaganda campaign designed to prepare the English public for the divorce and break with Rome, however, they took inside the walls a Trojan horse. When on 18 April 1530 the duke of Norfolk asked Chapuys point-blank whether Charles V would declare war on England if Henry remarried in defiance of the pope, the imperial ambassador daringly answered that a foreign invasion would be unnecessary since Henry's own subjects would rise in rebellion.[125] Clearly if the English people were to be expected to affirm their king's new order they would first need to be told what truth was now to be proclaimed and why. This process was initiated by the reading of foreign university opinions favourable to the king's cause to both Houses of Parliament in 1531, and followed in short order by the publication of Latin and English versions of the *Gravissimae Censurae*, and the best-known piece of Henrician government propaganda on the divorce, *The Glasse of Truthe*.[126]

These instalments were designed to present publicly the basis of Henry's scruple of conscience, and thereby refute the reports of 'maligners and raving babblers' that the king was seduced by 'affections' in pursuing the divorce.[127] Perhaps the most widespread of these rival versions of Henry's motivation was the persistent rumour that Wolsey, angered by Charles V's opposition to his bid for the papacy in 1522, had sought revenge by having John Longland, Henry's confessor, place a scruple in the king's mind regarding the validity of his marriage to Katharine. Wolsey's aim, so the story went, was to cement an alliance with the emperor's enemy, Francis I, by having Henry remarry one of the French king's sisters. Henry reportedly was originally unreceptive to Longland's doubts, but conveniently recalled them once his passion for Anne Boleyn had been kindled.

While the degree of truth contained in this account is open to serious debate, there can be no question about its currency. According to the recollection of George Cavendish, one of Wolsey's gentleman ushers, during the 1529 legatine court proceedings at Blackfriars, the Cardinal publicly asked Henry to declare whether he had been 'the chief inventor or first mover of this matter unto your Majesty; for I am greatly suspected of all men herein'.[128] The king's own refutation, however, seems to have had little impact, for slightly later allusions to the rumour survive in Tyndale's *Practice of Prelates*, Polydore Vergil's *Anglica Historia*, and the table talk of the Dean of Westbury; and by the reign of Mary, the story was regularly repeated in Catholic discussions of the English Reformation.[129] Moreover, the interest of king and Council in refuting this rumour should not be taken lightly. The Yorkshire rebels in the Pilgrimage of Grace considered Longland, also bishop of Lincoln, 'the beginning of all the trouble of your commons and the vexation that hath been taken of your subjects'.[130] As Chapuys' nephew informed Maria of Hungary, one of the rebels' first orders of business was to visit 'the bishop of Lincoln's lodging, where, failing to find him, they put to death his chancellor out of spite to his master, who is regarded by the people as one of the principal councillors who raised scruples in the king to repudiate your said aunt'.[131]

To this impressive catalogue of the vitality and political significance of the Longland–Wolsey rumour now can be added Elyot's *Pasquil the Playne*. At least two purely literary motives can be deduced in support of Sir Thomas's decision to characterize Harpocrates as his master's confessor. First, in Pasquil's debate with Harpocrates, it served to ease the transition between the discussion of physical and spiritual threats to the unidentified 'master'. Second, as Erasmus had written in his *Institutio Principis Christiani* that royal confessors were a monarch's last line of defence against flattery, Elyot's characterization of Harpocrates' negligence underscores Pasquil's sense of despair at the likelihood of reform.[132] Nevertheless, in making Harpocrates a flattering confessor whose failure to rebuke his master's bestial affections had subverted the common weal and brought the country to the brink of perpetual infamy, Elyot was sailing extremely close to the wind. It was all too easy for contemporary readers to see in Pasquil's babbling criticism of two counsellors' self-serving support of their master's private vices, defiant affirmation of a rumour the king and Council had publicly denied,[133] and intimations that those in the royal entourage like Longland had failed to live up to the standard of friendship commonly associated with their positions. Indeed, at several points in the dialogue the conduct Pasquil demands of Gnatho and Harpocrates appears coincident with what members of the early Tudor Council were already sworn to maintain.[134] Certainly someone in authority was bothered by this potential interpretation, for soon an altered second edition was issued with Elyot's name now affixed atop the epistle to the reader and all direct identification of Harpocrates as his master's confessor removed.[135] Sir Thomas had earlier generated suspicions of disloyalty by expressing reservations over Henry's proposed divorce during his audience with the king upon return from his embassy to the Court of Charles V,[136] and the publication of *Pasquil the Playne* constituted a still more daring flirtation with danger. Shortly after publication of his 1532 rejoinder to the English translation of the *Gravissimae Censurae*, Katharine's chaplain, Thomas Abell, was imprisoned in the Tower; had Elyot, like Abell, refused to alter his text, one suspects he would have met a similar fate.[137]

Clearly *Pasquil the Playne* offers scholars a more highly developed and realistic contemporary analysis of Henry VIII's divorce crisis than has hitherto been recognized. Indeed, the uncertainty over publicly opposing the Act in Restraint of Appeals expressed by George Throckmorton, a leading conservative spokesman in the House of Commons, suggests that Elyot's anonymously issued fictional meditation upon when, where, how, and whether to rebuke the vicious conduct of one's master spoke directly to one of the premier political concerns of late 1532 and early 1533.[138] For twentieth-century historians not well versed in the writings of the early Christian Fathers and accustomed to interpreting politics in terms of laws, institutions, and social and economic policies, it is perhaps difficult to appreciate the ease with which Elyot and some of his contemporaries viewed the 'Henrician Revolution' as fundamentally the tragic outgrowth of one of their king's extramarital affairs. Writing in the 1550s, however, George Cavendish had no such problem, and a look at some of his comments reminds us not to underestimate the degree to which certain Tudor Englishmen interpreted politics in terms of moral philosophy. Henry VIII, Cavendish remembered, became so 'amorously affectionate' for Anne Boleyn 'that will bare place and high discretion [was] banished for the time'.[139] Before long 'almost everything began to grow out of frame and good order':

> Is it not a world to consider the desire of wilful princes when they fully be bent and inclined to fulfil their voluptuous appetites, against the which no reasonable persuasions will suffice, little or nothing weighing or regarding the dangerous sequels that doth ensue as well to themselves as to their realm and subjects? And above all things there is no one thing that causeth them to be more wilful than carnal desire and voluptuous affection of foolish love. The experience is plain in this case, both manifest and evident, for what surmised inventions hath been invented, what laws hath been enacted, what noble and ancient monasteries overthrown and defaced, what diversities of religious opinions hath risen, what executions hath been committed, how many famous and notable clerks hath suffered death, what charitable foundations were perverted from relief of the poor unto profane uses, and what alterations of good and wholesome ancient laws and customs hath been tossed by will and wilful desire of the prince, almost to the subversion and desolation of this noble realm. All men may understand what hath chanced to this region; the proof thereof hath taught all us Englishmen a common experience, the more is the pity, and to all good men very lamentable to be considered. If eyes be not blind men may see, if ears be not stopped they may hear, and if pity be not exiled they may lament the sequel of this pernicious and inordinate carnal love, the plague whereof is not ceased (although this love lasted but a while).[140]

Even though England could never realistically expect a king entirely free from vicious affections, Elyot seems to have believed that had more inferior governors openly rebuked Henry's lechery before it became habitual, the course of English history might have been different. At any rate, those who promoted the king's lust for Anne Boleyn or looked on silently as it consumed their master failed to fulfil the obligations of friendship and inescapably shared responsibility for the country's subsequent misfortunes.

NOTES

1 G. Parfitt (ed.) *Ben Jonson: The Complete Poems*, New Haven, Conn., Yale University Press, 1982, p. 411.

2 D. W. Hanson, *From Kingdom to Commonwealth: The Development of Civic Consciousness in English Political Thought*, Cambridge, Mass., Harvard University Press, 1970, p. 128.

3 Cited in Erasmus, *Education*, p. 123.

4 S. E. Lehmberg, 'English Humanists, the Reformation, and the problem of counsel', *Archiv für Reformationsgeschichte*, 1961, vol. 52, pp. 74–90.

5 J. Guy, 'The King's Council and political participation', in A. Fox and J. Guy (eds) *Reassessing the Henrician Age: Humanism, politics and reform 1500–1550*, Oxford, Basil Blackwell, 1986, pp. 146–7.

6 E.g. A. B. Ferguson, *The Articulate Citizen and the English Renaissance*, Durham, NC, Duke University Press, 1965, p. 70; K. Sharpe, 'Parliamentary history 1603–1629: in or out of perspective?', in K. Sharpe (ed.) *Faction and Parliament: Essays on Early Stuart History*, Oxford, Clarendon Press, 1978, p. 37.

7 J. Spedding, R. Ellis and D. Heath (eds) *The Works of Francis Bacon*, 14 vols, London, Longman, 1857–74, VI, p. 441. A. B. Ferguson's, *Articulate Citizen*, the only book-length study of counsel in Tudor England, serves as a case in point. Because Professor Ferguson is concerned with charting a shift away from what he characterizes as a medieval propensity to explain politics primarily in terms of persons and moral complaint, his discussion of Tudor thinkers concentrates on those who conceived of counsel in terms of policies and institutions (see pp. 148–9 and *passim*).

8 C. Morris, *Political Thought in England from Tyndale to Hooker*, London, Oxford University Press, 1953, p. 23; A. Fox, 'Interpreting English Humanism', in Fox and Guy, *Reassessing the Henrician Age*, p. 25.

9 *Scriptores Historiae Augustae* (hereafter cited as *SHA*), *Severus Alexander* 65, 3: 'a state in which the prince is evil is better and almost more secure than one in which the friends of the prince are evil'.

10 *Confessio Amantis*, Book VII, lines 4157ff.

11 J. Hayward, *The Life and Raigne of King Henrie the IIII*, London, John Wolfe, 1599, pp. 6, 72. Cf. T. Gainsford's unpublished early Jacobean manuscript entitled 'Observations of state and military affairs, for the most part collected out of Cornelius Tacitus', Huntington Library MS. EL 6857, fo. 57: 'a good prince governed by evil ministers is as dangerous as if he were evil himself'.

12 I. Gentillet, *A Discourse upon the Meanes of Wel Governing and Maintaining in Good Peace, a Kingdome, or Principalitie, Divided into three Parts, Against N. Machiavell*, S. Patericke (trans.), London, Adam Islip, 1602, pp. 5–6.

13 The title-page of the 1539 *Bankette* advertises the work as 'newely augmented with dyuerse tytles and sentences'.

14 *Bankette of Sapience* facsimile in L. Gottesman (ed.) *Four Political Treatises by Sir Thomas Elyot*, Gainesville, Fla, Scholars' Facsimiles & Reprints, 1967, p. 130.

15 *The Dictionary of syr Thomas Eliot Knyght*, London, Thomas Berthelet, 1538, identified as item number 7659 in STC².

16 For a characteristic example of the expression 'company of friends' used in this context, see Suetonius, *Caius Caligula* 19, 1–2.

17 J. A. Crook, *Consilium Principis: Imperial Councils and Counsellors from Augustus to Diocletian*, Cambridge, Cambridge University Press, 1955, p. 23.

18 For a discussion of similar administrative phenomena in early Tudor England, see D. Starkey, 'Representation through intimacy: a study of the symbolism of monarchy and court office in early modern England', in I. Lewis (ed.) *Symbols and Sentiments: Cross-cultural Studies in Symbolism*, London, Academic Press, 1977, pp. 187–224.

19 Suetonius, *Divus Vespasianus* 21; Seneca, *De beneficiis* 6, 32, 2–4.

20 Gottesman, *The Image of Governance*, p. 315; *SHA*, *Severus Alexander* 31, 2.

21 Gottesman, *Pasquil the Playne*, p. 64.

22 Crook, *Consilium*, p. 30.

23 *Histories* 4, 7; cited in Crook, *Consilium*, p. 26.

24 *Divus Titus* 7, 2; cited in Crook, *Consilium*, p. 26.

25 *SHA*, *Severus Alexander* 65, 5; Crook's attribution of this sentence to Trajan (p. 26) is misleading.

26 T. Elyot, *The Boke named the Governour*, ed. H. H. S. Crofts 2 vols, London, C. K. Paul, 1880, I, pp. 11–12.

27 S. E. Lehmberg, *Sir Thomas Elyot, Tudor Humanist*, Austin, Tex., University of Texas Press, 1960, p. 45; Lehmberg, *The Reformation Parliament 1529–1536*, Cambridge, Cambridge University Press, 1970, p. 164; A. Fox, 'Sir Thomas Elyot and the Humanist dilemma', in Fox and Guy, *Reassessing the Henrician Age* p. 57.

28 Croft, *Governour*, I, pp. 8–24, 256–9.

29 Croft, *Governour* I, p. 5.

30 Ibid., p. 26.

31 Ibid., Elyot allows for the inclusion of virtuous men of lesser estate.

32 Ibid., p. 7.

33 Ibid., p. 6.

34 Ibid., pp. 31–5.

35 Ibid., pp. 53–71.

36 Ibid., pp. 72–91.

37 Ibid., pp. 91–8.

38 Ibid., p. 141.

39 Ibid., pp. 38–49, 169–203, 269–306; II, p. 433.

40 Ibid., I, p. 76.

41 Lehmberg, *Sir Thomas Elyot*, pp. 37–9; Fox, 'Sir Thomas Elyot', p. 57.

42 Lehmberg, *Sir Thomas Elyot*, p. 45.

43 STC² 20056.7. There is no mention of this edition in any previously published study of Elyot.

44 P. Hogrefe, 'Sir Thomas Elyot's intention in the opening chapters of the *Governour*', St Phil., 1963, 60, pp. 133–40; T. F. Mayer, 'Tournai and tyranny: imperial kingship and critical humanism', *HJ*, 1991, 34, pp. 257–77.

45 Croft, *Governour* I, p. 178.

46 Ibid., p. 20. Cf. Elyot's comment (ibid., p. 83) that had 'the isolencie and pryde of Tarquin' not excluded kings from the city, the Roman public weal would have been 'the most noble and perfect of all other'.

47 Croft, *Governour* II, p. 184, my emphasis.

48 K. J. Wilson (ed.) 'The letters of Sir Thomas Elyot', St Phil., 1976, 73, p. 53.

49 In his preface to the work, Elyot identifies the *Image* as the fulfilment of his promise in *The Governour* to write a book on 'the forme of good gouernance' (Gottesman, *Image*, p. 206).

50 See Note 9.

51 Croft, *Governour* II, pp. 128–9.

52 Ibid., pp. 132–66.

53 Ibid., p. 161.

54 Wilson, 'Letters', pp. 26, 35.

55 Croft, *Governour* II, pp. 165–6.

56 *The Correspondence of Erasmus*, R. A. B. Mynors and D. F. S. Thomson (trans), Toronto, University of Toronto Press, 1974– , II, pp. 249–50; *Opera omnia Desiderii Erasmi Roterodami* IV, ii, Amsterdam, North Holland, 1977, p. 119; *Hiero* 8.

57 *Politics* 1287b; *The Basic Works of Aristotle*, R. McKeon (ed. and trans.) New York, Random House, 1941, p. 1203.

58 *Prometheus Bound*, lines 226–7. Cf. Aristotle, *Politics* 1313b.

59 Croft, *Governour* II, p. 371.

60 Ibid., pp. 374–5.

61 E. J. Howard (ed.) *Of the Knowledge Which Maketh a Wise Man by Sir Thomas Elyot*, Oxford, Ohio, Anchor Press, 1946, p. 116.

62 Ibid., pp. 118–20.

63 Croft, *Governour* II, pp. 262–3.

64 Howard, *Of the Knowledge*, p. 219. Cf. Plato, *Republic* 586e–587b.

65 Plutarch, 'How to distinguish a flatterer from a friend', 20: 'The flatterer takes his place on the side of the emotional or irrational [part of the soul], and this he excites and tickles and wheedles, and tries to divorce from the reasoning powers by contriving for it divers low forms of pleasurable enjoyment.'

66 Croft, *Governour* II, p. 180.

67 Sir T. Elyot, *A Preseruatiue Agaynste Deth*, London, Thomas Berthelet, 1545, sig. D i.

68 Croft, *Governour* II, p. 179.

69 Sir T. Elyot, *The Castel of Helthe*, London, Thomas Berthelet, 1541, 4°, f. 62ᵛ.

70 Erasmus, *Opera omnia* II, v, Amsterdam, North Holland, 1981, pp. 101–2.

71 *Prometheus Bound*, lines 377–80.

72 *Tusculan Disputations* 3, 31; 'Letter of condolence to Apollonius', 2.

73 This passage is translated from the Latin dedicatory epistle to the 1542 edition of *Bibliotheca Eliotae, Eliotis Librarie* entitled *BONIS AEQVE AC DOCTIS VIRIS CONSTANTISS. AMICIS ELIOTA*, the corresponding portion of which reads as follows: '*humanum quidem est labi, errare, decepi: at labantem non sustinere, aut errantem in uiam non reducere, aut deceptum consilio aut opera non iuuare si possis, amicum praefertim, non modo inhumanum existimatur, uerum etiam bonis omnibus execrandum.*'

74 T. F. Mayer (ed.) *Thomas Starkey: 'A Dialogue Between Pole and Lupset'*, C4S, vol. 37, p. 132; Gottesman, *Pasquil*, p. 56.

75 Gottesman, *Bankette*, pp. 157, 174–5; *Image*, p. 209.

76 Howard, *Of the Knowledge*, p. 216.

77 Ibid., p. 210, my emphasis.

78 Erasmus, *Opera omnia* II, v, Amsterdam, North Holland, 1981, p. 102: '*Verum ut amica, salubris et in tempore adhibita oratio remedium est efficax ac praesentaneum, ita sermo inimicus aut pestilens aut non in tempore dictus letale venenum est.*'

79 'How to distinguish a flatterer from a friend', 20.

80 Gottesman, *Doctrinal of Princes*, p. 21; *De amicitia* 44.

81 *Galen on the Passions and Errors of the Soul*, P. W. Harkins (trans.), Columbus, Ohio, Ohio State University Press, 1963, p. 44.

82 'The maner to chose and cherysshe a frende', p. 16; cf. *De amicitia*, 88–9. This six-page collection of sayings was printed 'to fylle up the padges, that els wold haue ben voide' at the end of an anonymous and undated English translation of Plutarch's essay *Howe one may take profite of his enemyes* [STC² 20052]. The circumstantial evidence in support of attributing the work to Elyot is surveyed by Lehmberg (*Sir Thomas Elyot*, p. 128). While the identification is plausible, significant difficulties remain – such as the failure

of the translator of Plutarch's essay to render verse excerpts in rhymed metre, as was Sir Thomas's characteristic practice.

83 Cited in J. A. Fernández-Santamaria, *The State, War and Peace: Spanish Political Thought in the Renaissance 1516–1559*, Cambridge, Cambridge University Press, 1977, p. 265. See T. F. Mayer's essay on Reginald Pole as counsellor and resistor, Chapter 2 in this volume.

84 Croft, *The Governour* II, p. 184, my emphasis.

85 *Politics* 1313b.

86 D. J. White (ed.) *Richard Edwards' Damon and Pithias: A Critical Old-Spelling Edition*, New York, Garland, 1980, pp. 6, 101.

87 R. A. Rebholz (ed.) *Sir Thomas Wyatt: The Complete Poems*, New Haven, Conn., Yale University Press, 1978, pp. 192–4. For a discussion of the poem's historical context, see D. Starkey, 'The Court: Castiglione's ideal and Tudor reality', *Journal of the Warburg and Courtauld Institutes*, 1982, 45, pp. 232–9.

88 B. Castiglione, *The Book of the Courtier*, C. S. Singleton (trans.), New York, Anchor Books, 1959, p. 289.

89 A. Fox, *Thomas More: History and Providence*, Oxford, Basil Blackwell, 1982; see also Note 132 below.

90 Hanson, *From Kingdom to Commonwealth*, p. 125.

91 J. E. A. Jolliffe, *Angevin Kingship*, London, Adam and Charles Black, 1963, pp. 166–88.

92 M. Day and R. Steele (eds) *Mum and the Sothsegger*, EETS, old ser., vol. 199, p. 6.

93 M. James, *Society, Politics and Culture: Studies in Early Modern England*, Cambridge, Cambridge University Press, 1986, pp. 330–1; G. F. Lytle, 'Friendship and patronage in Renaissance Europe', in F. W. Kent and P. Simons (eds) *Patronage, Art, and Society in Renaissance Italy*, Oxford, Oxford University Press, 1987, p. 50. I owe the latter reference to the kindness of William Gentrup.

94 M. St C. Byrne (ed.) *The Letters of King Henry VIII: A Selection*, London, Cassell, 1968, pp. 48–9, 76–81.

95 T. F. Mayer, *Thomas Starkey and the Commonweal: Humanist Politics and Religion in the Reign of Henry VIII*, Cambridge, Cambridge University Press, 1989, pp. 154ff.

96 S. H. Thomson, 'Walter Burley's commentary on the *Politics* of Aristotle', in *Mélanges Auguste Pelzer*, Louvain, *Université de Louvain, Recueil de Travaux d'Histoire et de Philologie*, 1947, 3me Série, 26me Fascicule, pp. 571f. For a discussion of the differences between Burley's commentary and baronial theory, see E. Kantorowicz, *The King's Two Bodies: A Study in Medieval Political Theology*, Princeton, NJ, Princeton University Press, 1957, pp. 364–72.

97 Mayer (ed.) *'Dialogue Between Pole and Lupset'*, p. 121.

98 For a detailed history of Pasquino, examples of *pasquinate* and photographs of the statues, see M. dell'Arco, *Pasquino e le Pasquinate*, Milan, Aldo Martello, 1957; and R. Silenzi and F. Silenzi (eds) *Pasquino: Cinquecento Pasquinate*, Milan, Bompiani, 1933.

99 *CSPSp* IV, ii, 897; *L&P* V, 1658; VI, 299 (iii).

100 Gottesman, *Pasquil*, p. 42.

101 Ibid., pp. 42, 98.

102 Ibid., pp. 42–3; *Eunuchus* 252: 'Does someone say "no"? I say "no". Does one say "yes"? I say "yes" too.'

103 Ibid., pp. 43, 63, 66. Plutarch, 'On Isis and Osiris', 68: 'Harpocrates is to be

regarded as the representative and corrector of unseasoned, imperfect, and inarticulate reasoning about the gods by mankind. For this reason, he keeps his finger on his lips in token of restrained speech or silence'.

104 Ibid., p. 49. For the specific passage of Aeschylus in question, see Note 71.
105 Ibid., pp. 50–1.
106 Ibid., p. 53.
107 Ibid., pp. 55–6.
108 Gottesman, *Pasquil*, p. 79.
109 Ibid., pp. 77–8.
110 Ibid., pp. 85–6.
111 Ibid., p. 88
112 Ibid., p. 94.
113 Ibid., pp. 94–5.
114 This feature of the dialogue is heightened in the second and third editions by Elyot's addition of the following two sentences to Pasquil's explication of the passage of Aeschylus under discussion: 'Whan thou art sittynge in counsaile about maters of weighty importaunce, talke not than of daliaunce, but ommittinge affection, or dreede, speke than to the pourpose ... If thou be called to counsaile, after thou haste either herde one raissone bifore the/ or at the least weye, in the balaunce of thyne owne raison pondered the question: spare not to shew thin advise, & to speke truely/ remembring that god is not so ferre of, but that he can here the' (STC² 7672.5, fos 7–8).
115 Gottesman, *Pasquil*, pp. 69, 87.
116 Ibid., p. 98. The Privy Gallery was the main hallway in the Privy Chamber.
117 Ibid., p. 99
118 Ibid., p. 56.
119 Ibid., p. 58.
120 Ibid., p. 57.
121 E.g. ibid., p. 68; Sir T. Elyot, *The Castel of Helthe*, London, 1541, 4°, fo. 80ᵛ.
122 Wilson, 'The letters of Sir Thomas Elyot', p. 17.
123 The date is established by a letter from Elyot to Cromwell accompanying copies of the dialogue *Of the Knowledge Which Maketh a Wise Man* which alludes to the reception of *Pasquil the Playne* in its proem. Since Elyot's extant letters appear always to observe his correspondents' latest eminence, and Cromwell is addressed as Treasurer of the King's Jewels, it follows that Sir Thomas's letter was dispatched prior to his friend's appointment as Chancellor or the Exchequer on 12 April 1533.
124 The absence of any established licensing procedures for non-theological works, Elyot's past record of writing in support of official policy in *The Governour*, and the tendency for pasquinades to be strongly anti-clerical, all help explain why *Pasquil* was evidently published by the king's printer without its content having been scrutinized.
125 *CSPSp* IV, i, 290.
126 The *Gravissimae* and *Determinations* are reprinted in E. Surtz, S. J. Murphy and V. Murphy (eds) *The Divorce Tracts of Henry VIII*, Angers, *Moreana*, 1988; *The Glasse of Truthe* (STC² 11918; 1531) is reprinted in N. Pocock, *Records of the Reformation*, 2 vols, Oxford, Clarendon Press, 1870, II, pp. 385–421. The analysis presented in the following two paragraphs has benefited from my consultation of Dr Virginia Murphy's unpublished 1984 Cambridge University doctoral dissertation, 'The debate over Henry VIII's first divorce: an analysis of the contemporary treatises'.

127 Ibid., pp. 401, 419.

128 G. Cavendish, *The Life and Death of Cardinal Wolsey*, in R. S. Sylvester and D. P. Harding (eds) *Two Early Tudor Lives*, New Haven, Conn., Yale University Press, 1962, pp. 85–6.

129 *L&P* V, 1114; W. Tyndale, *Exposition and Notes . . . together with The Practice of Prelates*, H. Walter (ed.), PS, vol. 43, pp. 319–21; *The Anglica Historia of Polydore Vergil A.D. 1485–1537*, D. Hay (ed. and trans.), Camden Society, 3rd ser., vol. 74, pp. 325–7; W. Roper, *The Life of Sir Thomas More* in *Two Early Tudor Lives*, p. 214; N. Harpsfield, *The Life and Death of Sir Thomas More, Knight*, E. V. Hitchcock (ed.), EETS, orig. ser., no. 186, pp. 40–3; N. Harpsfield, *A Treatise on the Pretended Divorce Between Henry VIII and Katherine of Aragon*, N. Pocock (ed.), Camden Society, new ser., vol. 21, pp. 175 ff.; 'Vie de bienheureux martyr Jean Fisher', *Analecta Bollandiana* 1891, vol. 10, pp. 279–301; N. Sander, *The Rise and Growth of the Anglican Schism*, D. Lewis (trans.), London, Burns & Oates, 1877, pp. 15–16.

130 'The York Articles' (*L&P* XI, 705), reprinted with modernized spelling in D. Berkowitz (ed.) *Humanist Scholarship and Public Order: Two Tracts against the Pilgrimage of Grace by Sir Richard Morison*, Washington, DC, Folger Books, 1984, p. 167.

131 *L&P* XI, 714.

132 Erasmus, *Education*, p. 196: 'There still remains one holy stay – and even that often fails. I refer to those whom the common folks call "royal confessors". If they would be impartial and prudent, surely in that most intimate confidence they could help the prince with loving and frank advice'.

133 The thirty-fourth chapter of the first Statute of Westminster provided that anyone who should 'tell or publish any false news or tales whereby discord or occasion of discord or slander may grow between the king and his people' should be imprisoned until he disclosed the first deviser of the tale. Two statutes of Richard II repeated the substance of this chapter, adding only that spreaders of tales whose devisers could not be found were to be punished at the discretion of the Council.

134 Included in the text of the Councillor's oath sworn to by Elyot and other Council personnel are the following clauses: 'in every matter touching our sayd Soveraigne Lord, his honourable suretie, or profit that shall come to your knowledge, or that shall be commoned or treated in his Counsell, ye shall to the best of your wisedome give plaine and true counsell; Not letting so to do for meed, dread, favour or affection, of any person of what degree or condition soever he be . . . And if there shall come any thing to your knowledge that may be hurtfull, prejudicial or dishonourable to our sayd Soveraigne Lord ye shall let it to the best of your power, and assoone as yee may goodly may, shew it to our sayde Soveraigne Lord, or such of his Counsell, as ye shall thinke will shew it to him'. For the complete text of the oath used during the reign of Henry VIII, see fo. 87ᵛ of the royal precedent book (C193/1) preserved in the PRO. See also Note 114.

135 STC² 7672.5. There is no mention of this edition in any previously published study of Elyot.

136 *L&P* V, 1077; Wilson, 'Letters', p. 9.

137 STC² 61. Edward Lee composed a 'Confutation of Abel's Babbling' on behalf of the Council (*L&P* V, 1); I owe this point to Dr Virginia Murphy.

138 SP 1/125, fos 247–56, printed as Appendix 2B in J. A. Guy, *The Public Career of Sir Thomas More*, New Haven, Conn., Yale University Press, 1980, pp. 207–12.

139 Cavendish, *Life and Death of Cardinal Wolsey*, p. 77.
140 Ibid., pp. 31, 81–2.

4

Peace discourse and mid-Tudor foreign policy

Ben Lowe

The element of peace in Tudor intellectual, cultural and political life has generally been given but cursory attention and then dismissed with the implication that it was an impractical aberration of Erasmian idealism which astute statesmen could readily perceive.[1] For whatever serious consideration the 'pacifists' received at the time must have quickly dissipated after the failure of Wolsey's transparent Universal Peace of 1518, and most assuredly once the French and Scottish wars were launched in the 1540s.

In truth, however, Henry VIII faced sustained resistance at home by almost the entire Council for his continental and Scottish exploits, and there is evidence to suggest that he faced similar opposition among the people at large. There existed a perceptive cynicism toward the just war that went back at least as far as the fourteenth century, and a popular element vocalized its discontent during the Amicable Grant crisis of 1524–5.[2] Historians, however, have made little attempt to connect the declining respect for certain chivalric attitudes and the just war with the conversely growing appreciation for peace.[3] The links are tentative in many ways but they do exist and serve as part of an overall insistence on peace as an ethic (in public policy and personal behaviour) which describes to an increasing measure the course of sixteenth-century England.

The roots of this growing predilection for peace ideas can be discovered in the Hundred Years War when the connotations of peace expanded dramatically. The cruel militaristic forces unleashed during that conflict led to a wholesale re-examination of the institution of warfare and the manner in which it was legitimized; one of the most remarkable results of this refocusing on the problem of war was the early peace rhetoric which found an amazing coherence in the writing of men as diverse as John Gower, Geoffrey Chaucer, Thomas Hoccleve, John Lydgate and John Wyclif among others.

This chapter will consider briefly the peace paradigms which flourished during the latter half of the Hundred Years War and locate them within the political discourses available to writers of the day. The intention is to show that these various languages were transformed as ideas of peace

108

developed away from a purely anti-war or personal realm to encompass the benefits which peace brought in and of itself. These changes were largely the result of changing social, political and discursive contexts that created an escalating value for temporal peace. The military-political *milieu* in which peace ideas emerged in the late Middle Ages found parallels in the 1540s when war was once again found to be overly burdensome and destructive. In each case the exigencies of public policy absorbed any idealism about the possibilities for true and lasting peace, but leaders and writers pursued nevertheless an imperfect shadow of a condition both alluring and real. During the Hundred Years War the scholastic discourse which had couched most meanings regarding peace in a justification for wars on some level (although stressing increasingly humane and defensive types) was beginning to break down. From the time of Gratian to the later decretalists and theologians, the stipulations regulating war had exploded into an immeasurable and idiosyncratic number of categories. Yet these types of legalisms had lost their power to convince, especially when the economy was hopelessly faltering, ruthlessness and cruelty had become commonplace, and political stability was but a dim memory. For much the same reason overly abstract thinking unrelated to existing conditions was rejected among the humanists in the early sixteenth century, who also affected and were affected by peace ideas. The revived and/or changing languages of classical humanism, political economy, biblical exegesis and even 'secular' humanitarianism during the English Renaissance and Reformation each made room for new understandings of peace and its promise, even to the extent where some hope actually coincided with the traditional cynicism about human nature. This chapter, therefore, examines the actual impact of the *paroles*, or speech acts, regarding peace, on the *langues* of the time, while taking into account the expanded contexts in which they were expressed. From here we trace the coexistent emergence of a 'peace discourse', and discuss its *locus* in considerations of public policy during the 1540s.[4]

Early medieval thinkers did not conceive of peace in isolation from war or conflict, and by so construing the idea, exercised no sustained interest in peace as a condition in itself.[5] Augustine provided the touchstone and schema for most medieval discussions on peace. In the *City of God* especially, he looks on it as a condition brought about by war and victory, something that all creation desires but, because of sin, can find only temporarily, through fighting and struggle. Augustine and his successors therefore taught that spiritual, otherworldly peace was the only true and lasting peace and as such must be sought above all else.[6]

While this formulation of 'spiritual peace' carried great weight throughout the Middle Ages in the works of the canonists and scholastic theologians, it ceased to be the primary *locus* of peace discourse by the end of the fourteenth century. The monumental political, economic and social changes which arose out of the unprecedented destruction of the Hundred Years War (and before that, the Crusades), helped to create an intellectual environment wherein we find in England a typology of peace that embraced at least three newer notions.[7]

Those who wrote about peace in the fourteenth- and fifteenth-century vernacular, whatever their particular literary genre, were enamoured of the expanding possibilities for words and the consequent conceptual broadening which a formative language like English offered. The effect of what appeared to be a cataclysmic event may have helped to prod and enjoin writers of all persuasions to demonstrate greater rhetorical skills in the service of a righteous cause. The breakdown of protective social institutions to which the war gave rise provided the context for the first new manner in which peace was invoked by the 1380s. Here peace meant the restoration of order and stability along with an end to knightly lawlessness and corruption.[8] Tied inextricably to societal conditions and relationships, those who used peace in this way connected it most often with order, quiet, rest, concord and law. Gower, in his *Confessio Amantis* complains vehemently about the nobility's use of the just war to 'make weeres and to pile for lucre and for no other skyle', in a criticism that would become standard over the next century. Elsewhere, in Book Seven of *Vox Clamantis* he chastises the 'greedy lords' who 'deal in the blessings of peace, but inwardly, wars still stand first with them. As long as it can store up more loot through war than through peace, avarice does not know how to love the good things of peace'.[9]

Closely related to these connections between peace and order were the renewed emphases on peace as a rigorous Christian ideal that reflected the *imago Christi* in everyday life. For Wyclif, the Lollards, and even the many orthodox thinkers who were enamoured of this understanding of peace, the ability to live piously and chastely depended on the absence of war. Those who stressed this aspect of 'Christ-like' peace usually returned to the New Testament and in so doing often found themselves confronting the church, by arguing that its pastoral calling was being neglected for worldly gain through war. Wyclif was most vociferous in this contention, levelling the charge that all clerics from the pope to the parish priest were guilty of leading men to hell by teaching them to kill rather than to serve God and each other: 'If thei weren trewe procuratouris of pees, thei schulden gladly & ioiefully coste alle here worldly lordschipis & here flesch & blood & bodily lif to make pees & charite amongis cristene men'.[10]

The final context for the emerging peace discourse of the late Middle Ages focused on the practical benefits engendered by an end to war. In tagging peace with the related ideas of prosperity, wealth, profit and health, peace, in this particular guise, eschews the purely moralistic and ideological connotations or bases, and concentrates on the consequent rewards to the nation. Most of those who argued early on for peace from more pragmatic postures, such as Lydgate, Hoccleve and the writer of the 'Libell of Englishe Policye', made their appearance in the early fifteenth century. Thomas Hoccleve, in his *Regement of Princes* (1412), contends that lasting peace is possible because it is in the best socio-economic interest of both sides to avoid wars. He decries the French civil wars going on at the time, in which 'cornes wast', 'tymbred houses brent and drawen downe', and 'many a wif and maide hath be by layn'.[11] In much the same manner the Court poet and monk of Bury St Edmunds, John Lydgate, exhibits a strong and personal affection for the practical aspects of peace. Deeply disturbed by an interminable war that was reaching the centennial of its existence during his adulthood, Lydgate unequivocally calls for a permanent cessation of hostilities. In an early critique of war found in his *Troy Book* (1420), commissioned by Henry V, the monk links forcefully the common good with peace,[12] reiterating the classical proverb: 'Rem publicam ye must of riht preferre/ Alwey consideryng that pees is bet than were'.[13] In his 'A praise of peace', written after Henry V's death, between 1422 and the peace negotiations of 1443, Lydgate goes beyond pleas for peace with France, and demands an end to all war. After beginning the poem with a wordplay on the letters PAX he denotes the difference between inward tranquillity and outward peace.[14] The author includes numerous biblical, mystical and historical examples to prove that peace is undoubtedly the only sure protector of the common weal, and ends the poem with one of the most categorical pronouncements against war in his day:

> Al werre is dreedful, vertuous pees is good,
> Striff is hatful, pees douhtir of plesaunce,
> In Charlys [Charlemagne's] tyme ther was shad
>   gret blood,
> God send vs pees twen Ynglond and Fraunce;
> Werre causith pouert, pees causith habundaunce,
> And attween bothen for there moor encrees,
> Withoute feynyng, fraude, or varyaunce,
> Twen al Cristen Crist Ihesus send vs pees.[15]

By emphasizing the connection between the public welfare and peace, Lydgate is standing the Thomistic rationale for warfare on its head. Scholastic discourse could not incorporate fully the growing number of peace paradigms, and even though it still functioned as a valve to stem illicit warfare, the conceptual categories and linguistic forms it offered were too far removed from real events and concerns. The theologians had permitted going to war if it would benefit the common weal, which in its own way was a variation on the cruel-necessity argument found in Augustine.[16]

Lydgate's outlook, which would dominate the next century, laid bare such specious reasoning by blaming war for creating the need to restore a harmony that would exist already if peoples and nations lived in peace. Hoccleve, Lydgate and others, who for space cannot be considered here,[17] together demonstrate the complexity of the peace idea as it came to be expressed in the early fifteenth century, located increasingly in the language of political economy and less according to scholastic definition.

By the reign of Henry VI the ongoing war and the virtual collapse of royal government yielded an outcry against a conflict that was sapping the realm of its lifeblood, and precipitated a vigorous discussion about the possibilities for peace.[18] While the nation did not find itself in such a threatening dynastic crisis the following century, there were moments of rebellion and war when similar conditions existed and the spectre of irreparable harm to the public welfare was raised once again. During these times a transformed peace discourse helped to attune the nation once again to the overwhelming problem of war and violent conflict, offering an alternative that promised both a more productive and ethical outcome.

The early part of the sixteenth century witnessed the emergence of a peace ethic that found its basis in Erasmian opposition to war on both Christian and humanitarian grounds. Besides Erasmus, humanists such as John Colet, Thomas More, Richard Pace and Juan Luis Vives all took to offering extended disquisitions on the value of peace to the extent of making its attainment a moral imperative.[19] Their insistence that the way of peace was the only viable manner of behaviour among Christian peoples did much to override any vestiges of sacrosanct just war ideology, at least within their own circles.[20] Yet these writers did not just dally with the concept of true peace but each in his own way worked for it. The Universal Peace of 1518 was the high water mark of their (and Wolsey's) endeavours, but its pretensions proved illusory such that by the 1520s pessimism set in and the hope which carried their noble aspirations had all but dissipated.[21] Despite the failure of these men to inculcate an abiding love for peace among Europeans they made a significant contribution to the discourse itself and became the progenitors of a lasting ethic which finally separated the value of peace from considerations of legitimate warfare.

The access to medieval works which humanists and Protestants enjoyed by virtue of printing, and the 'knowledge explosion' which came in its wake, had an impact that while not easily determinable was certainly substantial all the same.[22] The printed word in itself might have contributed to an elevation of the peace idea by proffering a new dialogic means for two adversaries to come to terms.[23] But humanists had scant respect for scholastic technique and exhibited an outright disdain for the detached moralism that accompanied it. Their enchantment with antiquity tended to preclude the serious consideration of emergent ideas, even peace, which could be found in any product of the Middle Ages. Erasmus and his coterie of pacifists harkened back rather to ancient Rome and adopted the classical humanism of Stoic philosophy as their vehicle of social and political expression. For them, of course, the difference was that now in the Christian era there existed even a greater moral obligation and opportunity for bringing about *concordia* and *pax* among all people.

Early imperial Rome appeared to many humanists a golden age with the *pax Romana* having ensured effective government, economic prosperity and social tranquillity as the world had never witnessed before or since. Erasmus, More, Pace and Vives all admired the Stoic teaching that stressed the kinship of humanity and adherence to those natural laws that led reasonable creatures to live at peace and treat one another with love and kindness. Along with Scripture, classical *sententiae* denouncing wars were habitually used by humanists in England to convince readers of the morally superior condition of peace. Some of the more notable examples include, '*pax optima rerum, quas homini novisse datum est*',[24] '*dulce bellum inexpertis*',[25] and '*pax iniusta utilior est quam iustissimum bellum*'.[26] Overall, the writings of Seneca, Pliny, Sallust and Silius, informed much humanist opinion regarding war and peace, but it was Cicero's *De officiis* that became the prescribed standard by which princes should rule and conduct relations with one another.[27] In England alone this work was translated and reprinted continuously in the first half of the sixteenth century, sometimes twice in one year, and as the premier example of civic oratory, the writer was by far the most quoted expert on politics of the day. Yet Cicero argued in favour of the just war even as he concentrated on humane behaviour along with integrity and humanity in dealing with the enemy. Augustine had found his arguments little more than subtle casuistry to defend previous Roman conquests. Erasmus, however, accentuated Cicero's humanitarianism which most appealed to him, and connected it with similar emphases he found in the New Testament.[28]

The simple piety extolled by these humanists caused them to reject all scholastic *formulae*. On the topic of war and peace Aquinas, Bernard and even Augustine were not in accord with the 'philosophy of Christ' as taught in the Gospels, and as such were not to be followed.[29] Vives' gloss on Book Nineteen, chapters eleven and thirteen of the *City of God*[30] is a clear example of the limits to which Augustine would be followed by peace-loving humanists. It reveals a mind so dedicated to a vision of European peace that it rejects the rationales for just wars which had been espoused by this early church father (whom Vives in other respects admired tremendously), lamenting that 'the whole goodnesse of peace, and of that especially which CHRIST left vs . . . is gone. We have made a willing extrusion of it . . . And oh so we braue it, that we haue slaine thus many men, burnt thus many townes, sacked many cities!'[31]

Combining then the languages of classical (Stoic) humanism with the Christian, New Testament gospel, Erasmus deemed *concordia* the essence of *pax* and the foundation for peace in personal conduct, social and political correctives, and the basis for prosperity (*publica utilitas*):

> What in this world is more sweet or better than amity or love? Truly nothing. And I pray you, what other thing is peace than amity and love among men, like as war on the other side is naught else but dissension and debate of many men together?

By blending these various conceptions of peace into a plea for the good life, the Erasmians had not only fashioned peace into a personal ethic but also predicated it on more earthly and existential grounds.[32]

These like-minded humanists, inspired by the Stoics, also directed attention to the illogic and irrationality of war. Human beings were the only species that went to war, a fact that could make them inferior to the animal kingdom. In More's *Utopia*, Hythloday describes how the Utopians loathe war and consider it 'fit only for beasts and yet practiced by no kind of beast so constantly as man'.[33] As members of Henry VIII's diplomatic service, both More and Pace quickly became disabused of any idealism they might have at one time possessed. The latter did come to serve with great aplomb and seems to have maintained his optimism about the possibilities for universal peace, even after 1521 and the breaking of the 'universal peace'.[34] As late as 1523, after negotiating a peace treaty between Venice and the Empire, Pace reminded Charles V of his duty to secure peace in the Christian world and to punish those who disturbed it.[35] The Stoic and Christian bases for Pace's commitment to lasting peace in Europe are articulated clearly in the highly laudatory oration offered (and published) during the festivities celebrating the Treaty of Universal Peace in 1518, in which he declares that 'peace . . . is the heap and accumulation of all good things, which the great God has generously bestowed for the preservation of . . . mankind'.[36] Pace uses *concordia* and *pax* interchangeably in his oration, revealing his belief that both terms represented equally the desired absence of strife, war and even personal turmoil. Other humanists when writing in Latin likewise often refused to make any distinctions between these two terms.[37]

Erasmus himself, however, became so taken with the human, personal element that he never really moved the discussion of war and peace on to an institutional plane. Because evidences of familial feelings and conjugal love could be found among all people, he determined that each person was naturally a peaceful being. It is sin, especially greed, that has led to war and its consequent barbarism.[38] It is the duty of the prince, therefore, to exemplify godly behaviour and translate it into political policy. Since war is a human act, princes can simply decide to end it; it is not a 'prerogative of state' removed from individual behaviour:

> Most important . . . is the instruction of the prince in the matter of
> ruling wisely during times of peace, in which he should strive his
> utmost to preclude any future need for the science of war . . . A
> good and wise prince will make an effort to preserve peace with
> everyone.[39]

In the dedications to the Gospels in his New Testament paraphrase,
Erasmus entrusted contemporary monarchs with the responsibility for
preserving the commonweal through maintaining peace. To Francis I he
asserted that

> no kynde of people is more pernicious to the common weale then
> suche as put into princes heades those thinges that may stayre and
> moue them to warre . . . But how muche greater a poynt is it of a
> noble courage, for consideration to haue peace and tranquillitie of
> the common wealth conserued.[40]

Much the same caveat was made in the dedication to Charles V. Only
Henry VIII escaped the moral wrath of the Dutchman, who as late as
1523 still believed that England's attachment to peace lifted it above the
dynastic fray.[41] Holding to a similar belief, Pace praised the king in his
1518 oration for putting aside all enmity and quarrelling, for by being
'zealous only for the common tranquillity and health of all Christians,
you turned all your thoughts to health-bearing peace'.[42]

In many ways the tone of these humanists is just as moralistic and
pedantic as that of their medieval forebears, as if by calling attention to
the tragic situation and the consequent duty of each Christian to amend
would be enough to change human behaviour. If anything, the idealistic
tenor of their work was even more pronounced than that of Gower,
Wyclif or even Augustine.[43] The humanist ideal for peace was a simple
one, deceptively so, making it difficult to refute on rational or moral
grounds. By positioning the value of peace at such an elevated and unreach-
able height, these men helped mould the idea into an irrefutable and
uncontested virtue, or as Vives, recalling Silius, defines it, 'the chiefe good',
nothing of which is 'either more pleasant or more profitable: more wished
or more welcome'.[44] This approach to peace was instrumental in laying
the groundwork for the more practical considerations that would characterize the mid-Tudor period, when the ethic became less personal and
attached more to institutions and policy.

In the end the two languages of antiquity employed by humanists helped
to extol the value of peace and in turn, the ideas of peace also broadened
and transformed the idiomatic reservoir available to the users of these
languages. A discourse of peace was developing that eclectically combined
a number of linguistic conventions to match the political and economic

contexts that had necessitated a greater concentration on peace as an idea, and now also as a matter of state.

By the mid-Tudor period Protestants and political economists also had accommodated their rhetoric to incorporate the emergent peace paradigms. With many English evangelicals concerned with reform and its possibilities, they remained uncomfortable with the strict Augustinian justification for wars in a sinful world and the impossibility of true peace.[45] The Reformation also presented a natural challenge to social and political mainstays that were no longer serviceable in an age where reform and renewal were the watchwords. The 'purification of language' that accompanied regeneration of religion included dispensing with the antiquated features of some concepts with the intention of redefining them.[46]

Unmoved by the initial humanist optimism regarding peace, both English and continental reformers still could not avoid Christ's exhortation to become peacemakers. Among evangelicals the Bible was the hermeneutical handbook *par excellence*, the measure for separating the relative (and adiaphora) from the imperative; and those who attempted to abide by such a rigorous standard usually came to place peace in the latter domain. A scrupulous biblicism led some, like William Tyndale and Thomas Becon, to accept both Wyclif's *imago Christi* and Erasmus' *philosophia Christi* in making peace a matter of individual conduct *and* a devoted moral endeavour that clergy should relay to their congregations.[47] The majority of Protestants who went back to the New Testament found more that argued against war than for it. The hallmark of faith was a belief in the transforming power of Christ in the lives of individuals, who (in good humanist fashion) could then adopt a somewhat restrained postmillennial perspective on the coming era of peace.

Yet even with this in mind, these thinkers configured narrowly the means for engendering peace, for if sin and apostasy were the cause of war, then only by repentence could wars end. Reformers assimilated the peace value into their reluctant acceptance of recurring human conflict, demanding that before going to war all other remedies first be exhausted.[48] In the event of war, the Christian pleased God most by obeying his sovereign (the only possible means for remaining within grace in the event he shed innocent blood), but also by behaving in a Christ-like manner – even toward the enemy.[49] According to Tyndale, 'when you go to war it is important to love the one you fight as a brother or neighbour', even if you have to kill him: 'For thine heart loved him; and thou desiredst him lovingly to obey, and hast not avenged thyself in that state where thou art a brother: but in the worldly state, where thou are another manner person'.[50]

The struggle which this situation set up within the conscience of the believer led most Protestants, like Becon, to embrace peace also as the ultimate good, while accepting war as a flawed response to unremitting sin or as punishment from God: 'The occasion of all these cruel wars and other plagues, wherein we are so miserably oppressed, is the despising of God's word, and the wicked and dissolute manner of living'.[51] While the active pursuit of peace with an understanding of real-life situations was not simply a product of Protestantism, the ideological and practical components of mid-Tudor policy, where ideas of peace become a special concern, can find close affinity to evangelical struggles over the problem of war and the scriptural basis for an orderly and peaceful society. Unlike the humanists, these writers betrayed little trust in the personal actions of kings or in the eventual regeneration of humanity.

As the reformers lent credibility to their claims by speaking as biblical exegetes they nevertheless infused them with the concerns and rhetorical flourishes of humanism, while conversely, the humanists themselves seem to have accounted a greater debt to the Stoics. Those involved in policy-making at the time often identified closely with the language of either or both, as we have already seen with Pace and More. The wars of the 1540s introduced a new set of conditions that removed peace discourse from older theoretical and moralistic formulations into the even more rapidly changing and developing language of political economy. It is perhaps among the bureaucrats of Henry VIII's and Edward VI's wars that we find the most fluid and extended discourse of peace – always tied to specific conditions, shaped by both inter-factional and international political alignments, and offering practical considerations for policy development. And yet, the idea of peace here also begins to exhibit a certain autonomy that due to the overwhelming weight of its apparent teleology could nudge some close to treason if the circumstances warranted (as in the case of Stephen Gardiner) even if the writer/speaker was normally quite conservative in his own personal politics.

If at this point we turn to the conditions surrounding the wars of the 1540s we can find a fuller context in which to view closely the inter-relationship between a new discourse of peace and the concerns of policy. Fought in Scotland and France, each theatre in this renewed yet long-standing conflict was inextricably linked to the other. The failure of the Scots to honour the Greenwich marriage contract between Mary of Scotland and Edward of England formed the pretext for the Scottish war after July 1543.[52] It was Henry's intention that the two crowns become united under English hegemony so as to keep the north country from being an habitual beachhead for French or other foreign invasions of England. Raids were launched into Scotland by the duke of Norfolk and the earl of Hertford in 1542 and 1544 respectively, the latter in retaliation for the breached treaty, even though they both served foremost as pre-emptive strikes intended to keep the Scots off-guard while England invaded France.[53] Thus began the period known as the 'rough wooing' which lasted until the treaty of Utrecht (1546). The chronicler Edward Hall echoes the standard line of reasoning behind the Scottish incursions (which were used largely to screen the French campaign). He contends that the English had no choice but to invade Scotland:

> Beyng now enforced to the warre, which we have alwayes hytherto so much abhorred an fled, by our neighbour and Nephieu the kyng of Scottes, one, who above all other, for our manifolde benefites towardes him, hath moost just cause to love us, to honour us, and to rejoyce in our quietnes: We have thought good to notifie unto the worlde his doynges and behaviour in the provacacion of this warre, and likewise thee meanes and wayes by us used to exchue and avoide it.[54]

Turning to his other hand, in June 1542 Henry sent the bishop of Westminster to Emperor Charles to work out plans for a joint invasion of France the following year. Immediately, preparations were made and ships, weapons and new revenues were collected. The largest army up until the time of William III was assembled in Kent – a situation that prompted Becon, then in hiding, to write his treatise on war and peace.[55] Fulfilling an important formality, on 28 May 1543, Henry's Garter King of Arms, Christopher Barker, was sent to present Francis I with a list of grievances expressing 'righteous indignation' over the French alliance with the Turk, the suspension of a pension agreed to in 1532, the unlawful imprisonment of English subjects, and the provocation of the emperor.[56] Francis was called on to make an alliance with Henry and Charles to drive the Infidel from Europe, for 'the quiet of Christendom'. In an attempt to strengthen his position, Henry published the propagandist *Statutes of War* in 1544, wherein he still claimed a legal right to the French throne, and that he went to war, 'prouoked by the manyfolde iniuries commytted by the frenche king, both in his confederation with the Turke, and by his priuate displesures and wronges done to his highnes, against the common weal of Christendome'. It was an odd spectacle: a schismatic king allying with the emperor against the 'Most Christian King and his ally, the infidel Turk'.[57]

After several delays, and an assurance that the Scots would pose no immediate trouble, Henry landed in Calais on 14 July 1544 and began laying siege to Boulogne five days later. When Henry returned home on 30 September with the prize of Boulogne for his efforts he must have felt very satisfied by the results of the campaign. Yet on closer look it had not been a brilliant success. When one calculated the amount of money and manpower which were expended for a victory that gave Boulogne to England for only eight years with a pension that would be difficult to collect, there was really very little to celebrate.[58] In addition, there was a mounting shortage of men to serve in the garrisons at Boulogne, with the problem of mutiny and desertion always present.[59] On the Scottish front similar problems arose out of another spectacular victory. Hertford's complete rout of the Scots and the burning of Edinburgh in 1544, coming on the heels of the humiliation of Solway Moss two years earlier, left much of southern Scotland a wasteland. The campaign, however, was far from over, as the English still expected nothing less than complete surrender on the marriage issue and the right to keep Boulogne; but if they hoped to consolidate their gains in battle, a long-standing, expensive commitment of men and matériel would be required.[60]

The value of peace began making itself felt as those who sought to justify this enterprise went beyond the more traditional and negative breaking-of-contracts rationale and argued also in a positive manner for the restoration of the peace which would be a consequence of the marriage. In his account of Hertford's Scottish campaign William Patten claimed to witness

> his Grace's godly disposition and behaviour, in the fiercest time of war, seeking nothing more than peace, neither cruel in victory, nor insolent upon good success, but with most moderate magnanimity, upon the respect of occasion, using, as the poet [Virgil] saith *Parcere subjectis et debellare superabos*.[61] In peace again, wholly bent to the advancement of GOD's glory and truth, the King's honour, and the common's quiet and wealth.[62]

In 1548, Seymour, now the duke of Somerset, gave life to Patten's portrayal of him by producing his own tract which called on the Scots to submit to the treaty so as 'to haue vs [English] rather brothers, then enemies, rather Countreymenne, then Conquerours', and 'to make one Isle one realme, in loue, amitie, concorde, peace, and Charitie'.[63] Somerset has been the object of tremendous revision recently as historians try to strip away the benevolent veneer of the 'Good Duke'.[64] Yet attempts to discover the real motives behind his outward paternalism toward the commons cannot escape the plain appearance of the deeds (or attempted deeds) themselves.[65]

In reading his appeal to the Scots, one gets the sense that Somerset truly wants peace out of a moral (as well as financial) conviction, and that he is hoping to cater to a similar sensibility among his northern neighbours.[66] That the Protector would even use a literary device attests to some sympathy for the prospects of peace.[67] The good of orderly and spiritual peace is evident in the rhetoric as is an acknowledgement of the broader, economic benefits and unity that could come from adoption of the Protestant cause to which Somerset was personally committed. In the end, however, the duke made little impression as the Scots turned to their age-old ally against England – France – in an attempt to salvage their self-respect and autonomy. The French army arrived in 1548 and spirited away

Mary to wed the Dauphin. As the new decade dawned, England's initial triumphs had turned into disasters. The delicate peace with Scotland included no marriage contract and Boulogne already had been returned to France.[68]

The nature of sixteenth-century warfare, however, had tipped off many to this inevitable denouement. A much more realistic and less suppliant approach to military science, along with a heightened sensitivity to the practical benefits of peace, caused some members of the government to question early on the wisdom of these wars.[69] The late Henrician wars were supervised within the Council by Stephen Gardiner, bishop of Winchester; William Petre, Principal Secretary; and William Paulet (later marquess of Winchester), all of whom assisted in logistical planning, including the victualling arrangements.[70] Along with William Paget, these men were the most informed Englishmen on all aspects of the wars. As they deliberated over policy and attempted to bring about a conclusion favourable to England, they came to realize that it would most likely be a pyrrhic victory the longer it took to achieve, and so wrestled with when and how England could end the conflict with the least amount of loss in honour, resources and money.

There was an unusual amount of unity within the Council at the start of the Scottish campaign, with Henry intentionally putting an end to the recent political manslaughter that had culminated in the failed Prebendaries Plot of 1543. The reduction of faction at Court did not translate into uniform, unequivocal support for Henry's determination to invade France, and the king surely harboured no illusions that he could hope to gain enthusiastic backing. But he could control the activities to which his councillors directed their energies, and, considering the renewed campaign's massive expense in soldiers and supplies, he demanded nothing less than full attention to the war effort.

Gardiner handled the provisioning of the troops in Scotland while Hertford and the bishop's other political enemies, Lisle and Paget, continued to vent their lingering resentment by exposing him to a constant barrage of criticism and grumbling about unmet supply needs.[71] Even this sniping came to a halt for the time being when just before Henry's capture of Boulogne in September 1544, Emperor Charles began having serious reservations about the joint invasion and its prospects for lasting territorial remuneration. Right away and while still a favourite of the emperor, Winchester began his quest to maintain the Anglo-Imperial alliance. After Francis and Charles concluded the peace of Crépy on 18 September, this task became much more difficult, for by this time Henry was adamant about holding on to Boulogne while the emperor refused outright to support such a claim.[72]

As the need for peace became ever more a necessity, factions resurfaced at Court that coalesced around two different peace/alliance orientations.

Gardiner led the delegation that refused to give up hope for bringing the Habsburgs back into the English fold. Paget, according to his own political and religious proclivities, cast his lot with the reform element at the French Court, especially Madame d'Etampes, and worked to find some compromise that would bring an honourable peace to England.[73] Winchester, along with Hertford, pushed their case before Charles in November, and after much procrastination on the emperor's part, returned home unsuccessful. French negotiator Cardinal du Bellay and Paget meanwhile had entered into negotiations at Calais, as Henry consciously kept open this other avenue of accommodation as long as it appeared even slightly promising. Amid the constantly shifting international scene, Paget had the formidable task of juggling the various peace options coming out of France, depending on the ascendant position at Court at any particular moment. In the end, and after many months of sincere intentions on both sides, he, like Gardiner previously, came back to England empty-handed on 6 January 1546.[74]

Despite the failure of this mission the possibility loomed in Charles' mind that England, France and the German Protestants could eventually come to terms, leaving him potentially isolated and vulnerable. With the Schmalkaldic League particularly resurgent at the time, the emperor initiated once again negotiations for a renewal of the Anglo-Imperial alliance. Gardiner, its great champion, was dispatched quickly to Brussels and there the treaty of Utrecht was concluded on 16 January 1546, re-establishing the alliance but this time without the intention of invading France.[75]

Throughout these intricate and sensitive negotiations which impinged on princely honour and national prestige, the value of peace echoed clearly in the discourse of the protagonists. As potentialities for diplomacy grew concomitant with those for making war, the peace ideas were most often expressed in the developing language of political economy, which had in turn been affected by the Stoic-inspired humanists and the biblicism of the Christian reformers. Renaissance England is being characterized more and more as a transitional period with writers especially depicting the confusion, uncertainty and liminal nature of their changing world.[76] Doubts concerning many traditional practices, institutions and cultural norms extended beyond social displacements to include even conventional rationales for warfare. One need only look to the correspondance of Gardiner and Paget during the height of their diplomatic machinations to find this condition illustrated. Both men seem convinced that society must move beyond wars and concentrate alternatively on the superior condition which peace offers. They were particularly distraught, especially Gardiner, over the petty and dubious justification for their own king's latest act of chivalric fancy and futility.

A meeting with the French on 10 November 1545 in Antwerp, during

Winchester's final peacemaking mission, underscores the bishop's great exasperation over the war and his overwhelming desire for peace. With both nations in a financial bind, Gardiner pushed for peace at almost any price, even to the point of relinquishing Boulogne, which he considered a worldly prize, that if held on to would encourage only further greed and war.[77]

In a letter to Paget (who would join him at year's end) dated 13 November 1545, Gardiner laments England's isolation in the French war and muses about whether a dishonourable peace would not be preferable to continuing along a course that can bring only financial ruin:

> Our warre is noysom to all merchauntes that must trafique by us and passe the narowe sees as they crye out here wonderfully. Herwith we see at hom a gret apparaunce of lak of such thinges as the continuaunce of warre necessaryly requireth. And whenne, to put awaye this warre, we shewe ourself content to take a peace, we maye have it.[78]

Winchester's stress on profitable peace is indicative of the shift in peace discourse that many of his contemporaries had adopted, away from earlier platitudinous calls for restoration of goodwill among peoples or the ease of conscience, to the practical advantages which would come in bringing an end to war. Reiterating Lydgate's concern for protection of the commonweal, the bishop, however, infuses it with a more tangible quality. Yet Gardiner worries that France would now demand too much: 'Fye of such a peace as might be soo displeasaunte. And yet in the warre is miserie'. He concludes that the war should never have been started. For if one takes stock of the tragic situation at hand, the king was mired in a dilemma that held out two different options, neither of which was ultimately beneficial.

Winchester's critique highlights a problem that was recognized in much of the mid-sixteenth-century discussion on war and peace. He posed a moral quandary that humanists and Protestants had only tentatively and half-heartedly resolved, that is, deciding the greater sin, continuing a cruel war or accepting the terms of a dishonourable peace. Gardiner, himself, is not at all sure about what should be done:

> Shel he [the king] take these base and unsure conditions of peax? I dare not but saye, Naye; for I feare a myscontentement of the kinges Majestie to folowe it. What meane I thenne? To continue in war styl? . . . And yet, ye wyl saye, eyther we must take such a peace as we canne get or, of necessite, continue in wer; for there is noo thirde waye.[79]

The amazing admission here is that deep down, Gardiner acknowledges that the advantages of peace are of greater import than salvaging the king's honour (thereby tacitly rejecting the justification behind the war), even though in reality, such a course of action is unavailable to him. Because Henry's ego required so much stroking, the bishop actually fears for the king's mental health should a peace be concluded that did not include keeping Boulogne; but unconvinced that this can be accomplished he writhes in indecision, declaring at one point: 'I have wryten to youe vehemently for peace, and I have noted the sentence of oon that saide the worst peace is better thenne the best warre'.[80] As noted earlier, Gardiner is repeating a Ciceronian dictum that had gained great currency among the peace advocates of the Renaissance, but here it acquires fresh utility from the one person most responsible for overseeing the French campaign!

There were at least thirty deeply personal and confessional letters written to Paget in November, but no evidence of reciprocity on the secretary's part. Considering the past resentment and animosity between these two councillors, Gardiner's motivation seems hard to explain – unless perhaps they shared an affinity for peace that rested in common Christian, humanitarian, political and even commercial values that he could count on. The bishop's most recent biographer finds in all of this a man torn between loyalties to a 'warmongering monarch', the Habsburg alliance and to 'something of the humanist's ideal of peace between Christian princes'.[81] Throughout these letters he does betray a deep desire for *concordia* among all European Christians and anticipates the reputation England could gain by leading the way, not unlike the ambitions harboured by humanists of 1518 who sought 'universal peace' based on the shared humanity of all Christians.

Gardiner was not alone at Court in holding to these opinions as almost every member of the Privy Council wanted a quick peace. The Lord Chancellor, Thomas Wriothesley, expressed a prevailing sentiment when he wrote in November: 'I am at my wit's end how we shall possibly shift for three months following'. The French, however, still refused all compromise and so Gardiner drew back for the moment and left for home on 25 November. With the completion of the treaty of Utrecht, the French found reason to reopen negotiations the following April, and this time finally came to terms with the bishop, much to his delight.[82]

As a postscript, it should be mentioned that Gardiner's distress over the deleterious effects of war on the realm continued into the next reign, when clearly out of favour, he still expressed to Somerset the same concerns he had maintained under the old king, only this time addressing himself to the Scottish enterprise.[83]

Gardiner's colleague, Paget, while perhaps not as passionate in his quest for peace, was just as critical of wars that provide no clear advantage to the nation. More of a *politique*, throughout much of his term in royal service he played off war and peace policies to whichever could bring England the greatest advantage at the moment, hoping to avoid war when at all possible. In the 1545–6 negotiations he pursued a Protestant peace, while during Mary's reign he aligned himself with the Catholic cause. His letters demonstrate that an overriding concern for the nation's economic and political welfare led him to believe that the prospect of peace itself had the most to offer in any case, and that this should be the active direction of government policy.[84]

As mentioned, Paget was incidentally responsible for the peace of 1546. As leader of the commission sent to negotiate in Calais he seemed as bothered by his own king's recalcitrance as that of France. Writing to Petre, he encouraged his fellow councillor to use whatever influence he had to move Henry toward compromise, or else he might have to quit the conference in complete despair. The king at one point actually feared that Paget's insistence on an immediate peace would prevent him from seeking Henry's best advantage, and so sent his minister a sharp rebuke to that effect. The royal secretary quickly replied that nothing could be farther from the truth but that the financial burden of the war was becoming unbearable. On 23 May, once the king had sent his acceptance of the French terms, Paget 'burst into a paean of joy'. When it then appeared, however, that the French would balk due to a minor boundary dispute over the source of a stream, he once again wrote Petre a sombre letter exclaiming that peace must be had for 'I see the honour of it and the commodities so great both they be wrought at home, at your friend's hands abroad, and at your enemies' hands also'. The final treaty was signed on 7 July. It is indicative that by the end of the reign, Henry had moved Paget, that 'master of practices' into a position of chief adviser.[85] The councillor's political savvy extended to his use of a peace idea already an integral part of Tudor political discourse with its growing focus on strong, effective government, international status, and the economic welfare of the nation.

In the next reign the escalation of the Scottish war under Somerset found Paget once again advertising the benefits of a peace strategy. In April 1549, he wrote to the duke outlining 'certain points to be resolved upon in Council'. In this document he asserts that because of the broken marriage covenant 'we have bene in warre with the Scottes these viij yeres, and yet contynewe still endinge conquest of the realme vpon pretence of forfiture'. Then, setting out the major question concerning the war he wonders

> whether that his entent being not yet brought to passe yt be moste expedient to folowe the same by warre at this tyme till yt be atcheiued or rather to devise and effectually prosecute by some honorable practise to shyfte of the warre either vtterlye or at the least for a tyme.[86]

Paget went on and made the same case for the renewed French war, whether England should continue to fight 'or elles deuise by practise and treatie to set thinges betwene youe and them in some more honorable and suer stage'.[87] Yet this conflict dragged on ignominiously to the councillor's great chagrin.

With this predisposition toward peace, Paget played once again, in 1550, the role of peacemaker. After Charles V's candidate for pope was elected and Habsburg power again became ascendant, Henry II of France was prepared to come to terms with England. On 8 January he commissioned four ministers to treat with the English representatives (Paget, Petre, the earl of Bedford and John Mason). Once more Paget took the lead in the discussions, which began on 19 February. Three days later he wrote to Warwick in Boulogne, seeking advice and support for his 'peace at any price' stand.[88] The basis for Paget's dissatisfaction with the war is most vividly expressed when he blames the conflict for the economic and social evils plaguing England:

> The first, we must knowledg (which we cannot denye) the evil condition of our estate at home; which recognisaunce is the first degree to amendment. The next is, to know the cause of the evil; and that is warre, supposed to be, yf not the only, at least one of the chiefest amongst many great. How many, how great occasions of mischief the warre hathe engendred to England?[89]

He goes on to credit war with causing inflation (by supplying foreign armies with goods, which makes them scarce at home),

> idlenes among the people, . . . grudgings, devices to amend this and that, and an hundred myscheves more; which make my hart sorry to thynk upon; and these be the frutes of warre. Then yf the disease wil not be taken away, but the causes be taken away, also warre (which is one chiefe cause) must be taken away.[90]

The corrupting nature of war extends from personal vice to economic depression, and by arguing thus, Paget demonstrates the natural link that existed between spiritual, Christ-like peace and profitable peace which pervaded much thought on the subject by mid-century. In this case, as one disposed to realistic considerations of situations at hand, Paget believes that England should make peace and receive an indemnity, so that neither side would be dishonoured. He is proposing a way out of the impasse Gardiner had reached over Boulogne four years earlier. If his plan is not adopted he fears the result would be 'to lose Bulloin without any recompence, to lyve in warre without synews; and for lack of good opportunitie, to be forced to let things at home unredressed'. This is exactly what Henry did in 1523–4, when he squandered the fortune 'left by the king his father mervelous welthy, rich, and wel obeyed of his subjects, in peace'. By contrast, however, having been bequeathed a nation at peace with Spain, Flanders, Rome and Germany, his son 'entred the warrs to recover his right of France. But in conclusion what right get he?' He had to surrender Thérouanne and Tournai, getting nothing for the former and 600,000 crowns for the latter.[91] 'Thus being thus, as I take yt to be (praying your Lordship to let yt be loked up,) the exemple is much to move the place'.[92] Drawing from rather recent historical illustration, therefore, Paget finds Henry VII an exemplar of the practical value of peace and its corresponding relationship to strong government and a healthy economy and society. Finally, in another letter to Warwick, written on 15 March, the royal secretary confesses that there is an honour greater than that acquired by the repute of military victory:

> For my part I doubt nothing vtterly perswading to my self that peax is the furst degre to it [the peace treaty]. And as for the other degrees if your lordship and the rest of my lordes shall please to steppe, there is no doubt but you may shortly get up to the highest steppe, I meane the commyn welth & estate of the realme may be browght to a perfait & happy estate.[93]

The treaty was soon concluded and by 29 March he was back in London and the peace officially proclaimed.

In the end, Gardiner and Paget may not have offered a comprehensive anatomy of what plagued the commonwealth, or fathomed the depths of ongoing economic transformation (as did their contemporary Thomas Smith), but they did possess an astute understanding of the possibilities for peace in helping implement the needed correctives of policy.[94] They employed a rhetoric that purposefully eschewed the legalisms that Henry had originally called up in his *Statutes of Warre* to justify his incursions into Scotland and France. They had little use for any scholastic arguments that neglected the overwhelming pragmatism of good government, economic solvency and even Christan fellowship, and as such, continued to accommodate the idea of peace to those languages to which they now proved most conducive; and conversely, peace itself took on additional nuances of meaning and application as conditional understandings (*paroles*) interacted with already existent and adaptive discourses (*langues*) that had been part of the developing discussion on war and peace since the later Middle Ages.

The English Renaissance struggle over the language of peace beset other mid-Tudor bureaucrats and politicians as well. The same thoughtfulness for the state of the commonwealth can be found in the advice literature written by influential advisers to both the Protector and the king. In his *Defense*, dated September 1549, the Member of Parliament (MP) from Lancashire, John Hales, draws a strikingly more pointed correlation between problems of society and of war.[95] He begins by adopting the Protestant/Wyclifite argument that the pope is responsible for the ruinous conditions that plague the realm, for continuing 'to procure outwarde warres, to stur vp Rebellyons, to moue emongst vs seditions, till he hath recouered emonge vs his premacie'. While concerned specifically with the Scottish conflict, Hales despairs over the evils inherent in the institution of war itself, especially when contrasted with the fruits which always accompany peace:

> God graunt vs his grace and molifie our hartes that we maye receaue and followe his worde. Then no doubte he will withdrawe from vs these plages and power downe on vs his benedictions and send vs in steede of warres and sedition, peace and tranquyllytie, in stede of famyn, and scarcitie, abaundaunce and plentie, and in stede of syknes and sodeyne deathe, helthe and longe lyfe.[96]

All four medieval understandings of peace can be detected in Hales' statement. The dichotomy between tranquillity (orderly peace) and sedition is posited, and the spiritual and Christ-like forms are found in the Protestant providentialism that petitions God to change people's hearts so that they live according to Scripture. But that profitable peace is the rubric under which the others seem to fall in consequence is important since the other meanings are instrumental in the accomplishment of 'abaundance and plentie', and 'helth and longe lyfe'.

Another high-ranking government official of the time, William Thomas, clerk of the Privy Council, played a role for his king similar to that played by Paget for Henry. Both men were trusted implicitly by their sovereigns and seem to have developed close, personal friendships with them. As part of an embassy to demonstrate goodwill after the peace of 1550, Edward sent Thomas and the marquess of Northampton to France in May 1551 to invest Henry II with the Order of the Garter and to arrange a marriage between himself and the king's daughter, Elizabeth. Impressed with his senior clerk's service and interest in long-term planning (which is evidenced through a long list of topics submitted for Edward's special attention), the king took Thomas up on his offer to expound more specifically on current pressing issues, especially in the area of foreign affairs.[97]

Two of the treatises which resulted give us insight into what he believed should be the government's policy in making peace the springboard for a more stable alliance system, which would then lessen the probability of future wars. His overall philosophy is spelled out in 'What Princes Amitie Is Best', which begins with a quotation of Cicero hailing friendship and charity as the most perfect gift to man from the gods, 'ffor it maketh the prosperous thinges more resplendaunt, and adversities the more easie'. However, man's nature

> doth skarsely permitt any perfect amitie. Wherfore to treate of the politike amitie that is to saie the accustomable amitie that may be

had, it is first to be considered to what end the amitie of foreyn Princes doth serve, and what nede one Prince hath of thothers amitie.[98]

Thomas's construction of peace policies as part of the game of politics is almost Machiavellian in its shrewd calculation and cost-benefit analysis. He has internalized the Stoic and Christian values for peace and universal concord, but, as with many evangelicals of the time, finds none capable of living up to the standard which Christ taught.

At the same time, the practical benefits of peace, which appeal to a person's (or country's) selfish nature, can provide a basis for bringing about a lasting peace. For Thomas, then, the question is how does a nation maximize its own gain by avoiding war (now that the good of peace has already been established)? His answer focuses on alliances and deterrence. Achieving amity (an alliance) with a foreign power 'consisteth in two poinctes, one is giveng aide to resist an ennemye, & *ut sine iniuria in pace vivatur* [so as to live in peace and without injury], and thother in relieving his frendes cuntrey with those comodities that it wanteth'. Friendship with its nearest neighbours is especially important for England. Once alliances are struck, they must not be broken, because, 'being ones violated, without tyme againe can not be recovered' and 'the defyleng of that amitie muste breede extreame displeaser in the Prince that receaveth the iniurie, whereof foloweth the more hate of an auncient frende for the uncertayne amitie of a newe reconsyled foo'.[99] The object of foreign policy, therefore, should be perpetual peace with other nations, and Thomas is suggesting various means for achieving the alliances which would produce this state of affairs, thereby rejecting the medieval preference for tactical truces.

In specific reference to the state of peace just reached as a result of the treaty of Boulogne, Thomas applies his proposal for a stable alliance to England's own foreign policy, which he details in 'My Private Opinion Teaching Your Majesties Outwarde Affaires at this Present'. Referring back to the other treaties which were ultimately broken, he observes:

And bicause there be infinite reasons that thretten us with warre almost on everie hande: therfore it is to be forseene (as I have written in the discourse of Princes amitie) that we fall not into such a warre; as either we must be a praie to thenemie, or elles throwe ourselfes into the lappe of a deere purchased frende: thone and other being equallie preiudiciall unto us.[100]

Thomas then goes on to offer suggestions about how to stay friendly with France, the emperor and Scotland, while conceding that true peace is impossible when there are such divisive religious differences. But keeping the peace is not a vain hope: 'Preparacion doth not only discouraige thenemye, but also encourage the subiect; who systeyneng a soddayne warre onlooked for waxeth hardie'.[101] By raising money to equip a possibly necessary army 'your enemies shall either suffre your Maiestie in peace, or at the worse have small advantaige of you in warre'.[102]

Thomas's conclusion that strong alliances and defences do most in preserving peace is built on a steadfast belief in the abilities of Tudor government to fashion a workable policy of peace that looked beyond immediate slights to honour and expectations for heroism and glory. By the middle of the sixteenth century war was becoming too expensive and wasteful for English governments to maintain for any extended amount of time. The higher standards of conduct demanded of both crown and nobility, and their own growing sense of the responsibilities needed to meet those standards, left many members to conclude that war was an unproductive activity. The classical ideal of effective government office together with New Testament personal ethics enjoined princes to consider higher moral imperatives (as the political nation was still viewed as essentially the personal domain of royal activity) when establishing all policies. In the mid-Tudor wars of the 1540s, even more than the Hundred Years War, the religious and intellectual currents were transforming and being transformed by the economic and political realities that also took seriously the ethic of peace. The discourse that became the vehicle for fashioning this ethic demonstrates in this case both the autonomy of language and its direct association with historical change.

We have seen in this chapter the interactive nature of early modern political languages when through 'multiple contexts' a new idiom (or sub-language), such as that of peace, enters into the fray of current discourse. The Renaissance found writers resurrecting old rhetorics and fashioning new ones to give voice and definition to moral uncertainties, although events as unsettling as the Hundred Years War initiated profound questioning even in the later Middle Ages. New ways of thinking about war and peace (in the context of a growing belief in the necessity of peace) were all contingent on the replacement of older, worn out ideas that were perceived to be largely irrelevant to rapidly changing, troubling conditions. Attempts at 'purifying' language or refining meaning was one path taken, merely a small step removed from the more existential reformation that interested many contemporaries. The value of peace fits well into this purging mentality which characterized much of the sixteenth century. According to both humanists and Protestants (and they were not mutually exclusive) human beings had gone astray and left behind their true selves – becoming estranged from both God and one another. Restoration of the natural order, one that was also life-affirming, had to include peace. The ravages of war could not be easily tolerated in an age when the potential for destruction had increased exponentially. Nor could the financial and economic drain of war go unnoticed while personal and social reform were taking on added urgency in the midst of a concurrent demographical crisis.

Careful attention to the 'vocabulary, rules, preconditions and implications, tone and style' of peace discourse in mid-Tudor foreign policy yields a fascinating picture of how language is transformed by exigencies that became only more and more entrenched by virtue of their duration.[103] In England it was initially the circumstances surrounding the Hundred Years War that created fluid and mutable linguistic environments that expanded dramatically the connotations of peace between roughly 1370 and 1440. The incipient peace discourse which emerged highlighted new concerns and opened up additional doors to understanding current conditions. It was easy for contemporaries to detect in the wars of the 1540s features similar to late medieval conflicts, which, in turn, helped lead to a renewed attention to peace. This time the humanistic ethic and evangelical realism, both employing a hermeneutics derived from a persistent substratum of literary convention, gave the practical peace element a prominence in war policy-making which men high in government found compelling. The sixteenth century is thus a watershed of sorts in that peace – in the guise of benefit to the commonwealth – first assumes noticeable status in the making of war policy. Peace is valued for its own worth, released from the protocols of the *jus ad bellum* and *jus armorum*. It becomes an object of intense philosophical interest in and of itself.

Military and social historian J. R. Hale has well described this phenomenon where 'the appeal of "peace" . . . depends on what it has to offer'. He claims that the so-called 'military revolution' witnessed a corresponding 'revolution in the connotations of peace, not just as a pause between wars . . . , but as a positively attractive alternative to the perpetual preparation for recurrences of violence'.[104] In determining the role of ideas in this process, J. G. A. Pocock points out the utility of historians seeking junctures where a

> network or community of men of letters . . . employ the language of the professional corporations without necessarily belonging to them, and are capable, first, of adapting these idioms or rhetorics to the purposes of their own discourse; second, of generating and developing idioms and rhetorics of their own in the course of pursuing it.[105]

This type of study has the advantage of showing 'how the performance of speech acts not merely modifies language, but leads to the creation and diffusion of new languages . . . by the activities, practices and contexts of society'.[106] The development of the peace idea in its many manifestations within linguistic but also social, political, economic, religious and cultural environments, gave birth to a new language. Its emergence is explained as much as anything by a highly ethical purpose and a persuasive rhetorical style. For a discourse to become active and durable it must promote moral values that give it purpose and substance. The early modern peace discourse that flourished in England was kept vital by practitioners who felt themselves ensnared in a crisis from which true peace and concord offered the only hope of escape. It was a discourse born out of a prolonged and painful labour.

NOTES

1 See for example C. S. L. Davies, *Peace, Print and Protestantism, 1450–1558*, London, Paladin, 1976, pp. 160–4; J. J. Scarisbrick, *Henry VIII*, Berkeley, Calif., University of California Press, 1968, pp. 21–4. Robert Adams makes the mistake of equating the failure of the 'pacifist' humanist programme with a neglect of all peace ideas in policy, a situation which, as this study will show, was not the case. R. P. Adams, *The Better Part of Valor*, Seattle, Wash., University of Washington Press, 1962, passim.

2 Evidence of popular dissatisfaction with the war and the Amicable Grant can be found in H. Ellis (ed.) *Original Letters Illustrative of English History*, 3d ser., London, Richard Bentley, 1846, vol. 1, pp. 371–2; E. Hall, *Henry VIII*, London, T. C. & E. C. Jack, 1904, vol. 2, p. 38. See also R. B. Merriman, *Life and Letters of Thomas Cromwell*, Oxford, Clarendon Press, 1902, vol. 1, pp. 27–46; G. W. Bernard, *War, Taxation and Rebellion*, Brighton, Harvester Press 1986, pp. 5–11, 111–12.

3 The exception is A. B. Ferguson, *The Chivalric Tradition in Renaissance England*, Washington, DC, Folger Shakespeare Library, 1986. The chapters covering the mid-century and Sir Thomas Elyot are especially enlightening. That Henry's personal proclivity for war and military pomp went against the general opinion of his officials has been argued convincingly in S. Gunn, 'The French wars of Henry VIII', in J. Black (ed.) *The Origins of War in Early Modern Europe*, Edinburgh, John Donald, 1987, pp. 28–51.

4 This method of studying ideas and their impact on language is based on J. G. A. Pocock's signal essay, 'The concept of a language and the *métier d'historien*: some considerations on practice', in A. Pagden (ed.) *The Languages of Political Theory in Early Modern Europe*, Cambridge, Cambridge University Press, 1987, pp. 19–38.

5 J. M. Wallace-Hadrill, 'War and peace in the earlier middle ages', *TRHS*, 5th ser., 1975, vol. 25, pp. 159–61.

6 Augustine, *De civitate Dei*, in *Opera Omnia*, Paris, Gaume Fratres, 1837, vol. 7, 1.21, 26, 3.10, 19.7, 12(1), 13(1–2), 15, 21; Augustine, *Contra faustum manichaeum*, ibid., vol. 8, 22.70–9; R. S. Hartigan, 'Saint Augustine on war and killing', *JHI*, 1966, vol. 27, pp. 195–204.

7 The *Middle English Dictionary* lists nine categories of definition for peace, but because of overlap (especially concerning the absence of conflict or violence) they can be broken down essentially into the four I have determined here. S. M. Kuhn (ed.) *The Middle English Dictionary*, Ann Arbor, Mich., University of Michigan Press, 1981, vol. 14, pp. 862–70.

8 M. H. Keen, *The Laws of War in the Late Middle Ages*, London, Routledge & Kegan Paul, 1965, pp. 137–85, 241–5; J. Barnie, *War in Medieval English Society: Social Values and the Hundred Years War, 1337–99*, London, Weidenfeld & Nicolson, 1974, pp. 117–18, 125–8; W. Caxton (trans.) *The Book of the Order of Chyualry*, A. T. P. Byles (ed.), EETS, orig. ser., no. 168, London, Oxford University Press, 1926, pp. 121–5.

9 J. Gower, *Vox Clamantis*, in *The Major Latin Works*, E. W. Stockton (ed. and trans.), Seattle, Wash., University of Washington Press, 1962, bk 7, lines 31–6, vol. 3, pp. 254–5; Gower, *Confessio Amantis*, in *Complete Works*, G. C. Macaulay (ed.), Oxford, Clarendon Press, 1899–1902, bk 3, lines 2,359–64, vol. 2, pp. 287–90; Gower, 'Address to Henry IV', in *Political Poems and Songs*, T. Wright (ed.), Rolls Series 14, vol. 2, London, Longman, Green, Longman & Roberts, 1859–61, pp. 6, 15. *Confessio Amantis* was probably written in 1390 at the insistence of Richard II. For similar exhortations to orderly peace by three powerful clerics see T. Brinton, *The Sermons of Thomas Brinton, Bishop of Rochester, 1373–89*, M. A. Devlin (ed.), Camden 3d ser., vol. 85, London, Royal Historical Society, 1954, vol. 1, pp. 167–8; J. Bromyard, *Svmma Praedicantivm*, Venice, Cominicum Nicolinum, 1586, 'Bellum', bk 1, pp. 92–100; G. R. Owst, *Literature and Pulpit in Medieval England*, 2d edn., Oxford, Basil Blackwell, 1961, pp. 333–8; Owst, *Preaching in Medieval England*, Cambridge, Cambridge University Press, 1926, p. 204; A. Gwynn, 'Richard Fitzralph: Part III', *Studies*, 1934, vol. 23, p. 404.

10 J. Wyclif, *Of Prelates*, in *The English Works*, F. D. Matthew (ed.), EETS, orig. ser., no. 74, rev. edn, 1902, pp. 52–4, 73, 90–1. See Barnie, op. cit., pp. 123–4. For Lollard opposition to war and all killing see A. Hudson (ed.) *Selections from English Wycliffite Writings*, Cambridge, Cambridge University Press, 1978, pp. 27–8; G. F. Nuttall, *Christian Pacifism in History*, Oxford, Basil Blackwell, 1958, pp. 23–4.

11 T. Hoccleve, *The Regement of Princes*, in *Hoccleve's Works*, F. J. Furnivall (ed.), EETS, extra ser., no. 72, 1973, lines 5,081–9, 5,336–41, pp. 181–3, 192; V. J. Scattergood, *Politics and Poetry in the Fifteenth Century*, London, Blandford Press, 1971, pp. 99–100.

12 While there is some danger in interchangeably employing terms such as common good, common profit and common weal here, it can be done since we are relating the value of peace to a more general notion of material well-being among people.

13 J. Lydgate, *Minor Poems, Part 2: Secular Poems*, H. N. MacCracken (ed.), EETS, orig. ser., no. 192, 1934, p. 556; Lydgate, *The Poetry of John Lydgate*, A. Renoir (ed.), Cambridge, Mass., Harvard University Press, 1967, p. 100; C. Allmand, *The Hundred Years War*, Cambridge, Cambridge University Press, 1988, pp. 153–4; Scattergood, op. cit., pp. 100–1. Lydgate's citation is a version of Cicero's adage that the worst peace is better than the best war (Cicero, *Epistolae ad Atticum*, bk 7, epis. 14). This proverb would become even more prevalent during the Renaissance, especially among the 'pacifists' associated with Erasmus.

14 Lydgate, 'A praise of peace', in *Secular Poems*, pp. 786–7; Scattergood, op. cit., p. 102.

15 Lydgate, op. cit., 'Praise of Peace', lines 117–84, pp. 788–91.

16 The Thomist formulation of this argument can be found in the second part of the Second Part, question 40, in *Summa Theologica*. According to Aquinas, a man must take up arms on occasion 'for the common good or even for the good of his opponents'.

17 See for example 'The Libelle of Englyshe Polycye', G. Warner (ed.), Oxford, Clarendon Press, 1926, which posits peace as necessary for economic prosperity, as well as an early justification for deterrence as a national policy.

18 David Starkey claims that the 'commonwealth' idiom emerged in the 1450s as a response to the lack of good government and the squandering of the king's patrimony. See D. Starkey, 'Which age of reform', in C. Coleman and

D. Starkey (eds) *Revolution Reassessed: Revisions in the History of Tudor Government and Administration*, Oxford, Clarendon Press, 1986. I would go so far as to push the usage of the idea to a time earlier in the century when Lydgate and others were crying out against the devastation of war and its harm to the *res publica*. On the limitations of the commonwealth idea in the fifteenth century see B. Lowe, 'War and the commonwealth in mid-Tudor England', *SCJ*, 1990, vol. 21, pp. 173–4.

19 The following works of these authors (most in recent editions) contain their most significant discussions on war and peace: J. Colet, *Ioannis Coleti Enarratio in Epistolam S. Pauli and Romanos*, J. H. Lupton (ed.), Ridgewood, NJ, Gregg Press, 1965; T. More, *Utopia*, E. Surtz (ed.), New Haven, Conn., Yale University Press, 1964; R. Pace, *Oration to Peace*, London, Richard Pynson, 1518, repr. in J. G. Russell, *Peacemaking in the Renaissance*, Philadelphia, Pa, University of Pennsylvania Press, 1986, pp. 234–41; J. L. Vives (ed.) *Saint Avgvstine, of the Citie of God: with the Learned Comments of Io. Lodovicvs Vives*, J. Healey (trans.), London, G. Eld & M. Flesher, 1620, STC 917.

20 Erasmus' attack on the just war was also a repudiation of the Thomist position: 'Ye say ye make war for the safeguard of the commonweal, yea, but noway sooner nor more unthriftily may the commonweal perish than by war'. Erasmus, *Erasmus Against War (Bellum Erasmi)*, J. W. Mackail (ed.), Boston, Mass., Merrymount Press, 1907, p. 60; see also the prefaces in Erasmus, *The First Tome or Volume of the Paraphrase of Erasmus upon the Newe Testamente*, London, Edward Whitechurche, 1548, STC 2854; and *Education*, pp. 251–2.

21 The signatories of the peace which was concluded on 18 October 1518 were England, France, the Empire, the Papacy, Spain, Denmark, Scotland, Portugal, Hungary, the Italian states, the Swiss Confederation and the Hanseatic towns. A few days later, it was announced that a meeting had been arranged between the English and French kings (later known as the Field of the Cloth of Gold). Around this time, Erasmus published three of his most pacifistic works: *Bellum Erasmi* (1514–15, for Leo X, also known as the adage, *Dulce bellum inexpertis*), *Querela Pacis* (1517), and *Institutio Principis Christiani* (1516, with Henry VIII receiving a personalized copy the following year).

22 According to Elizabeth Eisenstein: 'Increased output directed at relatively stable markets, in short, created conditions that formed new combinations of old ideas at first and then, later on, the creation of entirely new systems of thought'. E. L. Eisenstein, *The Printing Revolution in Early Modern Europe*, Cambridge, Cambridge University Press, 1983, pp. 43–4. While the development of the peace idea can hardly be called a new system of thought, it was, nevertheless, significantly transformed by humanists who considered it such a valuable concept in all of its manifestations that they fashioned it into an ethic applicable to all Christians.

23 As Walter Ong has stated, 'the word moves toward peace because the word mediates between person and person. No matter how much it gets caught up in currents of hostility, the two persons keep talking, despite themselves they are not totally hostile': W. J. Ong, *The Presence of the Word: Some Prolegomena for Cultural and Religious History*, New Haven, Conn., Yale University Press, 1967, pp. 192–5. See also R. Callois, *Man and the Sacred*, M. Barash (trans.), Westport, Conn., Greenwood Press, 1980, p. 177, which contrasts the hostile nature of oral culture with the peace norm that exists in typographic societies. Lydgate was especially attracted to the possibilities of eloquent language 'in reforming men and creating order'. To him, the poet civilizes

the reader and has a duty to set out instructive examples in a way that would convince as well as delight (L. A. Ebin, *John Lydgate*, Boston, Mass., Twayne Publishers, 1985, pp. 16–18). For Ebin, Lydgate's genius lies in the way he helped to embed certain values into English culture. She claims that the poem, 'A praise of peace', 'moves toward the realm of artifact, both in its transformation of mutable events into finely crafted structures and in its distillation of permanent values from impermanent events (p. 91)'.

24 'Peace is the best of all things given to man by nature' (Silius Italicus, *Punica*, 11.592–3); referred to by Pace (op. cit., p. 235) and found in Erasmus' *Querela Pacis*, B. Radice (trans.), in *Collected Works of Erasmus*, A. H. T. Levi (ed.), vol. 27, Toronto, University of Toronto Press, 1986, p. 299, and in the anonymous, Erasmus-inspired poem, *A Pretye Complaynt of Peace*, London, John Byddle, 1538, sig. C1ʳ.

25 'How sweet is war to to those unfamiliar with it'. Originally taken from the Greek poet Pindar's proverb *glukus apeirois polemos*, this saying served as the title of Erasmus' most anti-war adage (*Adagia* 4.4.1). See also Pace, op. cit., p. 237; R. Taverner, *Proverbes or Adagies with New Addicions Gathered Out of the Chiliades of Erasmus*, London, n.p., 1539; G. Gascoigne, *Dulce bellum inexpertis*, in *The Complete Works of George Gascoigne*, J. W. Cunliffe (ed.), Cambridge, Cambridge University Press, 1907–10, 1:142–84.

26 'The worst peace is preferable to the best (or most just) war' (Cicero, *Epistolae ad Atticum*, bk 7, epis. 14; *Ad familiares*, 6.6.5). Perhaps the most common of all anti-war slogans, Lydgate repeated it (op. cit., p. 183) as did Erasmus in *Querela Pacis* (op. cit., pp. 310–11) and *Panegyricus ad Philippum Austriae ducem* (in *Collected Works*, vol. 27, p. 55), Colet in a celebrated sermon preached around 1513 (J. B. Gleason, *John Colet*, Berkeley, Calif., University of California Press, 1989, pp. 256–9), the writer of the advice manual, *The Institucion of a Gentleman* (London, Thomas Marshe, 1555, sigs., F2ᵛ–F3ᵛ), and Stephen Gardiner in two of his letters written during the wars of the 1540s (no. 86, to Paget, 13 November 1545, and no. 117, to Somerset, 28 February 1547), both in J. A. Muller (ed.) *The Letters of Stephen Gardiner*, Cambridge, Cambridge University Press, 1933, pp. 189, 265.

27 Cicero, *De Officiis*, 1.53–6, 100, 107, 2.32; Seneca, *Epistulae morales*, 91.17–18, 94.61–9, 113.27–31, and *Quaestiones naturales*, bk 3; Sallust, *Bellum Catilinae*, 1–3, 9, and *Bellum Iugurthinum*, passim.

28 Adams, *Better Part of Valor*, pp. 7–8; Matthew 5: 9, John 14: 27, 16: 33, I Peter 3: 11, Hebrews 12: 14.

29 Erasmus, *Education*, p. 251.

30 Vives presented Henry VIII a copy dedicated to the king during his stay in England between May 1523 and November 1528.

31 Vives, op. cit., pp. 719, 723.

32 E. V. Arnold, *Roman Stoicism*, Cambridge, Cambridge University Press, 1911, pp. 408–36.

33 More, op. cit., p. 118; cf. Cicero, *De Officiis*, 1.11–14.

34 Pace regarded highly the role of education, especially the knowledge of many languages, in helping to ease international strife and prepare one for noble service as a diplomat/peacemaker. This position was expressed in his famous rejoinder to an aristocrat who, during a dinner conversation in 1517, confessed to Pace his complete disregard for 'book learning' and knowledge of foreign languages. R. Pace, *De Fructu*, Basil, 1517, preface cited in F. J. Furnivall (ed.) *Early English Meals and Manners*, EETS, orig. ser., no. 32, 1868, pp. xii–xiii. See also Russell, op. cit., pp. 15–16, 70–1.

35 *CSPSp*, 3: 572–3; *L&P*, 3(2): 1629; Russell, op. cit., pp. 55–6.

36 Pace, *Oration to Peace*, pp. 238–9; Silius, op. cit., 11.592–3. Pace frequently remarks fervently on the tremendous unity of Christian monarchs in support of this treaty, which has given him a 'secure hope' for perpetual peace (pp. 238–41).

37 Pace, *Oration to Peace*, p. 235. He also quotes Sallust here: '*nam concordia parvae res crescunt, discordia maxime dilabuntur* [for peace makes small states grow, while discord harms the greatest empires]'. Sallust, *Bellum Iurguthinum*, 10: 6.

38 D. Erasmus, *The Complaint of Peace*, W. J. Hirten (ed.), New York, Scholars' Facsimiles & Reprints, 1946, p. viii.

39 Erasmus, *Education*, pp. 205, 239; J. A. Fernandez, 'Erasmus on the just war', *JHI*, 1973, vol. 34, pp. 211–12.

40 Erasmus, *First Tome or Volume*, sigs 1ᵛ–2ʳ.

41 Ibid., sigs 1ʳ–7ᵛ

42 Pace, *Oration to Peace*, pp. 238–9.

43 Alistair Fox has argued recently that it is this 'transcendental bias of Erasmus's humanism, . . . insufficiently concerned with practicalities' that put off many English humanists who were most interested in translating 'wisdom into political action': A. Fox, 'English humanism and the body politic', in A. Fox and J. Guy, *Reassessing the Henrician Age*, Oxford, Basil Blackwell, 1986, pp. 50–1. This position is expanded upon by Fox in *Politics and Literature in the Reigns of Henry VII and Henry VIII*, Oxford, Basil Blackwell, 1989, p. 210.

44 Vives, op. cit., p. 719. The author makes this comment in his gloss on bk 19, ch. 11. Cf. Silius, op. cit., 11.592–3.

45 See T. Becon, *The New Policy of War*, in *Early Works*, J. Ayre (ed.), PS, vol. 2, 1843, pp. 249–50.

46 In discussing how ideas of law, liberty, authority and tradition underwent such a process during the development of resistance theory, Donald Kelley could have been talking just as easily about the problem of war, where likewise, 'as always large social conflicts were accompanied by struggles for language, and so the process of "politicization" exemplified by the Reformation was implied from the beginning in the arguments of the theologians and scholars': D. R. Kelley, 'Ideas of resistance before Elizabeth', in *The Historical Renaissance: New Essays on Tudor and Stuart Literature and Culture*, H. Dubrow and R. Strier (eds), Chicago, Ill., University of Chicago Press, 1988, p. 48.

47 Zwingli charged a friend in 1519 to 'seek out the pastors in your region and instruct them that they should be friends of peace and preach without ceasing about peace'. Quoted in J. T. Johnson, *The Quest for Peace: Three Moral Traditions in Western Cultural History*, Princeton, NJ, Princeton University Press, 1987, p. 149.

48 J. Calvin, *A Short Instruction for to Arme All Good Christian People Agaynst the Pestiferous Errours of the Common Secte of Anabaptistes*, J. Veron (trans.), London, Dumfrey Powell, 1548, sig. D2ᵛ; W. Tyndale, *Expositions of Scripture and Practice of Prelates*, H. Walter (ed.), PS, vol. 43, 1849, pp. 26–7; R. Bainton, *Christian Attitudes Toward War and Peace: A Historical Survey and Critical Re-evaluation*, New York, Abingdon Press, 1960, pp. 128–9.

49 J. R. Hale, *War and Society in Renaissance Europe, 1450–1620*, Baltimore, Md, Johns Hopkins University Press, 1985, pp. 36–7.

50 Tyndale, op. cit., p. 63; D. D. Smeeton, *Lollard Themes in the Reformation*

Theology of William Tyndale, Kirksville, Mo., Sixteenth Century Journal Publishers, 1986, p. 237. For Tyndale's exposure to and connection with Erasmian humanism, M. M. Knappen's *Tudor Puritanism*, Chicago, Ill., University of Chicago Press, 1939, especially pp. 3–30, is still very helpful.

51 Becon, op. cit., pp. 238, 244. Similar thoughts are expressed in a homily for Lent found in *Postilles or Homilies Vpon the Epistles and Gospels from Ester vntyll Trinite Sondaye*, R. Taverner (ed.), London, Richarde Bankes, 1540, STC 2967, sig. Z2^r.

52 *L&P*, 18(1): 804

53 G. J. Millar, *Tudor Mercenaries and Auxiliaries*, Charlottesville, Va, University Press of Virginia, 1980, pp. 66–8; G. R. Elton, *Reform and Reformation, 1509–1558*, Cambridge, Mass., Harvard University Press, 1977, pp. 304–6; R. B. Wernham, *Before the Armada: The Growth of English Foreign Policy 1485–1588*, New York, Norton, 1972, p. 154.

54 Hall, op. cit., vol. 2, p. 320. For the Council's even more direct linkage between the French and Scottish campaigns see G. Redworth, *In Defence of the Church Catholic: The Life of Stephen Gardiner*, Oxford, Basil Blackwell, 1990, p. 210.

55 Becon, op. cit., pp. vii–ix, xvii; D. S. Bailey, *Thomas Becon and the Reformation of the Church in England*, Edinburgh, Oliver & Boyd, 1952, pp. 18–22; Scarisbrick, op. cit., pp 434–5; C. S. L. Davies, 'The English people and war in the early sixteenth century', in A. C. Duke and C. A. Tamse (eds) *Britain and the Netherlands, Vol. VI: War and Society*, The Hague: Martinus Nijhoff, 1977, pp. 2–3.

56 *L&P*, 18(1): 606, 622, 754.

57 *Statutes and Ordynances for the Warre*, London, Thomas Berthelet, 1544, STC 9334, sig. A1^v; Scarisbrick, op. cit., p. 440; Millar, op. cit., pp. 66–8, 97, 127.

58 J. Guy, *Tudor England*, Oxford, Oxford University Press, 1988, pp. 190–2; C. Barnett, *Britain and her Army, 1509–1970*, London, Allen Lane, 1970, p. 15; Scarisbrick, op. cit., p. 448; Elton, op. cit., pp. 394–5.

59 *L&P*, 19(2): 489.

60 M. L. Bush, *The Government Policy of Protector Somerset*, Montreal, McGill-Queen's University Press, 1975, pp. 9–11.

61 '[to ordain the law of peace]: to be merciful to the conquered, and to keep the proud from waging war'. *Debellare* here is translated more literally and within its immediate literary context than the usual 'to beat down', 'subdue', or 'to tame in war'. Virgil, *The Aeneid*, bk 6, lines 852–3.

62 W. Patten, *The Expedition into Scotlande of . . . Edward, duke of Soomerset*, repr. in *Tudor Tracts 1532–1588*, A. F. Pollard (ed.), New York, Cooper Square, 1964, pp. 57–62.

63 E. Seymour, *An Epistle or Exhortacion, to Vnitie & Peace, Sent from the Lorde Protector, & Others the Kynges Moste Honorable Counsaill of England to the Nobilitie, Gentlemen and Commons, and Al Others the Inhabitauntes of the Realme of Scotlande*, London, Richard Grafton, 1548, STC 22268=9181, sigs A2^v–A8^r.

64 Bush's *The Government Policy of Protector Somerset* was the first study to suggest that Somerset's sympathy for enclosure restrictions and other reform efforts was part of a calculated plan to obtain the necessary support to wage war in Scotland. Since then, several leading Tudor scholars, including G. R. Elton (*Reform and Reformation, 1509–1558*) and J. Guy (*Tudor England*), have incorporated in some fashion this interpretation into their syntheses of

the period. For a concise look at the controversy from another convert, see G. J. R. Parry, 'Inventing "the good Duke" of Somerset', *JEccH*, 1989, vol. 40, pp. 370–80. Others, such as B. Bradshaw, in 'The Tudor commonwealth: reform and revision', *HJ*, 1979, vol. 22, pp. 455–76, and P. Williams, in *The Tudor Regime*, Oxford, Oxford University Press, 1979, without accepting A. F. Pollard's overly romantic portrait, remain more sparing in their criticism.

65 This current inability to take Somerset at face value is most recently observed in John Guy's declaration that 'seeking to appear virtuous and to be held in wide esteem, he [Somerset] courted mass popularity while sugar-coating his natural severity with talk of clemency and justice'. Guy, *Tudor England*, p. 201; Bush, op. cit., p. 5.

66 Paul Crowson goes so far as to say that 'Somerset had a genuine belief in Anglo-Scottish collaboration on the basis of the Treaty of Greenwich; he believed in equal partnership between the two countries and in the joint creation of a unified kingdom of Greater Britain': P. S. Crowson, *Tudor Foreign Policy*, New York, St Martin's Press, 1973, p. 169.

67 If we accept Ong's contention that 'when hostility becomes total, the most vicious namecalling is inadequate: speech is broken off entirely', then the fact that there was dialogue (not simply conditions) indicated hope for peace. Ong, op. cit., p. 193.

68 Davies, 'English people and war', pp. 3–4; Guy, op. cit., pp. 201–3; Crowson, op. cit., p. 39.

69 There is also evidence of significant popular dissatisfaction with both Edward's and Mary's wars against France, especially toward conscription. See P. Clark, *English Provincial Society from the Reformation to the Revolution: Religion, Politics and Society in Kent 1500–1640*, Hassocks, Harvester Press, 1977, especially pp. 72, 104; Elton, op. cit., pp. 394–5.

70 The best studies of Henry's final war with France are C. S. L. Davies, 'Supply services of English armed forces, 1509–1550', PhD diss., Oxford University, 1963; D. L. Potter, 'Diplomacy in the mid-sixteenth century: England and France, 1536–1550', PhD diss., Cambridge University, 1973; G. Redworth, *In Defence of the Church Catholic: The Life of Stephen Gardiner*, Oxford, Basil Blackwell, 1990, ch. 9; S. R. Gammon, *Statesman and Schemer: William, First Lord Paget, Tudor Minister*, Hamden, Conn., Archon Books, 1973.

71 Redworth, op. cit., pp. 210–12.

72 *CSPSp*, 7: 364; *L&P*, 19(1): 249.

73 G. R. Elton, 'Tudor government: the points of contact, part 3: the Court', *TRHS*, 5th ser., 1976, vol. 26, pp. 222–3, 226–7; Gunn, op. cit., pp. 44–7; Redworth, op. cit., pp. 217–18.

74 Redworth, op. cit., pp. 219–26; Potter, op. cit., pp. 50, 117–21.

75 *L&P*, 21(1): 71; D. L. Potter, 'Foreign policy in the age of the Reformation: French involvement in the Schmalkaldic War, 1544–1547', *HJ*, 1977, vol. 20, pp. 525–44.

76 This approach to the period has been seized most readily by 'new historicist' scholars who have rejected Tillyard's more unified and confident 'Elizabethan world picture'. For the best introduction to new historicism see J. E. Howard, 'The new historicism in Renaissance studies', *English Literary Renaissance*, 1986, vol. 16, pp. 3–33; also S. J. Greenblatt, *Renaissance Self-Fashioning, from More to Shakespeare*, Chicago, Ill., University of Chicago Press, 1980.

77 J. A. Muller, *Stephen Gardiner and the Tudor Reaction*, New York, Macmillan, 126; repr. Octagon Books, 1970, pp. 114–18.

78 Gardiner, op. cit., pp. 185–6.

79 Ibid., pp. 186–9.
80 Ibid., p. 189. Some movement by the French the next day raised Gardiner's hopes for peace once again. Sensing the dangerous sentiment inherent in the 13 November letter, in another one written to Paget the following day, he asked the recipient to burn it once it was read. Gardiner, op. cit., p. 191.
81 Redworth, op. cit., p. 230.
82 Muller, op. cit., pp. 117–20; Crowson, op. cit., p. 129.
83 In a strongly worded, anti-war, pro-peace letter to Somerset dated 28 February 1547, before his confinement, Winchester repeated Cicero's remark that any peace is preferable to the best war, and proclaimed the dire need for 'quyet, tranquilitie, unitie, and concord', especially during the new king's minority. Gardiner, op. cit., pp. 265–7.
84 Gunn, op. cit., pp. 44–7; W. K. Jordan, *Edward VI: The Young King*, Cambridge, Mass., Harvard University Press, 1968, pp. 230–1.
85 *L&P*, 21(1): 691, 763, 771, 831, 849, 855, 862, 891; Gammon, op. cit., pp. 103–7.
86 W. Paget, *The Letters of William, Lord Paget of Beaudesert, 1547–1563*, B. L. Beer and S. M. Jack (eds), C4S, 1974, vol. 13, pp. 30–1.
87 Ibid., p. 31.
88 Gammon, op. cit., pp. 169–72.
89 J. Strype, *Ecclesiastical Memorials*, Oxford, Clarendon Press, 1822, vol. 2, pt 2, p. 439.
90 Ibid.
91 Ibid., pp. 440–1.
92 Ibid. In other letters to Somerset and the Council, Paget makes similar comments on the disastrous nature of the present wars. See Paget, op. cit.: To Somerset, 2 February 1548–9; To Somerset and Council, 28 August 1549, also entitled 'A Discourse to the Duke of Somerset and Counsaill', pp. 24, 75–7.
93 Paget, op. cit., p. 98.
94 Even when Paget became a proponent of war as he did in 1556–7, he seemed interested in the long-term benefits of maintaining the Spanish alliance above all else. Relatively unconcerned with nationalistic glories, he conceived of war in the further interest of lasting peace, as a means to intimidate France and Scotland, preventing future wars, and for protecting commerce with the Low Countries. Through Paget's unique insight, war could be envisioned as a means for ushering in a secure peace. See Gammon, op. cit., pp. 191–2; D. M. Loades, *The Reign of Mary Tudor*, New York, St Martin's Press, 1979, pp. 393–407.
95 Hales' criticism of Tudor wars goes back at least as far as 1542, when he praised King Henry's 'tender care of his subjects not wasting their lives in war but providing that they may live in peace and quiet', *L&P*, 17, Appendix 1: 706.
96 J. Hales, *Defence of John Hales* (1548) n *A Discourse of the Common Weal of this Realm of England*, E. Lamond (ed.), Cambridge, Cambridge University Press, 1929, pp. lv, lxvii.
97 E. R. Adair, 'William Thomas: a forgotten clerk of the Privy Council', in *Tudor Studies*, R. W. Seton-Watson (ed.), New York, Russell & Russell, 1924; repr. 1970, pp. 141–4.
98 W. Thomas, *The Works of William Thomas, Clerk of the Privy Council in the Year 1549*, A. D'Aubant (ed.), London, J. Almon, 1774, pp. 147–8.
99 Ibid., pp. 148, 151–4.
100 Ibid., p. 180.

101 Ibid., pp. 180–91.
102 Ibid., p. 193.
103 Pocock, op. cit., p. 21.
104 Hale, op. cit., p. 97.
105 Pocock, op. cit., p. 25.
106 Ibid., p. 29.

5

Foundations of political economy: the new moral philosophy of Sir Thomas Smith

Neal Wood

Fortune has not altogether favoured Sir Thomas Smith (1513–77). While he held important posts, he never attained the high office commensurable with his exceptional talents, and only recently has it been convincingly demonstrated that he and not John Hales was the author of *A Discourse of the Commonweal of This Realm of England*.[1] On the basis of this masterful treatment, he can be called the founder of the science of political economy, to become perhaps Britain's outstanding contribution to social history.[2] Nothing quite like the volume had appeared prior to Bodin in English or continental thought. The traditional economic concerns of scholasticism seem by comparison narrow and formalistic. Possible intellectual precedents had been established by Oresme, Carafa, Molinaeus, and the School of Salamanca, but the *Discourse* bears Smith's own unique humanistic stamp.[3] A few English economic pamphlets of the preceding hundred years may have shaped his ideas, as possibly did the unusual interest in economic affairs of previous English political thinkers like Fortescue, Dudley and More.[4] Among Smith's famous continental contemporaries, however, one searches in vain for a counterpart to the searching economic analysis of the *Discourse*, for instance, in the works of Machiavelli and Guicciardini, in Claude de Seyssel's *The Monarchy of France* (1515). Philippe de Commyne's *Memoires* (1524, 1528), Erasmus' *Institutio Principis Christiani* (1516) and Juan Luis Vives's *On Education* (1531).[5] In France, at any rate, before the second half of the century little about social and economic conditions can be found except in cahiers, laws and edicts.[6]

One can only conclude that Smith in the *Discourse* is a true pioneer, an evaluation admitted by historians of economic thought. A 'remarkable' book is the verdict of Eli Hecksher, 'the first work representing, on the whole, the outlook of a mature mercantilism'.[7] In the opinion of George Unwin the *Discourse* was 'the most advanced statement of economic thought in Tudor England'.[8] Somewhat less laudatory is Schumpeter's remark that 'most of it was sound common sense', and that 'in its impli-

140

cations, it approaches the status of analytic work'.[9] More generous is Hutchison's appraisal that Smith's outlook was a harbinger of an independent subject of economics, separated from philosophical and moral concerns.[10] Nevertheless, despite these favourable evaluations, the full measure of Smith's accomplishment remains to be taken.

Smith's long and distinguished career as academician and man of action was ideal preparation for his intellectual endeavours. Of humble agrarian origins, he went up to Queens' College, Cambridge, where after his degree he remained there as a fellow, gaining a reputation as a brilliant classicist, accomplished orator and skilful teacher. Appointed the first Regius Professor of Civil Law in 1540, he became Vice-Chancellor of the University in 1543, and Provost of Eton College in 1547. On the death of Henry VIII, Smith entered Parliament, holding his seat during the successive reigns of Edward VI, Mary and Elizabeth. Principal Secretary of State from 1547 to 1549 under Somerset and knighted in 1548, he specialized in finance and economics, and became known as an expert in the field. He was Elizabeth's ambassador to France from 1562 to 1566 and again in 1572 when he negotiated the treaty of Blois. Close friend of William Cecil and Francis Walsingham, he entered the Privy Council in 1571, and was named Principal Secretary of State the next year, holding the position until 1576, the year before his fatal illness and death.

Proficient in six languages, Smith found time amid his many activities to write a variety of works, although only three were published during his lifetime: treatises in 1542 on a new pronunciation of Greek and on English orthography, and in 1571 a tract publicizing a cherished project for the colonization of Ireland.[11] In addition, he produced in 1554 an important economic memorandum, 'For the Understanding of the Exchange', composed verse, translated the Psalms, penned a dialogue in 1561 on the perils of Queen Elizabeth's spinsterhood, and in 1562 completed a monograph, *The Wages of a Roman Footsoldier*.[12] His fame now rests upon the *Discourse* (1581) and *De Republica Anglorum* (1583), both published posthumously.

The subsequent argument that with the *Discourse* Smith in the conventional guise of 'moral philosophy' in fact launches a new mode of social and political discourse, that of political economy, will proceed in a number of stages. Initially, consideration will be given to the style and form of the work, emphasizing some characteristics that may signal its novelty. Second, attention will be given to his notion of human nature which informs so much of his economic thought. Next his conception of methodology and economy will be examined. An attempt will then be made to relate some aspects of the doctrine of the *Discourse* to the broad outlook of *Republica*. Finally, the question will be briefly addressed as to what there was about Smith's historical context (apart from the inherited realm of traditional ideas and concepts) that may have spurred him on in thinking as he did.

Written by Smith in July–September 1549 at Eton during 'some vacation from other business', the *Discourse* was published anonymously and posthumously by 'W. S.', probably his nephew William Smith, who dedicated it to Queen Elizabeth.[13] 'Vacation from some other business' presumably refers to his enforced retirement from government because of his opposition to Somerset's policy of debasement. Perturbed by the appalling economic situation and increasing disorders of the realm – most notably Kett's uprising in East Anglia and the Western Rebellion in Cornwall and Devon – Smith wrote to Cecil on 19 July 1549 of the 'miserable estate, our commonwealth', and evidently intended the manuscript (to help remedy Somerset's disastrous economic programme) for Cecil's eyes only.[14] Circulated in manuscript before publication, the 1581 edition has been reprinted four times, together with four other versions, including that of Mary Dewar. It is a relatively short work, something over forty thousand words, written in the form of a three-part dialogue. The *Discourse* is a treatise on inflation – the so-called 'dearth' – its causes and remedies. Smith opens by explaining that he is responding to 'the manifold complaints of men touching the decay of this Commonweal that we be in, moved more at this present than of a long time past has been heard'.[15] He proposes to do so by describing the 'griefs', mainly in respect to mounting prices, that give rise to these complaints by identifying their causes and by proposals for reform, allotting the three parts of the dialogue to each of the topics.[16]

Smith says at the outset that he intends the work to be part of 'Moral Philosophy' since it pertains to the 'policy or good government of a Commonweal'.[17] Later he notes that moral philosophy is devoted to the proper ethical guidance of individual and family, and to 'how a city or realm or any other Commonweal should be well ordered and governed in time of peace and also war'.[18] He sees the *Discourse* as a modest effort in the spirit of Plato's ideal of the philosopher-king to apply knowledge to the problems of government, and in doing so he thus continues the traditional intellectual preoccupation with the question of counsel.[19] Nothing, however, could be so far removed as the *Discourse* is from either the intention of Plato or the conventional understanding of the nature of moral philosophy. The ordering of state and society so as to create the proper conditions for the realization of the morally virtuous life was one of the commonly accepted goals of moral philosophy, exemplified during the Middle Ages and Renaissance by the popular mirror of princes' literature. In a way Smith shatters this mode of discourse. He may occasionally pay lip-service to moral concerns, but makes no reference to the education of the prince or the structure of his rule, focusing instead upon how governmental policy can best handle deteriorating economic conditions.

While 'commonweal' or state figures in the title, it is used infrequently in the text.[20] Any idea of the state in the *Discourse* seems at least in part to be absorbed by an elementary notion of the economy. Politics, indeed, appears to be all but reduced to economics and the manipulation of the economy by government for the advancement of the common interest defined by the people in their parliament.

Eschewing moralizing rhetoric, Smith in hardheaded and realistic fashion presents an impressive array of economic facts and figures. His use of statistics is limited by the scanty and inaccurate data available and is often more confusing than helpful to the modern reader. Nevertheless, the grounding of his argument in empirical, quantitive fact marks a new and distinctive approach, possibly reflecting the previous English penchant for collecting data in municipal census, inquests, Royal Commission reports, and economic pamphlets. Besides his empiricism, he is eminently common-sensical, writing in ordinary language about complex subjects with considerable clarity. Smith is never an impassioned moralizer like so many of his contemporaries. Always matter of fact, he is seldom given to exaggerated statement. He is the first to admit that the cause of current problems is the individualistic drive for money, power and status. But he accepts this, refraining from utopianism or a call for spiritual rejuvenation. Smith is the dispassionate recorder of observable behaviour, the investigator of its causes with the aim of designing policies for the restoration of unity and order to the state. He does not propose sweeping governmental reforms, nor does he inculpate specific social groupings for current troubles. Responsibility for the ills of England seems to lie less with individuals than with impersonal economic forces. Not so much that no one is blameless, but all are in some sense victims, if unwitting ones, of the inexorable dynamic of the economy. Displaying no special nostalgia for the good old days, Smith looks to the future convinced that it can be moulded by men seizing the initiative and acting positively, constructively, and rationally, instead of passively responding and succumbing to the vagaries of fortune.

If Smith has thus transformed the common meaning of moral philosophy, his employment of the conventional dialogue form may also indicate something of the novelty of the enterprise. His use of the dialogue for a technical subject – even for a memorandum of economic advice – was not extraordinary. The unique character of Smith's dialogue is in its *dramatis personae*. They consist of five active participants: a knight, merchant, doctor of divinity, husbandman and craftsman. Smith presents a conclave of a single learned individual and 'members of every estate', who in congenial debate will arrive at the truth of the matters under discussion.[21] For a distinguished Cambridge scholar, Essex landlord and man of affairs to compose a dialogue on 'moral philosophy' whose cast includes two gentlemen and three practical men of the lower orders, all making

positive contributions to the conversation, is uncommon. It seems to be
an approach with little precedent in previous intellectual dialogues and
possibly reflects the radical character of the work. Smith himself poses as
a mere *rapporteur* who 'will declare unto you what communication a
knight told me was between him and certain other persons of late about
this matter', the troubles besetting England.[22] We have in effect the record
of the meeting of a 'dining society' of four stalwarts of the local community, and an outsider in the person of the doctor, spending a lively
evening over venison pasty and claret. The knight, a landlord and Justice
of the Peace, has spent the day with other justices of the county testifying
before a royal commission on enclosures. After the rigours of the meeting,
he is taking refreshment with 'an honest husbandman whom for his hon-
esty and good discretion I loved very well'.[23] Perhaps he is a tenant of
the knight, obviously a middling farmer. The scene may be Saffron
Walden, Essex, where Smith was born and near which he lived. They are
joined by the merchant, 'a man of good estimation and substance', and
then by Doctor Pandotheus (to worship or stretch out to God), the only
one mentioned by name.[24] He is a highly respected theologian, probably
a Cambridge don, who voices Smith's own views, taking the leading role
in the conversation, summarizing points and drawing conclusions. The last
participant is a master craftsman, a capper or manufacturer of caps, like
the others a pillar of the community, 'an honest man'.[25] Possibly for the
first time in English history, for that matter in world history, we have in
literary form a symposium of those whose vital economic interests are
threatened by the ills of their country: representatives of the gentry and
clergy, and lower-class spokesmen for the mercantile, agricultural and
manufacturing sectors.

A final formal characteristic of the dialogue deserves comment. Although
Smith is obviously at ease with the classics, he does not rely excessively
upon them, nor is overburdened by their authority. Except for single
passing references to Erasmus and 'Utopia', no modern authors or works
are cited.[26] Plato, Aristotle and Cicero are the most frequent ancient
sources. The 'divine philosopher', Plato, is mentioned (along with Cicero)
for perceiving that we are not born to ourselves alone, praised for his
idea of the fusion of knowledge and political power symbolized by the
philosopher-king, and upheld for his notion that all are covetous of
money.[27] Aristotle, 'the sharpest philosopher of wit that ever was', is
named in only four passages for his insight that coinage was devised
simply to be a convenient means of exchange.[28] 'That wise and politic
Senator' and 'great clerk', Cicero, is credited with holding that a state is
held together by reward and punishment, and that no law can satisfy
everyone, but at best should be advantageous to most and hurt fewest.[29]
Among other ancients cited, none significantly, are Columella, Vegetius,
Vitruvius, Pythagorus, Solon, Pliny, Pomponius Mela, Cato and Polyd-

orus.[30] Smith, therefore, is his own man. He adheres to literary convention by paying lip-service to the ancients as seals of approval for certain points, but is not substantively indebted to them. This admirable independence of mind may suggest an awareness of the new approach to moral philosophy that he is inaugurating.

Smith's economic analysis and recommendations seem to rest upon his conception of man. Although he never systematically treats human nature, saying relatively little about it, the few remarks on the subject in the *Discourse* and *De Republica Anglorum* leave the reader with few doubts about his viewpoint. At the beginning of the *Discourse*, citing Cicero (presumably *De officiis*) that we are not created for ourselves alone, but for the benefit of our country, parents, kin, friends and neighbours, Smith concludes that of all living creatures we are most like God and have a natural potential for doing good.[31] Despite this human potentiality, the astute and practical Smith knows that in reality it is seldom realized. Tarnished by selfishness, he writes in *Republica*, man is a frail vessel who cannot hold absolute and uncontrolled power 'without swelling into too much pride and insolence'.[32] Physically

> the nature of man is never to stand still in one maner of estate, but to grow from the lesse to the more, and so to decay from the more againe to the lesse, till it come to the fatall end and destruction, with many turnes and turmoyles of sicknesse and recovering, seldom standing in perfect health.[33]

Men are of such evil that they must always war among themselves. Their chief aim in society and state is 'honour and profitt';[34] in any undertaking, according to the *Discourse*, each seeks to enhance his advantage and increase his profit.[35] Buying cheap and selling dear seems to be a behavioural law of man's fallen nature.[36] All are naturally avaricious and will follow the path promising the greatest remuneration. By his fallen nature man is weak and selfish, ambitious, avaricious and lustful, an egoist with little concern for the good of others. These few passages indicating Smith's view of human nature would have been endorsed by most of his contemporaries.

Despite his apparent acceptance of the Christian position, Smith is saying something more. Since humans are fundamentally egoists who cannot be changed, we must make the best of it, and instead of trying futilely to remould the imperfect human raw material, use that very selfishness for the welfare of all. 'Can we devise', Smith queries rhetorically, 'that all covetousness may be taken from men?'[37] 'No, no more', he replies, 'than we can make men be without ire, without gladness, without fear, and without all affections. What then? We must take away from men the occasion of their covetousness in this part.'

He illustrates his view by reference to enclosure. Smith thinks that the rural decay of England and the threat of popular uprisings can be ended not by prohibiting enclosure, to which so many of the current ills are traceable, but by prudent governmental policies which attempt to resolve the crucial problem of overspecialization in livestock production and the decline of arable and diversified farming. He offers a defence of enclosure, as Starkey had previously done, providing the process is moderate and rational, regulated by the state.[38] Pandotheus takes up the knight's point that the wealthiest counties (Essex, Kent, Devon) are those with most enclosures and that farming is better done on individual holdings than on common ones, by stating that he is not opposed to all enclosure. If arable is not converted into pasture as part of enclosure, and not done forcibly and violently, but gradually with the approval of the commoners concerned, each receiving his due share of the enclosed land, the result may benefit all.

The vital problem for Smith is not so much enclosure *per se*, as how to restrain naturally profit-seeking men from converting arable to pasture for grazing, which in the light of existing market conditions is obviously the most lucrative and sensible course of action. Considering the greed of men, which in no practical way can be eliminated, the best must be made of human nature by measures for discouraging the conversion of arable to pasture and the profit-seeking fixation with production of livestock. Governmental intervention and regulation must assure that tillage is as profitable as grazing. This can be accomplished in several ways.[39] The farmer who relies on the cultivation of arable, the producer of corn for instance, should be as free to sell his commodities at all times and in all places, at home and abroad, as are all other producers, for example, graziers. Wool must be subject to the same export restrictions as corn, and duties on raw wool increased. If necessary, grazing land must be more heavily taxed than arable. Once the profit from arable is widely perceived from these measures to be as much as from pasture and grazing, much of the enclosed land converted to pasture will be reconverted to arable, and wasteland will be fully exploited for cultivation.[40]

Thus rather than attempting the remodelling of man, the lover of lucre, that very love must be manipulated so as to encourage farmers to return to the plough. Governmental policies and laws should aim at canalizing the pursuit of narrow self-interest for the good of the whole society. Far from being an inherently destructive force, self-interest is the dynamic of the economy, which when properly utilized by government can advance the common interest. Smith takes pains to explain the principles to be followed by government in the matter:

> We must understand also that all things that should be done in a
> Commonweal be not to be forced, or to be constrained by the

straight penalties of the law, but some so and some other by allurement and rewards rather. For what law can compel men to be industrious in travail and labor of his body or studious to learn any science or knowledge of the mind? To these things men may well be provoked, encouraged, and allured as if they that be industrious and painful be rewarded well for their pains and be suffered to take gains and wealth as reward for their labors. . . . Take these rewards from them and go about to compel them by laws thereto, what man will plow or dig the ground or exercise any manual art where is any pain? Or who will adventure overseas for any merchandise? Or use any faculty wherein any peril or danger should be, seeing his reward shall be no more than his that sits still?[41]

After this pronouncement, Smith cites a letter of Cicero to Atticus stipulating that the state is maintained by reward and pain.[42] Citizens should be moved to do good by reward and abstain from evil by pain.

Smith's intellectual posture, resulting perhaps from his own practical experience as administrator and public official and possibly from his reading of Machiavelli, is essentially utilitarian. Man, ever striving for happiness, seeks to enhance pleasure and reduce pain. Human pleasure (and thus happiness), however, as conceived by Smith, depends primarily upon increase of profits and decrease of monetary losses. He offers a rudimentary model of economic man, a highly acquisitive, individualistic being who acts rationally in choosing the most efficient means of maximizing profits and minimizing losses. This profit-orientated behaviour not only drives the economy, but also enables the government to utilize it for the common interest. Anticipating Bernard Mandeville by a century and a half, Smith clearly recognizes that 'private vices' yield 'public benefits' only when mediated by government.[43] Governmental policy and law from Smith's perspective can be effective instruments of social control only when they are premised on this fact of human nature, advancing human pleasure and happiness by rewarding socially useful types of action and causing citizens to avoid pain resulting from penalties for the violation of legal prohibitions. It must be made more profitable and pleasurable for subjects to comply with the law and much less so for a lack of compliance. Laws, however, cannot realistically be framed that will inconvenience no one.[44] Their aim, instead, should be the profit and pleasure of the greatest number, and the disadvantage and pain of the fewest. The guiding assumption of policy and law-making, therefore, should be the greatest happiness of the greatest number, in terms of the felt pleasures of profitability of the many and pains or monetary losses of the fewest, achieved through the legal application of reward and punishment.

Smith, of course, does not express his views in this full utilitarian manner, but such appears to be the direction he is taking, one which becomes the course of future political economy. If the economy is a mechanism, as he suggests, then its prime motive force is precisely those human passions aiming at pleasure, and hence happiness, through increasing profits and decreasing losses, by producing more and cutting costs, and by buying cheap and selling dear in the market. A contemporary of the 'Commonwealthmen', Smith's position could not be more different from theirs, although beginning with similar assumptions about human nature. His outlook is far removed from the uncompromising denunciation of human greed and their call for religious and spiritual renewal. While they are doctors of the soul, Smith is the physician of the body politic who accepts the soul for what it is. Smith's response to them is that unfortunately we must put up with the unregenerate nature of human egoism, which if history has any lessons, is a universal constant. If, however, we are to survive in peace and prosperity, living the kind of civilized life we have constructed, in contrast to the misery and backwardness of most of the world, then this is the only way, assigning to responsible, limited government the onerous and complex task of guiding us.

Notwithstanding his advocacy of economic individualism, Smith does not argue that free vent given to the pursuit of personal gain by all will automatically produce the common good. He is not an early advocate of the doctrine of the natural harmony of interests. That conception is presented in the *Discourse* only to be discarded. In an exchange between the knight and Pandotheus the former reasons that a commonwealth is little more than an atomistic collection of individuals, and what is profitable for one is profitable for all, to the advantage of the entire state.[45] One should always strive to promote whatever commodity is produced, for such behaviour can only be to the common interest. Smith in the guise of Pandotheus admits his agreement with much of this classic brief for the natural harmony of interests, possibly one of the first in social discourse. But he would make the qualification that individuals should 'not purchase themselves profit by that which may be hurtful to others'.[46] The common interest depends upon the advancement of our own commodities as much as possible, providing it does not hinder others in promoting their commodities.[47] Were all men, for example, to follow the lead of the enclosers and convert arable to pasture, the result would be disastrous: 'What should ensue but a mere solitude and utter desolation of the whole realm, furnished only with sheep and shepherds instead of good men?'[48] The questions raised by much of the discussion are who shall determine whether the actions of the profit-orientated individual are harmful to others, and who is to take the measures necessary to curtail such abuses? From subsequent remarks, it appears that Smith thinks that men, as pursuers of self-interest, should be encouraged to seek their own advantage, but always within the limiting framework of the common interest.[49] Society may well be an arena of competing social atoms, but government should serve as arbiter of the common interest, as defined by the people in their Parliament, intervening when necessary through prudent policies and laws to secure the welfare of the whole. Instead of the natural harmony of interests, Smith clearly favours an artificial harmony of interests, with government having the function of managing egoistic individualism for the public welfare. The profit motive is the motor of society, but government must be its regulator for the benefit of all.

Smith's attitude toward human nature is further illustrated by his constant anxiety over insurrection to which economic considerations prove so central. Acknowledging and hopeful of making the best of the fallen nature of man, he wishes to capitalize on both its strengths and weaknesses for the sake of reforming and strengthening the state. The *Discourse* was begun in the summer of 1549 during the uprisings in the east and south-west. These serious outbreaks must have weighed heavily on his mind as he was writing, and he returns time and again to the spectre of civil disorder. There is a constant stream of references to the disturbances and their possibility of continuing in the future unless reform becomes the order of the day.[50] Yet he never expresses the moral outrage of the Commonwealthmen for the predicament of the rebels, nor their stern and unrelenting admonitions of all parties to the turmoils. Rather, he takes a matter-of-fact view of the troubles, trying to show how they have been provoked, and how they can best be prevented from recurring.

Smith is basically a social environmentalist who subscribes to the age-old doctrine of human malleability so dear to the ancients and to Renaissance thinkers like Machiavelli, Pico, Erasmus, Vives and More. All of us, according to the doctrine, are in varying degrees plastic creatures whose natures – at least up to a point – can be shaped by upbringing and education, by social, political and legal institutions and arrangements. What, Smith essentially asks, do we expect other than seditious conflict and desperate protest in light of the dire straits of many commoners, their impoverishment, unemployment, and homelessness due to enclosure and the decline of manufactures in decaying towns, all discontents fuelled by sectarian religious zeal? Covetousness and pride may be the origin of the upheavals, but this is no time, he implies, for righteous condemnation and pleas for moral regeneration. Material improvement in town and country and an end to religious controversy, brought about by cool and prudent heads, are the only antidote for the poisons of the commonwealth. Certainly the ruthless and repressive measures of the French, should not be emulated.[51] Instead every effort should be made to reduce the likelihood of civil disorder through a rational assessment of the situation and rational policies of reform.

Smith's procedure in the second part, extending into the third, is to 'discuss and search what should be the causes of the said common and universal dearth [inflation] of all things'.[52] After rejecting various explanations, Pandotheus concludes that the 'chief cause of all this dearth of things and of the manifest impoverishment of this realm . . . is, the debasing or rather corrupting of our own coin and treasure', later repeating that the debasement of the coinage is the 'chief and principal cause of this universal dearth'.[53] Quoting Aristotle's axiom, *Sublata causa tollitur effectus*, translated as 'the removal of the principal cause takes away the effect', Smith stresses the crucial practical consequences of his method.[54] If the prime cause of inflation can be discovered and defined, then the effects can be corrected by removing that cause. In the search for the fundamental cause of inflation, he warns that 'because there may be divers causes of one thing and yet but one principal cause that brings forth the thing to pass, let us seek out that cause, omitting all the mean causes which are driven forward by the original cause'.[55] Several analogies are then employed to illustrate that secondary causes should not be confused with the basic cause. Throughout he resorts to the Aristotelian vocabulary of efficient, formal and material causes. The most telling and certainly the most original of the analogies to illuminate the idea of a primary cause as differentiated from secondary causes is drawn from mechanics: 'as in a clock there may be many wheels yet the first wheel being stirred it drives the next, and that the third, and so forth until the last that moves the instrument that strikes the clock'.[56]

Before discussing the truly innovative quality of Smith's clock simile, his economic argument must be summarized. He lists various common explanations of the cause of inflation: high prices charged by tenant farmers for their commodities, excessive rents set by landlords, enclosure and conversion of arable to pasture, and alteration of the value of coinage.[57] Smith admits that all these accompany the inflation amidst not a shortage, but a plentiful supply of goods. Nevertheless, this is no proof that these developments are the cause of inflation. The familiar story of Tenterden steeple and the sanding of the nearby harbour, whose source was said to be Thomas More, and was used by Hugh Latimer to absolve preachers from responsibility for the recent civil disorders, is cited by Smith to support his own reasoning.[58] The building of the steeple had nothing to do with the sanding of the harbour, he points out, although the two occurrences were coeval. The farmers' mark-up of food prices, he continues, is due to the increase in rents, which landlords are compelled to charge because of the inflated cost of commodities. Landlords are thus forced to enclose land, reduce their labour costs and enhance profits by the conversion of arable to pasture. 'Thus', Smith maintains, again relying on the clock analogy, 'one thing hangs upon another and sets forward one another but first of all is the chief cause of all this circular motion and impulsion'.[59]

His initial attempt to account for the 'circular motion' or flow of economic phenomena in the 1549 draft is that the debasement of the coinage is the 'first original cause' of the inflation.[60] He is forced, however, because of events since 1549, to qualify this explanation in his revision of the 1549 draft (probably in 1576, the year before his death) for posthumous publication in 1581.[61] The knight in the new version asks why it is that inflation still remains even after the coinage has been restored to its original value.[62] To which Pandotheus replies that while the price spiral in the first instance was caused by the debasement of the coinage, 'two special causes' account for the continuation of inflation even after the renewal of the value of the coinage.[63] One is the rack-renting of landlords in response to the general increase in prices following debasement, compelling farmers to contribute to inflation by their high food charges. A second 'special cause', Smith contends, probably influenced by reading Bodin's *Résponse au Paradoxe de Monsieur de Malestroit* (1568), is the recent influx of gold and treasure from the new world.

Smith's clock analogy likening economic life to a mechanism of interdependent constituents with a prime mover whose motion is transferred to every other part, each responding to the movement of the other, is remarkable.[64] Although the mechanical clock dates back to the thirteenth century, only in the fifteenth century were portable clocks made possible by the invention of the coil spring.[65] By the sixteenth century domestic clocks, still fairly crude by modern standards, were relatively common, too expensive, however, for any but affluent households. Hans Holbein's drawing of 1526, 'Sir Thomas More and the family', preparatory to his painting, now unfortunately lost, shows that the More ménage possessed a clock.[66] Likewise Smith may have had one at home or in his study at Eton where he penned the *Discourse*. So it is perhaps not surprising that he should use the clockwork comparison to explain the circular movement of the economy. No one before seems to have employed the analogy to describe the economic operations of society.[67] The frequency of its subsequent use in this manner is unclear, but two centuries after Smith, Sir James Steuart in his *Inquiry into the Principles of Political Oeconomy* (1767) compares the 'modern economy' to a watch.[68]

The implications of Smith's clock analogy are momentous. For he is apparently striving to express the view that the diverse economic phenomena of a state operate as an integral whole, possessing at least for analytic purposes an autonomy from the rest of state and society. In this sense he can be said to have discovered the economy as distinct from the rest of society. Like a clock the economy is an equilibrium of moving parts, each part transmitting motion originating in the prime mover to another part in a dynamic circular process or flow of interaction and interdependence. Once the motion of the prime mover becomes defective, at least by the logic of the analogy, the defect is passed on to other parts of the economic mechanism. As in the case of a clock, the circular economic motion can be adjusted and corrected, but only by experts, or such is the implication of Smith's conception. Informed governmental policy devised by specialists can adjust the economic mechanism just as master craftsmen repair clocks. Ignorant tampering with either mechanism will simply compound the difficulties. Moral philosophy for Smith is concerned with policies for the well-ordering of the commonwealth. Since the state's primary objective in his view is the economic well-being of all, he has in effect made economics the essence of moral philosophy, transmuting it into political economy, an intellectual step of the first magnitude.

Not only is Smith struggling to delineate the distinctive realm of the economy, but also to show that the economic mechanism is not confined to a specific state. Once more Smith seems to be among the first, after the 'Libell of Englische Policye' and Clement Armstrong, to perceive that the economic mechanism transcends state boundaries, interacting with other economies.[69] A national economy is an integral component of the international economy. Plato, Aristotle and the scholastics fully recognized that the social division of labour was an important foundation of the state. Smith, however, realizes that the social division of labour of one state cannot be divorced from that of other states. According to the divine plan for mankind, he asserts, no country is capable of producing all the commodities required for its own use. What one country lacks, another is capable of producing, and there is a year by year variation in the needs of one, and the ability of others to supply those needs. Each nation, therefore, requires the assistance of others in making up its deficiencies. Through the ensuing mutual aid in the form of exchange of goods 'love and society . . . grow amongst men all the more'. Although

> God is bountiful unto us and sends us many great commodities, yet we could not live without the commodities of others. And for example, of iron and salt though we have competently thereof, yet we have not the third part to suffice the realm; and that can in no wise be spared if we will occupy husbandry. Then tar, rosin, pitch, oil, steel, we have none at all; as for wines, spices, linen, cloth, silks, and collars, though we might live so–so without them, yet far from any civility should it be.[70]

Again, he emphasizes that no country can lead an isolated economic existence, and set its prices at will in disregard of prices elsewhere:

> but since we must have need of other and they of us, we must frame out things not after our own fantasies but to follow the *common market of all the world*, and we may not set the price of things at our pleasure but follow the price of the *universal market of the world*.[71]

Rejecting the ideal of economic autarky, part of the notion of self-sufficiency so beloved by the ancients, Smith offers a justification for the pursuit of international commerce. He envisages the national economic clockwork as part of the mechanism of an international economy character-ized by constant flux and transformation. Any change in production, the national market, the price mechanism and the value of coinage cannot be made unilaterally, but always within the totality of 'the common market of all the world'.[72] Reciprocal economic relationships involving all the complexities of the international trade that has become imperative for advanced nations mean that national economic policy can never occur in isolation. Indeed for Smith this is a sure sign of the high level of European civilization. Such a situation redounds to the good of all concerned, he suggests, since a rationally organized commerce among nations will draw them more closely together, tightening the mutual bonds of friendship. The implication is that such commercial interdependence appreciably con-tributes to and strengthens international stability, order and peace. Smith has anticipated one of the hallmarks of eighteenth- and nineteenth-century political economy for which international trade is conducive to universal peace; giving rise to goodwill and refinement of manners among nations.[73] In his opinion the common interest of the English cannot in the final analysis be considered apart from the larger context of the common interest of the international community.

By drawing a parallel between the state and the household or family in his discussion of economic matters, Smith also is doing something of significance. His use of it does not contradict, but rather complements, his conception of the interdependence of national economies. While he never relates the two ideas, his reasoning might be that just as households are economically interdependent, so are states. Smith is not the first to compare the state to a household, nor is he the first to utilize the analogy for economic argumentation, but he seems to be the first to use it exten-sively in this way to make a number of major points. He may have been familiar with the passage in *The Education of a Christian Prince*, where Erasmus maintains that the attitude of the prince in respect to economic matters should be like a 'good *paterfamilias* towards his household', a kingdom being little more than a 'great family'.[74]

The analogy is employed by Smith in order to articulate some basic economic precepts. He never explicitly maintains that the state is like a household, sometimes only comparing the proper action of the state to that of a prudent farmer. His parallels between state and household, none the less, are too noticeable to be discounted. Following Aristotle, in *Republica* Smith sees the origins of the first state in the patriarchal house-hold, and in general the rule of the family as being similar to the govern-ment of existing polities: the aristocratic regime of the parents, and the democracy prevailing among their children.[75] But in the *Discourse* he implies that the state is the household in macrocosm by his comparisons of the economic life of each. First, England should not retain all commodities produced at home, but sell them abroad to be able to import needed goods, being sure to export more than is imported.[76] So the prudent farmer, dependent solely on the revenue from his husbandry, should not buy more than he sells in the market. Second, in arguing that coinage in a state is simply a medium of exchange allowing for easy and efficient receipt for surpluses and hence the power to purchase goods needed and in short supply, Smith points out that a farmer, instead of risking the spoilage of a hoarded surplus of grain, can exchange it for a commodity like money that will not spoil, and that can be used at any time to supply his wants.[77] Third, a ruler should not discourage an increase in population just because many subjects are more difficult to govern than a few.[78] No more should the master of a household reduce the number of his employees or sell his land because of the trouble entailed in managing large numbers of workers or vast acreage. In both cases the lesson is to employ as many people as possible in useful activity instead of depriving them of jobs. Finally, in commonwealth as well as household, the more people set to work, the greater profits for their respective heads.[79] It is significant that in these examples Smith is dealing with some urgent economic problems of the age: balance of trade, coinage, population and employment.

After Smith the household-state similarity comes to the fore in reference to economic questions, culminating in the conception of 'political economy'. Writing in 1576 in his *Six Books of the Commonwealth*, Bodin also notes the origins of the state in the household, claiming that it is the archetype of successful government.[80] Both household and state seek to acquire goods to provide for the prosperity of their members, and in each prudent management depends upon a single all-powerful ruler. The absolute sovereign is the manager of the public economy for the welfare of his subjects. From Bodin's analogy several salient economic conclusions follow. If the king heads a household writ large, the promotion of the public interest is essentially to his advantage. Therefore, the ruler should take suitable measures to encourage production, expand exports and reduce imports, just as the wise household head should increase revenues over expenditures. In keeping with this reasoning, Gerrard de Malynes in 1601 declares that 'a common wealth is nothing but a household or family', and hence the prince like a shrewd householder should strive to secure a favourable balance of trade.[81] Somewhat later, Antoine de Montchrétien, relying on the household-state simile, is the first to use 'political economy' in the title of a book: *Traicté de l'oeconomie politique* (1615).[82] In doing so he is applying the Greek, *oeconomia*, or science of household management, to the state, conceiving of it as the great household, the locus of economic production and exchange supervised by the royal *paterfamilias*.

Even in later pre-classical political economy the household–state analogy proves useful for illustrative purposes.[83]

A final trait of the *Discourse* may be relevant to our thesis that Smith founded political economy. In the Ford Lectures of 1975, Joan Thirsk suggests that he, long before Defoe's *Essay on Projects* (1692–3), was among the first to be preoccupied with 'projects', thus foreshadowing the growing interest of the late-seventeenth-century political economists.[84] She defines project as 'a practical scheme for exploiting material things . . . capable of being realized through industry and ingenuity'.[85] Smith, some of his contemporaries, and his successors, whether enterprising businessmen or theoreticians, increasingly devoted their energies to the question of turning out in manufacturing and agriculture a growing variety of consumer goods ranging, for example, from luxuries (silks, laces, carpets, tapestries, dyes) and 'trifles' (looking and drinking glasses, brooches, cards, tennis balls, pins, needles) to necessities (oil, salt, pitch, tar, flax, rosin, steel and iron, tools).[86] Production of this kind would prevent the drain of English financial resources for the costly import of these and similar commodities, create sorely needed employment at home, and open up seemingly limitless opportunities for investment and profit-making. Smith and William Cecil were evidently the leading projectors in governmental service.[87] So over a century earlier than Defoe's dating of the beginning of the 'Age of Projects' as 1680, Smith pointed the way to be taken by inventive entrepreneurs and political economists.[88]

Among the major features of the *Discourse* are what amounts to a secular and amoral conception of the state, largely subsumed under an embryonic notion of the economy, and an idea of rational, economic man, highly individualistic in his behaviour. In view of the fact that some fifteen years after the *Discourse* Smith composed a work on English government, *De Republica Anglorum*, the crucial question arises as to whether its doctrines are in harmony with his previous broad outlook. Does the second book confirm or substantiate our estimate of the first? Written in Toulouse about 1565 while he was ambassador to France, *Republica* seems to have been originally intended to introduce French readers to the nature of the English polity. Smith probably touched up the book in 1576, the year before his death, as he did to the *Discourse*. Published posthumously in 1583 under Smith's name (unlike the *Discourse*), *Republica* went through fifteen later reprintings, four Latin editions, and several chapters were translated into Dutch and German in the late seventeenth century. For the student of Tudor state and society the volume is indispensable. As Maitland comments: 'No one would think of writing about the England of Elizabeth's day without paying heed to what was written about that matter by her learned and accomplished Secretary of State'.[89] Of relevance for our purposes, however, are not the details of the English constitution and governmental and social structure, but Smith's remarks, mainly of Aristotelian inspiration, on the nature of the state that introduces them. Over half of the first three sections of the work is allotted to the subject.

Smith employs the conventional 'common wealth' for state in the institutional sense, and adheres to the traditional classification of Aristotle in distinguishing different commonwealths or constitutions by their different forms of government, the rule of one, the few or the many: monarchy, aristocracy or democracy.[90] Each of these three simple constitutions is subject to corruption and may change respectively into tyranny, oligarchy and ochlocracy or mob rule. In reality, Smith observes, states are mixtures of at least two of these simple modes of government, and are identified by the mode that tends to predominate.[91] The government of every simple form is thought by the citizens to be just and lawful. The 'just' in each is 'the profite of the ruling and most strong part', or in other words the interest of government, whether it is that of one, the few or the many. On his identification of justice with ruling-class interest, he acknowledges his agreement with Thrasymachus in Book One of Plato's *Republic*, who, he says, is not as misguided as the Platonic Socrates suggests, a refreshing instance of Smith's candour and analytic acumen.[92] He adds, however, that if it is to be maintained that justice is always perceived by citizens to be in the interest of the ruling-class, then we must always mean the genuine interest or profit, not merely the appearance of interest or profit. On this point Smith seems to accept the correction made by Socrates to Thrasymachus' original formulation and agreed to by the latter.[93]

Smith appears to be arguing, although he is none too clear, that the genuine profit or interest of government is identical with the genuine profit or interest of the citizens. Any action of government in its own true interest must be in the true interest of the people, the common interest. The true interest of the government, therefore, must always forward the common interest. This interpretation of Smith's meaning seems to be supported by his single consideration of a corrupt constitution, tyranny as compared to monarchy.[94] A monarch is supported by the people, rules by law and equity, and aims at the profit or interest of the people as much as at the advantage of the ruling-class or governing part. In contrast, a tyrant rules without the support of the people, fails to comply with law or equity, and is solely concerned with his own narrow self-interest to the detriment of the common interest, seemingly pursuing a spurious instead of genuine interest. And Smith's readers all know, although he never says as much, that tyrants usually come to a sticky end.

The important point about all this, if we keep in mind the *Discourse*, is that Smith in *Republica* has secularized the state. In contrast to the attitude of most of Smith's Tudor contemporaries, the state is given no high moral or religious purpose, nor is any mention made of the law of nature or of God. The just and rightful always seem to be defined in terms of the state's primary economic objective: the genuine 'profit' or 'wealth' or interest of the 'people' whom he identifies with 'the whole body of the three estates of the common wealth'.[95] Fundamentally, he offers an economic interpretation of the 'common wealth' (in the senses of both state and common interest).

Smith's amoral and secular approach to the state in *Republica* is also reflected in his handling of the problem of civil disobedience and even more directly in his famous definition of the commonwealth. Is it just, he asks, for the citizen of a corrupt state to obey its government and laws?[96] Or is resistance to such an unjust regime the just course of action? Smith might have replied to his own questions as did Commonwealth preachers of his day that our duty is always to obey the higher authorities unless we are commanded to violate God's law. In that case passive disobedience is the only licit response. On the contrary, he might have agreed with his former pupil, Bishop John Ponet, that the evil laws of a corrupt state contravene the laws of God and nature, thereby relieving us of the obligation of obedience.[97] Indeed, Ponet contends, citizens have a moral duty of disobedience, and depending upon the circumstances, may actively resist, resorting if necessary to insurrection and tyrannicide. The ever prudent Smith hesitates to commit himself, failing to come down clearly either on the side of passive disobedience or active resistance. His amoral position on the matter is rendered conspicuous by his failure to invoke the divine or natural law. Instead, he comments with bland neutrality that many great men in the past have resisted and overthrown tyrannical governments. Then in true Machiavellian vein he remarks that ordinary people have judged such actions to be just or unjust according to whether their result has been successful or unsuccessful, and that the judgment of 'learned men' has depended on the intentions of the actors and 'the estate of the time then present'.[98] For Smith moral considerations simply do not enter into the matter, apparently because the state is not an ethical entity in any conventional sense. His pragmatic conclusion is cautionary. It is always a dangerous enterprise to change existing laws and governments, or to disobey established authority. So Smith does not rule out civil disobedience or active resistance, and certainly not on moral grounds, only warning of the hazards of such action.

His matter of fact, amoral and secular attitude toward state and government is perhaps most strikingly illustrated by his classic definition of the commonwealth: 'a society or common doing of a multitude of free men collected together and united by common accord and covenants among themselves, for the conservation of themselves in peace as in war'.[99] And somewhat later he again refers to the state in terms of 'common and mutual consent for their preservation'.[100] In the first place, the full force and novelty of his stance can be best appreciated by comparing his definition with those of Cicero and Bodin, and of three of his contemporaries: Sir Thomas Elyot, Thomas Starkey and Richard Morison.[101] Unlike them (Morison excepted), Smith does not refer in his definition to justice, right, equity, the rule of reason, God or morality. The defence and promotion of Christian worship and values seem to have no part in Smith's conception of the state, unlike the position of Starkey and the Commonwealthmen.

Smith, nevertheless, appears to agree with Cicero, Bodin and Starkey that the aim of the union is the common interest. Previous to giving his definition, Smith stresses that the goal of the simple uncorrupt commonwealth is the 'common profit' as distinct from the 'private profit' of the rulers. And in the definition this is apparently the meaning of 'conservation of themselves in peace as well as in warre', a point twice repeated.[102] 'Common profit' or common interest and 'conservation' in this context, in agreement with Hobbes, signify much more than 'bare Preservation'.[103] They have to do with the individual's quest for honour and gain, with his 'ease' and 'pleasure', and with 'quiet', social peace and security.[104] There is an undertone of economic individualism, reminiscent of the *Discourse*, in these passing observations. Order, protection, the material well-being of a citizenry guarded against foreign encroachments and free from internal strife, the preservation of lives and possessions are the referents of 'common profit' and 'conservation'. Smith would probably have approved of the view of the anonymous author of *Policies to Reduce this Realm of Englande* (1549) who defines 'the Floreshing estate of a realm' as one which 'consisteth chiefly in being stronge against theirvasion [*sic*] of eneymies, not molested with cyvile warres the people being wealthie, and not oppressed with famine nor penury of victuelles'.[105]

Among the startling features of Smith's definition is its individualism. Elyot tends to emphasize the organic nature of the state resting not directly on the individuals composing it, but only indirectly through the mediation of the 'estates and degrees' to which they belong, and that have mutually agreed to an order based on justice. Morison also sees not individuals, but corporations such as 'cities, towns, and shires' as the foundation of the state, and so does Bodin. On the other hand, Smith seems closer in spirit to Hobbes than to traditional corporativism, conceptualizing the state as a 'society' or collection of individuals who as individuals have agreed directly, not indirectly as with Elyot and Morison through the orders to which they belong, to unite for their common interest by covenanting (giving their 'common and mutuall consent') each with every other.[106] The basic units of the state, for Smith, therefore, are unmediated consenting individuals acting for their own interests. They are persons, who, he asserts in another context, know 'howe to demeane and order their matters, best for the conservation of themselves, and ech of their families, generally and particularly'.[107] A state or 'politique body' is composed of the bodies of its citizens.[108] It is in effect a mixture of these individuals, not a compound, as it were, in which their individuality disappears in a new whole.

The introductory chapters of *Republica*, therefore, apparently do not deviate from the secularism, rationalism, economism and individualism of the *Discourse*, thus indicating no fundamental change in Smith's position. Before ending our discussion of his second book, a highly speculative matter must be raised, which if correct, may even serve to reinforce our conclusion. Throughout *Republica* as already noted, Smith always employs 'common wealth' for the state conceptualized institutionally and never 'state' itself. Why is this the case? We know that the use of 'state' by humanists of the period was not a rarity, and that *l'état* and *lo stato* had already become commonplace on the continent.[109] As early as the 1530s Starkey sometimes appears to use 'state', perhaps for the first time in English, in a way that anticipates the modern meaning.[110] Ponet does likewise even more than Starkey.[111] Smith's friend, Thomas Wilson, employs 'state' institutionally in his dialogue on usury, published after the drafting of *Republica* but before the revision of 1576.[112] Consequently, it seems likely that Smith was familiar with the books of both Ponet and Wilson and with the budding convention of 'state'. Moreover, while 'state' never appears in Smith's two books, in the second he uses 'society' frequently, and perhaps without much precedent in previous Tudor social and political thought.[113] That he relies on 'common wealth' for state, defining it as a 'society' is in itself suggestive. 'Common wealth', as the word literally denotes, is the common economic interest; and in the institutional sense of state, as Smith says in his definition, it consists of individuals sharing a common end, composing a society or fraternity designed to forward that economic interest. Smith may have observed that the use by his contemporaries of 'state' signified a definite legalistic and jurisdictional whole. But he seems to have been primarily interested in the *Discourse*, at any rate, in the interrelationships of the social division of labour that result in the production of common wealth or profit. The basic unit of production is the household, the archetypal 'society', according to Smith in *Republica*, the origin of other kinds of societies.[114] Unlike the household, however, each of the others he mentions, 'cities, towns, nations, and kingdoms', is not simply a society but a 'societie civill', society organized by government and law, possibly the first use of the expression in English.[115] He unambiguously equates 'common wealth' or state with civil society.[116] After Smith 'civil society' was to become a common term in the seventeenth and eighteenth centuries. Was Smith's preference (and the evident preference of later English thinkers) for 'commonwealth', 'society', and 'civil society' over 'state' possibly because he and his successors conceived of the state fundamentally as an economic arena of profit-seeking individuals competing and co-operating for the production of wealth? Did it reflect the gradual absorption of the English state by the economy? Was it because the dominant propertied classes in Parliament were fashioning a political community or civil society to which the state was increasingly subordinated, in roughly the same way that ancient Roman republican aristocrats came to think of themselves 'much less as administrators than possessors' of the state?[117] Unfortunately, any answers to these questions must be purely conjectural.

How then do we account for Smith's new moral philosophy that laid the foundations of political economy? No doubt humanism, particularly the commonsensical, practical approach of Aristotle and the conceptual apparatus of Cicero helped to shape Smith's outlook, as did the realism of Machiavelli.[118] Of equal importance may have been the century-old tradition of English economic pamphleteering and the recent spate of empirical, quantitative surveys. The inherited ideas and modes of procedure at Smith's disposal, however, cannot solely explain his pioneering venture. Mounting economic and social troubles may well have been decisive. Smith admits as much in giving his reason for writing the *Discourse*. Burgeoning inflation and the increasing impoverishment of the lower orders, the dispossession and dislocation of the peasantry and rise of a rural 'proletariat', growing unemployment and the decline of once flourishing towns had all reached crisis proportions by the end of the decade when Smith penned his 'memorandum' for Cecil.

But an explanation of Smith's new moral philosophy in these terms is surely a statement of the obvious. Was there anything unique about the economic conditions perceived by Smith, and differing from what had occurred before in human history, that can elucidate his new moral philosophy? Smith and his contemporaries appear to have recognized not simply a quantitative, but a distinctive qualitative difference. Something new and unsettling was happening, and they were groping to identify it. They, in fact, as we know and they obviously did not, were among the earliest witnesses of and commentators on some of the effects of an incipient capitalism that for the first time in the world appeared in England. Not that growing economic and social adversities can be solely attributed to agrarian capitalism in its infancy, or to the rural putting out system in textile manufactures, or to the rise of a metropolitan market centring on London with the complex system of credit and exchange being erected.[119] But these economic developments were far from negligible, and were to have momentous consequences for the future. Smith's recognition of the novelty of the troubles is reflected in a number of ways, among which are his implied acknowledgement in the *Discourse* of the triadic organization of the social relations of agricultural production, rendered more explicit in *Republica*, and his worry over the decay of formerly thriving textile towns.[120] Furthermore, he discerns a direct causal link between deteriorating material conditions and multiplying delinquency, crime, vagabondage, civil turmoil and insurrection. He was enough of a social environmentalist to understand that order could be established only if pressing social and economic problems were resolved, and for him rational governmental policies and their implementation are important means of recovery.

The intellectual significance of Smith's accomplishment can perhaps best be indicated by reference to the views of his younger contemporary, Thomas Wilson (1525–81). They were friends, fellow Cantabrigians, humanists, active in government and economic experts.[121] Both thought that something unprecedented was happening in English society in the form of acquisitive individualism and both believed that it was traceable to natural human egoism.[122] Here, however, they parted company, representing contrasting outlooks. First drafted in 1569 and not published until 1572, Wilson's *Discourse Upon Usury* is a lengthy and learned critique in dialogue form not against all interest, but 'pure interest', involved in the promise to pay a fixed amount required by the lender for the loan of a sum of money for a stated period of time, with no risk to be incurred by the lender in case of default by the borrower. Usury is simply money made from money. Essentially the problem with Wilson's argument is his failure to appreciate that most of English agriculture, manufacturing and foreign commerce was being increasingly financed by the very credit arrangements he so scathingly condemns, and that his recommended law against usury if implemented would all but destroy the English economy. It is unimaginable that the worldly-wise Smith, who never mentions usury or interest in his two books, or refers to any of the many business transactions involving the payment of 'illegitimate' interest, so meticulously catalogued by Wilson, could possibly have agreed with his friend. The economic individualism, so blandly accepted by Smith, is for Wilson most virulently and destructively manifested in the spreading contagion of usury. He finds the principal cause of the unbridled profit-seeking in a tidal wave of covetousness that threatens to engulf society, and differs markedly from Smith in his moralizing and censorious attitude.[123] He evidently feels that the only hope for his country is in spiritual renewal.

The difference in attitude of the two thinkers, who otherwise had so much in common, could not be more pronounced. While Wilson is the traditional humanist moralizer obsessed by profit-seeking individualism, the increasing covetousness of the age, Smith is willing to seize the bull by the horns. Instead of excoriating economic individualism, he wholeheartedly embraces it, seeing in it a bright prospect for the future, a means of revitalizing England, providing it is harnessed and used constructively for the welfare of all. Wilson is more of a romantic, in love with the sterner, heroic qualities of the past. On the other hand, Smith appears to have discarded any romantic notions that he may have harboured for the glorious days of yore. He exhibits instead a highly rationalistic, realistic and calculating style of thinking. Smith is writing his *Discourse* from the standpoint of a public official who must always strive for what is possible of accomplishment in a most imperfect world. Smith is never a moral crusader or radical reformer, or utopian thinker; he is a secular analyst of social forces and their harmful effects, and a proponent of constructive policies designed to curb them. A person of empirical temper, moderate and tentative in outlook, Smith hopes to check and reduce inflation, prevent the drainage of gold and silver from the realm, and increase and diversify agricultural and manufacturing production, all for the prosperity and strength of the Tudor state and well-being of its people.

Smith, consequently might be termed an early 'theorist' of emergent capitalism. He is not the discerning economic analyst or technical innovator that, for example, Petty and Locke were, but he manifested something of the spirit of capitalism. His writings reflect in concentrated form, possibly for the first time, something of that spirit in their individualism, secularism, rationalism and economism. It was the beginning of the unromantic spirit and 'anti-heroism' that in the epoch to come would contribute to a civilization dedicated to the progressive 'disenchantment of the world', to use the glosses of Schumpeter and Weber on Marx's initial insight. Such, more than anything else, may have been Smith's intellectual response to the structural changes occurring in English society, a response that put in place a new moral philosophy and the foundations of political economy.

NOTES

1 On Smith see M. Dewar, *Sir Thomas Smith: A Tudor Intellectual in Office*, London, Athlone Press, 1964; 'The memorandum *For the Understanding of the Exchange*: its authorship and dating', *EcHR*, 1965, 2nd ser., vol. 17, pp. 476–87; 'The authorship of the *Discourse of the Commonweal*', *EcHR*, 1966, 2nd ser., vol. 19, pp. 388–400; and the introductions to Dewar's editions of Smith's two major works, *A Discourse of the Commonweal of This Realm of England: Attributed to Sir Thomas Smith*, Charlottesville, Va, University Press of Virginia, for the Folger Shakespeare Library, 1969 (hereafter *D*); *De Republica Anglorum*, Cambridge, Cambridge University Press, 1982 (hereafter *R*).

   Also of value are A. B. Ferguson, *The Articulate Citizen and the English Renaissance*, Durham, NC, Duke University Press, 1965, pp. 279–314, 355–62, 385–96; E. A. J. Johnson, *Predecessors of Adam Smith: The Growth of British Economic Thought*, London, King, 1937, and New York, Prentice-Hall, 1937, ch. 2; W. R. D. Jones, *The Tudor Commonwealth 1529–1559*, London, Athlone Press, 1970, pp. 105–6, 141–2, 197–201; D. McNally, *Political Economy and the Rise of Capitalism: A Reinterpretation*, Berkeley, Calif., University of California Press, 1988, pp. 25–8, 194–5; J. Thirsk, *Economic Policy and Projects: The Development of a Consumer Society in Early Modern England*, Oxford, Clarendon Press, 1978, pp. 13–15, 16, 18, 24, 27, 29, 33, 47, 55, 67, 78, 127.

   My thanks are due to Ellen Meiksins Wood for her helpful comments on the original draft of this chapter; and also to Ted Winslow and the Political Economy Seminar of the Department of Economics, York University, for the opportunity to present publicly for the first time my views on the subject.

2 To avoid any misunderstanding, my usage of 'political economy' should be made clear. Political economy is a systematic mode of social discourse focusing on the problem of the 'wealth of nations'. It is policy oriented and hence political, designed to make recommendations for governmental action in respect to economic matters. It is concerned with the function of state and government, conceived of either positively or negatively, in contributing to the wealth of nations. The history of British political economy can be divided chronologically between a 'pre-classical' phase, largely mercantilistic in outlook (Malynes, Misseldon, Mun, Petty, Locke, Child, North, Barbon, Davenant) and a 'classical' *laissez-faire* phase (Adam Smith, Malthus, Ricardo, James Mill, J. S. Mill).

3 T. Hutchison, *Before Adam Smith: The Emergence of Political Economy, 1662–1776*, London, Basil Blackwell, 1988, pp. 15–16; E. Roll, *A History of Economic Thought*, London, Faber & Faber, 4th edn, 1973, pp. 40–59; J. A. Schumpeter, *History of Economic Analysis*, E. B. Schumpeter (ed.), New York, Oxford University Press, 1954, pp. 162–4.

4 Among the English economic pamphlets were the 'Libell of Englische Policye' (1436), 'The Comodytes of England' of the mid-fifteenth century, Clement Armstrong's tracts of the 1530s and the anonymous 'Policies to Reduce this Realm of England unto a Prosperous Wealth' (1549). On these works, see Ferguson, op. cit., pp. 99–106, 153–4, 236–9; S. T. Bindoff, 'Clement Armstrong and his treatises of the commonweal', *EcHR*, 1944, ser. 1, vol. 14, pp. 64–73.

Smith was probably unfamiliar, even in manuscript, with Thomas Starkey's 'Dialogue between Pole and Lupset', completed in the early 1530s, but not published until the late nineteenth century.

5 Erasmus, surprisingly, has more to say on economic questions than any of the others; see *Education* ch. 4 'On tributes and taxes'. L. K. Born (trans.), New York, Columbia University Press, 1936, pp. 215–18. Vives' book, widely circulated on the continent and highly regarded by More and Erasmus, is more than a specialized treatise on education, touching on a vast range of subjects, including the nature of politics and the state. See J. L. Vives, *On Education*, F. Watson (trans.), Cambridge, Cambridge University Press, 1913, pp. 42, 258.

6 C. W. Cole, *French Mercantilist Doctrines Before Colbert*, New York, Octagon Books, 1969 (1931), ch. 1.

7 E. F. Hecksher, *Mercantilism*, M. Shapiro (trans.), London, Allen & Unwin, 1934, vol. 2, p. 227. Hecksher and Schumpeter were writing before Dewar attributed the authorship of *D* to Smith. Of economic historians, Hecksher seems to be the most appreciative of *D* for example, vol. 2, pp. 20, 46ff., 131, 227ff., 278–9, 293, 301, 310, 313–14.

8 Quoted in Dewar's introduction, *D*, p. xvi.

9 Schumpeter, op. cit., p. 166.

10 Hutchison, op. cit., pp. 20–1.

11 Like Sir William Petty, Smith was a dedicated advocate of Irish colonization.

12 Dewar, 1965, op. cit., persuasively argues that 'For the Understanding of the Exchange' was not written by Sir Thomas Gresham, but by Smith. This important and influential document deals with the questions of recoinage, the exchange rate, the foreign debt and the carrying trade. In *The Wages of a*

Roman Footsoldier Smith engages in extensive and systematic calculation of the current English equivalent of the value of Roman money.

13 *D*, p. 11.

14 Quoted in Dewar's introduction, *D*, p. xxiv.

15 *D*, p. 11.

16 *D*, p. 13; for these issues in other Tudor contexts, see Norman L. Jones and Paul A. Fideler, chapters 6 and 7 in this volume.

17 *D*, p. 12.

18 *D*, p. 29.

19 *D*, pp. 29–30.

20 Throughout this chapter, unless otherwise specified, 'state' is employed in the broad generic sense of the personalized or institutionalized organization of authority and power over a people usually inhabiting a particular territory. Smith seems to use 'common wealth' as state in an institutionalized rather than a personalized sense, anticipating in a way the early modern conception of the state fashioned by Bodin, Hobbes and others. From their viewpoint, the state is a secular, institutional whole, a legal, constitutional order characterized by sovereignty, one which is distinct from government and often from society. See Q. Skinner, *The Foundations of Modern Political Thought*, Cambridge, Cambridge University Press, 1978, vol. 2, pp. 349–58, and 'The state', *Political Innovation and Conceptual Change*, T. Ball, J. Farr and R. L. Hansen (eds), Cambridge, Cambridge University Press, 1989, pp. 90–131; also N. Wood, *Cicero's Social and Political Thought*, Berkeley, Calif., University of California Press, 1988, pp. 123–5.

21 *D*, p. 12.

22 *D*, p. 13.

23 *D*, p. 15.

24 *D*, pp. 15–16.

25 *D*, p. 16.

26 *D*, pp. 75, 105. This second obvious reference to More is in the section, pp. 102–16, of the 1549 draft omitted in the 1581 edition.

27 *D*, pp. 16, 29, 31, 107, 118 and possibly the reference on p. 114 to the tale of the Gyges ring, which could have been derived from Plato's *Republic*, 359d–360d.

28 *D*, p. 106; also pp. 71, 72, 105.

29 *D*, pp. 16, 59, 116, 134.

30 *D*, pp. 28, 29, 31, 59, 75, 91, 134, 141.

31 *D*, pp. 16–17.

32 *R*, p. 54. Smith refers to Plato, perhaps with *Laws*, 691c–d, in mind.

33 *R*, p. 51.

34 *R*, p. 62.

35 See in general, *D*, pp. 54, 55, 58–60, 118, 119.

36 For example, *D*, pp. 47–8.

37 *D*, p. 118.

38 *D*, p. 50. T. Starkey: 'A Dialogue between Pole and Lupset', T. F. Mayer (ed.), C4S, no. 37, pp. 65–6. The first technical defence of enclosure is probably in John Fitzherbert, *The Book of Husbandry* (1523). Starkey and Smith, however, must have been among the first to offer non-technical arguments for enclosure.

39 *D*, pp. 54–6.

40 Also see *D*, p. 91.

41 *D*, pp. 58–9.

42 *D*, pp. 59–60.

43 M. M. Goldsmith, *Private Vices, Public Benefits: Bernard Mandeville's Social and Political Thought*, Cambridge, Cambridge University Press, 1985, esp. pp. 114–15.
44 *D*, p. 116.
45 *D*, pp. 51–3.
46 *D*, p. 51.
47 *D*, p. 52.
48 *D*, p. 53.
49 *D*, pp. 54–61.
50 *D*, e.g. pp. 49, 50, 89, 92, 126.
51 *D*, pp. 92–4.
52 *D*, p. 38.
53 *D*, pp. 69, 101.
54 *D*, p. 95.
55 *D*, p. 96.
56 *D*, p. 96.
57 *D*, p. 97.
58 *D*, p. 98. Hugh Latimer, *Sermons*, G. E. Corrie (ed.), Cambridge, Cambridge University Press, 1844, vol. 1, pp. 250–1. Latimer cites More as the source.
59 *D*, p. 98.
60 *D*, p. 101.
61 Pp. 102–16 of the 1549 draft were replaced probably in 1576 by Smith with a new section for the version to be published posthumously in 1581, pp. 143–6 in Dewar's Appendix A of *D*.
62 *D*, p. 143.
63 *D*, pp. 144–5.
64 Ferguson, op. cit., p. 385: 'In its economic aspects, at least, the commonwealth has become for Smith a mechanism of forces, impersonal and amoral in character, subject to analysis and manipulation by intelligent policy'.
65 On clocks in medieval and early modern Europe, see D. J. Boorstin, *The Discoverers*, New York, Random House, 1983, pp. 36–53, 64–72; C. M. Cipolla (ed.), *The Fontana Economic History of Europe*, London, Collins/Fontana, 1972, vol. 1, pp. 87–8; vol. 2, pp. 282–3; L. White, jr., *Medieval Technology and Social Change*, Oxford, Clarendon Press, 1962, pp. 120–8.
66 For the drawing see D. Piper (ed.) *The Genius of British Painting*, London, Book Club Associates, 1975, p. 68. The new clocks contributed to an acute awareness of time and abhorrence of idleness; in Thomas More, for example. See R. Marius, *Thomas More: A Biography*, London, Dent, 1985, pp. 12, 165, 224–5, 229.
67 However, the clock analogy, first applied by Nicole Oresme (1330?–1382) to the workings of the universe constructed by the divine clockmaker, became commonplace in this regard in the early modern period. See Boorstin, op. cit., pp. 71–2.
68 On the clockwork analogy and Steuart, see A. O. Hirschman, *The Passions and the Interests: Political Arguments for Capitalism before its Triumph*, Princeton, NJ, Princeton University Press, 1981, pp. 86–7.
69 Ferguson, op. cit., pp. 308–9.
70 *D*, p. 62.
71 *D*, p. 86; my emphasis.
72 *D*, p. 86, also p. 99.
73 This seems to be at odds with Smith's mercantilism.
74 Erasmus, op. cit., pp. 170–1.

75 *R*, pp. 58–60.

76 *D*, p. 63.

77 *D*, p. 73.

78 *D*, pp. 87–8.

79 *D*, p. 89.

80 Jean Bodin, *Six Books of the Commonwealth*, M. J. Tooley (ed. and trans.), Oxford, Basil Blackwell, 1967, p. 7.

81 G. de Malynes, *A Treatise of the Canker of England's Common Wealth* (1601), in R. H. Tawney and E. Power (eds) *Tudor Economic Documents*, London, Longman, Green, 1924, vol. 3, p. 386.

82 See E. M. Wood, 'The state and popular sovereignty in French political thought: a genealogy of Rousseau's "General Will" ', *History of Political Thought*, 1983, vol. 4, pp. 298–300; MacNally, op. cit., pp. 68–72.

83 For example, see J. Locke, *Some Considerations of the Consequences of the Lowering of Interest and Raising the Value of Money* (1692), in *The Works of John Locke*, London, 9th edn, 1794, vol. 4, pp. 19–20, 72.

84 Thirsk, op. cit., p. 9.

85 Ibid., p. 1.

86 For some of Smith's references and recommendations for their production in England, see *D*, pp. 18, 62–6, 77–8, 87–8, 90–1, 121–6.

87 Thirsk, op. cit., p. 33.

88 Ibid., p. 9.

89 Quoted in Dewar's Introduction, *D*, p. xxii.

90 *R*, pp. 49–51.

91 *R*, p. 52.

92 *R*, pp. 49–50; Plato, *Republic*, 338c–e.

93 Ibid., 340c–e.

94 *R*, pp. 53–4.

95 *R*, p. 54.

96 *R*, p. 52.

97 J. Ponet, *A Shorte Treatise of Politike Power*, Strasbourg, heirs of W. Kopfel 1556, STC 20178.

98 *R*, p. 52; cf. Machiavelli, *The Prince*, ch. 18; *Discourses*, 1, ch. 9. According to the listing given in J. Strype, *The Life of the Learned Sir Thomas Smith*, Oxford, Clarendon Press, rev. edn, 1820, pp. 276–7, Smith had in the library of his Essex country home in 1566, *The Prince*, *Discourses* and *Florentine History* of Machiavelli.

99 *R*, p. 57.

100 *R*, p. 59; also p. 61.

101 Cicero, *De re publica*, I. 39: 'an assemblage of people in large numbers associated in an agreement in respect to justice and a partnership for the common interest'. (Loeb Classical Library trans. with slight variation).

Bodin, op. cit., p. 1: 'a rightful government of many families and that which is common to them under a sovereign power'.

T. Elyot, *The Book Named the Governor*, 1531, ed. S. E. Lehmberg, London and New York, Dent, Everymans Library, 1962, p. 1: 'a body living, compact or made of sundry estates and degrees of men, which is disposed by the order of equity and governed by the rule of reason'.

Starkey, op. cit., p. 34: 'the gud ordur & pollycy by gud lawys stablyschyd & set, & by hedys & rularys put in effect by the wyche the hole body as by reson ys governyd & rulyd, to the intent that thys multytude of pepul & hole commynalty so helthy & so welthy havyng convenyent abundaunce of al thyngys necessary for the maytenance therof, may wyth dew honowr reverence & love relygyously worschype god, as fountayn of al gudnes maker & governour of al thys world, every one also dowyng hys duty to other, wyth brotherly love one lovyng a nother as membrys & partys of one body'. Mayer's editorial symbols have been omitted.

R. Morison, *A Remedy for Sedition*, 1536, quoted in G. R. Elton, *Policy and Police: The Enforcement of the Reformation in the Age of Thomas Cromwell*, Cambridge, Cambridge University Press, 1972, p. 202: 'a number of cities, towns, shires that all agree upon one law and one head, united and knit together by the observation of the laws'.

102 *R*, pp. 61, 63.

103 T. Hobbes, *Leviathan*, 1651, Harmondsworth, Penguin, 1968, ch. 30, p. 376.

104 *R*, pp. 62, 63.

105 Tawney and Power, op. cit., vol. 3, p. 313.

106 Hobbes, op. cit., ch. 18, pp. 228–9.

107 *R*, p. 61.

108 *R*, p. 51.

109 The conclusion of Skinner, 1978, op. cit., vol. 2, pp. 349–58, refers to both Starkey and Ponet. See also his essay, 1989, op. cit.

110 For example, Starkey, op. cit., p. 33. Also see the valuable explication of Starkey's terminology in T. F. Mayer, *Thomas Starkey and the Commonweal: Humanist Politics and Religion in the Reign of Henry VIII*, Cambridge, Cambridge University Press, 1989, esp. ch. 4.

111 See the separately paginated text of the original edition of the *Shorte Treatise* in W. S. Hudson, *John Ponet (1516?–1556): Advocate of Limited Monarchy*, Chicago, Ill., University of Chicago Press, 1942, pp. 27, 59, 98, 105, 110, 111.

112 T. Wilson, *A Discourse uppon Usurye: By waye of Dialogue and oracions, for the better vanitye and more delite of all those that shall reade thys treatise*, R. H. Tawney (ed.), New York, Harcourt Brace, 1925. Wilson's dialogue is found on pp. 173–384 of this edition. For examples of his use of 'state' in the institutional sense see pp. 204–5, 222, 270–1, 311, 329, 375, 385.

113 In addition to his definition of 'common wealth' (p. 57), Smith employs 'society' no fewer than eight times in *R*, pp. 57, 58, 59, 60.

114 *R*, pp. 58–60.

115 *R*, pp. 57, 59, 60.

116 *R*, p. 57.

117 M. Gelzer, *The Roman Nobility*, R. Seager (trans.), Oxford, Basil Blackwell, 1969, p. 137.

118 On the possible influence of Cicero, see N. Wood, 'Cicero and the political thought of the early English Renaissance', *Modern Language Quarterly*, forthcoming; for the application of Machiavellian realism to the modern economic sphere by early Tudor thinkers, consult Ferguson, op. cit., p. 201.

119 For early English agrarian capitalism and related matters, see the works cited in N. Wood, *John Locke and Agrarian Capitalism*, Berkeley, Calif., University of California Press, 1984, n. 6, pp. 117–18. Wood's position and that of the authors cited are at variance with the provocative thesis of A. Macfarlane, *The Origins of English Individualism: The Family, Property and Social Transition* and *The Culture of Capitalism*, both Oxford, Basil Blackwell, corrected edn, 1979, and 1987 respectively. English capitalism and individualism, according to Macfarlane, do not emerge in our period, but are at least as old as the thirteenth century.

120 *D*, pp. 118–19; 123–6; *R*, pp. 74–7.
121 For Wilson's life, see Tawney's introduction to Wilson, op. cit., and *Diction-ary of National Biography*; Dewar, 1964, op. cit., esp. pp. 125, 134–5 discusses Smith and Wilson. Norman L. Jones's essay includes much attention on Wilson and the usury dilemma (Chapter 6 in this volume).
122 Wilson, op. cit., pp. 177, 182.
123 Ibid., pp. 177, 258, 314, 353, 379, 384.

6

William Cecil and the making of economic policy in the 1560s and early 1570s

Norman L. Jones

Few policy-makers allow the historian to see the alignment between their intellectual processes and the ways in which they respond to the mundane demands of governance. Sir William Cecil, Principal Secretary to Queen Elizabeth, who became Lord Burghley in 1571, is one of those rare politicians who did. His copious notes and ruminations, scattered on hundreds of sheets through the State Papers and other Elizabethan collections, let us follow his concerns on an almost daily basis while allowing us to watch how he brought his education, his religion – his very world view – to bear on issues that he, the second most powerful person in England, found worthy of governmental attention.

Like notes that any of us make to ourselves, his were skeletal and assume a world of knowledge inaccessible to the reader, but once in a while, thanks to his academic training, he worked out his thoughts syllogistically. This habit of self-debate lets us follow the way he framed policy issues and to deduce why he responded to problems as he did. For instance, the economic problems of the 1560s were a constant concern to Cecil and the Privy Council. In particular the economic distress provoked discussions of bankruptcy, usury, poor relief and the role of wealth in the commonwealth, discussions that led to proposals for legislation in the Parliaments of 1562–3, 1566 and 1571. Cecil, in considering these problems, left us seventeen folios covered with syllogisms that knit all these issues together under the rubric of usury.

These folios, covered with his unmistakable long, thin pen strokes, are undated and unpaginated. The British Library catalogued them as two documents because the paper size changes, but they were almost certainly written in late April 1571.[1] The Bill Against Usury had received its second reading in the Commons on 19 April and Burghley seems to be taking this into account, probably in preparation for the debate on the Bill in the Lords. As the leader of the government Burghley's response to the Bill is of more than passing interest, but his reflections are about more than usury. The usury Bill itself was one of a group of Bills that had originated in the early 1560s in response to the disturbed times.

When Elizabeth brought Cecil into her new government at the beginning of her reign he was presented with a number of difficult issues. In an advisory document sent to Cecil in the last days of 1558 by Armigal Waad, a close associate of the new Principal Secretary, the 'Distresses of the Commonwealth' were diagrammed under seven heads: the poverty of the queen; the penury of the noble men, and their poverty; the wealth of the meaner sort; the dearth of things; the divisions within the realm; the wars; and the want of justice.[2] Together they formed a tangled ball that had at its heart an economy weakened by war, inflation and natural disaster. Lord Paget, a leader of Mary's Privy Council, summed up the situation when he remarked dryly, 'God save us from the sword, for we have been plagued of late with famine and pestilence'.[3]

The disastrous war with France had cost the realm its last continental possession, Calais. With that had gone the trade that had passed through it, to the great distress of the merchant community and the crown's coffers. Although the treaty of Cateau-Cambresis ended the Anglo-Spanish war against the French and the Scots in early 1559, England was again at war with the Scots by 1560 and intervened – disastrously – in France in 1563. The wars, and royal policy, fed the scourge of inflation. Throughout the 1550s money had been called in, melted down, adulterated and reissued. As its value deflated prices inflated, part of the 'great inflation' that plagued the century, forcing real incomes to lag behind the escalating prices.

In the early 1560s Elizabeth and Cecil set out to remedy the inflation, believing, on the advice of experts like Sir Thomas Gresham, father of Gresham's Law, that bad money drove out good. They succeeded in returning the coins to a standard weight, but their attempts caused widespread economic confusion. Interfering in the market by means of proclamations and trying to reassure the public, the Privy Council was surprised at the reluctance of Her Majesty's subjects to believe that the government meant well by calling in the coins. As one contemporary observed

> The crying down of the money made great dearth and in many places the people would not sell for money, but upon trust because they knew not the certainty of the fall, and in many places the price of things was double increased.

The same observer commented: 'Immediately after gold was abated in value by proclamation nothing is the better cheap either coming from beyond the sea or at home, but rather increased in price'.[4]

The restoration of the coinage was followed in 1563 by the worst outbreak of plague in the reign and bad harvests. In the same year increased English export duties prompted Margaret of Parma, regent in the Spanish Netherlands, to close Antwerp to English merchants, blocking up England's chief continental outlet for cloth and forcing her merchants to move to Emden, establishing there a short-lived and unsuccessful staple. As Cecil informed Sir Thomas Smith in 1564,

> We here do see it very necessary to return to the Low Country, for although it were to great purpose to divert some part of our trade from them ... yet ... our country shall not be presently able to endure and hold out. One of our greatest lets is the lack of revenue for the Queen of the custom. The second is the sudden stay at home of the people, that belong to clothmaking.[5]

Trade with Antwerp reopened in 1565, but, despite an initial burst of trade, the market remained unstable and English cloth exports were under stress. January of 1569 saw another stoppage of the trade with Antwerp, as the Netherlands sank slowly into the revolt against Spain. Merchants and labourers in the cloth trades did not flourish in the 1560s. Indeed, many responded as did John Isham, who seems to have concluded that retiring to the country was better than struggling to keep his export business afloat.[6] Other merchants sought out new markets, beginning the great expansion of Elizabethan trade that we associate with the reign. But in 1571 when Cecil was thinking about usury he was looking back over thirteen years of economic distress that had had alarming effects on the social fabric.

Further in the back of his mind were economic forces that were even more difficult to control than inflation, war and foreign trade: famine and disease. Harvests were undependable. For example, 1555 saw the worst crop failure of the century; in 1561 the grain rotted in the summer rains; in 1563 and 1566 the harvests were bad again. The final years of the 1560s had better yields, but the effects, and threat, of bad harvests were constant. Wide fluctuations in the food supply, in turn, caused dramatic price swings, exacting a heavy toll on a society that was primarily agricultural. A bad harvest emphasized the social divisions between the poor and the better off, the griping stomachs of the poor pushing them toward riot and revolt. Hungry, agricultural labourers reduced their consumption, hurting those who sold to them. Their masters, with less produce to sell, curtailed their spending. Reduced spending meant hard times for the merchants and occupiers were sold to the agricultural sector. The poor then swelled the ranks of the seasonal labourers, travelling in search of work and food.

Government intervened to protect the food supply and to control the population. The obsession with masterless men that marked the period stemmed from this hungry migration. In 1568 the Privy Council ordered a national crackdown on 'rogues, vagabonds, and Egyptians'. At the same time, Parliament, Privy Council and local governments struggled to deal with the needs of the 'truly needy' poor. Believing that those who were poor by accident of age and physical deformity – orphans, widows, the aged, the maimed – were the responsibility of their immediate neighbours, they combined their desire to control the unemployed with the need to look after the deserving. Parliament passed statutes for the relief of the poor and the punishment of vagabonds in 1563. In 1572 the two issues were combined in an omnibus statute entitled 'An Act for Punishment of Vagabonds, and for Relief of the Poor and Impotent'.[7] Feeling their way toward the creation of that great Elizabethan institution, the Poor House, parliamentarians also gave more and more towns the right to create courts of orphans to care for the children of deceased citizens, safeguarding their inheritances by lending out the principal at interest and using the income to support the children.

As English people understood them, the economic ills of the country grew out of the greed, social climbing and lack of discipline that disturbed the divinely ordained structure of the Commonwealth. Convinced that social hierarchy and economic hierarchies were fixed, many saw social climbing as a sin, economic aggrandizement as sinful and anti-social, and economic and social change as threatening. To modern eyes the distresses caused by disordered hierarchy look like the effects of economic depression and class division, but contemporaries did not think in such categories. Rather than depersonalizing the causes into abstractions, they personalized them, identifying misbehaviour, sloth and sinful natures driven by greed as the roots of social distress. Thus all would be well if disordered lives could be ordered.

A 1559 proposal sent to Cecil asking for laws preventing labourers and servants from leaving their hundred, fixing their wages and forcing them to carry work permits exemplifies this drive for order. These seemingly draconian measures would, the document declares

> reduce servants to obedience which by degrees shall reduce to obedi-ence to the prince, and to God also, which is now by looseness of times, come to such contempt, that there is now none other remedy left, but by awe of law to acquaint men with virtue again.[8]

Although these proposals did not become law, statute after statute con-firms their belief that disordered people create a disordered state. For instance, the price of leather goods was high not because of deflated coinage or competition but because 'divers and sundry covetous and greedy persons now of late having more regard to their own singular lucre and gains, than unto the maintenance and preservation of the common-wealth' were exporting tanned leather.[9] This language recurs again and again as Parliament, led by Cecil, framed laws to cope with the rising tide of inflation, the increasing numbers of poor, the declining prosperity of the 'better sorts', and the sinful greed of the human race.

The concepts he used to address these issues were in common circu-lation, and it is clear that Cecil was not an innovative thinker when it came to economic problems. His friends and advisers were not, either, and they tended to see greedy usurers as the cause of bankruptcy, the enemies of the upper classes, and the oppressors of the poor. Usurers may have even caused plague, as William Bullein suggested in his 1564 *Dialogue . . . Against the Fever Pestilence*:

> I heard a friend of mine say, that he had written a book against extortioners and usurers, which if they amend not, he will name them, and paint them forth, not only them, but their parents which are dead, which used that vile trade of usury, procuring Gods vengeance, in casting the pestilence upon cities, towns and countries; causing poverty, breaking up houses most ancient, selling to lend upon gain, destroying hospitality, with infinite encumbrances by forfeiture statutes etc. Oh that the usurers' goods were confiscated after their deaths to the common poor.[10]

Before Cecil put his thoughts on usury on paper in 1571 the air was filled with plans to solve the nation's economic problems by controlling usury.

That usury was a problem in the 1560s is hard to deny, even if we dissent from Bullein's argument that it caused plague. The inflation, devaluation and the illegality of all lending at interest had combined to make the price of credit extremely high. In 1559 John Young noted that interest rates had risen sharply since the passing of the 1552 law prohibiting lending at interest, as, he claimed, he was able to prove by the brokers' books in London. That spring he reported the best rate available, given to credit-worthy merchants – not 'needy bankrupts, nor light and rash young men' – was 20 per cent. For others, such as gentlemen called into military service by the queen, the rate was 30, 40 or even 50 per cent. The costs of brokers, drawing the documents and conveyancing added another 5 per cent to the cost of the money, 'as those which have borrowed money in London (among whom I myself have been one) to my great loss, can be a good witness'.[11] Other contemporaries confirmed Young's observations. Thomas Wilson, writing a decade later, said 'men now can get no money, but after xxx or xx at the least in the hundred'. My own research in the legal records confirms them too. Of ninety-three loans made in Devon in the late 1560s most carried rates of interest between 15 and 40 per cent.[12]

Tudor people were not naive about the effects that the cost of money had on business, government and society but they tended to analyse them according to the broad principles of moral theology rather than the amoral ones of modern economics. Reporting the bankruptcy of many people in Flanders and London because of the default of Philip II and the French king in September 1561, one remarked: 'Many that were worth 100,000 li. were suddenly not worth a halfpenny. The plague of God upon the usurers whose money caused all these alterations of wars'.[13]

God was at the heart of the matter for many, since He had forbidden usury, a prohibition maintained by the canon law as well as the statute law. Defining usury as 'an act of oppression and extortion sprung from covetousness, which arises from a lack of trust in God', Richard Porder, in a 1570 Paul's Cross sermon, unravelled the knot of economic disaster and suffering caused by usury, foreshadowing much of what Cecil would write in his notes on the subject. Arguing that loans at interest should not be made even to the rich, he showed the effect such 'innocent' loans would have:

> For, first they [the rich] lend for usury, which is against the common law; then they lend to the rich man, who having the money, doth engross the markets, bringeth heaps of commodities into his own hands, and so maketh a Monopolion, and dearth without need. The meaner sort are thereby prevented of their markets, and must glean after the engrosser, and take small leavings or sit still, and so remain mean, or rather become poor: the common sort weep through the dearth, for the rich will be sure to make his common weal to bear out his loss, and pay for that usury, and when many are beggared for ever, one is helped with a halfpenny, which is the usurers charity.[14]

Those who lend at usury, Porder believed, are idolaters, worshipping money when they should worship God, destroying their neighbours and nation in their frenzy to consume.

Some who take usury do so in order to gain monopolies, 'and free markets to be bound to their covetous desires'. Others borrow in order to lend again at a higher rate, lacking goods to set themselves up in honest business. These generally end up bankrupt. In the mean time, they drive up the prices of goods because interest paid must be added to the price paid. Again and again Porder stressed that lending at interest was a form of theft that oppressed the borrowers, drove up prices, interfered with free markets and fair prices, created artificial shortages and cooled charitable impulses. And in the end lending at interest destroyed the wealthy borrowers as surely as it oppressed the poor. Porder wrote:

> usury contracts and bargains are the chief maintainers of this occupation of bankrupts. For every man will give credit now: even he that scarcely has credit himself, because he would have gain by the loan. Whereby too much credit is amongst men: though none lawfully.[15]

Porder's arguments were echoed by many other commentators at the time. Bishop Jewel of Salisbury preached on the same theme and with the same moral, and Thomas Wilson confirmed it in his well-known *Discourse upon Usury* in 1569. The hard times had called their attention to the problems of the economy and at their root they found the greed of the usurers.

Because usury was at the centre of discussions concerning the economy it cropped up in everyone's economic policy, whether dealing with the poor, with bankruptcy, with the price of land, with food shortages, or with Roman Catholics who, as idolaters, were supposedly more given to usury than godly Protestants, causing God's wrath to descend on England.

The economic distress of the time provoked demands for government action in Parliament and out, but what was to be done? The causes of the distress set men to pondering, and their pondering was guided by their academic training. Clearly, they believed, usury was at the heart of their troubles, but what it was and how to control it was debatable because it appeared in so many places. Usury itself was the subject of a series of Tudor Bills and statutes, but it was linked to proposals to curb bankruptcies, to establish non-profit banks for the poor, to regulate foreign exchange and to care for orphans.

The crime of lending at interest had entered English law from the canon law in 1487, becoming an offence against the king punishable by forfeiture, fine and imprisonment. Sharpened and reconfirmed by an Act of 1495, the total prohibition of lending at interest stood until repealed by 37 Henry VIII c. 9 in 1545. This Act gave statutory force to the theory of usury being advanced by continental scholars like Charles du Moulin, setting a legal minimum of 10 per cent for usury; anything less than that was no longer usury. As one commentator put it, the Act of Henry VIII took away 'that usury, which under pretext of interest, being not above ten in the hundred, might then be committed unpunished, because the same was left at large, to the conscience of the lender'.[16]

The result was offensive to many, since open usury began to be practised in England. Pressure built for repeal, and under the godly influence of the Edwardian reformers the toleration of usury was stopped. An Act of Edward VI declared that usury, being prohibited by the Word of God, was completely and totally forbidden.[17]

This statute proved to be very unpopular in some circles. Urban oligarchs disliked it especially, since it, in effect, outlawed the operation of the courts of orphans which, by lending out the inheritance of minor orphans, supported them until their majority on the interest, preserving their estates. London's aldermen had a Bill introduced to legalize its Court of Orphans in the second session of Mary's first Parliament. There it was joined by a Bill that sought total repeal of the Act Against Usury. Ultimately, the Bill 'for the qualifying the statute of usury of orphans' was defeated in the Commons.[18]

In 1563 another attempt at total repeal came in the Bill 'for punishment of usury and unlawful bargains' which passed the House of Commons on a division, 134 to 90. Sent to the Lords, it met with fierce resistance, dying on the third reading. Cecil, then in the Commons, seems to have had something to do with the Bill's demise, since he informed Sir Thomas

Smith at the time, 'Many other good laws are passed in the nether house; as for toleration of usury under ten per cent (which notwithstanding I durst not allow)'.[19]

Ironically, not all who were concerned about the oppression of the poor were in favour of the total prohibition of usury. Some believed that the ban actually increased misery. Guido Cavalcanti, an Italian merchant and diplomatic Man Friday for Cecil, argued that the poor would benefit more if lending at interest was harnessed by the creation of 'poor men's banks' or *monte pietatis* like those functioning throughout Italy. Better, he believed, to allow usury at a controlled rate than to drive up the cost of money by making lending at interest illegal. 'If', he asked Cecil, 'minimal interest is damnable, how much more damnable would excessive interest be?'[20] Cavalcanti's call for a poor men's bank based on a mortuary tax and lending to the poor at minimal interest echoed calls already made by natives, such as John Young, who gave the queen a new year's gift in 1559 entitled 'A Discourse of John Yonge gentleman for a Bank of money to be established for the relief of the common necessity'. He urged 'that your highness would commit the same to be penned in better form and order, and upon deliberation had, to be debated in Parliament when your grace shall see occasion'.[21]

Thomas Lupton the poet made a similar proposal in 1570 in an elaborate plan for the creation of a pension scheme for maimed soldiers, impecunious young merchants and artificers, debtors in prison and other deserving poor. The entire scheme, which also funded schools, would cost 'only' £59,000, and was to be supported by the interest from loans at 5 per cent made to gentlemen who were in danger of forfeiting their lands.[22]

Schemes of this sort bore fruit in the Parliament of 1571 when a Bill for poor men's banks was introduced in the Commons. It failed, but it was a blood relative of the attempts to repeal the Edwardian prohibition of usury and resurrect the Henrician statute with its tolerance for loans under 10 per cent.[23]

The poor were increasing in number in the 1560s, and one of the most noticeable and frightening signs of the increase was the jump in bankruptcies. We have already seen how bankruptcy and usury were linked, so it is not surprising that Bills for the control of bankrupts were introduced in 1563 and 1566. Failing in both those sessions of Parliament, another Bill for bankruptcy was introduced in 1571. This time it passed, becoming the grandfather of modern bankruptcy law.[24]

Bankruptcies among merchants and the resulting loss to their creditors confirmed the evil of usury in people's minds; the manipulation of the foreign exchange in order to cloak usurious loans therefore became a target of reformers. For instance, in 1570 Richard Taverner presented Cecil with a proposal for the creation of a royal exchange. Its purpose was to stop the usury contained in 'dry exchange' – currency speculation – by bringing all exchange transactions under one, supervised, roof. Unless something was done, he argued,

> the riches of the city of London, and in effect of all this realm, shalbe in short time, in the hands of a few men, having unmerciful hearts, and being unnecessary members of the common wealth. And a great number of the rest of the subjects of this realm, being in their diverse vocations, necessary members of the common wealth, by the unmerciful dealing of these usurers, dry exchangers, and corrupt chevisaunces, shalbe either driven to bankruptcy, or else so much impoverished that they shall not be able to do unto the Queen's Majesty, and unto the realm in time of wars, any such favours as they would willingly do, if they were of ability.[25]

Given the perceived connections between usury and bankruptcy, poverty, business prosperity and charity it is not surprising that Parliament dealt with it, but there were fundamental ideological and political differences on usury in the English polity. Demonstrated by the sharp contrasts between the usury law of 37 Henry VIII, permitting lending at rates up to 10 per cent, and 5&6 Edward VI, which forbade all lending at interest, these differences forced policy-makers to ask hard questions about usury. Their answers, reflected in their responses to the Bill against usury of 1571, demonstrate that they were deeply divided over the questions of what usury was, when and how it should be regulated, and, most importantly, what God wanted Parliament to do about usury. William Cecil, recently created Lord Burghley and made Lord Treasurer of England, found himself in the middle of this debate and his attempts to answer these questions are fascinating because we can see how he, as a leader of the government, approached the solution of pragmatic problems.

The immediate cause of Cecil's thoughts on usury was the passage of a usury Bill in the House of Commons in April 1571. Sitting for the first time in the Lords, he did a careful formal analysis and consulted experts about the matter. What we cannot know is if he was responsible for the appearance of the Bill, but the notes he left us show us how he, Lord Treasurer of England and Prime Minister in all but name, analysed the issue of usury.

Faced with the question of whether or not usury could be tolerated, and, if it could, how it should be regulated, he fell back on the method of analysis he had learned at Cambridge. Posing a series of questions, he started with God's law, and he concluded with the problem of policy.

Usura

Questions
1 Whether it be against nature or not.
2 Whether it be forbidden [unlawful] by gods Word or no.

3 Whether it be a [ceremoni] judicial or moral law.
4 Whether it be wholly forbidden, or but where it is used with the poor.
5 Whether (if it be not unlawful by god's law) yet it be convenient to prohibit it by man's law.
6 Whether in making a law for it, it be convenient to prohibit it generally, and to provide for particular cases that may chance or to leave them to the construction of the Chancery.[26]

Cecil's analysis began with natural law and divine law because he knew the essential issue in the usury debate was what God's opinion on usury really was. He clearly believed that human law must conform to God's law, and that God was the ultimate arbiter of this legal issue.

The basic definitions of usury used by William Cecil and his contemporaries were inherited from scholastic theology, deriving ultimately from biblical precepts. Tudor people knew that God had first forbidden lending at interest in Exodus 22: 25, translated by Nicholas Sanders: 'If thou shalt give money to loan unto my poor people which dwelleth with thee, thou shalt not be instant upon him as an importunate wringer, neither shalt thou oppress him with usury'.[27] Ezekiel went so far as to describe usurers as idolaters, oppressors of the poor and robbers: 'Such a man shall not live . . . he shall die and his blood will be on his own head'.[28] In Psalms it is announced that usurers shall not dwell in the tabernacle of the Lord, and in Leviticus people are ordered not to oppress their brethren with interest.[29] As if these condemnations of lending at interest were insufficient, Christ himself ordered in Luke 6: 35 that you shall, in Sanders's translation, 'Give to loan, hoping for nothing out of the loan itself, or respect thereof [Date mutuum, nihil inde sperantes]'.[30]

In the hands of Thomas Aquinas these biblical condemnations were united with Aristotelian logic to create a legal standard against which the behaviour of lenders could be measured. Arguing that to pay for the use of money was to pay twice for one thing, the great Dominican theologian proclaimed that to charge interest was to commit an unnatural, sinful act. In *Summa Theologica* usury was defined as unnatural, and clearly forbidden by God's word, because money is barren. Consequently, Aquinas and Gratian agreed that intentionally lending at interest without sharing in the borrower's risk was the sin of usury. By the late fifteenth century, however, Conrad Summenhardt, Gabriel Biel and others of the Tübingen School had launched an attack on the classical definition of usury because of their understanding of what sin was and when it occurred. Whereas in Aquinian scholasticism the act itself was sin, for these nominalists intention was the arbiter of sin. For them, loans made with good intentions were permissible.[31] John Eck, Luther's great antagonist, popularized the nominalist argument in favour of intent, to the great pleasure of his patrons, the Fugger banking family from Augsburg. He cogently argued for the legitimacy of 5 per cent as a legal rate of interest, attacking those who believed that all interest had to be forbidden at all times.[32]

By the time of the Reformation, European theologians were divided in their thoughts on usury, some holding with the Aquinian prohibition of all loans at interest and others siding with those who believed that if the borrower and the lender were in charity with one another usury could not occur. Luther took a conservative stance on usury, unwilling to license it even though he did insist that magistrates were permitted to allow it, if it was carefully controlled. Swiss reformers tended to take the nominalist stance, edging cautiously toward the idea that lending at interest was permissible as long as the golden rule was observed.

The quintessential argument about usury from the Protestant side came from Charles du Moulin who published his *Tractatus contractum et usurarum reditumque pecunia et monetarum* in 1547, even though it was completed in 1542. Interestingly, he built his disquisition on a reinterpretation of scripture. Rather than reading it as Aquinas had read it, he developed the familiar argument that Jewish law did not bind Christians because it was a judicial rather than a moral law. This allowed him to assert that what had been a prohibition of lending at interest was now no more than a principle of equity – do not oppress your neighbour. Thus he could interpret Christ's 'lend, hoping for nothing in return' as nothing more than edification of the conscience. Just as no one really expected the magistrate to turn the other cheek, so it was unrealistic to expect that loans be without interest. Instead, Christ's message was that people should govern themselves with a spirit of love and charity.[33] Scripture was not a code of rigid precepts governing exterior actions; it established an ideal of beneficence and altruism by which Christian behaviour was to be guided.

It followed that du Moulin believed that lending at interest was permissible if the borrower and lender had an equality of contract. To the destitute poor one must make donations; to the working poor one lent without interest; to the rich merchant one charged interest because he would use the money to make money and could afford to pay for the loan.[34]

Jean Calvin, writing after du Moulin, took much the same line. He too began with the question of whether the laws of the Jews are binding on Christians, concluding that they were not. Rather than forbidding all lending at interest, Christ had intended to remind people that they had to help the poor freely. We must follow the rule of equity, applying tests to determine what kind of loan the supplicant needed. We should not charge interest to paupers, and we should be sure that our loans help our poorer brethren. The borrower must be able to make a profit by the use of the money, and we should regard public utility if we are to make loans. Moreover, we must be sure that the loan is made in accord with natural equity, and it should not exceed the legal rate of interest.[35]

These arguments were brought to England by Martin Bucer, fleeing Strasbourg to Cambridge. In 1550 he delivered a lecture on Ephesians 4, describing the various kinds of theft and including usury in his list. However, he specifically exempted loans at interest that did not harm the borrower. Worse, he told the students that they could lend at interest in order to support their studies since loans supporting the deserving poor – widows, orphans, students and clergy – were licit. His argument upset John Young, a fellow of Trinity College, and a debate ensued. This exchange, in which Bucer adopted the arguments of du Moulin and Young defended the more traditional Aquinian attitude toward lending, put the contest, between those who believed all loans at interest were against God's law and those who believed that the intent of the lender and the status of the borrower determined the propriety of the loan, on the English stage.[36]

These arguments were widely known among educated English people, provoking Thomas Wilson, the noted rhetorician, civil lawyer and diplomat, to write his classic *Discourse upon Usury* in 1569. He dedicated it to John Jewel, the first Elizabethan bishop of Salisbury, because Jewel shared his determined opposition to any concession to the sin of usury. Jewel wrote to Wilson:

> For what man would not be afraid to live desperately in that state of life that he sees manifestly condemned by heathens, by Christians, by the old fathers, by the ancient counsels, by Emperors, by bishops, by decrees, by canons, by all sects of all regions and of all religions, by the Gospel of Christ, by the mouth of God? . . . *ut vivat liber, usura pereat.*

None the less, the fact that they felt the need to write against usury proves that their traditional beliefs about the sin were being challenged theologically and in practice.[37]

When Cecil asked his questions about usury he was aware of this intellectual history of the debate, and he clearly knew the arguments being used on both sides of the issue. The debate in the Commons turned around the validity of the Aquinian interpretation versus the nominalist position. Since both Wilson and Jewel sat in the Parliament of 1571 we know a great deal of how they probably argued. What we can see in Cecil's notes is probably how he would argue the issue.

After he had asked his questions, he proceeded to posit the three competing definitions of usury in Latin. The first, Aquinian, definition was that usury arose from an agreement to pay in money more than the value of a thing. The second, Aristotelian, definition said usury is the fruit of money which is lent. The third, nominalist, definition said that it is the price of money lent under contract. Which was correct? Was lending at interest overcharging for a good, the product of money's activity, or the price paid for money over time?

Setting out to answer these questions, Cecil dived into his list of six questions.

1 Whether it [usury] be against nature or not.

The fact that Cecil saw fit to begin with this question shows how thoroughly his thinking was grounded in scholastic principles and Aquinian theology. Aquinas had taken from Aristotle the idea that what was natural was good, making the unnatural use of a thing a sin. Thus Cecil had to work out the natural use of money and whether it could be either rented or expected to multiply. His method, in keeping with his question, was scholastic. He writes:

1 It is against nature to do wrong any wise, but by usury wrong is done. Ergo [it is wrong].
2 It is wrong that a man should pay for the use of his [own]; in usury of money a man pays for the use of his own, and that against his will.
3 When the money is delivered it is his own and yet he pays for the use thereof, and also renders it again. Ergo [it is wrong].

Objection

So does a man for his house or horse when he borrows him.

Response

That is a *location* [rental] where the property remains still.

Drawing the distinction between fungible and non-fungible goods, he is rehearsing an ancient argument over whether a man can have the thing itself and the use of the thing if it is consumed by use, or, as he so charmingly puts it, 'a man cannot have his cake and eat it also'.

Working along the same lines, he took up the Aristotelian contention that lending at interest is contrary to nature because money is a measure of value, having no value in itself, and therefore is sterile. That being the case, to demand interest is to pervert the proper end of money. Thus lending at interest is unnatural, and therefore it is a sin.

From these two arguments Cecil could be expected to draw the conclusion, as Aquinas had, that charging interest on non-fungible goods or money was unnatural and sinful. Naturally, what was sinful should not be permitted by human law. Most conservative commentators on usury took this route when demanding secular prohibition of the crime, as did Dr Thomas Wilson, in the debate on the Bill Against Usury in the Commons in 1571.

> First endeavoring to prove that the common state may be without usury . . . He made a definition of usury, showing that it was the taking of any reward or sum over and above the due debt. To take

any thing for that which is not mine is robbery: forthwith upon the delivery of loan money it is not mine, and the law is that *mutuum* [a loan] must be free. And here showed the difference between location and *mutuum*, the one implying a contract, the other none.[38]

Wilson proceeded in his argument to discuss the place of usury in the Word of God, as did Cecil with his second question.

2   Whether it [usury] be forbidden by God's Word or no.

At first glance the answer to this question was a resounding yes. Cecil notes that it is forbidden in Exodus 22, Leviticus 25 and Deuteronomy 23. It is dissuaded in Nehemiah, Psalms and Ezekiel. He copied the passages, in Latin, from Exodus, Leviticus and Deuteronomy into his notes, but he found something especially interesting in Exodus 22: 25. 'Si pecuniam mutuam dederis populo meo pauperi qui habitat tecum, non urgebis eum quasi exactor, *nec usurus opprimes* [If thou shalt give money to loan unto my poor people which dwelleth with thee, thou shalt not be instant upon him as an importunate wringer, neither shalt thou oppress him with usury'].[39] Beneath the italicized clause he wrote '*neque inferes ei morsum*' [in this he infers biting]. This reference to biting makes it clear that Cecil was asking whether or not this meant a total prohibition was required, or if it meant only that oppression was forbidden.

The issue of whether all loans at interest should be illegal, or only loans which, in the words of Chrysostom, 'bit like an asp' was an important one. If all loans bite, all should be outlawed, but if they did not, those that were not 'biting' could be legalized: a total prohibition of usury was not necessary.

The origins of this question are in humanist linguistic scholarship. Students of Hebrew had discovered that in the original the word translated by St Jerome as *usura* was *neshek*, meaning 'to bite'. This led some to argue that the Latin translation should be *morsus*, 'bite'. The Hebrew did not always use *neshek*, but its presence in the text gave those who supported liberalizing the law a claim that God did not forbid loans when the borrower and lender were in charity with one another. This etymological argument had been used by Bucer, among many others, to justify his position on usury, and it had direct bearing on the Parliamentary deliberations on the proposed toleration of lending at 10 per cent.[40]

In the Commons debate Mr Clarke argued for the total prohibition of lending at interest, insisting that God's law abolished any contradictory common law and clinching his argument with this quotation from the Vulgate Bible: 'The very word of the Psalms answers to the question *"Domine, quis habitabit in tabernaculo tuo?"* he said, *"qui iuvat proximo suo et non decepit et qui pecuniam suam non dedit ad usuram"*.' Sir John

Wooley answered this with an argument for liberalization that ended with a new translation of Psalm 14:

> As for the words of scripture, he says the Hebrew sounds this in answer of this, '*quis habitabit in tabernaculo tuo?*' it is said, '*qui non dat pecuniam suam ad morsum*': so that it is the biting and oversharp dealing which is disliked and nothing else. And this he said was the mind and interpretation of the most famous learned man Beza in these days and of one Bellarmine who said that the true interpretation of the Hebrew word is not *usura* but *morsus*.[41]

People wishing to enter the debate over the shape of the proposed usury law had to decide what the proper translation was before they could conclude their own analysis. Cecil therefore spent half a folio on a response to the two propositions. 'It is', he began, 'no argument *ab etymologia ad rem* [from the history of the word to the thing] for etymologies comprehend not always the sense of the word'. For instance, the Bible forbids you to steal ['*Non facies furtum*'], yet *furtum* comes from *furno*, which has nothing to do with theft. He adds that *bona* comes from *beando*, and 'extortion' from *extorquendo*. None of which roots has anything to do with the thing named by the word. Here we have something of a puzzle, for Cecil's etymology is wrong in all cases, leading us to suspect either that he was misled or that he may have deliberately used roots which proved his case, even if they were not the real roots of the words.[42]

Cecil's rejection of the argument from etymology is important because the belief on the part of those who would tolerate usury that only 'biting' loans were forbidden by God created an easy justification for liberalization. Moreover, it was a position popular with French-speaking theologians and they liked to use it when constructing justifications of lending at interest to support the 'truly needy' – widows, orphans, students and ministers. By finding it fallacious Cecil was kicking one of the legs from under poor men's banks and the courts of orphans.

There was, however, another arrow in the quiver of those who believed that God had not intended to outlaw all lending at interest. Cecil's third question was aimed at testing the Christian's relationship to the Hebrew law.

3 Whether it be a judicial or moral law.

Once he had concluded that usury was unnatural and forbidden by scripture, Cecil took up the question of whether the prohibition was binding on Christians. Here he faced a thorny Reformation problem. Although Luther had propounded the principle of *sola scriptura* and proclaimed the return to a scriptural faith, he and his fellows had been quickly forced by radical literalists to deny that the letter of the Jewish law was binding on Christians. Luther, and more emphatically Calvin, made a distinction between judicial laws, which are valid only in the time and place for which they are made, and moral laws, which are universally applicable. Therefore the judicial laws of the Jews bind Christians only in so far as they are examples of the equity God requires. They are not to be imposed literally on Christians.

Calvin had dismissed the Aristotelian argument that money was barren as frivolous. The etymological argument that it was expressly forbidden by God in scripture he took more seriously, but the crux of the matter was the law of equity. All the scriptural discussion of lending led one to conclude that God disliked oppression, not interest. 'We see', he wrote, 'that the end for which the law was framed was, that men should not cruelly oppress the poor, who ought rather to receive sympathy and compassion'.[43]

Thus for Cecil to answer his questions about usury he had to resolve for himself the problem of whether the anti-usury passages in the Old Testament applied to everyone at all times – were a moral law – or whether they formed a judicial law, binding only the Jews at the time they were promulgated. If they were a moral law, lending at interest must always be forbidden. If they were a judicial law, the judicial law of England need not slavishly follow their lead so long as the rule of equity was not broken.

His analysis of the question of whether the biblical prohibition of usury had to be enforced by Parliament begins with an objection: that it was a judicial law not a moral one. He answers with two responses. The first is summarized in his comment that to argue that it was a Jewish law and does not apply to 'us' is to argue to the person, not to the thing.

His second response was to observe that it was a moral law, and that it still prohibited usury, for under the precept 'you shall not steal' usury is prohibited because it is a form of theft. Besides, all judicial laws are reducible to moral laws at some point. Moral law that gave rise to the judicial law was based on God's general prohibitions of theft and oppression, especially oppression of widows and orphans.

Cecil's conclusions on this point are unclear, but he seems to have been influenced by friends and legal experts he consulted. In particularly, 'Mr Throckmorton' (perhaps Sir Nicholas Throckmorton) helped him by showing him that one could tolerate usury in human law without conceding that the Old Testament was not binding on Christians.

Throckmorton had insisted that usury was purely an internal matter. Summarizing the argument Cecil wrote 'Nothing external is evil *nisi quatemus interna actio animi accedit* [unless it proceeds from an internal action of the soul]', drawing the moral, 'lending of money is external. Ergo if it be not with an evil conscience it is not evil'. If correct, this argument, which rested squarely on nominalist analysis, had important implications for law. It meant that human law, incapable of knowing a person's intent, could not regulate sinful behaviour.

These implications were clear to Cecil, since the argument sent him into an extended analysis of the human conscience and its relationship to sin and law. He began with a 'syllogism of conscience' derived from Gratian:

Major:	Nothing evil should be done;
	Reason
Minor:	This is evil;
	Conscience
Conclusion:	Ergo, this should not be done.

It was a line of argument that had been used in the Commons by his friend and collaborator Sir Thomas Norton. A prominent lawyer, Norton opposed liberalizing the usury law: 'since it is doubtful what is good, that we should be mindful of the true old saying *quod dubitas ne feceris* [don't do what is doubtful], and for that *quod non ex fide est, peccatum est* [what is not from faith is sin]'.[44]

Cecil, however, did not fully agree with Norton, recognizing that Norton's argument rested on the idea that conscience is law understood naturally. Therefore he countered by noting that a conscience too free would make a man presumptuous; one too strictly controlled would make a man desperate; and both those conditions could lead a man into sin because he could not act against the prompting of his erring conscience. To the proposition that anything contrary to a formed conscience is wrong and sinful Cecil appended the vitiating qualification that to act contrary to an overly timorous or scrupulous conscience is not always sinful.

For a lawmaker this was not, however, the key point. An erring conscience was not an excuse that human law could recognize. Decisions in conscience lead to actions, and actions fall into three categories. There are those which are, of themselves, good or bad. A correct (*recte*) conscience will not err in distinguishing between them. And then there are indifferent actions. But ignorant deeds are not excused in law, even if God Himself might excuse them. The law works on facts, asking the classic questions who, what, where, when, by whose aid, why, and in what manner about circumstances arising from human actions. The only time the law can forgive an illegal action is when the actor is, like a small child, incapable of knowing the law.

What he concluded from these ruminations is not certain, but he seems to have been reasoning away from the argument that conscience and sin could reside within the same paradigm as human law. As he says on another folio, '*nihil externum est peccatum vero quo ad Deum sed ad hominem pene omnia. Nam alias multa absurda. Homo omnium rerum mensura.* [Nothing external is truly sin to God, but men punish all. For anything else would be absurd. Man is the measure of all things.]' Thus the issue of sin is God's concern, not the magistrate's. Human law must be made to fit humans.

To this point Cecil was debating the crucial issue of how much God's scriptural prohibition of usury (whatever it was) bound human lawmakers to prohibit it. Having, perhaps, concluded that there was a distinction between divine and human responses to sinful actions, he turned to another important issue, that of whether there was a qualitative difference between usurious loans made to the poor and loans made to those who could afford to pay interest.

> 4 Whether [usury] be wholly forbidden or but where it is used with
> the poor.

This was a crucial question because in the debate over the Bill Against Usury in 1571 demands for a total prohibition were met by a distinction between permissible usury which did no damage, and usury which oppressed the poor. Certainly people who wished to establish a poor men's bank or a court of orphans tried to justify themselves by arguing that such a difference existed. 'For surely', said a member of the Commons,

> there can be no sin where there is no breach of charity. To do
> that therefore to another which we would to our selves (the state,
> circumstance and case to our selves counted) is commendable and
> not to be improved. If we our selves be to borrow, who is it that
> would not in extremity give a little to save much money?[45]

To answer the question of whether the status of the borrower determined the legality of the loan, Cecil sorted through the arguments used by Aquinas and Dr Wilson, juxtaposing them with arguments used by du Moulin, Calvin and Bucer and embodied in two of his consultants, Mr Skinner and Dr Huick. Skinner insisted that the argument from etymology was a good witness to the essential illegality of usury, while Huick took a more liberal position. He rejected the traditional definitions as false, arguing pragmatically that if usury is, as it was at the time, totally prohibited 'other contracts secret will follow whereby men shall be more impoverished as buying of 20 li. in wares for 60 li.'[46] From this Cecil drew a moral: 'Usury lawful to a rich, unlawful to a poor man'.

These conflicting opinions were analysed under the proposition that if usury is illicit it should be punished consistently. However, he raised an objection. Was not the prohibition a general one rather than a specific one? After all, there is a general prohibition against killing, but magistrates are permitted to kill under certain circumstances. Thus, even if usury is generally permitted by God the test of circumstance might reveal times when it would be wrong not to permit usury. That being the case, the taking of interest on a loan is not a sin in itself, but must be judged according to a test of circumstance. As a member of the Commons said:

nothing is to be said in that degree sin in it self, but by the circumstance so is it known whether it be good or bad. To kill is prohibited,
yet sometime not to kill is evil: Phineas killed, and was therefore
commended. And thefts at times have been in scripture approved. . . .
That all should be well it is to be wished, but that all may be well
done among men it is more than to be hoped for. We are no saints;
we are not of perfection to follow the letter of the gospel. . . . Surely
there can be no sin where there is no breach of charity.[47]

Even if people could not be expected to follow the letter of God's law,
and even if God's opinion on the subject was debatable – so that not all
usurious loans were *malum in se* – the policy-maker still had to face the
question of whether it should be prohibited by human law because of its
economic effects.

5 Whether, if it be not unlawful by God's law, yet it be convenient to
prohibit it by man's law.

The answer to the question seems to have been a qualified 'Yes'. Cecil
knew that the Athenian, Roman, Spartan and other laws controlled usury.
However, the shape of the law used to control it was an important
problem.

Therefore, Cecil turned to an analysis of the nature of law. Unfortunately, the folio containing his thoughts seems to be missing, but we can
get an idea of its content from other notes. In so far as his tangled,
abbreviated Latin can be deciphered, he seems to assume that the function
of human law in this case is to correct deficits in equity. As long as there
is not a consistent violation of equity in the loan, there is no need to
totally outlaw usury. As he points out, if the prohibition is to be considered universal, unique cases cannot be considered; but, if lending is
tolerated by law, then the law must be ready to consider unique cases. If
unique cases are to be considered, the equity of each case is the subject
of the law. This reasoning leads him to consider the limits of the law and,
citing Menander's warning that laws must be looked into sharply to avoid
over subtle interpretation, he concludes that the right of a judge is restricted by the penalties of the law.

None of this seems to make much sense, unless taken together with
Cecil's next question.

6 Whether in making a law for it, it be convenient to prohibit it
generally, and to provide for particular cases that may chance or to
leave them to the construction of the Chancery.

Having decided that usury could not be left unregulated, Cecil began an
analysis which seems to a modern eye to be the heart of the matter. He
asked what the social and economic consequences of usury were. Usury's

negative effects were detailed in a series of six interrelated observations that are easiest understood if reproduced as he wrote them.

1   It decays merchandise ergo it is hurtful.
    Merchandise rests in exchange properly, wares for wares.

> Improperly wares for money.
> Unnaturally money for money.
> Ergo [it is hurtful.]

2   Merchants may not be infinite in the common wealth but by taking usury they may be infinite. Ergo [it is hurtful.]
3   The rich merchants gain without peril. Ergo [it is hurtful.]
4   The oftener anything is sold the dearer it is. But by usury both the price and the thing is sold. Ergo [it is hurtful.]
5   It decays charity for now no part of liberality is left but giving and that is too chargeable to be often or much used.
6   It makes many bankrupts.

In this list Cecil incorporated all the major secular arguments against usury made by contemporaries. They explain much of the hostility toward usurers for, even though usury was ungodly, seen in this light the usurer's activities also were anti-social and hurt his neighbours.

Many feared that the return on money lent at interest would be so high that people would cease to trade. Doctor Wilson told the Commons that allowing lending would hurt the Queen and the commonwealth because men, 'not usinge their owne money, but findinge greater gaine in usury, doe employ the same that way, soe that her custome must decrease'. The damage to the commonwealth came from increasing prices for 'who soe shall give hire for money is to raise the same in the sale of his comodity: all trades shall bee taken away, all occupacions lost, for eich man seekinge most ease and greatest gaine without hazard or venture will further employ his money to such use'.[48] Of course bankruptcy was another result of this combination of increasing interest rates and rising prices.

Worse, charitable giving would end if people were permitted to earn interest on their money. No longer would they lend to the poor without charging, and few could or would give outright.

These arguments make a grim assessment of human motivations and demonstrate the assumption that no one would borrow unless driven by necessity or greed. Only those who are striving to live beyond their stations could possibly support legalized lending at interest if this scenario was followed.

However, those who had a different assessment of human nature and who believed that capitalization of business benefited the commonwealth were represented in the list of eight reasons usury should be permitted. For them usury preserved trade, aided the indigent, allowed the maximization of profits, was permitted by laws, was a voluntary contract, helped the church, helped orphans and the poor, and was given not to the poor but to the rich.

These arguments were aimed at proving that not all lending at interest was bad or illegal. By pointing out that some laws permitted taking interest he was reminding himself that the Romans had allowed interest of up to 12 per cent and that on the continent many principalities permitted 5 per cent. By reminding himself that the church, widows and orphans could be helped by loans he was stressing that good ends could be achieved by lending at interest. His last point, however, was the most potent pro usury argument.

This was du Moulin's belief that it was permissible to lend at interest if the borrower was using the money to make a profit for himself. It was not permissible, however, to lend at interest to the poor. The quality of the borrower determined the proper response to the request for a loan. Cecil took over du Moulin's argument and schematized it, showing that beggars deserve gifts; the working poor deserve loans; rich men deserve to pay rent for their money. He summarized the argument in English: 'Christ meddles not with contracts, but with justice of contracts'. Thus if the borrower could afford to pay interest there was no reason not to charge it.

None of these reasons seems to have fully convinced Cecil of the desirability of deregulating lending at interest. Nor was he persuaded by arguments of those who, like Serjeant Lovelace, urged that it was impossible to make a law to control usury. Lovelace told the Commons that he hated usury, but

> to prohibit it with so sharp and extreme a law as to lose all, he thought it would be the ground of greater covetousness. Withall he added that to prohibit the ill of covetousness in generality were vain, void and frivolous, since that the speech and the act itself is indefinite, comprehending all kind of our actions and doings, and therefore as utterly vain it were to prohibit it in vain words of a generality.[49]

Cecil therefore asked himself if a law should not be made if many absurdities were likely to arise from it. He seems to have concluded that to permit an evil in order to achieve a good end was wrong.

Before he ended he addressed one other argument. To those who argued that nothing external is prohibited as sin unless it arises from an internal action he responded: 'That opinion is true in theology, but not in human law, for it punishes the external'. Nevertheless, there are many cases in law in which the intention is obvious, such as when a person ships wool to Castile. And there are many cases where the law refuses to punish because the action arises from the state of mind, as in *fellonies lunatici*.

After this exhaustive consideration of the pros and cons of legalized usury he opted for a middle position in his conclusion. Having clearly concluded that usury was wrong and forbidden by God, he also seems to have decided that the definition of usury allowed some lending at interest to be done, so long as it was permitted in order to prevent a greater evil. Three precepts guided his conclusion.

1   Merchandise must be exercised by justice, for else might pirates be sometime allowed.
2   We must help men as the Word prescribes.
3   Many things be permitted, but not to be drawn in an example.

The first seems to rest on the principle of equality of dealing and upon a suspicion that profits would be maximized at the expense of the common weal. He was not willing to let the market regulate itself for, as he noted, 'mercantile fraud is prohibited by the commandment "you shall not steal" ', drawing the moral that justice should not encourage iniquity.

The second point demonstrates both his commitment to obeying the law of God and his belief that Christians have a duty to help one another. It is difficult to know from these notes which of the many arguments about usury's effect on the poor Cecil accepted, but it does not seem that he supported the pro-usury arguments about lending at interest being good for the poor. God had commanded that men be helped, and the law should do nothing that would undermine charity.

His last point emphasizes that he took a conservative stand on usury. Even if exceptions had been allowed in the prohibition of usury, whether by God or by human law, they were not to be construed to mean that the divine law against usury was abrogated.

What this conclusion meant in practice is that Cecil had rationalized the shape of the Act Against Usury that emerged from Parliament in 1571. The Bill had proposed that the statute passed in 37 Henry VIII be revived. If it had been, all loans at less than 10 per cent interest would have been permitted without regulation. It would have legalized the taking of interest for the support of orphans and the poor, encouraged capitalization of business by moderating interest rates and let money-lenders come out of the closet.

People who supported the toleration of moderate usury because of its positive effects were opposed by those who believed that God had damned usury and no human excuses could justify legalizing it. When the 1571 Bill was introduced in the Commons, they attacked it vigorously, insisting that Parliament had no right even to consider repealing a law that conformed to God's law.

When the Bill was committed, after a debate that demonstrated how far apart the two positions were, it was rewritten. We cannot prove that Cecil took a hand in shaping the new Bill, but it conformed neatly to the views he expressed at the end of his ruminations. It did not allow usury. Instead, it made a distinction between heinous usury – interest over 10 per cent – and petty usury. This was necessary because, as the statute says, 'all usury being forbidden by the law of God is sin and detestable'. Aware that judges might deliberately misinterpret the statute, the men who drafted it ordered that it should be 'most largely and strongly construed for the repressing of usury'.

There was to be no toleration of usury – else piracy might be allowed. This also meant that charity was not threatened. The help that the Word commanded Christians to offer to the needy was not threatened because the profits that people could make from lending were controlled, as was the interest rate. Charitable lending was not dried up, since a little interest was tolerated and the borrower always had recourse to law to stop oppression.

In his third conclusion Cecil had observed that many things were permitted that were not to be made into precedents. That precisely describes the way the statute dealt with the courts of orphans. Having outlawed all lending at interest, the authors added a proviso ordering that it was not to be used to stop the 'finding of orphans'. In short, all usury was illegal except that usury which was specifically permitted by an exception.[50]

Cecil's notes on usury were part of a policy debate that had been raging since the late 1540s. The compromise statute of 1571 settled the issue in law, representing, as Cecil's notes represent, the way in which theological positions and philosophical principles were brought to bear on economic and social problems. Tudor people believed usury was at the root of bankruptcy, poverty, declining trade, and the decay of the upper classes, so it was necessary to deal with it. That, in turn, required definition and definition sent men back to their books.

The attempt made by Cecil, the most powerful man in the English government, to define usury shows how closely his approach to legislation was linked to his religion and his education. He was facing pragmatic issues, but in order to find a solution to those problems he used his university training to define usury and to debate within himself the nature and function of law. The result was a pragmatic statute that stood until 1624, when the economy and conceptions of human and divine law had changed to such an extent that the compromise of 1571 no longer worked. After wrestling with usury for a quarter of a century, Parliament, undoubtedly under Cecil's influence, had succeeded in finding a compromise that brought together the conflicting views of usury. It was a compromise that was possible only because it was reached at a normative level, literally blending divergent philosophical positions. It stands as a monument to the legal statesmanship of William Cecil, Lord Burghley, Lord Treasurer of England; to the small band of parliamentary leaders in the Commons; and to the parliamentary process. In a thoroughly pragmatic way law was created in response to economic troubles under the influence of theology and philosophy.

NOTES

1 BL Lansdowne, 101, nos. 24 and 26. Because these are unpaginated and are clearly part of the same exercise, I have considered them together.

2 PRO SP 12/1/fos 147–54.

3 HMC Salisbury, 9, I, 151.

4 BL Add. 48, 023, fo. 354.

5 BL Lansdowne 102, fo. 98.

6 G. D. Ramsay (ed.) *John Isham, Mercer and Merchant Adventurer: Two Account Books of a London Merchant in the Reign of Elizabeth I*, *Northamptonshire Record Society*, 1962, vol. 21, lxxx–xci. For English trade with the Netherlands in the 1560s, see G. D. Ramsay, *The Queen's Merchants and the Revolt of the Netherlands: The End of the Antwerp Mart*, Manchester, Manchester University Press, 1986, vol. 2.

7 5 Eliz. I, c. 3, An Act for the Relief of the Poor; 5 Eliz. I, c. 20, An Act for the Punishment of Vagabonds calling themselves Egyptians; 14 Eliz. I, c. 5. See Paul A. Fideler's essay on Tudor poor relief policy, Chapter 7 in this volume.

8 Hatfield House, Herts., Cecil Papers, 152, fo. 96v.

9 1 Eliz. I, c. 10, *The Statutes of the Realm*, 12 vols, London, Dawsons, 1963 (reprint of 1810–28 edn), vol. IV, pt. 1, pp. 370–1 (hereafter *Statutes*).

10 W. Bullein, *A dialogue bothe pleasant and pietifull, Against the Fever Pestilence*, fo. 52v. (London, J. Kingston, 1573 STC 4037).

11 Bodl., Laud 683, fos 145–7. John Young's new year's gift to Queen Elizabeth, 1559.

12 N. L. Jones, *God and the Moneylenders: Usury and Law in Early Modern England*, Oxford, Basil Blackwell, 1989; I had not seen Young's observation when I wrote the book.

13 BL Add. 48,023, fo. 356v. See Neal Wood, Chapter 5 in this volume, for Sir Thomas Smith's 'amoral' analysis of the economy.

14 R. Porder, *A sermon of gods fearefull threatenings for Idolatrye*, fos 59–59v (London, H. Denham, 1569–70 *STC* 20117).

15 Ibid., fos 101v–102.

16 PRO SP 12/75/fo. 112. The comment is by 'Mr Taverner'.

17 5 & 6 Edward VI, c. 20, *Statutes*, vol. IV, pt. 1, p. 155.

18 Corp. London RO, Repertories 13, fo. 12v. CJ I, 30; 31; 33–5.

19 T. Wright (ed.) *Queen Elizabeth and her Times: A Series of Original Letters*, 2 vols, London, H. Colburn, 1838, II, 126.

20 PRO SP 12/75/fos 107–10. 'Contro le eccesive usure'. I have translated 'usure' as 'interest' in my quote in order to make Cavalcanti's meaning clear. The original reads: 'Se l'usura per minima che sia edannabile, tanto piu devono essere dannate le eccesive?'

21 Bodl., Laud 683, fos 138–138v.

22 Bodl., Jones 17, fos 8–26.

23 PRO, SP 12/77/fo. 113vff.

24 13 Eliz. I, c. 7. W. J. Jones, 'The foundations of English bankruptcy: statutes and commissions in the early modern period', *Transactions of the American Philosophical Society*, 1979, vol. 69, no. 3. BL, Lansdowne 13, fos 54, 55.

25 PRO, SP 12/75/fo. 113v.

26 This list of questions originally began with what is now number 2. The question now numbered 1 was added after Cecil had reached the question currently numbered 5. The words in brackets were crossed out.

27 N. Sanders, *A breife treatise of vsurie*, fo. 5 (Louanii, ap. J. Foulerum, 1568 *STC* 21691), in D. M. Rogers (ed.) *English Recusant Literature*, 1972, vol. 97.

28 Ezekiel 18: 13.

29 Psalms 15: 5; Leviticus 25: 35–7.

30 Sanders, op. cit., fo. 7v.

31 J. T. Noonan, *The Scholastic Analysis of Usury*, Cambridge, Mass., Harvard University Press, 1957, is the standard study of these complex doctrines.

32 H. A. Oberman, *Masters of the Reformation*, D. Martin (trans.) Cambridge, Cambridge University Press, 1981, p. 138.

33 J.-L. Thireau, *Charles du Moulin (1550–1566) Etude sur les sources, la méthode, les idées politiques et économiques d'un juriste de la Renaissance*, Geneva, Droz, 1980, pp. 357–84.

34 Ibid.

35 L. Calvin, *Opera*, X, 1, pp. 245–8.

36 M. Bucer, *Praelectiones Doctiss. In Epistolam D.P. ad Ephesios . . .*, Basel, Apvd Petrvm Pernam, 1562, pp. 168–9, and 'Tractatus de usuris', *Scripta Anglicana*, Basel, ex Petri Pernae, 1577, p. 792.

37 T. Wilson, *A Discourse Upon Usury*, R. H. Tawney (ed.), London, G. Bell, 1925. John Jewel, *Works*, J. Ayre (ed.), Cambridge, Cambridge University Press, 1847, II, p. 851. N. L. Jones, op. cit., 24–34.

38 T. E. Hartley (ed.) *Proceedings in the Parliaments of Elizabeth I, 1558–1581*, Leicester, Leicester University Press, 1981, p. 233.

39 The translation is Sanders's in Rogers, op. cit., fo. 5.

40 Bucer retranslated the Hebrew in Psalm 15 this way: 'Qui non dederit pecuniam suam ad usuram mordentem, & munus non acceperit adversus innocentum'; 1577, op. cit., p. 793.

41 Hartley, op. cit., pp. 231–2.

42 I owe a debt of gratitude to my colleagues Frances Titchener and Mark Damen for their etymological detective work on this.

43 Calvin, op. cit., pp. 245–8.

44 Hartley, op. cit., pp. 236–7. Norton and Cecil were drawing on Gratian, who glossed Romans 14: 23, saying ' "Omne, quod non est ex fide", id est omne, quod contra conscientiam fit, "peccatum est" '. A. Friedberg (ed.) *Decretum Magistri Gratiani*, Graz, 1959, I, pp. 1,226–7.

45 Hartley, op. cit., p. 235.

46 Huick was referring to the way 'coloured' contracts were created in order to hide interest in the guise of a legitimate sale at a price higher than the market price. For a discussion of how this was done, see N. L. Jones, op. cit., pp. 118–44.

47 Hartley, op. cit., pp. 234–5.

48 Ibid., pp. 232–3.

49 Ibid., p. 235.

50 13 Eliz. I, c. 8, *Statutes*, vol. IV, pt. 1, pp. 542–3.

7

Poverty, policy and providence: the Tudors and the poor

Paul A. Fideler

A nation's government and policy, wrote Sir Thomas Smith, should fit the people agreeably 'like a garmet to the bodie or shoe to the foote'. When the fit is proper, the realm enjoys ease, pleasure and profit; but, if 'too litle or too great', it does 'hurt and encomber' convenient use.[1] The crafting of the Poor Law was an important and sustained policy endeavour in the sixteenth-century Tudor years. Signs of preoccupation with poverty abound from Thomas More's *Utopia* to William Perkins's *Cases of Conscience* and from the calls for poor law reform in the 1520s and 1530s to the culminating statutes of 1598 and 1601. Nevertheless, we have no comprehensive study of the intellectual fabric from which the Old Poor Law was fashioned. Instead we have clusters of interest in the policy ideas of particular Bills, statutes, decades and reigns. Unfortunately, there is no consistency of question or method across these studies, and they yield little overall perspective on the role of ideas, perceptions, and social and political thought in the Old Poor Law's formation.[2]

To be sure, recently we have learned much about the dimensions of poverty and the institutional development of poor relief from the work of social historians. Yet, these same historians have insisted that it is no longer satisfactory to assume a direct causal connection between changing numbers of poor people and the shape and goals of poor relief policies and institutions.[3] More attention to the intellectual dimensions of policy formulation is needed. As Donald R. Kelley has argued, historians must try to account for the 'inside' as well as the 'outside' of the past. The inside suggests 'the general meaning of a particular field of experience' to those who lived it. This is best done through the pursuit of ideology, according to Kelley, because it occupies the 'pivotal and almost inaccessible juncture between society and consciousness'.[4] Martin Rein, a current policy analyst, emphasizes the importance of perceptual 'frames', or 'visions' and 'structures', in policy development. A frame provides an individual with 'a way of inquiry, of making sense as well as masking sense of the world', and the encouragement to act.[5] Clearly, the historical study of policy requires attention to the inside of the story, the ideologies, frames and intentions of those who studied and designed measures on poverty and poor relief, as well as to the statutes and initiatives that formed its outside and the shifting demographics and social conditions of its context.

This chapter seeks to characterize the important constellations of ideas, aspirations and perceptions that informed English analyses of poverty and formulations of poor relief and anti-vagrancy policy in the sixteenth century. Sketching these background configurations and the shifts among them requires that I work on a Tudor canvas, not just a Henrician, Edwardian or Elizabethan one. My focus will be particularly on Christian humanism and Calvinist Protestantism; Lutheranism and a more Italianate humanism which veered toward the assumptions of political economy will also be addressed, although in less detail. These frames of thought were enmeshed in a 'relational network' of ideas and perceptions, including inherited medieval ones, within which Tudor people sought to understand and respond to poverty.[6] I hope to demonstrate that fundamental shifts in Tudor thought on poor relief policy can be discerned from a humanist and value-driven to a more providential and pragmatic hue and in the locus of policy development from the central government to the localities.

Thomas Starkey's lament in the early 1530s that the realm is presently 'more pore than hyt hath byn in tyme past, & such poverty reyneth now that in no case may stond wyth a veray true & floryshchyng commyn wele' captured well the mood of Tudor social commentary throughout the sixteenth century.[7] This widely shared perception grew out of a variety of impressions and judgements, including fear of uprisings, discomfort with begging, exasperation with vagrancy and crime, a view of the poor as virtually an unpredictable and dangerous race apart, the assumption that poor labourers were too lazy and unskilled to produce a vigorous economy, and the distinct impression that the numbers of indigent and vagrant people were all the time expanding. The provocative reform languages embedded in humanism and Protestantism, however, were crucial in calling attention to the poverty problem. Both thought systems, although from different premises and for different reasons, challenged the medieval accommodation with poverty; they also directed attention away from God's poor toward man's. Each urged nothing less than the attempt to revivify the common weal.[8]

These new frames of thought contended with conventional wisdom on poverty that rested on several centuries of custom, local relief practices, canon law, statutes and inherited patterns of thought, much of which survived into the seventeenth century.[9] Medieval thinking on poverty had been shaped by notions of *caritas, humilitas, fortuna* and the *imitatio Christi*. Great spiritual merit was conceded to the voluntary, supererogatory poverty of the few regular clergy. The remaining faithful were expected to be patient in the poverty that fortune might send or charitable with whatever excess goods they enjoyed. Property itself was considered a potential good, not only for the opportunities it offered for charitable acts but also for the discipline required to acquire it.[10]

Lollardy represented the kind of heresy that could develop when Augustinian ideas of election and a semblance of the *imitatio Christi* were brought together as John Wyclif had done: in theory dominion became the privilege of the elect. Wyclif and the Lollards called for an unworldly, Christ-like church,[11] and William Langland praised the working poor. Having conceded the spiritual importance of voluntary poverty, no matter how cautiously, Wyclif and Langland had released the genie of inverted merit. The justification of wealth and rank became ever more difficult and always open to challenge, as the Peasants' Revolt (1381) illustrated so well.[12]

The social theory embedded in the Statute of Labourers (1349) held that work was available for all able-bodied people who wanted it. Unemployed, poor and healthy people were looked upon as criminal and suffered harsh punishments; the impotent were considered deserving of assistance and were permitted to beg.[13] There was much almsgiving in the fourteenth and fifteenth centuries, and private charity constituted the largest category of poor relief well into the sixteenth century. Nevertheless, it was understood that institutional efforts directed by the church were an essential supplement to voluntary giving. Monasteries, religious fraternities and the beneficed clergy were the most usual ecclesiastical sources of support for the poor. The statute of 1388 (12 Rich. II, c. 7), which urged villages and towns to maintain their own beggars, was the beginning of the interlocking of ecclesiastical and secular supervision of poor relief, which would be so central to policy developments in the sixteenth century.[14]

A growing distress with vagrancy in the localities and the refinement of Christian humanist discourses of social criticism sparked concern about man's poor and government's role as a remediating force in the early decades of the sixteenth century. Attracted to Cicero's emphasis on civil concord in *De officiis*, Erasmus, Thomas More, Juan Vives and other humanists concluded that much contemporary poverty was a manifestation of lost fellowship. Cicero had insisted that thoughtful people can discover that societies are bound together by justice and that the most natural of all human activities is liberality. Consequently, those who cultivate *sapientia*, strength of mind for good fellowship, citizenship and counsel, make a better preparation for service to the commonwealth than those who build up their bodies for war. In the best commonwealths 'war [will] give place to policy and triumph to eloquence'.[15]

The *Institutio Principis Christiani* was Erasmus' elaboration of very general principles of statecraft that, if widely acted upon, could yield a society of justice and liberality. Erasmus' work and *Utopia* were both written in 1515, and More probably saw the *Institutio* in draft.[16] The well-educated prince, according to Erasmus, unlike sixteenth-century monarchs, would not pursue extravangances or wars. The uncomplicated laws in his state would make clear the folly of idleness and greed and, yet, be humane enough to eschew harsh punishment for theft. However, Erasmus' most signal contribution to the humanist policy commitment was the claim he made for the role of reason in the kingly office. The prince, imitating God's 'supreme judgment' in his rule of the universe, should 'cast aside all personal motives, and use only reason and judgment'.[17]

In *Utopia*, unique for many reasons, More brought reason and the humanist policy impulse to bear on poverty and generated three challenges to traditional analyses. First, he moved the focus of policy discourse from Christian *humilitas* to classical *humanitas*, from poverty of the spirit and self-denial to the cultivation of intellect and modest physical pleasure.[18] Second, in Book One he presented a structural analysis of the source of most poverty, wrong-headed statecraft (e.g. the legalization of enclosure) which institutionalized greed on the one hand and vagrancy and crime on the other. More insisted that poverty is largely a creation of man, not a divine visitation. And this man-made calamity had a withering effect on human personality: in the thrall of systemic poverty an individual was a kind of fallen being, impervious to the blandishments of the *studia human-itatis* and thus prevented from possessing his or her full humanity. Third, More stimulated confidence that government policy, conceived in the spirit of Cicero's *sapientia* and Erasmus' wise prince, could remediate poverty and other shortcomings of the common weal. Altogether, More's deep analysis of poverty within a context of classical values threw down the gauntlet to conventional wisdom. The ignorance, idleness, surliness and debauchery, on which popular attitudes (and vagrancy legislation) rested, were symptomatic of the poor's deprived and untutored humanity, not their inherent depravity.

The implication for any 'state' worthy of the name was unavoidable: a more profound solution to the poverty problem must be undertaken than merely to punish vagrants and to encourage patience in the working poor and impotent. But what was to be done? The Utopians, for their part, had designed a counter-society to contemporary England and Europe. They eschewed private property, avoided greed, and achieved a peaceful and modestly prosperous commonwealth, ruled benignly by their *intelli-gentsia*.[19]

Being at one and the same time the elusive, ironic and didactic work that it was, *Utopia*, as George Logan has shown, confounded its readers right from the start.[20] It continues to bedevil the critic and the historian. Surely Logan and Quentin Skinner are correct when they assert that in *Utopia* More was challenging from the inside the pieties of the humanists themselves, e.g. their continuing commitment to social hierarchy and their reliance on *sententiae* and exhortation rather than social analysis.[21] Just as surely Logan, Skinner, J. H. Hexter, Brendan Bradshaw and Dermot Fenlon are correct in their general agreement that *Utopia* was More's view of a desirable polity, either a truly Christian one or, in Skinner's designation, *'de optimo reipublicae statu'*. However, the interpreters cannot agree on whether More intended that contemporary Europeans should try to replicate Utopia's institutions.[22]

Interesting as these exchanges are, I suggest that they are essentially moot, for *Utopia* represents the Renaissance equivalent of a 'critical theory' of society.[23] The book probably produced a 'curse of enlightenment' for sixteenth-century readers who took it seriously. Existing social and political institutions were drained of all but perverse significance, and the alternative world suggested was compelling to imagine but seemingly impossible to reach. Furthermore, *Utopia* offered transforming assumptions and insights to those wrestling with the 'social question': an array of subtle tools of analysis; a set of high-minded assumptions about human potential; a seductive presentation of the efficacy of policy; and a model of the good society. While all of this did have its inspiring side, it was also a constant reminder of the shortcomings of the existing order, as well as the stark challenges involved in moving from here to there.[24] As I shall point out, the immediate shadow cast by *Utopia* is discernible into the 1550s in the quarrels that the men of *negotium*, like Starkey, Richard Morison, Smith and even Martin Bucer, had with it, as they sought ways to understand and ameliorate the common weal's ills.

Added to *Utopia's* importance in reinvigorating the theoretical analysis of poverty was its contribution to the tactical discourse on poor relief. More had articulated a humanist conceptual vocabulary of policy which Juan Vives applied in his plan for Bruges. This language incorporated four principles: human perfectibility; *mediocritas* in goods;[25] the transforming value of education; and intellectual elitism. Vives held that natural and man-made calamities, as well as individual stupidity, meant that indeed 'the poor ye always have with you'. Nevertheless, even though his plan 'will not prevent a man from becoming a pauper', it will remove him quickly from that condition and restore him to usefulness, virtue and active participation in civil concord.[26]

By the later 1520s the other reform discourse of the sixteenth century, Protestantism, in this case its Lutheran version, was circulating and challenging the ideological assumptions of humanism. Tudor dissenting Protestants throughout the sixteenth century expounded a coherent plan for social reform based on their understanding of human nature and agency, societal destiny and the efficacy of faith.[27] The Protestant discourse can easily be overlooked, however, because its short-term goals were indistinguishable from those of the humanists and most government men: reaffirmation of social hierarchy and avoidance of rebellion; greater liberality to the deserving poor and the elimination of vagrancy; and the achievement of concord and common weal. Protestants viewed with alarm the greed and illiberality of the rich, the surliness of many of the poor, the apparent spread of idleness, and the generally contentious tenor of the times.[28]

Yet Protestants did not share the humanists' degree of commitment to reason and its instrument, policy, as the means with which to achieve greater societal concord. The Protestant plan was rooted in the central tenets of Reformation biblicism, God's omnipotence and providence and human beings' impotence and submission to divine intention. Most important of all, the faithful must consciously involve themselves in God's plan for society rather than design a faulty one through reason and policy and fail. Lutherans were encouraged to practise exemplary Christian patience in whatever social rank they found themselves, while Calvinists were expected to pursue Christian social concern zealously. In either case, however, participation in the total rearranging or overturning of society's institutions was never intended. Protestant reform aspirations were essentially conservative; they sought to alter human predispositions but not to restructure society's institutions.

Luther had revealed his deep disagreement with Erasmus about human nature in *The Freedom of a Christian*, emphasizing that the flesh is unregenerate and does not affect the 'inward self'. It makes no matter if the body is free, active and healthy or imprisoned, ill and weak. 'This sort of thing never touches the soul a little bit, nor makes it free or captive, religious or sinful'.[29] Luther scorned the possibility for spiritual conditioning implicit in the 'works' of medieval Christianity as well as in humanism's commitment to the restorative powers of education. All institutions in the world were, to Luther, factories of pride; yet, he did concede that intelligent men were able to found kingdoms and commonwealths, to govern them with good counsel, and to design many positive supports for social cohesion.[30] Nevertheless, he did not expect government to be an agent of social or economic amelioration; at best it could prevent evil. Luther was drawn to the quiet, bucolic atmosphere of the medieval social ideal far more than to the dynamic, urban one that was gathering momentum around him.

A person's position in the world was passed on from the hand of God through other men. Accepting one's calling was essential. It was the structure through which God demands obedience, and the practice of one's calling within existing social institutions was the best expression of social love.[31] Nevertheless, Luther regretted that many merchants, labourers and citizens of all degrees did not live fully Christian lives. Without strong and harsh oversight by the state, commerce would become corrupted and society anarchic. Thus, Charles Trinkaus probably comes close to the mark in his estimation that Luther's ethical position remained 'sentimental' when all was said and done: it allowed an experience of inner righteousness while the intractable outer world was treated with wary shrewdness.[32]

If, according to Luther, it was folly to think of perfecting society, he nevertheless was convinced that proper faith could make *some* difference for the better in the world. In 1523, three years before Vives published his Bruges plan, Luther had drafted a poor relief proposal for Leisnech. Luther's design, like Vives' and others drawn up for Venice, Ypres, Lyons and Geneva from the mid-1520s onward shared many tactical similarities. Begging was prohibited, alms collected and distributed centrally, the poor surveyed periodically by elected overseers to ascertain need, hospital care provided to the impotent, and education or apprenticeship provided to poor boys and dowries to girls.[33]

The premises that informed Luther's plan were quite different from the 'humanitas-concord-policy' register of Vives'. Luther stressed the challenge that Christian love 'may be led into channels of truth and works of kindly benevolence'. Parishioners were required to give money or in kind to the parish fund, the Common Chest; the distribution of relief was the responsibility of ten overseers elected annually in the parish. This was to insure that the possibility of unChristian impulses in private acts of charity would be eliminated. As Luther put it, the overseers were to distribute from the fund 'for the sake of God and the common good, with a clear Christian conscience, laying aside all considerations of fear, favor, malice, profit or other likely motive'.

William Tyndale, the principal colporteur of Lutheran doctrine in England, imparted a particular tone to his formulation of Lutheranism that gave it a much livelier cast than the original. To Tyndale, proper faith should make individual and social life better. This commitment stemmed from the importance that he placed on the divine compact. If men seek to bind themselves to God, to accept the general contract proffered, 'then God hath bound himself unto us, to keep and make good all the mercies promised in Christ throughout all the scripture'.[34] In his elaboration of the famous 'lilies of the field' passages (Matthew 6: 28), which had so attracted Francis of Assisi and other medieval practitioners of the *imitatio Christi*, Tyndale gave the compact idea a utilitarian significance with regard to worldly prosperity that was important. Christ promised the faithful man, according to Tyndale, 'an hundred fold, even in this life, of all that thou leavest for his sake'.[35]

As Luther had been, Tyndale was very concerned to clarify the significance of works. He made explicit often the Lollard and Lutheran formula that proper works follow *from* faith. They were, in effect, the outward signs of one's inner rectitude. Real, achievable 'apostolic poverty', according to Tyndale, was nothing more, or less, than to be 'content with a competent living', whether it be acquired through inheritance or with one's own labour, and 'doing service to the commonwealth', so that 'my neighbour may have a living by me as well as I'.[36] And, 'as riches do not exclude thee from the blessing, so does not poverty certify thee'. Only 'trust in the living God' can do that.

The immediate impact of Lutheranism *per se*, separate from official anti-Romish doctrine in the 1530s and 1540s, is difficult to ascertain. In their formulation by Tyndale, Luther's ideas served more as a beginning reorientation of English social thought that will blossom later under the influence of Calvinism. Doctrinally more appealing at Court were Melanchthon's moderate views on human will and reason and his emphasis on obedience to authority.[37] His 'middle way' on reason was written into the official *King's Book* (1543), the Forty-Two Articles (IX) and the Thirty-Nine Articles (X).

The Council at the instigation of Cardinal Wolsey developed the government's first response to the localities, beleaguered with vagrancy and other poverty-related problems.[38] Wolsey began with an enclosure commission in 1517 and proceeded to use the policy devices available to him, proclamations, commissions, letters and his personal orders, to move against an array of festering problems. By the time of his fall, Wolsey had begun efforts to minimize the social dislocations caused by enclosure, to enforce vagrancy regulations in London and several large towns, to train physicians and encourage public health efforts, and to assess national grain supplies for their accessibility during bad harvests. Throughout the remainder of the century the Council acted on pressing issues of social need, and, in the process, supplemented the growing body of Tudor poor relief and vagrancy legislation. Further steps were taken to oversee grain storage; Books of Orders were published instructing local officials about proper actions during plague outbreaks and dearth; and copies of the poor laws were distributed.[39]

In 1531 Parliament finally responded to local officials' growing perplexity with vagrancy. The statute, 22 Henry VIII, c. 12, took note of the 'great routs and companies' of vagabonds that disturbed the realm and reaffirmed customary appraisals and treatment of the homeless poor. Justices of the Peace were required to search out the deserving poor and license certain of them to beg. Vagrants were to be arrested, whipped and settled in their places of birth or where they last resided for three years.[40]

At the same time, more strategic thinking was being directed to the poverty problem. Perhaps as early as 1530, Christopher St German, soon to become a strong defender of the royal supremacy but apparently not in service to the crown, drafted among other reform statutes a bold plan for a national poor relief policy. It would have established a standing council to oversee government make-work projects and regulate wages and the prices of essential goods, all this to be paid for by graduated taxes on every household, church, abbey and college in the realm. A special fund would be raised to care for the impotent. Common Chests were to be instituted in every town, city and county.[41]

A companion to the 1531 statute was needed, and William Marshall, translator of the Ypres poor relief plan and employed by Thomas Cromwell, was the author of an even more remarkable Bill presented to Parliament in 1536.[42] The Bill was a Christian humanist-inspired proposal to rescue the realm's poor by means of government policy. It acknowledged many causes of poverty beyond 'visitacion of god' and the pauper's 'own default' and insisted that a way must be found 'to helpe and sucour' all the different types of poor and 'to preuent that other shall not hereafter fall into like mysery'. A national 'councell to auoide vacabunds' would provide wages, food and medical care for the able-bodied unemployed who would be put to work renovating ports, building roads and dredging and cleansing waterways. These endeavours were to continue until 1540 and be financed by the king's benevolence and yearly levies on church dignitaries and the wealthier laymen. At the local level parishes were to appoint overseers who would supervise a voluntary fund of money and kind to provide relief and hospital care. Each bishop was to provide a sermon for Sundays and holy days that praised charity and impugned sloth.[43]

Marshall's Bill must have shocked the Parliament. It was withdrawn almost immediately and a substitute (27 Henry VIII, c. 25), itself surprisingly innovative, was quickly introduced by the government and passed.[44] It appropriately announced its intention to clarify and extend the mandate of the statute of 1531. Local officials and householders should receive the poor and vagrant 'most charitably'. The clergy were to exhort liberality to raise voluntary donations to parish funds, from which the impotent would be relieved and the able-bodied put to work. Most, but not all, corporate and private almsgiving was prohibited and some begging was allowed to continue. Idle children were to be apprenticed.[45]

The history of policy is filled with unforeseen consequences and, as the Pilgrimage of Grace illustrates so well, profound ironies. The towns and localities distant from London evidently never knew about the statute of 1536 or ignored it entirely. Local records show no traces of the legislation's influence, and Parliament did not renew the statute in 1536 or 1539.[46] If there had been any local knowledge of the statute, officials and parish leaders would probably have been intimidated by its demands on them. On the other hand, it should have had a calming effect on the poor since its provisions urged gentleness and care towards even the vagrant poor. Instead the government found itself almost immediately involved in a confrontation with the enraged poor commons of two shires in the north about culpability for the poverty and suffering there.

Robert Aske and the Pilgrimage's other leaders, whose numbers included lords and gentlemen, complained about abusive taxation, the dissolution of the monasteries, the quality of the king's new 'base' councillors and the theology of the new bishops; they saw themselves as defenders of the church and the poor against the intrusions of inappropriate policy.[47] In his public pronouncements Henry alternated between hurt that his subjects in the north did not appreciate his care in keeping them so long in peace and prosperity and outrage that the commons of 'the most brute and beestelie' shire of the realm would fain have any opinion about his rule.[48] I suggest that what we have in the Pilgrimage is a 'dialogue by other means' about counsel and policy: life was recapitulating the theory, or the art if you prefer, of Book One of *Utopia*. The men of the north implored the king to consider the consequences of his policies: were not his taxes making them poorer and his new religion depriving them of their spiritual contentment and needed monastic alms? Probably unaware of *Utopia*, the views of Aske and his men nevertheless paralleled Hythlodaeus': badly conceived policy creates poverty and makes criminals of poor men.

The crown's weapons included propaganda. Another of the new men, Richard Morison, fresh from Padua, was pressed into the fray by Cromwell and delivered in short order two pamphlets against the Pilgrimage. Morison certainly did know *Utopia* and disparaged a 'certain commonwealth' that 'we imagine' and those who say that poverty causes men to become thieves. He insisted that such a place would be a 'common woe' and that sedition itself and not wrong-headed policy was the real cultivator of poverty.[49]

It seems likely that the government, anticipating its planned dissolution of church properties, had wanted the 1536 Poor Law to provide stimulation and direction on vagrancy and poor relief for the localities. The dissolution began with the monasteries in 1536 and 1539 and turned to the chantries and certain religious hospitals and fraternities in 1545 and 1547. The end result was that by 1550 most of the established forms of institutional relief, including about half (260) of the endowed almshouses, had been closed. The cumulative effects of this were disastrous for poor relief in the realm in the short term and served to put additional exigency on local officials and church leaders.[50] Eventually, the twin pressures of 'civic circumstances and humanist rhetoric', according to Paul Slack, forced local innovators into practical arrangements that simulated the statutory plan of 1536: prohibition of begging; a centralized fund; oversight of the poor; make-work for the able-bodied; and relief for the impotent.[51]

During the years of bold humanist theorizing and statute drafting that preceded 27 Henry VIII, c. 25, a less critical and value-charged approach to the analysis of poverty, one that centred the problem in the shifting and evolving economic life of the realm, was formulated. Although not published until the nineteenth century, Thomas Starkey's 'Dialogue between Pole and Lupset' provides a sounding of a thoughtful mind at

Court in the 1530s.[52] Starkey was interested in the high proportion of beggars, but also in the work habits of labourers, the use being made of England's natural resources, and the variety and degree of imports. These were the kinds of issues that would be taken up by Sir Thomas Smith at mid-century and Sir Francis Bacon at its end. Starkey was particularly concerned with what he perceived to be excessive worldliness and lack of common purpose among the various degrees of society. As bleak as all this might have appeared to him, Starkey was convinced that government could restore the common weal by enforcing labour and vagrancy laws, developing a plan for the realm's economy, and instituting municipal responsibility for poor relief. In short, what was needed was 'the gud ordur & pollycy by gud lawys stablyschyd & set, & by hedys & rularys put in effect' that the political body will be ruled by 'reson' and achieve health, prosperity, proper worship and brotherly love.[53]

Starkey was aware, however, that intellectual cant could impair policy: in the 'Dialogue' Lupset cautions Pole that Plato's (and More's?) 'vayne imygynatyon' not be allowed to interfere with a careful and accurate understanding of conditions in England, lest the resulting policies be formulaic and ineffective.[54] And, as T. F. Mayer has shown, Starkey's understanding of what policy actually is changed in the course of the six years or so during which he was seeking a role of influence at Court. Early in the 'Dialogue', for instance, he was convinced that reason and nature were independent from God; but further on he decided that the soul contained a 'sparkle of the godly and eternal reason'. In 'What is policy', his response to Cromwell's request for a treatise on Aristotle's understanding of policy, Starkey's attention ranged from human nature, to the origins of civil society, to constitutional forms. He concluded that policy in the hands of wise men was the instrument that transforms the multitude into a Christian polity. Lastly, in his *Exhortation* Starkey declared that 'faythful love & charytabul faythe' allowed a person to live 'like a chryst, lyke a god, lyke reson hyt selfe'. Whether Starkey's faith was Italian Evangelical as Mayer maintains or Protestant as Cromwell thought, he saw policy's civil dimension as a means to its religious ends and was forging a polyvalent, humanist and providential, language of reason and policy.[55]

Parliament's first attempt at a comprehensive poor law after the ignored statute of 1536 was the Vagrancy Act of 1547. The statute noted 'the foolish pity and mercy' of earlier anti-vagrancy efforts; the indigents' 'perverse nature and long accustomed idleness' had been more than a match for inappropriate compassion. The new law combined branding and forced slavery for hardy vagrants with succour for impotent poor and victims of calamity, all paid for through voluntary contributions to a parish fund. Two years later in 1549 another statute, claiming that the 'extremity' of some statutes had prevented their implementation, repealed all legislation having to do with vagabonds, aged and impotent persons except the statute of 1531. The government had reverted to its two-category definition of poverty, the impotent to be relieved and the hardy to be punished.[56] The harsh tone of this legislation must nevertheless be put in the context of the broader policy goals of the government to get at the roots of 'poverty making'. Protector Somerset's endeavour to diminish enclosure by taxing sheep and reviving the anti-enclosure commissions is but the most obvious example of this: more than 40 per cent of the statutes passed in the first two parliamentary sessions of Edward VI were concerned with social and economic issues.[57]

If the government had hoped that the official reformation of religion would stifle 'hot gospelling' on the social question, whether from traditional Lollard and populist sources or continental Anabaptist ones, it was mistaken. Religiously fuelled social criticism persisted from several quarters. Advanced Protestants in the Edwardian years, Thomas Lever and Hugh Latimer, for example, fanned the flames of smouldering urbanphobia and attributed the suffering of the realm's poor to the habits of London's pagan and rapacious rich.[58] And, well before the uprisings of 1549, Henry Brinkelow had thrown down the gauntlet for the 'oppressed and over-yoked' commons, declaring the government's efforts deficient in both curbing clerical abuses and orchestrating a more just and prosperous commonwealth. Very much in the spirit of later medieval social commentary, Brinkelow saw the poor commons as victims of 'wicked' laws, their related oppressions and the fornicating, covetous and idolatrous population of London. The cause of all this, he declared, was the still thwarted reformation of religion. Since the unregenerate episcopate persists in forcing a Catholic-like religion on the realm, the continuing obfuscation of God's word prevents the realization of just social relations.[59]

Robert Crowley, who became a fully committed Puritan after the Marian exile, sustained the medieval populist social analysis with *The Vision of William concerning Piers the Plowman* (1550) and a series of pamphlets defending the rights of the poor. In his remedy for sedition, *The Way to Wealth* (1550), Crowley accused gentlemen, merchants and lawyers of oppressing the poor in a variety of ways, from raising rents to enclosing arable land. These excesses far outweighed the poor's lack of respect for the law and their social superiors. Yet, even though the king, 'Goddes minister to revenge the wronges done vnto the innocent', had failed in his job, rebellion was not permissible. Oppressions and evil rule are visited on a realm by God; the only justifiable remedy is for each man to examine his conscience, acknowledge that evil times follow from sin, and reform his life. Crowley concluded with a line worthy of Langland or Wyclif himself but which also captured the deepening providentialism of mid-sixteenth-century Protestant discourse: 'let thy desire be that Goddes will be fulfilled in the'.[60]

Complementing this provoking rhetoric was a constant undertow of class resentment and economic grievance in the Tudor years that kept the poor commons susceptible to recruitment into most insurrections regardless of the immediate causes. Kett's Rebellion in 1549, however, was the one Tudor rising driven primarily by economic and status issues. Its 'discourse of confrontation' suggests that the initiative for change on the social question was shifting from the government to the grass roots (although not without the government's encouragement in this instance). The instigators were aggrieved primarily at local officials who seemed to be thwarting the desire for social and economic mobility at or near the bottom of society. The rising began as a quite ordinary local riot of tenants against unloved landlords and in succeeding transformations developed first into a great demonstration about injustice and finally into a bloody insurrection of national significance.[61] Somerset's measures from June 1548 to June 1549 against enclosure and pardoning those who had thrown enclosure open seemed to signal that the Lord Protector sided with the ambitious small farmers and businessmen against the large landlords, their lawyers and the control they maintained over the courts and markets.[62] In effect, the aspirations of the poor commons had been whetted by central government policy and blunted at the local and county level by conservative interests.

The Court propagandist at this time, John Cheke, reminded Robert Kett and his followers of the contradiction involved in seeking social advancement through rebellion: insurrection breaks down social distinctions. It is not that Cheke would ridicule the desire for mobility, however, just the means. Since rebellion levels the social order, the insurrectionists were guaranteeing that children of the poor would no longer move up in society and provide succour to their families. Even more interesting was Cheke's identification of the instrument of mobility in the first place; it is providence, not reason or state policy. Thus, the ultimate presumption of the rebels was that they would put their faint wisdom in the place of God's plan to advance whom he chooses.[63]

Many assumptions about the importance of biblical and populist-inspired social commentary in the 1540s and 1550s and the general policy climate of the Edwardian years have been challenged in recent years.[64] Nevertheless, one prominent figure of those years and beyond, Sir Thomas Smith, seems to be gaining in stature. Smith, doctor of civil law and regius professor, privy councillor, emissary and ambassador, as well as mentor to William Cecil, was a man of learning and much practical experience. Through his responsibilities and personal connections at Court from the 1530s to the 1570s he was a crucial bridge from the Cromwellian policy-making environment to that of Cecil.[65] Equally important for this study of policy thought was his place between Starkey and Bacon. In his ingenious dialogue, *Discourse of the Commonweal*, written in 1549 and published in

1581, Smith recast policy discourse on the poverty problem, even more fundamentally than Starkey had, without focusing on poverty *per se*. As Neal Wood argues (Chapter 5 in this volume), Smith was actually crafting a kind of political economy.[66] Thus, to Smith poverty was less a problem in and of itself and more a consequence of dearth, dwindling national wealth, enclosure and the decay of towns and villages. Smith examined these problems deftly and independently and offered proposals that would change England for the better, not attempt to restore it to an order already lost. For example, he refused to condemn all enclosure outright, although it was mostly an evil; the decay of towns and villages and a damaging increase in imports were related to changing consumer fashions which English craftsmen were ignoring. Consequently, the economic culture of the towns must change: new crafts would have to be instituted, perhaps by attracting foreign craftsmen into England. Smith was convinced that the de-valuation of currency was the prime cause of the intractable dearth so complained about, and he urged a restoration of former currency names and values. Only in a country like 'Utopia', he chided, which had no contact with other nations, could the delusion persist that precious metal and currency values could be changed dramatically.[67]

The ideological assumptions that Smith brought to the purposes, mechanics and efficacy of policy make an interesting contrast with those of the policy formulators of two decades earlier with the exception of Starkey. To Smith, poverty was more an economic fact than a moral or spiritual condition. Its waxing and waning was dependent on a complex of forces, some resting in human nature, some in the quality of statesmanship, some in unfolding economic trends and forces. And, when he discussed the need to keep servingmen and yeomen exercised and fit for war or analysed which craftsmen actually created revenue for the realm, Smith could sound almost like William Petty.[68]

Smith had no doubt that experience, indispensable as it was, required supplementation by formal learning and that in any kind of governance – family, city or commonwealth – the most learned are chosen to govern the rest.[69] Nevertheless, policy, even in the hands of the wise where it belongs, had its limits. 'All things that should be done in a commonwealth be not to be forced', wrote Smith, 'but some so and some other by allurement and rewards rather'.[70] Smith regarded human nature as irremediably covetous; thus, in what may be yet another allusion to *Utopia*, he maintained that this covetousness could no more be purged from human inclination than could ire, fear or gladness.[71]

In the *Discourse*, Smith, as Starkey had earlier, used a polyvalent, humanist and Protestant language of social analysis and policy; he did it with insight and sophistication. Smith was humane and hopeful, yet reconciled to the shadow of cupidity that fell across the human soul; he was an advocate of policy, yet aware of its limits in the face of worldly allure and profit. More than any of his predecessors he secularized the idea of poverty and transformed the reform expectation from the quest for a static common weal to acceptance of the contingency and meliorative possibilities of historical development. It was in this form that the Burghleys and the Bacons would take it up.

By the later 1550s the government had developed a broad range of initiatives to curb vagrancy and facilitate proper care for the poor. In addition to the spate of legislation since 1531 and the continuing efforts of the council on several fronts, the government had embellished several lines of urban policy that extended back to the fifteenth century. These included redistribution of a portion of tenths and fifteenths to poorer communities, defence of monopolistic privileges in certain towns to sustain their economic livelihood, and obliging owners to restore land to tillage and rebuild decayed housing.[72]

In spite of these efforts, at the grass-roots level villages and towns were trying to cope with the poor in ways independent of the government. Censuses and surveys of the poor were undertaken, and plans were made for setting the able-bodied poor to work. Perhaps of most significance was the introduction of mandatory poor rates in London, Norwich and York by 1550 and subsequently in Colchester, Ipswich and Cambridge. In 1557 these developments were buttressed with scriptural imperative by Martin Bucer. Drawing on the Acts of the Apostles, Bucer made a compelling justification for congregation-centred poor relief and cautioned against the 'uncertyn sophistrie' of those who use 'Vtopia' as a model. Deacons, men above reproach in the parish, should be given the responsibility to visit the poor, distinguish genuine need from bogus, and supervise, distribute and account for poor relief funds. Unsentimental in his approach to vagrancy, Bucer thought that all sturdy vagabonds should be expelled from the congregation. On the other hand, he sounded almost like Vives in his plea that every congregation should bring up its youth virtuously, trained in 'good Artes', so that each can 'declare hymself to others a true, and profetable member off Christ'.[73]

The advance of Calvinist thought in England was well under way by the turn of the 1550s. After the temporary set-back of Mary's reign, the influence of the Genevan faith spread rapidly with the return of hundreds of exiles from the shelter of Calvinist congregations on the continent and the publication of *The Institutes of the Christian Religion* in English in 1561.

Calvinism was much more a faith of action than was Lutheranism. In contrast to Luther's redoubt of inner freedom, a Calvinist's energy was supposed to flow outward into the vibrant domain where human agency and divine providence worked inseparably. Challenged, instead of being put off, by emerging capitalism, statism and the new science, Calvinist

Protestantism engaged the 'modern' and attempted to shape it to the framework of biblical Christianity.[74] During the very years when Smith and Bacon were applying their political-economy oriented humanism to a close analysis of the generation of poverty in the realm, Puritans, from biblical premises, were in their own spirit of a 'new science' attempting to understand and act upon the world as it really was.[75] As we shall see, one consequence of this hard looking at the world was a distinct perspective on the poverty problem, which ignited the charitable concern of the congregation, informed the policy initiatives of the ministry–magistracy alliances in many localities and provided ideological justification for the national codification statutes of 1598 and 1601.

The conceptual vocabulary that English Calvinists developed in approaching the social question incorporated the consequences of justification, the merits of commerce and material aspirations, and the relationship among calling, human will and divine providence in cultivating Christian community. Justification, the result of God planting faith in a person, was literally 'to pass over from death to life'. And, even though justified people cannot achieve perfection, they should attempt the imitation of Christ to the degree of their 'puny capacity' to make 'some progress in the way of the Lord'.[76]

One's social rank was not fortuitous. Place was decided by God, and the elect were to be found in all degrees. A reformed society should literally glow from top to bottom with the cumulative inner light of its saints.[77] Calvin, like most Protestant divines, held that asceticism is an 'inhuman' philosophy that reduces a person to a 'block'; nevertheless, comfort must be pursued with moderation. The proper route to appropriate 'riches and honors' is trust in God's blessing, not the practice of 'wicked arts'.[78] Calvin thought that unregenerate merchants, craftsmen and traders sullied commerce, but that the activity itself was without inherent fault. More to the point, commercial activity was a pungent example of mutual dependence among people; and, if carried out in the proper spirit of Christian duty, it could bring great benefits to a community.[79]

When Calvin dealt with the 'king as god' issue, which appeared frequently in Scripture, a quite different tone from Erasmus' was present. Commenting on the passages in Proverbs, 'By me kings reign, and princes decree justice', Calvin played down the credit that could be attributed to human wisdom in carrying out the kingly office. The authority of kings and other earthly governors is of 'the providence and holy ordinance of God'. He is 'present, and also presides among them, in making laws and in executing equitable judgments'.[80] In making less of the prince's independent judgment and reason in the practice of rule, Calvin was at the same time making more of the monarch's role as a conduit through which providential intentions for the realm were transmitted. We have already noted movement toward the identification of reason and policy with providence in the polyvalent language of Starkey and, in his own way, of Smith.

Calvinists brought three scriptural imperatives to their reflections on poor relief: 'But there will be no poor among you' (Deuteronomy 15: 4); 'Blessed is he that considereth of the poor, the Lord will deliver him in the time of trouble' (Psalm 41); and 'If anyone will not work let him not eat' (2 Thessalonians 3: 10). By the first, they were inspired to attain a degree of liberality within the community that would render begging unnecessary. The second encouraged belief in the worldly return of charity. From the third, Calvinists were drawn to a contempt for the healthy unemployed. Such persons perverted the meaning of dependency and deprived the deserving poor of alms to which they were entitled.[81] Thus, the presence of begging should be a source of shame to an entire congregation. As Perkins put the matter, begging 'doth proclaim to the world, in the ears of all men, the shame either of the Magistrate, who restrains it not, having authority: or of the wealthy and able, that they have no mercy or compassion'.[82]

Growing numbers of vagrant poor people in the Elizabethan years ensured that the sense of crisis over the social question would continue, particularly in the first two and the last decades of the reign.[83] Local officials, long since swamped by vagrancy and poverty in their towns and villages, had been pressuring Parliament to establish a mandatory rate. Halfway measures, which embarrassed or inconvenienced non-contributors more than anything, were enacted in 1552 and 1563. A fully mandatory rate was included in the statute of 1572.[84]

Furthermore, reform in the labour market had been long overdue; the last wage legislation had been passed in 1514–15. While the evidence is not conclusive, it appears that the government was attempting to enforce the 1514–15 wage rates in the north but allowing them to be superseded in the more prosperous south at the discretion of local officials. The pressure from the localities for a more coherent labour policy and the government's recognition that coinage reform alone was ineffective in preserving social peace, produced a climate for parliamentary legislation.[85] Several Bills were introduced in 1559 on apprenticeship regulations, retention of artificers in the towns and wages. Four years later the so-called Statute of Artificers (5 Eliz., c. 4) was passed. It was wide-ranging and established the legal framework of English labour policy for two centuries.[86] The Act touched artificers, labourers, servants of husbandry and apprentices. Certain categories of persons were to be forced into service; wages and hours for artificers would be settled in each county annually by the Justices of the Peace; and apprenticeship qualifications were designed to keep the social order perpetuating itself as nearly as possible.[87]

Local initiative in poor relief intensified in Puritan areas during the Elizabethan years. Although there had been a decrease in oral, symbolic and ritualized sacralization in communities as Protestantism took hold, coherence was being cultivated by a new 'mental and imaginative "set"', dominated by the printed page, the catechism and the sermon.[88] This tendency was most pronounced in the 'Puritan citadels' during the last half of the sixteenth century. By the late 1560s and 1570s alliances between Puritan ministers and social activist magistrates in towns like Bury St Edmunds and Warwick, and in the rural parishes of Suffolk were producing an atmosphere that reaffirmed or provoked reforms like those already begun in Norwich and York in the late 1540s.[89]

Sir Francis Walsingham, Secretary of State after 1573 and a committed Puritan, had reported on the reforms at Norwich to his confidant, Burghley. This sort of activity probably contributed to the continuation of Council-centred initiatives to the localities. At the same time, pressure from below directed at Parliament intensified, now from Puritan officials like John Aldrich, city councillor of Norwich in 1549 and mayor and MP in 1572 and 1576. The immediate help that Aldrich and others wanted was a mandatory rate and more intervention against vagrancy.[90] Thus, we can be fairly confident that Puritan ideas of social reform were being transmitted between the government and the towns by the 1570s.

The concern of the government with the poor commons and vagrancy may have been intensified by the Northern Rebellion in 1569, as well. Northumberland and the other northern earls had used religious propaganda, the offer of wages, and threats to dragoon poor men into their ranks.[91] While the actual violence of the rising was confined to the siege of Barnard Castle and a skirmish at Hexton, the mere fact that the rebel numbers had been swelled by the poor and destitute probably contributed to Parliament's willingness to legislate again on vagrancy.

The statutes of 1572 (14 Eliz., c. 5) and 1576 (18 Eliz., c. 3), taken together, may be considered not only an anti-vagrancy measure, but a more general anti-poverty undertaking as well. Noting that the realm was 'exceedingly pestered' with vagrancy and crime, the 1572 statute classified vagrants elaborately by type, in much the way that Thomas Harman had done in his *A Caveat for Common Cursitors*, which nomenclature William Harrison appropriated in 1577.[92] The statute authorized 'grievous' whipping and other corporal punishments to hardy recalcitrant vagrants. On the other hand, it acknowledged several categories of acceptable unemployment; relief for the impotent and work for the unemployed was to be financed by mandatory contributions to the parish fund. The 1576 Act continued the provisions of 1572 and added the establishment of Bridewells, or houses of correction, in every county so that youth may be 'accustomed and brought up in labor' and rogues deprived of the excuse that 'they cannot get any service or work'. Materials for work were to be acquired for the houses of correction from the parish fund, and collectors would sell the finished goods from which returns the workers would be paid and the stock refurbished.[93]

The policy assumptions embedded in these statutes – the distinction between legal and illegal unemployment, severe punishment for the illegal variety and make-work for the legal, succour to the impotent, attention to the proper cultivation of poor youth, overseers and a parish fund to which contributions were mandatory – were the core of the 'Tudor' Poor Law, which was codified with a few embellishments in 1598 and 1601. From the 1570s forward the challenge was more the realization of policy than its formulation. Henry Bedel, vicar of Christ's Church, London, put the matter succinctly: 'Good and godly laws' exist for collecting relief for the poor; but 'how loosely' they were enforced 'appeareth in the treasure of the poor'.[94]

In these years, educated Puritans often would have encountered Christian humanist and classical literature that urged the social benefits of hard work, education and liberality to the poor.[95] However, to the degree that they worked within an ideological framework of personal responsibility and agency and societal aspiration and causation it was that of Calvin, Bucer and Perkins, not Erasmus, More and Vives. If it is time to 'bring the state back in' our analyses of social process, Patrick Collinson, Margaret Spufford and Peter Lake are also correct in insisting, albeit from different vantage points, that religion and what people actually believed must not be consigned to the periphery in explaining Tudor social and political behaviour.[96]

In the 1590s and first years of the seventeenth century the providential language of social reform was brought to great clarity in the work of William Perkins, the Cambridge Puritan. Perkins, as earlier Protestants had, embraced a moderate worldliness, was friendly to commercial activity and eschewed apostolic poverty. He also disagreed with the humanists' view that 'policy', government initiative conceived by human reason, was the primary means for achieving a peaceful, prosperous and harmonious commonwealth. On the contrary, the proper undertaking for society's regeneration was to search out the providentially designed 'inner commonwealth', that lay inchoate in humankind, and bring it to life. 'God hath ordained and disposed all callings, and in his providence, designed the persons to bear them'. While *election* applied to individual saints, *vocation* advanced the divine plan for all human beings and, as such, was immensely important.[97] This was a message of divine concern to persons at all levels in society. Thus, the poor must not despair even though the world will hold them in 'contempt and reproach'. Their ranks have no fewer worthy souls than any other, and for them the all-important value of poverty of the spirit should be easier to achieve.[98]

Perkins's technical discussion of poor relief is found in *Cases of Conscience* (1606); the work provided a summary and a systemization of

Puritan approaches to poor relief and vagrancy that had been developing throughout Elizabeth's reign. His most general assumption was that all human beings are either givers or receivers of alms. Perkins identified three degrees of want: extreme necessity, great need and common necessity. Succour must be given to the first two categories, and the deserving poor may be assisted at home. Responsible charity, e.g. giving to the poor, free lending and remitting due debt, should be provided first to one's own, then to members of the church and finally to neighbours; but, except in cases of extreme necessity, alms should not be given to the degree of creating suffering in the donor. Almsgiving should be consecrated to God and carried out in faith, simplicity, love, justice and cheerfulness. Nevertheless, all superfluity should not be directed to works of charity: some should be saved for church and commonwealth.[99]

As Bucer had done, Perkins and other Puritan writers showed little sympathy for vagrants. Unable to accept that there were not divine callings for everyone, Perkins thought vagrants undeserving of help because they apparently refused the elementary obligation of choosing theirs and were members of neither congregational nor civil communities. His reluctance also stemmed from his caution about the danger of indiscriminate almsgiving. As we have seen, on both counts Anglican preaching was less strict. Nevertheless, Christopher Hill's contention that Perkins was responsible for a new callous regard for the poor is unwarranted, in my judgement.[100] He shows an incomplete understanding of the social activism cultivated by the providential ideology, and he fails to acknowledge that unfriendliness toward vagrants was widespread in Tudor England and had deep medieval roots. Nor were non-Puritans shocked with Perkins's attitude. Smith, for one, after reciting the whipping and forced service held out for vagabonds in the 1572 statute, concluded with no apparent opprobrium, 'so much our policy does abhor idleness'.[101]

No later Elizabethan matched or even attempted an analysis of the economic, social and policy dynamics of the realm on the scale and with the subtlety of Smith's *Discourse*. Yet in Francis Bacon that spirit lived. He used a polyvalent language of social analysis similar to Starkey's and Smith's and played a significant parliamentary role in achieving the Poor Law codifications at the turn of the century. Bacon sought particularly to understand the relationship of population to natural resources in the creation of poverty and the effectiveness of hospitals and houses of correction in its remediation. With regard to the first, he was concerned that the proper balance be sought between a population and the resources needed to support it. A 'smaller number, that spend more, and earn less' wears a country out sooner than 'a greater number that live lower and gather more'. He concluded that multiplying nobility, clergy and scholars relative to the common people would quickly bring a state to 'necessity' because these ranks 'bring nothing to the stock'. This led Bacon to oppose the establishment of additional grammar schools. The expanding number of schools was causing too few 'servants of husbandry, and apprentices for trade', while more scholars 'are bred than the state can prefer and employ'.[102]

Bacon was convinced that large hospitals for the poor were a mistake; they required very careful management usually only available in London. And, even more to the point, they became the receptacles of the most despicable sort of poor and were avoided by those who 'have been somebody' but have fallen on hard times. Much better, according to Bacon, would be combined workhouses and hospitals of moderate size to accommodate the poor of every sort 'as the country breeds them'. Hardy beggars could be put to work, the impotent relieved, and the partially impotent given tasks they are able to perform.[103]

If a run of good harvests and preoccupation with recusants, mission priests, the threat of Spanish invasion and the Admonition Controversy had eclipsed the social question in the later 1570s and 1580s, it returned forcefully in the 1590s. Dramatic price rises and wage declines in the mid-1590s led to a full-blown subsistence crisis for the poor and attendant insecurities for the government. As early as 1593 a committee had been appointed in the House of Commons to evaluate the poverty statutes. Later, in the 1597–8 session seventeen Bills related to poverty were introduced, some of them probably products of the 1593 committee. Nevertheless, another study committee was appointed; serving, among others, were Bacon, Thomas Cecil, Edward Coke, Sir Robert Wroth (a Puritan social reformer), Miles Sandys, Edward Hext (a Somerset justice) and Anthony Cope, who was experienced in Lincolnshire efforts to employ the poor.[104] Bacon seems to have been a prime mover in calling attention to the plight of the poor and the extent of idleness in the realm. Early in the session he urged the revival of legislation against enclosure, to which he attributed depopulation, idleness, decay of tillage, withering of charitable institutions and ultimately the impoverishment of the realm.[105]

In addition to two new enclosure statutes, a new vagrancy Act, and an Act authorizing the erection of workhouses, a definitive Bill on poor relief was passed after considerable committee work and debate. The statute, 39 Eliz., c. 3 (1598), called for the designation of four overseers of the poor in each parish to assist the churchwardens. The overseers were to raise funds and gather materials by means of a parish tax (the poor rate) for relief of the 'lame ympotente olde blynde' and to put poor children and unemployed and healthy adults to work. The infirm were to be relieved and housed in 'convenyent Howses of Dwellinge' (the hospitals that Bacon later objected to). Family members were expected to attempt to relieve their own poor before turning them over to the parish. The statute 39 Elizabeth also carried forward the principle that Justices of the Peace could tax for poor relief outside of beleaguered parishes and it established the responsibility of all parishes for the support of county hospitals and almshouses. These provisions were reaffirmed with slight alterations and extensions in 43 Eliz., c. 2 (1601), the so-called 'Elizabethan' Poor Law.[106] This codification, supplemented by the Act of Settlement (1662), shaped English public poor relief until 1834.

The government's elaborate plans and initiatives of the 1530s had been provoked by Christian humanism's infatuation with reason, critical analysis of society, and commitment to policy. However, as the Pilgrimage of Grace and Kett's Rebellion revealed, Henrician and Edwardian policy endeavours propelled the state too quickly and alarmingly into the traditional domains of custom, church and local jurisdiction. By mid-century a more 'empirical' and less 'critical' approach to policy was developing from the influence of newly imported Calvinist Protestantism and the beginnings of indigenous political economy. During the second half of the century the initiative in developing poor relief and anti-vagrancy policy switched primarily to the local level; after 1570, in the ministry–magistracy alliances of the Puritan strongholds, municipal plans reached 'state of the art' for the Tudor years. The government continued its overriding interest in preserving order, but by comparison to the mid-1530s and the Somerset years the later Tudor state was much less, if at all, committed to revivifying the common weal rapidly through policy. More often than not it responded to requests from innovators in the counties and localities for specific assistance or institutionalized the repertoire of actions that seemed to work, as in the Poor Laws of 1598 and 1601.

The culminating Tudor Poor Laws were less dramatic certainly than the plans of St German and Marshall in the 1530s. The statute of 1598 emerged from a parliamentary committee of government men, lawyers, Puritan reformers and at least one thoughtful political economist. The result was legislation well calibrated ideologically and institutionally to the English realm. Perkins thought it 'an excellent statute and being in substance the very law of God'.[107] He hoped it 'is never to be repealed' and was almost right. Returning to Smith's metaphor with which I began this chapter, the fabric of ideas proved to be resilient and the fit of the policy garment to the social and political body quite good. It remained usable for more than two centuries.

NOTES

1 Sir T. Smith, *De Republica Anglorum*, London, H. Midleton f. G. Seton, 1583 *STC* 22857, pp. 17–18. Work on this chapter was advanced by two research opportunities for which I am very grateful. A travel stipend in the autumn of 1987 from the Folger Institute Center for the Study of British Political Thought allowed me to participate in A. J. Slavin's seminar, 'Property, Power and Politics', and to report there on some preliminary ideas about

sixteenth-century policy thought. An early draft of this chapter was completed during a three-month fellowship in residence at the Folger Shakespeare Library in the spring of 1990. I would also like to acknowledge with deep appreciation the encouragement I received on this project at different times from J. G. A. Pocock, A. J. Slavin and the late Roger Howell, jr. They, of course, bear no responsibility for anything I say herein.

2 For an overview of this scholarship, see the Introduction and pp. 271–5 of the Critical Bibliography.

3 P. Slack, *Poverty and Policy in Tudor and Stuart England*, London, Longman, 1988, pp. 2–7, argues that perceptions of poverty and its significance were more important than the actual numbers of poor in stimulating policy. A. L. Beier calls for a 'more impressionistic', less quantitative, approach to policy research that will place more attention on 'contemporary opinion'; see 'Poverty and progress in early modern England', in A. L. Beier, D. Cannadine and J. M. Rosenheim (eds) *The First Modern Society: Essays in English History in Honour of Lawrence Stone*, Cambridge, Cambridge University Press, 1989, pp. 236–8. M. K. McIntosh, 'Local responses to the poor in late medieval and Tudor England', *Continuity and Change*, 1988, vol. 3, pp. 234–5, concedes the influence of the 'new learning' on Edwardian and Elizabethan policy.

4 D. R. Kelley, *The Beginnings of Ideology*, Cambridge, Cambridge University Press, 1981, pp. 4–5; I subscribe to Kelly's broad definition of ideology as 'a distinctive and more or less coherent conglomerate of assumptions, attitudes, sentiments, values, ideals and goals accepted and perhaps acted upon by a more or less organized group of persons' (p. 4).

5 M. Rein, 'Value-critical policy analysis', in D. Callahan and B. Jennings (eds) *Ethics, the Social Sciences, and Policy Analysis*, New York, Plenum, 1983, pp. 96–9.

6 The term is Dominic LaCapra's, and he is urging a more catholic approach in deciding what constitutes a 'source'; see his 'Rethinking intellectual history and reading texts', in D. LaCapra and S. L. Kaplan (eds) *Modern European Intellectual History: Reappraisals and New Perspectives*, Ithaca, NY, Cornell University Press, 1982, p. 64.

7 *T. Starkey: 'A Dialogue between Pole and Lupset'* (1529–32?), T. F. Mayer (ed.), C4S, vol. 37, 1989, p. 61.

8 Christian humanism emerged the earlier of the two. Whether it was the first Tudor language of reform, however, has been challenged by David Starkey. He finds a 'commonwealth' language in the middle decades of the fifteenth century which revived the idea that king and kingdom were separate and held mutual obligations to one another (*regnum politicum et regale*). The commonwealth discourse, of which Starkey finds evidence in Fortescue, held that a revived Council would protect the king's prerogative, provide him with disinterested advice and plan for the public welfare. See D. Starkey, 'Which age of reform?', in D. Starkey and C. Coleman (eds) *Revolution Reassessed*, Oxford, Clarendon Press, 1986, pp. 15, 21, 22. For Christian humanism as an ideology, see M. Todd, *Christian Humanism and the Puritan Social Order*, Cambridge, Cambridge University Press, 1987, esp. ch. 2.

9 For the persistence of Catholic allegiance and practice well into the Protestant era, see C. Haigh, 'The continuity of catholicism in the English reformation', in Haigh (ed.) *The Reformation Revised*, Cambridge, Cambridge University Press, 1987, Introduction, Conclusion and pp. 176ff. Todd in her characterization of Christian humanism as 'Catholic' presents a similar challenge to

'discontinuity' in Tudor pedagogy and social thought (op. cit., p. 136 and chs 3 and 5).

10 Thomas Aquinas, *Summa Theologica*, English Dominican Fathers (trans), 3 vols, New York, Benziger, 1947, vol. II–II, q. 25, art. 1, p. 1,286; q. 66, art. 2, p. 1,477; q. 184, art. 1, p. 1,950; and *Summa Contra Gentiles*, English Dominican Fathers (trans), 4 vols in 5, London, Burns, Oates & Washbourne, 1923–9, vol. III–II, chs 125, 128.

11 H. B. Workman, *John Wyclif*, 2 vols, Oxford, Clarendon Press, 1926, vol. I, pp. 98–9, 104, 119; vol. II, pp. 13–14.

12 R. Hilton, *Bondmen Made Free*, New York, Viking, 1973, ch. 3.

13 *The Statutes of the Realm*, 12 vols, London, Dawsons, 1963 (repr. of 1810–28 edn; hereafter *Statutes*), vol. I, p. 308.

14 B. Tierney, *Medieval Poor Law*, Berkeley, Calif., University of California Press, 1959, ch. 1; McIntosh, op. cit., pp. 214–16.

15 *The thre bookes of Tullius offyce*, R. Whittinton (trans.), London, W. de Worde, 1534 *STC* 5278, C.5.b, C.8.b, D.2.b, I.6.b.

16 For a comparison of the *Institutio* and *Utopia*, see A. Fox, 'English humanism and the body politic', in A. Fox and J. A. Guy (eds) *Reassessing the Henrician Age*, Oxford, Basil Blackwell, 1986, pp. 37–8.

17 Erasmus, *Education*, p. 159.

18 This commitment was ambivalent in More and Erasmus because of their own predilections for voluntary renunciation of comfort and physical pleasure.

19 T. More, *Utopia, The Complete Works of St. Thomas More*, vol. 4, J. H. Hexter and E. Surtz, SJ (eds), New Haven, Conn., Yale University Press, 1965, pp. 127, 131–3, 147, 159, 179–81, 195–7.

20 G. Logan, *The Meaning of More's Utopia*, Princeton, NJ, Princeton University Press, 1983, Prolegomena.

21 Ibid., 257–9; Q. Skinner, *The Foundations of Modern Political Thought*, 2 vols, Cambridge, Cambridge University Press, 1978, vol. I, ch. 9, esp. pp. 255ff.; and 'Sir Thomas More's *Utopia* and the language of Renaissance humanism', *The Languages of Political Theory in Early-Modern Europe*, A. Pagden (ed.), Cambridge, Cambridge University Press, 1987, pp. 123–57.

22 Fenlon and Skinner maintain that More did intend that European states should emulate Utopian institutions, while Hexter, Bradshaw and Logan believe that he did not. Bradshaw summarizes his own views and those of Hexter, Fenlon and the early Skinner in 'More on Utopia', *HJ*, 1981, vol. 24, pp. 5, 27. See also Skinner, 1987, op. cit., pp. 124, 156–7; and Logan, op. cit., p. 270.

23 My allusion is to the Frankfurt School of social theorists, Theodor Adorno, Max Horkheimer, Herbert Marcuse and Jürgen Habermas, who beginning in the 1930s brought together Kantian and Hegelian critical philosophy with Marxian and psychoanalytic thought to form a deep structural analysis of the sway of capitalism over modern life and consciousness. A useful introduction to Frankfurt School critical theory, particularly as Habermas formulates it, is R. Geuss, *The Idea of a Critical Theory*, Cambridge, Cambridge University Press, 1981, esp. pp. 52–4 and 76–95.

24 More's understanding of pride's hold on the souls of his contemporaries and the Utopians' measures to prevent that spiritual crippling is similar to the psychoanalytical depth of Frankfurt theory. And the number of institutions in Utopia, beginning with the family, that must be different from those in contemporary Europe to make pride-free living possible parallels the counter-status quo implications of critical theory. Not surprisingly, the acquisition of critical theory tends to develop in stages, beginning with the awareness of

suffering or injustice, and proceeding to enlightenment and the desire for emancipation. The process can readily culminate in frustration, however, because of the fundamental level of change that its implementation seems to require. Finally, the fact that one can use critical theory to analyse the social environment without ever acting on it (or be dissuaded from acting because its implementation and likely consequences are so daunting as to require one's total commitment) suggests, at least, the *otium–negotium* dilemma of Renaissance humanists. See p. 273 of the Critical Bibliography for studies of critical theory.

25 Todd makes much of *mediocritas* in arguing for Christian humanist influence on Protestant social thought well into the seventeenth century (op. cit., pp. 129–30, 152).

26 J. Vives, *De subventione pauperum* (1526), *Some Early Tracts on Poor Relief*, F. R. Salter (ed.), London, Methuen, 1926, pp. 9, 20–1, 22, 27, 33, 36, 44–7; for a fuller discussion of More's discourse and Vives' elaboration and dissemination of it, see P. A. Fideler, 'Christian humanism and poor law reform in early Tudor England', *Societas*, 1974, vol. 4, pp. 275–9.

27 I use 'dissenting' to distinguish biblically informed and relatively independent Protestant discourses on poverty, which included views on the role of government, local and parish undertakings on poor relief, from 'official' religion, which was in many respects the creature of the government and less indigenously Protestant as a result.

28 This recitation of society's problems was *de rigueur* in Tudor social commentary.

29 M. Luther, *The Freedom of a Christian* (1520), *The Reformation Writings of Luther*, B. L. Woolf (trans.), London, Lutterworth, 1952, pp. 357–8.

30 B. A. Gerrish, *Grace and Reason: A Study in the Theology of Luther*, Oxford, Clarendon Press, 1962, pp. 13, 70–1.

31 R. M. Douglas, 'Talent and vocation in humanistic and protestant thought', in T. K. Rabb and J. E. Seigel (eds) *Action and Conviction in Early Modern Europe*, Princeton, NJ, Princeton University Press, 1969, pp. 291–5; D. C. Ziemke, *Love for the Neighbor in Luther's Theology*, Minneapolis, Minn., Augsburg, 1963, p. 72; and E. Troeltsch, *The Social Teachings of the Christian Churches*, O. Wyon (trans.), 2 vols, New York, Macmillan, 1931, vol. II, pp. 540–1, 557.

32 C. Trinkaus, 'The religious foundations of Luther's social views', in J. H. Mundy (ed.) *Essays in Medieval Life and Thought*, New York, Columbia University Press, 1955, p. 72.

33 M. Luther, *Ordinance for a Common Chest* (1523), Salter, op. cit., pp. 80–96; H. J. Grimm, 'Luther's contributions to sixteenth-century organization of poor relief', *Archiv für Reformationsgeschichte*, 1970, vol. 61, pp. 222ff.; for additional references on continental poor relief in the 1520s and 1530s, see pp. 271–5 of the Critical Bibliography.

34 W. Tyndale, *Prologue upon the Gospel of St. Matthew* (1536), *Doctrinal Treatises and Introductions to Different Portions of the Holy Scriptures*, H. Walter (ed.), Cambridge, Cambridge University Press, 1848, pp. 469–70; see also *The Work of William Tyndale*, G. E. Duffield (ed.), Appleford, Sutton Courtenay, 1964, xxxii; and W. A. Clebsch, *England's Earliest Protestants*, New Haven, Conn., Yale University Press, 1964, pp. 187–8.

35 W. Tyndale, *An Exposition upon . . . Matthew*, Duffield, op. cit., pp. 283–4.

36 W. Tyndale, *The Prologue into the Fourth Booke of Moses called Numeri,*

The Works of the English Reformers: William Tyndale and John Frith, T. Russell (ed.), 3 vols, London, E. Palmer, 1831, vol. I, p. 43.

37 P. Melanchthon, *A Civil Nosegay*, J. Goodale (trans.), London, R. Wyer f. J. Goodale, 1550? *STC* 17788, passim, but esp. B.iiii.a–B.v.a.; and *The Confession of the Fayth of the Germaynes*, R. Taverner (trans.), London, R. Redman, 1536 *STC* 908.

38 For the difficulties in the villages and towns, see McIntosh, op. cit., pp. 218–25.

39 Slack, op. cit., pp. 116–17, 138–9; see also J. J. Scarisbrick, 'Cardinal Wolsey and the common weal', in E. W. Ives, R. J. Knecht and J. J. Scarisbrick (eds) *Wealth and Power in Tudor England*, London, Athlone Press, 1978, pp. 45–67.

40 *Statutes*, vol. III, pp. 328–32.

41 J. A. Guy, 'The Tudor commonwealth: revising Thomas Cromwell', *HJ*, 1980, vol. 23, p. 685; and *Christopher St. German on Chancery and Statute*, Selden Society, suppl. ser. 1985, vol. 6.

42 *Forma subventionis pauperum* (1535), W. Marshall (trans.), Salter, op. cit., pp. 32–79. For a description of the poor law draft and Marshall's authorship of it, see G. R. Elton, 'An early Tudor poor law', *EcHR*, 2nd ser., 1953, vol. 6, pp. 55–67.

43 It is in the St German and Marshall drafts, not in More's private-propertyless Utopia as Logan mistakenly suggests (op. cit., p. 268), that we find sixteenth-century analogues to modern 'welfare state' policy. A welfare state can be said to exist only in conjunction with a capitalist or mixed economy.

44 G. R. Elton, *Reform and Renewal*, Cambridge, Cambridge University Press, 1973, pp. 123–4.

45 *Statutes*, vol. III, pp. 558–62.

46 The 1531 vagrancy statute was continued in 1536 and 1539; the 1536 statute was listed in the margin of the 1539 continuation statute, but only the 1531 statute was discussed in the text (ibid., pp. 655, 725); for the apparent local ignorance of the 1536 statute, see McIntosh, op. cit., p. 213.

47 Important recent studies are persuasive in tracing the unrest to over-zealous goals and implementation of the government's church reform policies; see M. Bowker's treatment of the Lincolnshire rising in *The Henrician Reformation*, Cambridge, Cambridge University Press, 1981, ch. iii, esp. p. 149; C. S. L. Davies, 'Popular religion and the Pilgrimage of Grace', in A. Fletcher and J. Stevenson (eds) *Order and Disorder in Early Modern England*, Cambridge, Cambridge University Press, 1985, p. 68.; and M. E. James, 'Obedience and dissent in Henrician England: the Lincolnshire rebellion, 1536', *P & P*, 1970, vol. 48, pp. 3–78.

48 Henry VIII, 'Answer to the Petitions . . .', SP, vol. I–II, no. LXVIII, p. 463.

49 Sir R. Morison, *A Lamentation . . . of Seditious Rebellyon* (1536), *Humanist Scholarship and Public Order: Two Tracts Against the Pilgrimage of Grace by Sir Richard Morison*, D. S. Berkowitz (ed.), Washington, DC, Folger Shakespeare Library, 1984, p. 86; and *A Remedy for Sedition* (1536), ibid., pp. 111, 119, 128, 136, 144–6. A. J. Slavin has generously allowed me to read his as yet unpublished essay, 'Richard Morison's two treatises: poverty and sedition'.

50 McIntosh, op. cit., pp. 225, 228; Slack, op. cit., pp. 118–19.

51 Ibid., 121.

52 The indispensable study of Starkey is now T. F. Mayer, *Thomas Starkey and the Commonweal*, Cambridge, Cambridge University Press, 1989.

53 Starkey, op. cit., pp. 34, 113–17.

54 Ibid., p. 18.

55 Ibid., pp. 20, 96; Mayer, op. cit., pp. 205–6; T. Starkey, *An exhortation . . . to vnitie and obedience*, London, T. Bertheleti, 1536 STC 23236, 5b–6a; for the mixing of 'languages' or 'paradigmatic structures' into ambivalent or polyvalent expression, see J. G. A. Pocock, *Virtue, Commerce, and History*, Cambridge, Cambridge University Press, 1985, Introduction, esp. pp. 9, 25.

56 1 Edward VI, c. 3 (1547) and 3 & 4 Edward VI, c. 16 (1549–50), *Statutes*, vol. IV–I, pp. 5–8, 115–16; see C. S. L. Davies, 'Slavery and Protector Somerset: the Vagrancy Act of 1547', *EcHR*, 2nd ser., 1966, vol. 19, pp. 533–49.

57 W. K. Jordan, *Edward VI: The Young King*, Cambridge, Mass., Harvard University Press, 1968, p. 391 and ch. XIV, passim.

58 T. Lever, 'A fruitful sermon made in Poules Church, etc.', *Sermons*, E. Arber (ed.), London, A. Murray & Son, 1871, pp. 24, 29; H. Latimer, 'Sermon of the plough', *Works*, G. E. Corrie (ed.), 2 vols, Cambridge, Cambridge University Press, 1844–5, vol. I, p. 61.

59 H. Brinkelow, *The Complaynt of Roderyck Mors, etc.* (1542), J. M. Cowper (ed.) EETS, extra ser., no. 22, pp. 73–4; and *The Lamentacyon of a Christen Agaynst the Cytye of London, etc.* (1545), ibid., p. 119.

60 R. Crowley, *The Way to Wealth* (1550), *Selected Works* EETS, extra ser., no. 15, pp. 132–8, 141–2, 145.

61 S. T. Bindoff, *Ket's Rebellion, 1549*, London, Historical Association, 1949, pp. 7, 23.

62 S. K. Land, *The Norfolk Rising of 1549*, Ipswich, Boydell, 1977, p. 72.

63 Sir J. Cheke, *The hurt of sedicion . . . to a commune welth*, London, J. Daye & W. Seres, 1549 STC 5109, B.iii.a.

64 G. R. Elton, 'Reformation and the "commonwealth-men" of Edward VI's reign', in P. Clark, A. G. R. Smith and N. Tyacke (eds) *The English Commonwealth 1547–1640*, Leicester, Leicester University Press, 1979, pp. 23–38, calls into question the existence of the commonwealth 'party' and the reform reputation of the Edwardian years; M. L. Bush maintains that Somerset was less interested in social reform than in a military adventure against Scotland: *The Government Policy of Protector Somerset*, Montreal, McGill-Queen's University Press, 1975, pp. 57–85.

65 For what is known about the details of Smith's life and his very uneven public career, see M. Dewar, *Sir Thomas Smith: A Tudor Intellectual in Office*, London, Athlone Press, 1964.

66 See Neal Wood, Chapter 5 in this volume, especially pp. 141, 143, 152.

67 Sir T. Smith, *A Discourse of the Commonweal of this Realm of England* (1581), M. Dewar (ed.), Charlottesville, Va, University Press of Virginia for the Folger Shakespeare Library, 1969, pp. 49–54, 99–113, 121–6.

68 Ibid., pp. 83, 87–92.

69 Ibid., pp. 24–30.

70 Ibid., pp. 58–60.

71 Ibid., p. 118.

72 R. Tittler, 'The emergence of urban policy, 1536–58', in J. Loach and R. Tittler (eds) *The Mid-Tudor Polity, c. 1540–1560*, London, Macmillan, 1980, pp. 74–7.

73 M. Bucer, *A Treatise, How Almose Ought to be Distributed* (1557?), The English Experience, no. 779, pp. 10–11, 13–14, 17–18, 24–26.

74 C. H. George and K. George, *The Protestant Mind of the English Reformation*, Princeton, NJ, Princeton University Press, 1961, pp. 3, 16; C. Trink-

aus, 'Renaissance problems in Calvin's theology', *Studies in the Renaissance*, 1954, vol. 1, p. 78; Troeltsch, op. cit., vol. II, p. 601; R. H. Tawney, *Religion and the Rise of Capitalism*, New York, Harcourt, Brace, 1926, p. 84; C. Hill, *Society and Puritanism in Pre-Revolutionary England*, New York, Schocken, 1964, pp. 271, 275.

75 Trinkaus identified this scientific quality in Calvinism; it sought to sweep away the distortions, 'idolatrous, anthropomorphic, and mystical', that interfered with the proper understanding of the world (1954, op. cit., p. 61).

76 J. Calvin, *Institutes of the Christian Religion*, J. T. McNeill (ed.), F. L. Battles (trans.), 2 vols, Philadelphia, Pa, Westminster, 1960, bk III, ch. vi, par. 5, pp. 688–9.

77 Ibid., ch. ii, par. 7, p. 551; par. 28, pp. 573–4.

78 Ibid., ch. x, pars 1–4, pp. 720–2.

79 A. Bieler, *La Pensée Economique et Sociale de Calvin*, Genève, Georg, 1959, ch. ii, passim.

80 J. Calvin, 'On civil government' [*Institutes of the Christian Religion*, bk IV, ch. xx], *John Calvin on God and Political Duty*, J. T. McNeill (ed.), New York, Liberal Arts, 1950, p. 46.

81 Anglican preaching was less concerned with indiscriminate almsgiving and thus encouraged more liberality toward vagrants. For example, Henry Bedel, vicar of Christ's Church, London, implored: 'Though some [beggars] make an occupation of it . . . yet as Paul doth bid thee especially remember the household of faith, so he doth not deny thee to do good to all [1 Timothy 6] (*A Sermon Exhorting to Pity the Poor*, London, J. Awdely, 1573 *STC* 1784, D.i.a.).

82 W. Perkins, *Cases of Conscience* (1606), *Works*, 3 vols, London, I. Legatt, 1612–13 *STC* 19650, vol. III, p. 145.

83 McIntosh, op. cit., 231; A. L. Beier, 'Vagrants and the social order in Elizabethan England', *P & P*, 1974, no. 64, pp. 5–6; P. Clark, 'The migrant in Kentish towns 1580–1640', in P. Clark and P. Slack (eds) *Crisis and Order in English Towns*, London, Routledge & Kegan Paul, 1972, pp. 117–18.

84 McIntosh suggests that the 1552 statute was more appreciated by local officials than any earlier Tudor legislation on vagrancy and poor relief (op. cit., pp. 229–30).

85 D. Woodward, 'The background to the Statute of Artificers: the genesis of labor policy', *EcHR*, 2nd ser., 1980, vol. 33, pp. 38, 41–4.

86 Ibid., p. 42.

87 *Statutes*, vol. IV–I, pp. 415–20.

88 C. Phythian-Adams, 'Ceremony and the citizen: the ceremonial year at Coventry 1450–1550', in Clark and Slack, op. cit., pp. 57–85; J. Bossy, 'Holiness and society' (rev. art.), *P & P* 1977, no. 75, pp. 119–37; P. Collinson, *The Birthpangs of Protestant England*, New York, St Martin's Press, 1988, p. 99.

89 P. Collinson, *Godly People*, London, Hambledon, 1983, p. 449; Slack, op. cit., pp. 149–50.

90 Ibid.; J. A. Guy, *Tudor England*, Oxford, Oxford University Press, 1988, pp. 279–81.

91 A. Fletcher, *Tudor Rebellions*, 2nd edn, London, Longman, 1973, pp. 91, 95–101.

92 T. Harman, *A Caveat for Common Cursitors* (1566), *The Elizabethan Underworld*, A. V. Judges (ed.), London, Routledge, 1930, pp. 61–118;

W. Harrison, *The Description of England* (1577), G. Edelen (ed.), Ithaca, NY, Cornell University Press, 1968, pp. 180–1.

93 *Statutes*, vol. V–I, pp. 590–4.

94 Bedel, op. cit., D.iv.a.

95 Todd, op. cit., chs 2, 3 and 5, amasses impressive evidence for this in the 'Oxbridge' curricula, student notebooks and sermons of university-trained clergymen.

96 M. Spufford, 'Puritanism and social control?', in Fletcher and Stevenson, op. cit., pp. 41ff., esp. 43–4; P. Lake, *Anglicans or Puritans?*, London, Unwin Hyman, 1988, Introduction, esp. p. 6; and Collinson, 1988, op. cit., pp. 35–6. See also T. Skocpol, 'Bringing the state back in: strategies of analysis in current research', in P. B. Evans, D. Rueschemayer and T. Skocpol (eds) *Bringing the State Back In*, Cambridge, Cambridge; University Press, 1985, pp. 3–37.

97 Perkins, *A Treatise of Vocations, etc.*, op. cit., vol. I, p. 751; Trinkaus, 1954, op. cit., p. 77.

98 *Vocations*, op. cit., vol. I, p. 768.

99 Perkins, op. cit., vol. III, pp. 143–8.

100 C. Hill, 'The Puritans and the poor', *P & P*, 1952, no. 2, p. 41; 1964, op. cit., ch. vii.

101 Smith, 1583, op. cit., pp. 114–15.

102 F. Bacon, 'Of seditions and troubles', *The Works of Lord Bacon*, 2 vols, London, W. Ball, 1838, vol. I, p. 272; Advice to the King, Touching Sutton's Estate, *The Works*, J. Spedding, R. L. Ellis and D. D. Heath (eds), 14 vols, London, Longman, 1868–90, vol. XI, pp. 252–3.

103 Ibid., 251–2.

104 Slack, op. cit., p. 126; E. M. Leonard, *The Early History of English Poor Relief*, London, F. Cass, 1965 (repr. 1900), p. 74.

105 Sir S. D'Ewes, *The Journals of all the Parliaments during the Reign of Queen Elizabeth*, P. Bowes (rev.), London, John Starkey, 1682, p. 551.

106 *Statutes*, vol. IV–I, p. 896–8, 962–5.

107 *Vocations*, op. cit., vol. I, p. 755.

8

The Tudor State, Reformation and understanding change: through the looking glass

A. J. Slavin

'When *I* use a word,' Humpty Dumpty said in rather a scornful tone, 'it means just what I choose it to mean – neither more nor less.' 'The question is,' said Alice, 'whether you *can* make words mean so many different things.' 'The question is,' said Humpty Dumpty, 'which is to be master – that's all.'
(Lewis Carroll, Through the Looking Glass, 1872, ch. VI)

Nothing is today more greatly needed than clarity upon ancient notions. Sovereignty, liberty, authority, personality – these are the words of which we want alike the history and the definition; or rather, we want the history because its substance is in fact the definition.[1]

Once upon a time historians of England did not have to worry about Humpty Dumpty's reply to Alice, in making sense of the words they used to describe things. They had confidence in a knowable past and believed they could enter into some dialogue with it through the philological methods of the German School. Archival study gave direct access to a phenomenal world and had as its chief concern the story of the building of the modern sovereign state. This building had an architecture resting on the solid foundation of events, each marking a turning in the road leading from 1485 to 1832 – framing dates in state-building and the shaping of democracy.

It is now rarely asserted that the accession of Henry VII ended the divisions and civil conflict that had haunted the fifteenth century or that the first Reform Bill marked the triumph of democracy. Even the notion that in the Tudor era an ascendant Commons had emerged as a force capable of limiting royal power has been modified almost beyond recognition. We are now told that what was forged in the furnace of the Reformation was a nation-state about the core of royal sovereignty.

223

Parliament appears as a body confined in the main to legislation in aid of the crown.[2]

Dissenters have raised questions about the phenomena of the allegedly new-built Tudor state and the language required to describe it correctly. Was it despotic or even absolutist? Did the frequency of Tudor rebellion signify the state's inability to exercise univocal authority and maintain law and order?[3]

Questions about events have been problematized by the intrusion into discussion of questions of a conceptual nature. Historians inclined toward theory have asked whether there emerged at any time in the sixteenth century in England a state to which we can rightly ascribe the chief attribute of sovereignty: the possession of final and absolute authority in the political community and the jurisdiction appropriate to it. If such a state came into existence in the 1530s, as has been maintained, what was the locus of sovereign power? What type of state was displaced by the one created in the crisis of the Reformation?

Historians ascribing the adjective sovereign to the Henrician state have extended the definition beyond final authority to embrace within sovereignty the idea of an impersonal and privileged rational-legal and constitutional order whose agents possessed the power to control a given territory.[4]

It remains unclear how applying such concepts to the events of the period can be reconciled with what we know of some deeply laid social bases of Tudor political life: e.g. the existence of concrete personal rights, social duties and local political obligations. These were in their actual existence tied closely to irrational traditions of kinship, property systems, customary law and other matters not easily contained within conceptual formulas, and were rooted in belief systems – especially religious beliefs.

Tudor people submitted to power embodied in real agents but never to constructs, even when such concepts as sovereignty did struggle to the surface. This is the point of reference that informs the way in which I take up questions about the Tudor state and how it stood in relationship to the society it governed and the means to govern rulers possessed. I shall argue that in the absence of a monopoly of violence, command over the economy or any other array of sanctions adequate to the extension outward from the centre to the periphery of royal prescription at a time of religious upheaval, Tudor state-builders governed more by the distribution of gifts than by prescriptive acts.

In so doing I propose to focus on alternative ways to read the Tudor evidence, in the belief that applying to that evidence a language suitable to describe modern national sovereign states inhibits understanding of state and society. Quite different vocabularies of political change seem to fit the Tudor facts better and to have greater explanatory power in respect of the events under description.

Among the alternate vocabularies I find especially useful concepts deriving from the analyses of belief and state-building put forward by Max
Weber, Emile Durkheim and their followers. Many of their ideas bear
on the root assumption of the Tudor modernists: that through some
revolutionary process at work in the sixteenth century England became a
modern society, politically.[5]

Recent work bearing directly on the issue of sovereignty runs contrary to
very old traditions which ascribed to English monarchs certain imperial
powers without in any way rising fully to either the concept of sovereignty
or the idea of unitary authority lying behind it.

A point drawn from Sir Thomas Smith by Professor Wood bears repeating: that Tudor writers saw in the state Aristotle's household writ large;
or Bodin's insistence that successful contemporary states (even those he
called sovereign *ex post facto* in the process of creating his own theory)
had household origins and that these remained the very model of good
government.[6]

Contemporaries who used the adjective 'sovereign' to modify the noun
'state' seemed downright old-fashioned in coming to grips with the new
thing, in at least two ways. Not only did they refer to it often by reference
to an Aristotelian *oikonomia*. They insisted on the substantial sameness
of the state throughout the Tudor age.

Elizabeth's personal motto *semper eadem* itself challenged novelty,
insisting on tradition in much the same way that Henry VIII's draftsmen
did in shaping the preamble to the Act of Appeals. They referred to
'sundry old authentic histories and chronicles' and grounded Henry's
restraint of papal jurisdiction by affirming the traditional nature of his
'power, preeminence, authority, prerogative and jurisdiction'. The statute
had in it not a word to suggest the empire that Henry governed was a
sovereign state, except by implication in the limited medieval sense whose
context was the attempt to protect both centralized and segmentary territorial states from the universal claims of popes and emperors.[7]

The language of the Act is dualist, despite its use of the corporate
analogy to identify a unitary body politic. This dualism has been explained
by saying that the language reflected the existence in the body politic of
lay and ecclesiastical jurisdictions embodied in competing court systems,
with the implication that legislation in the 1530s resolved this dualism. In
point of fact neither the arguments nor the Act resolved the deep irrationality of English law. The example of matrimonial law is a case in point.
And in other areas of the law both disputes and competition over jurisdiction ran right through the Tudor century and beyond, despite claims by
historians about the unitary state.[8]

Grindal reminded Queen Elizabeth of this, in arguing that religious
policy made by the state was bad policy, because truths of religion 'were

to be judged . . . in the church, in synod, not in the palace'. That the archbishop laboured under house arrest and was later deprived does not mitigate the sting of a rebuke rooted in old notions of what were the powers, attributes and jurisdiction of the state.[9]

Historians who claim that Henry VIII and his ministers reconstructed the body politic on unitary lines in fact run against the language of their main statutory texts. This has encouraged them to look for proofs behind the words of statutes and to reach into contemporary pamphlets, broadsides and treatises whose meanings are themselves problematic.[10]

Nothing better illustrates this than the disagreements evident in recent accounts, in which the creation of the sovereign state is a main tenet. One discovers wide differences on the date of the appearance of sovereignty, who its main discoverers were, and even the locus of final authority. And nowhere is the possibility for confusion more evident than when we seek clarity about the claim that statute discovered an ancient imperial sovereignty but was itself not instrumental to it.[11]

We meet this argument in works claiming that in 1500 the term 'state' had no meaning in English beyond the condition of the prince or kingdom but that by Elizabeth's time the word signified the state in the modern sense. This claim denies to the 1530s revolutionary significance, by denying that changes in a single decade uniquely shaped the Tudor state while embracing the notion that the shift from realm to state was underpinned by the longer process of Reformation which made the Tudor state unitary in nature.[12]

The unitary character of the rebuilt state turned on the claim that the crown used Parliaments to make law equally binding on church and state. This claim has been tied to the seemingly contradictory assertion, that Henry's kingship and royal supremacy were in no sense equivalent to a parliamentary sovereignty. The clear words of the statute ascribed to the monarchy powers merely rediscovered and affirmed by Parliament. To resolve the tension, it has been said that Henry VIII's government was modelled on Constantine's after his conversion to Christianity – in the sense that the crown assumed full responsibility for the right ordering of the church.[13]

Byzantinism was not an idea congenial to Tudor writers in the 1530s or after, however. Archbishop Parker held that the Supremacy was ordained by God and could be traced back to Anglo-Saxon times only. Byzantinism also worried Henrician common lawyers. St German had in 1531 advocated a theory of parliamentary sovereignty, arguing that it was the king-in-parliament who had full authority over the souls and bodies of subjects. Two years after the passage of the Act of Appeals he claimed that all law was properly made only when made by the king, Lords and Commons, because in their assemblies they fully represented the various estates of the people who were equivalent to the 'whole catholic church thereof'.[14] Moreover, there is evidence that even the chief ministerial upholders of the Supremacy were at odds with the king on this most essential point. Cromwell apparently refused to support any view of an imperial kingship on a Byzantine line, one that asserted the monarch's absolute right to govern the church without the consent of Parliament. Cromwell allegedly went so far as to delete from a draft of the Commons' Supplication a reference to England as an empire, apparently because he meant to neutralize Henry's absolutism in practice.[15]

St German countered any tendency toward a Byzantine theory by reasserting a venerable element in English thought, conveying something akin to what Fortescue had signified (*regnum politicum et regale*) in his contrast of French absolutism and English mixed monarchy. Cromwell's ideas may well have been close to St German's, if both men regarded suspiciously the authority Henry VIII claimed as deriving from a mixture of the medieval theories taken by canonists from civil law (*lex regia* and *dei gratia*). If such phrases signified Constantine's delegation of legislative power from the people and made the expression of the royal will law, with divine sanction, the main point becomes suspect. If Henry had truly emulated Constantine's autocracy, the king's claims should have reached beyond ecclesiastical policy and intrusions into doctrinal debates and tested other realms of law. Constantine's absolutism was of an altogether wider scope, as we know from any discussion of imperial decrees and rescripts. English judges were fond of repeating Bracton's maxim, that English kings were under God and law (*sub deo et sub lege*). Law made the king.[16]

Foxe and Cranmer may have thought otherwise, if recent interpretations of the *Collectanea satis copiosa* are correct in maintaining that its redactors believed Henry was under God but not the law because the king made law. But their reputed ideas run up against the fact that Henry VIII never made law on his own in the tradition of imperial decrees. Not even the debate hovering around the Act of Proclamations invokes Byzantinism in that sense. Later in the century and elsewhere in Europe the notion that the power to make law inhered entirely in the ruler was essential to theories of sovereignty. But English theorists resisted this formula, as we shall see.[17]

Henry VIII's actual practices on a very wide front implicated the feudal language of suzerainty rather than the language of sovereignty. The 1536 Statute of Uses extended rights to tax on a feudal basis. His claims of authority over Ireland and Scotland were defined in terms of suzerainty, in the Irish case until 1542 at least and in the matter of Scotland until his death. The doctrine of naturalization and denization in England turned on the feudal notion of allegiance.[18]

The language of sovereignty is slippery when applied to Henrician state-building. If we are to get back to the other side of the looking glass, where words stay in place, the journey will require that we track closely the nature of Tudor society in relationship to its governing institutions while developing a vocabulary suitable to events.

A step along the track is to focus on the way in which social and political changes correlate or cluster in a society experiencing state-building. Max Weber was much concerned to shape a theory of political development making use of both concepts.[19] Under his influence and that of Durkheim, Mauss, Moret and Davy elaborated the idea that in state-building a culturally dominant focus on exchange functions and gift relationships gave impetus to a whole range of changes tending toward the consolidation of the state where before a state was lacking or did exist but had a segmentary character. By this they indicated a state that was not centralized or rationalized and was in fact a loose confederation of units and jurisdictions subject to strong pressures from patrimonial kingship.[20] They argued that in such societies a dominant focus controlled the pace of change and determined the boundaries of any institutional set making up the state.[21]

The importance of such ideas is apparent from any consideration of Weber's *The Protestant Ethic and the Spirit of Capitalism*, his other classic works on legal and economic development, and Durkheim's main studies of related problems. In these Weber analysed secular social and economic change in terms of a specific constellation of legal and religious ideas, attitudes, habits and values making up a total belief system that was itself the ground of political culture and political change. This kind of analysis has dominated subsequent work to define modern state-building in terms combining modernizing centralization and the resolution of aspects of irrationality informing traditional cultures.[22]

However much they might dispute the 'generously stimulating tyranny' of Weber's classic theory, historians who otherwise have little traffic with the human sciences have taken seriously his attempt to explain state-building by the linkage of rationality and modernity. But debates over Weber's theory of the rise of capitalism have obscured his other concerns for the dynamics of state-building and his work on developments in the English political system in particular. Historians have paid scant attention to Weber's studies of charismatic leadership and its routinization through bureaucratization, or the creation of a modern rational-legal order out of the traditional ordering of society, though these ideas are implicated in all debates over the alleged appearance of a sovereign state in the aftermath of Henry's alleged revolution in government.[23]

There has been even less notice of Weber's analyses of how the monarchical institutions characteristic of early modern states were dependent for their development on the existence of what he called patrimonialism. For Weber, patrimonialism signified the practice of monarchs voracious in the actual expansion of their powers into new areas of claim on the basis of a merely discretionary personal power. The authority of such rulers had been traditional, in the sense of being rooted in the givenness of a past order, an order said to be sacred and of divine institution.[24]

It is worth recalling here that Henry VIII augmented his power by ruthlessly widening the scope of property claims and attacking all groups inhibiting these claims, without much regard for geography or status. In justifying these new claims both the royal language and iconography remained traditional.[25] On Weber's account this is no surprise, because patrimonial monarchs extended their real power and authority by incorporating into their *Hausmacht*, originally on traditional grounds, resources foreign to it. A case in point is the centralizing Yorkist and Tudor policy of fiscal feudalism. The crown required the resources essential to its actual exercise of power but in invading others' rights used such customary devices as *quo warranto* proceedings and acts of resumption. It was careful not to raise questions about the legitimacy of actions which rested on traditional and deeply rooted norms of power and authority in a segmentary state. Wherever subjects resisted, the gap between royal claims and popular belief was an important measure of dislocation in the relationship of society to polity. Henry VIII marked his accession by sacrificing ministers who were accused of exceeding the boundaries of traditional claims and their basis in beliefs.[26]

He could not validate the claims made by Henry VII by reference to sovereign powers, because the patrimonialism of the crown in its drive for resources was itself a condition necessary for the creation of a unitary state out of the segmentary medieval state. Weber's theory of patrimonial monarchy thus has advantages in decoding data and in the ordering of that data as we try to evaluate modern claims made about the nature of the Tudor state. It sheds light on recent discussions of household government in the general context of arguments over the reform of law and institutions, in particular relationships among courts, councils and the royal Court.[27]

The earlier Henrician efforts at territorial consolidation, improved administration of finances and experiments in direct lay taxation had not removed Henry VIII as far from Lancastrian kingship as the theory of the modern state implies. For example, the war efforts early in the 1520s were to show clearly how limited the royal powers of prescription and enforcement were in respect of taxation, well before the greater challenges in the 1530s resulting from the alterations in religion.[28]

Such gaps between royal aspiration and achievement strike me as giving support to Weber's contention, that a deep conflict pervaded English society in the Reformation era, between what he called the existing traditional socio-political order and any efforts to shape a new order based on an absorption of resources and the rationalization of institutions: what we may in keeping with Weber's meaning call a modern social order and the state apparatus appropriate to it.[29] Weber regarded the roots of the conflict as in the broadest sense religious, because religion set the seal on acceptable change. It informed the law and its interpretation and supported every other system expressing any idea of right order. Within its domain lay the mandate to rule, in codes defining access to power, for example in the idea of legitimate succession by birth.[30] In attacking the traditional religion after 1529, Henry VIII brought into question the link between political rule over society and the idea of a transcendent world order that was its sanction. Tradition legitimized authority. When Henry VIII made even greater claims to take into the crown foreign resources, mobilizing the wealth of the church for example, and thereby altering old relationships of society to polity and the belief system upholding both, we may question whether the 'points of contact' model of Tudor political cohesion satisfies the demand to explain how a government of the limited means Henry VIII commanded managed the changes in behaviour necessary to support expanded claims.[31]

Weber had used the words tradition and traditional to point toward a system of imperative co-ordination (in the sense of effective authority) over a given society. The legitimacy of that authority rested on the sacredness of an order whose origin was shrouded in the deep past – the claim that the order had always existed.[32]

Hence Weber's concept of a traditional order rooted in irrationality is polar to any concept of the order of a state rooted in the rationalization of institutions and beliefs. In a modern legal-rational order institutions have a high degree of independence from the sacred, on the basis of functionally specific and rational norms. Any effort to shape such an order forced into opposition the most conservative bearers of ideas about government in relation to society, ideas rooted in theological, ritualistic and kinship-based norms of conduct. To the degree that the Tudor state and its government were embedded in such traditional notions the potential for conflicts multiplied.

Weber argued that in the struggle for change within a traditional society, in situations where blind adherence to the old order by partisans of traditionalism spurred the ruler's quest to extend the span of control over resources, the results achieved might exceed those intended by the innovators, as resistance triggered even more radical claims by the state. Because tradition signified a complex system of codes, an artifact made within the culture and usually transmitted in recognizable forms over long periods, it shaped actions and set boundaries to acceptable change. Tradition provided an index of the means necessary to overcome the inertial energy of accustomed forms and regulated the ways in which people confronted the everyday ethical and aesthetic valuing that determines what is a fitting way of life.[33] Traditions were dynamic, even dialectical, informing politics, economics, kinship – flowing from their source in religion to all the main structures of society. They were not things which once were and suddenly passed away. As forces of change impinged on traditions some lost coherence while others disintegrated. The result was social disorganization and social delinquency, the fear of chaos we find so loudly voiced in the Tudor obedience literature.[34]

But by itself the enervation of traditions did not produce new forms of the state. In societies in such rapid flux the disruption of traditional frameworks might as easily produce what contemporaries called disorder, for example in the struggles in the 1530s and 1540s to define new articles of faith and to validate the crown's claims to the property of the church. What the Tudor discourse on disorder masked was the fact that there had been the disruption of an old order without the creation of a stable new socio-political order. By recurring to Weber's root ideas undergirding patrimonial monarchy and its exercise, *Hausmacht* and imperative co-ordination, we may illuminate matters of mid-Tudor social and political change without invoking the idea of sovereignty and the modern freight of values carried with it.

Weber's theories direct our attention to the growing tension within society over the givenness or assumed validity of royal authority and the belief system sanctioning it, the very idea of right order itself, at a time when the royal attack on property and religion bred confusion about proper roles for persons and institutions.[35] In the controversialist literature of the period there is ample evidence of the tensions at the heart of the matter: upholders of tradition seeking compromise, partisans of traditionalism urging all out resistance to royal concerns, innovators rethinking the relationship between canon law, scripture and the law made in Parliament.[36]

There is reason to stress the consequences for subjects of this confusion in a new intermingling of religion and politics. We think of modern political life in terms of citizenship, in which most if not all obligations are circumscribed by the demand for an active participation in making law and interpreting it in the decision of public questions. This part-taking assumes political roles are clearly distinguishable from others. In Tudor England political roles for most persons were not clearly distinguishable from other social roles, for example membership in kinship or analogous groups such as guilds and chantries. Political life was embedded in other roles, and we hear relatively little, and that at infrequent intervals, of any direct and majoritarian political decision-making.[37] In so much as it existed it was masked in primarily juridical forms having religious sanctions. It is noteworthy that in all of the sessions of the Reformation Parliament we have a record of only one majority vote. In the Pilgrimage of Grace there was a unique demand for a system for the redress of grievances, but it took the form of a Parliament in the north, away from the influence of London and the Court.[38]

There were other demands for regular accountability from rulers to society. Thomas Starkey proposed checking royal power by asserting the rights of noble counsellors at a time when there were still occasional meetings of Great Councils. But these had passed into oblivion by the end of the sixteenth century, and demands by rebels for changes in the king's advisers, for example the demand in 1536 that the king purge Cromwell and Cranmer from his council, were backward-looking and infrequent.[39] Demands for accountability took the form of adhesion to traditions of claim and sanction. Consider taxation. It is no longer clear, as has been maintained, that Henry VIII, during the time of Cromwell's dominance, abandoned extra-consensual claims touching taxation of the sort said to be typical under Wolsey and revived in the 1540s. Henry obtained the consent of Commons and Lords for the attack on church wealth, but together with consensual moves the king used threats to levy huge fines on individuals and coerced surrenders of church property. The taxes levied in 1536 elicited widespread opposition as reaching beyond legitimate royal authority.[40]

As the stakes grew larger, with the monasteries down and a political elite to keep in alignment with the government in the wake of the Pilgrimage of Grace, by repeated distributions of gifts, one sees a mixture of negotiations for exchanges of episcopal land and surrenders under duress. The context in which we may best understand these negotiations is the long history of royal limits put upon the absolute immunity of church property and papal authority.[41] This mixture of law, threat and negotiation in the expansion of royal resources at a time of crisis is typical of patrimonialism. The monarchy widened the scope of its fiscal power by absorbing claims to the property of others, as it was simultaneously meeting a clamour for reversal of new claims by groups both close to the ruler and those remote from his authority in space and status.

That the king disliked traditionalists' complaints but often bowed to them appears in a wide variety of evidence. Consider the case of Alderman Rede, a member of the London City elite who refused in 1544 to give a benevolence. He was impressed on the king's authority to serve in the war against Scotland, taken prisoner there, and then ransomed because of pressure brought to bear on the Privy Council from the corporate bodies of London.[42] Rede's case grows in interest in the light of the recent discussions of the celebrated debates over arbitrary levies a century later. At issue were claims by the crown to take property from subjects in the name of the general good, even by coercion. These were upheld by royal justices on the basis of precedents, in decisions highlighting the irrationality of the legal system, a feature appearing again in the opinions on arbitrary levies by royal judges under Charles I and Charles II, in the case *Craw* v. *Ramsey*. The judges opined that a clearly wrongful escheat taken by Charles I was made for the common weal (*pro bono publico*) and should stand. During the 1665 session in Exchequer Chamber, Bridgeman CJ wrote that upholding royal rights to take was necessary whenever 'the King's Revenue falls short of answer to the public charge'. He argued that his brethren ought to declare for the king, not on the merits, but on a reading of the king's ancient feudal prerogative, the basis for which was the form of an oath found in a statute of 18 Edward III. This bound judges to aid their monarch in all jurisdictional matters touching his patrimony.[43]

What is noteworthy in this evidence from the 1530s, 1540s, 1620s and 1660s is, first, the cleavages on matters of policy, which if not attended to might erupt into conflicts capable of threatening the regime on a wide front, and second, the authority appealed to is that of irrational precedent touching feudal rights, with no idea of sovereignty. Henry's retreats stand in sharp contrast with Stuart claims made good. The study of tax protests bears on this point. Rumours of a royal attack on property rights in the Amicable Loan Revolt played a prominent role in triggering resistance where wholly secular interests were engaged. Archbishop Warham sided with East Anglian peasants and yeomen who said they wanted to support the king but were unable to do so because of their poverty as well as with pauper priests in Kent. Where the property of lay holders alone was at issue, taking lands from wealthy gentry raised the objection that strength would follow possession and weakness dispossession, that there would be an unwarranted shift in power from subjects deprived of lawful rights.[44]

The crux of the matter is whether traditional limits on royal claims to take had given way generally, under the real pressures of royal patrimonialism. Throughout the fifteenth century and into the 1530s English kings had appropriated ecclesiastical monastic wealth on relatively narrow fronts, after the great scare over Lollardy, and with little evident dissent except from those injured. And in the 1530s there was a revival of arguments from Roman law about the prince and absolute property rights. But efforts to attach chantries produced second thoughts and retreat.[45] The contrast in the history of confiscatory policy touching different religious endowments is especially illuminating. Expediency may explain the Marian retreat from restoring religious endowments and the 1559 actions in respect of episcopal lands, but lacks power to explain why Henry VIII and his government contemplated seizing chantry lands as early as 1535–6, drew back, came forward again in 1545, only to retreat once more before settling the confiscation by statute in 1546–7.[46] Did the 1547 statute signify a breakthrough to a new set of popular attitudes of acceptance of expanded claims? Hardly, if we stress the large-scale depredations by persons responsible for chantry endowments or evidence bearing witness to the careful preservation by hiding of tangibles connected to the obits and other aspects of chantry obligation.

At least part of the answer to the question about fiscal stop and start lies in recognizing the difference in the structure of belief undergirding the function of monastic and obituary endowments. These differed radically in terms of the spiritual concerns of donors for themselves and their ancestors, in the sense of the interest at stake within the economy of salvation. The fate of the chantries belongs to a larger history and unwritten history of gifting and gift relationships, the dynamics of exchange and the basis for gifting in which economic values and religious beliefs were inextricably linked. This linkage in turn was crucial to the view taken of the legitimacy of political actions. Donors were perhaps more likely to resist attacks on chantries because their beliefs in the efficacy of prayers and masses for the dead were more closely engaged.[47]

As the Reformation unfolded it is clear that old institutions and old religious symbols had taken on new meanings among common folk, and had assumed different shapes and even shifts in function, at different rates in different places. In the extreme case, when Purgatory was called into question as a necessary doctrine, many in the society experienced a remarkable and rapid shift in practice, if not in belief, for example in London and the south-east in particular but in other regions as well. In many places endowments were overthrown without any resistance, at least in part because new ideas of salvation put forward by the government drew support from traditions of native dissent and continental infiltrations. But much recent work has shown how careful we must be in assuming anything about the pace of change in belief and practice and their interrelationship in national terms.[48]

We see the matter in microcosm in Cromwell's man Thomas Wriothesley. He has been consigned to the Catholic Reaction by many historians. But he played the key role in the destruction of the shrines of Becket at Canterbury and St Swithin at Winchester. As late as 1535 however, when his mentor was receiving advice to down the chantries, Wriothesley was buying letters of admission to the Guild of St Mary at Boston, the most richly endowed chantry under English administration, in terms of its privileges for the remission of temporal punishment arising from mortal sins. When he died in 1550, Wriothesley left a request that Bishop Hooper, that great enemy of the doctrine of purgatory, preach his funeral sermon.[49]

The matter of habit, attitude and belief in relation to endowments commands attention because the crown has been said to have had two motives in the attacks on chantries: to pay debts from the wars in the 1540s, as the recoinage failed to meet the demands for money and rising direct taxation pushed people to resistance; and to meet pressing needs to widen the scope of the means available to the monarchy in the exercise of gifting, even in the obvious forms of patronage, as the transference of monastic lands out of crown hands went on apace.[50]

Gifting was itself deeply implicated in social custom and belief systems in ways of valuing bringing together tangibles and intangibles. It was of supreme importance in the exchange networks of the era. As the monarchy tried to bind to it members of the politically valid nation it risked alienating them not only by its fiscal patrimonialism but also by its religious policies. The government was under pressure nearly everywhere 'to butter the rooks' nest', but some means employed in regions where traditional values and beliefs remained intact proved dysfunctional, as the history of resistance reveals.[51]

What impelled innovators to go so far toward uprooting religious traditions in their efforts at fiscalism in the process of state-building is a question to which Weber and his followers have provided an answer, in setting forward ideas about political modernization. They found a tendency for attacks on any part of a belief system to become holistic. Innovators may seek at first to relieve deformities in the order they value as natural. Given the centrality of religion, that is its dominant role as the cultural focus of traditional societies, efforts to reconfigure religious institutions entailed redefinition of doctrine.[52]

In the English case the monarchy had played the central role in weakening the relationship between an old authority grounded in the Catholic religion and the sense of solidarity in the community of the realm. This necessitated redefinition of the relationship, as royal agents pressured the people on a wide front touching church property, taxes, oaths and worship, and demanded an appropriate theory to legitimize the crown's absorption of religious authority. Once any part of the pastness and sacredness of tradition on which the social and religio-political order rested had been touched, the innovators were brought face-to-face with the fact that in pushing the church from its lofty eminence they had implicated their own authority in its crisis.[53]

This followed from the binary character of all relations of power and authority. Any proposal to alter them from one side only called into question the contractual values at the heart of the quid pro quo by which England had remained in the Roman communion for a millennium and Rome had sanctioned the exercise of royal power.[54]

It is a strong argument, that the extent of the reforms was a consequence of the intolerable strain put upon relations with Rome from the purely dynastic matter of the Divorce. Recent studies demonstrate how the pace of the challenge to tradition was dictated from the outset by strains that had their origin within the law of contracts. As the English pressure on Rome mounted, the boundaries of diplomacy cracked and the result was a weakening of Roman authority on a wide front. The monarchy mobilized all resources, first to justify its demands, and then to achieve a significant differentiation of religious institutions, by separating them and their operation from their traditional sources of authority.[55] The Divorce was a Trojan Horse, and resolving it led to the refurbishing of old institutions and the erecting of new ones. Both renovation and creation released radical forces in society, energies which proved difficult to channel or control. Regulating the changed vectors and integrating them into a redefined monarchy by declaring the king Supreme Head (*supremum caput in ecclesia*) went beyond the modification of traditions and tended toward the reordering of the entire political system.

Yet there is scant evidence either that any holistic plan to shape a modern sovereign state was intended by Henrician agents or that they possessed the means to do so. In every part of the realm, in town and shire communities, the breaking of old bonds and the refusal of many to accept new ones, gave rise to resistance. Allegiance to older ideas of community and the relationship of state to society endured in the face of the best efforts of the government to instil loyalty to concepts not yet susceptible of absolute clarity. The revival of King John's reputation competed for attention with the campaign against 'idols'.[56]

The history of rebellion in the 1530s and 1540s shows how difficult it was for the leaders of reform to go beyond the small initial premisses of the Divorce Crisis toward the wider secularizing reordering of society sometimes ascribed to them. They could succeed only if royal agents vigorously pursuing the goals of patrimonialism mustered larger forces than traditionalists. And this proved difficult, whenever the direction of change challenged traditional elites in ways that threatened the social bases of their political status and the values underlying them. Recent historiography reveals this difficulty in the careful attention given to the 'feudal' reactions among parts of the landed aristocracy. They regarded the changes of the 1530s as a threat to their existence as leaders of local society. At the very least a basic transformation of their place in the socio-political order was explicit in the moves of the patrimonial monarchy, and many magnates regarded the threat of marginalization in their exercise of power locally as unacceptable. In some regions the threat seemed to be one of actual liquidation.[57]

Nowhere is this more evident than in the tightening of the screws by the government directed against Catholic landed families and their priests generally. No matter what strategies of survival they shaped against the force of an increasingly repressive government, they were met by ever more stringent statutes, from 1536 through 1585 and after. They experienced the changes as marginalizing in multiple senses, in terms of their perception of the common good, strongly held personal values, and the ability to maintain worship, kinship and other networks of affinity giving meaning to their lives.[58]

Many recent studies focus on the difficulty encountered at the centre by resistance at the periphery to motifs of reforms embodying both material interests and their ideological underpinnings. Waves of propaganda sought to mobilize assent to new policies and doctrines and were supported by vigorous traditional gifting to persuade the 'outliers' not to work against the policy radiating from the centre. When this failed, various pressures, including overt force, might be used against the geographically remote upholders of traditionalism who were also off-centre religiously, economically and in their allegiance to ancient and segmentary institutions and symbols of social and political life. The 1536 risings provide important examples, as do those in 1569 and 1570.[59]

Resistance to the ingressive monarchy reveals how in England the state was itself nascent rather than the mature intentional agent of change. The process by which dissidents identified themselves politically with the monarchy's state-building was limited by the highly stratified and segmented nature of Tudor political society. The English system of politics from the later Middle Ages well into the modern period was characterized by a multiplicity of hierarchies of status and very deep pockets of status incongruity, or lack of equilibrium between groups we may consider dyads: lords and peasants, merchants and craftsmen, clergy and laity, patrons and clients. Despite efforts to resolve the most gross elements of disequilibrium incompatibilities of status persisted everywhere.[60]

Differences in status and rights were mediated by attitudes, beliefs and their embodiment in institutions. These differences inhibited state-building, despite the movement to forge out of the numerous hierarchies of status a system of compromises in which something like a countrywide political consciousness might take shape. There is ample evidence from diverse regions of inhibitions to community-building directed from the centre, particularly in the interests expressed by the higher social groupings in their corporate bodies, which upheld local rights and privileges against service and subservience to the state as the means to betterment. But even at lower social levels corporate bodies played a crucial role in promoting localism against the centre.[61] It was a problem for state-building that regional elite groups enjoying privileged status might also have little by way of common interests, except when brought together in such emergencies as those producing 'national' associations of bond and oath to safeguard Queen Elizabeth.

The problem reached into urban as well as rural society. The merchant elites of London and the outports are an excellent case in point. The outport merchants were, like the London ones, divided between wholesalers and retailers, as well as between chartered men and the interloping traders whose voyages were regarded as depredations against royally sanctioned privileged societies. This high degree of dissociation within and among elites spurred competitions even with the monarchy, whenever domination seemed at issue. And they could be induced to co-operate with other elites usually only in the face of any threat from the lower social orders, and not always then.[62]

This principle informed Lord Burghley's action, in drawing up for Queen Elizabeth I a list of about 2,500 men whose allegiance could guarantee the queen's security on the throne. It had been stated clearly by the duke of Norfolk in 1537 for his titular county, when he said the yeomen and other leaders sworn to overthrow the landed classes had no hope of success 'bicause we bee to manie jantylmane heere in thys countrye'. But perhaps the best evidence for the vertical strains in society appears in studies of the middling ranks of landed families in Tudor England.[63]

The regional landed elites in England during the Reformation era were factious and rebellious. Periodically, in 1536, 1537, 1549, 1553, 1569 and 1572, in one constellation or another, their adherence to the regime was put under strain. Their reluctance to close ranks with the monarchy stemmed in large measure from the fact that they could not easily distinguish their political role from their other roles in society. What was crucial for them in any political change emanating from the monarchy was its potential impact upon the traditional bases of their power.[64]

This power had for centuries arisen out of their possession of broad landed estates and the offices attaching to them, from which they secured the loyalties of their dependants and administered from their households the territories in which they had effective authority. Their ideas about property were fundamental to their conception of their roles and the legitimacy they ascribed to the political order. For them property was power.

They were as much proponents of *Hausmacht* as was Henry Tudor. This was the source of their good lordship, entailing the bundle of rights and mutual obligations upon which all questions of status and honour rested. In their politics they were much less concerned about the quantity of value in their land expressed in money than they were about the kind and quality of their social relationships expressed through land. In this they resembled the king closely.[65]

Moreover, what historians have condemned as bastard feudalism was in fact the normal and legitimate form of aristocratic social organization. The transformation of the basis of magnate affinities from the heritable fief to indenture was not of necessity destructive for public order. And close study of lordship has revealed that the change was pervasive in an age of an economy increasingly monetized, in an arc of work being done on clientage and patronage reaching from the fourteenth century well into the sixteenth century. Studies of clientage suggest caution in relegating even middling men to an inferior place in patrimonial politics, by labelling them in a pejorative manner.[66]

Middling lords as well as magnates were able to control a defined regional territory effectively by a process of diffusion of authority, working out from the home council into the wider affinity to exercise influence over landed men outside the network of their bonds and indentures. This they did by multiplying offices through the division of stewardships and also through direct expansions of their households. But it was never the case that even the greater nobility engrossed the services of the gentry, and there is ample evidence to show that in regional politics many gentry existed outside the framework of any relationship of clientage.

The implications of this are important. For the gentry so described were mainly concerned to preserve their own ancient patterns of patrimony and lineage, giving less attention to any other set of relations. It seems likely that these independent gentry helped to shape a pattern of regional politics in which they simultaneously resisted royal power and eroded magnate power by stratagems of inactivity in response to calls to arms by their betters.[67]

It is too early to say with assurance that this pattern of evasion explains the general failure of solidarity on magnates and tenants in Tudor rebellions, but studies of the north may well support this contention. Wherever good lordship rooted in tangible counters existed, that good lordship required a variety of services for its maintenance: marriage brokering; securing positions of power and honour in local administration for followers through influence at Court; providing aid, counsel and various forms of advocacy both legal and extra-legal – feuds as well as mediations. That is, the relationships of good lordship were themselves aspects of the gift relationship at the root of patrimonial power, and the values expressed in it were feudal and traditional in the fullest sense. It was the absence of bastard feudalism rather than its presence that multiplied difficulties for the patrimonial monarchy.[68]

Policy caused difficulties for patrimonial rulers whenever royal acts undermined traditional attitudes of loyalty by regarding patrimonies as fungible assets. It was essential to the landed elites in the more conservatively organized regions on the whole, in or out of magnate affinities, that the monarchy do nothing to erode traditional forms of social relationship and social action. The danger of disruption was great.

Yet Henry VIII's proposed legislation in the 1530s struck just such blows at the fabric of aristocratic life and generated a tremendous force of opposition at Westminster and in the regions, when the king proposed to reform the law that permitted evasion of the monarch's feudal interests in land. Henry VIII had to retreat in 1532 from an effort to reform the practices of uses and trusts. It was only after the defeat of the risings in 1536 and 1537, in which some northern lords were executed and others had their wings clipped, and when for reasons not connected immediately to the risings the Percy earldom collapsed and the Poles were decimated, that the king took up this struggle again, seeking to widen the provisions of the 1536 statute.[69] But even the 1540 legislation compromised the issues, and we may say with accuracy that resolution of conflict revealed the contradiction in ascribing to Henry VIII the full powers of prescription we associate with modern sovereignty. His bargains struck with the landed classes suggest patrimonialism in its clearest operations. There were limits set to even Henry's ability to expand the basis for royal gifting at the expense of the landed classes who had their own exchange networks to tend.

The question of what were the ties that held and what were the ones that broke is thus central to our understanding of the impact of royal policy and the nature of the political system. There is a sense in which it is less important to know whether the dangers perceived by the landed elites were real than it is to know the strength of such perceptions and the forms that reaction took. If the monarchy aimed at extending its territorial control, substituting royal domination for regional patterns of power, while simultaneously eroding the position of the church in regions of strong religious conservatism, then neither prescriptive behaviour nor a radical expansion of gifting were likely to be adequate to overcome the deep distrust of unpopular policies.

This was especially true in the north where the aristocracy were slower to achieve literacy than were their counterparts in the south and relied more on face-to-face communications in important matters, with all the great pressures of conformity inherent in speech.[70]

Hence the crown did what it could do, expanding its patrimonial functions and hoping for the best. The attempted regional mobilization of sentiment failed, not only in the 'backward' Tudor north or the western fringes. It failed also in some areas within the south where the crown had entrenched itself over the centuries.[71]

Even had royal policy in these areas attracted unwavering support on the basis of extended patrimonialism, to describe that success as the achievement of a univocal sovereignty, in the way that term has been applied to the sixteenth century, remains wide of the mark. A regime too weak to command obedience to its main policies of reform had to settle for outward conformity rooted in negotiations. The bargaining was tantamount to the acceptance of inward opposition, a recognition at the centre of the assertion by M. E. James, that there was a very slow growth of agreement to reform in the north where the keeping up of honour and appearance were no little things.[72]

What is at issue is a grasp of how government in a traditional society nudged that society toward change and its acceptance, breaking old rules and conventions in the act of doing so. Understanding this dynamic requires that we bring into a fruitful relationship discourse about prescriptive aspects of power and its distributive aspects.

In speaking of the distributive aspects of power (and hence of sovereign, final authority) we touch again the essence of patrimonial politics. The essence is economic: the attempts by rulers to concentrate access to resources and distribute them to those committed to the government as the maker of political change. Exchange and gifting were the means of co-optation and the essence of all further attempts to build solidarity. The aggressive Tudor policy of territorial consolidation which has been treated chiefly under the guise of the rise of the sovereign territorial state has a more important dimension in the concept of *Hausmacht* and the acts of appropriation by which it was expanded.

Whenever the monarchy was itself the prime mover in efforts to transcend other loyalties, gifting was central to its efforts. The royal campaign to reconstruct borough governments through rechartering may have had as its goal to win support for royal policy through commitment rather than coercion. Town charters were officially acts of royal grace – no matter what petitioning there had been when the initiative was local, as Professor Tittler has shown. But in some cases there was coercive pressure, and the gift of a new charter was as welcome as the plague to dominant segments of the urban community experiencing royal intrusion. Perhaps of even greater importance is the demonstration that much urban reform, for example rebuilding in the sixteenth century, was not the result of central initiative and had behind it a long medieval tradition of local initiative; this is a demonstration that strikes at the heart of any revolutionary interpretation of the Henrician age.[73]

The gifting practice aimed at social and political loyalty that has attracted most attention to date from Tudor historians has been the distribution of former monastic lands and their appurtenant tithes, offices and buildings. But there has been little effort to discipline the data by fitting it to the theory of patrimonialism and the role within it of the gift relationship: how gifts express mutuality of obligation and mobilize the non-material as well as material resources of society for change.

There has also been attention to other tangible property: lands, offices, capital goods, patents, consumption, wages, marriage and wardship, titles and honours. On the side of intangibles entering into gifting, historians have done only scattered research. There has been some scrutiny of education, literacy and access to schooling as socially empowering or disenfranchising, especially of the ratio of opportunity between London and other towns. The role of women in domestic politics beyond their place as marriage counters has drawn attention recently. But gifting with ritual objects of little or no intrinsic value has hardly been approached.[74]

The importance to Tudor rule of this fuller range of gifting showed most strikingly in the creation of a class of centralizing agents (*ministeriales*) supporting a dynasty seeking to extend its territorial power in an unprecedented way. This ministerial class was a closed cadre in some sense, however open recruitment to it might have been. Once selected, the new *ministeriales* appeared to those outside the circle as restricted, segregated and focused on the royal Court, at a time when in official propaganda there was an emphasis on the formation of the larger community of the realm in terms of old corporate analogies.[75]

To the Tudor *ministeriales* and their dependants Parliaments were crucial occasions for the operations of patrimonialism. In a politics based on exchange Westminster was the centre of the social season, the place where status was confirmed among local elites, an important marriage-market for a tightly connected ruling class and an important job market. It was also the focus of patronage through private acts, the place where patents and monopolies were made and undone, and the symbol of the ostensible unity of the politically valid classes. Exclusion damaged the interests of peers, as their concerns at Westminster reached well beyond saying yea or nay to crown initiatives.[76] Things bargained at Westminster were as much a part of the patrimonial outreach of members of both houses as was the relentless search for the means to control society-wide political activities by the crown.[77] For patrimonialism required the relentless mobilizing of pressure groups for the crown's ends, not only in London and Westminster but also in towns and counties whose stories are now being carefully told, in new studies illuminating the conflicts arising out of royal attempts to co-ordinate the regions by acts of grace and acts of coercion.[78]

The operation of the metropolitical exchange system, with its triple centres in Parliament, Court and Chamber, was in effect an elaborate system of domestic diplomacy, in which marriage and wardship figured prominently alongside advocacy by patrons who maintained their own place in the political sun by proximity to the patrimonial regime at the centre. Yet this diplomacy internal to England, which has been less studied than the external diplomacy of the era, was an extension of the basic mechanism of exchange, a process of contracting interests and reconciling divergences of interest. What went on at the centre went on also between the centre and the peripheral foci of political power in a traditional society in crisis.

In a modern system of politics this harmonizing of interests might have as its focus the formation of constituencies disciplined by the notion of loyal political opposition. There was no idea of legitimate opposition to the monarchy in the Tudor state. Faction and party connoted illegitimacy and threatened to extend outward from the royal Court to the counties rivalries embedded in the segmentary features of the Tudor state. Henry VIII lacked extensive power of command and prescription rooted in a monopoly of violence. He chafed at this limitation and was inclined toward extreme brutality in reaction to any signs of less than warm support for his centralizing policy, being much given to hectoring and purges.[79]

His lack of prescriptive power, or rather the means to enforce what he had prescribed, was critical to the resolution of rebellions in the 1530s and 1540s. Henry VIII might exact a high toll in revenge from the lower ranks of rebels, but he was often driven to bargain with those in the upper ranks. And he could not generally control the regions in his segmentary state without gifting the locally powerful leaders. His efforts at control were complicated by the high degree of dissociation among the regional elites, for example the interests of lords in the home counties as contrasted with those of marcher lords on a permanent war footing.

The constant drain of resources away from the crown by extensive gifting from the 1540s through to the 1590s entailed a real decline in Elizabeth's distributive power, which had consequences for her power to prescribe. This change historians have interpreted in many ways, but here it is interesting to widen the view by taking into account the relationship between theories of sovereignty and the decay of power in the monarchy in the 1590s.

A good start towards this wider view is to look more closely at royal power as it appeared to men learned in the law in Elizabethan and early Stuart England. Common lawyers seeking to understand earlier events employed several 'languages' in discussing political and constitutional questions, retaining vocabularies from scholasticism, scriptural study and the common law tradition of interpretations reaching back to Bracton. They also took into account the ideas then in circulation from the continent deploying a language fully absolutist and embodying a zeal for Roman law principles.

Faced with the actual rise in royal power under Henry VIII, and knowing well the Roman texts, they showed little interest in applying Roman maxims to English government. They conceded that the king was sovereign in the sense of being a prince independent of any foreign authority. But they put no stock in the idea of an undivided sovereignty of the kind Bodin treated in the French context.

English rulers were said to possess a bundle of feudal and royal powers, in sum the prerogative, conferring on them the first place in politics and some legal privileges. But their powers and rights were also said to rest on their real property, something private and personal in nature, regulated by law without being completely defined by it. Commentators believed that in respect of making new law there existed power-sharing, because under Elizabeth clearer boundaries were set to royal authority, even in respect of the Supremacy, than had been the case under Henry VIII. Sir Thomas Smith admitted only that the king was absolute in his discretion in coining money, making war and concluding peace. It remained for

Gentili and James VI to argue for unrestrained royal absolutism early in the seventeenth century.[80]

These later comments throw fresh light on Henry VIII. Good King Harry had in fact behaved like a lord of old, maintaining a formal harmony between his crown and his outliers, while close to home he demanded more by way of support of the new order of things. He acted a very traditional role, at times seeming closer to the intimate kingship of Beowulf in his great hall than that exercise of power characteristic of his Hanoverian heirs. In his Privy Chamber Henry was a great ring giver, a *hlaflord*, who at the new year gifting ceremony was observed leaning casually on a cupboard while a servant took careful note of incoming gifts. Those closest to him were no longer spear-thegns, to be sure; but neither were they the civil servants of a sovereign state. And those more remote from the centre were perhaps closer to spear-thegns than we admit in our discussions of the changes emanating from the palace.[81]

It is no accident that in his refurbished style of patrimonial rule Henry VIII and his ministers should make much of the common weal and even the commonwealth, for these were motifs of ancient, even Davidic, kingship. In groping toward a language of social well-being leaders of reform were impelled less by modernizing impulse than by a recognition of the precariousness of their regime and the need to cover the nakedness of their situation in the fig-leaf of a decent old imagery.

Recent work on the Henrician Court and the Privy Chamber in particular reminds us of the degree to which the refurbished Henrician monarchy poured new wine into old bottles. Its politics were the politics of intimacy. Its administrative and political reforms were distilled out of traditional fruits and either failed or went sour within two decades. Cromwell's own style of power was, like his king's, personal to the core, resting as it did on the manipulation of royal household offices and the familiar mingling of his own servants with those of the king.[82]

The tensions and contradictions between events and concepts that I have addressed here seem ample reason for applying to Tudor England the sort of framework Weber developed to comprehend political change in traditional societies. In the throes of the real revolution inseparable from rapid religious changes, the entire social system was under enormous strains. Dysfunction and violence were endemic, in the name of a return to the ancient and right order.

It is my central contention that the evidence supports a view of the nature of the reforming monarchy as embodying the still-dominant force of feudal and quasi-feudal institutions and ideals. We should raise the flag of caution against any who would say that by 1500, or even by 1700, the whole structure of the modern national state had developed.

We should show equal caution in stating that Tudor rulers were unalloyedly sovereign rather than being a curious compound of *rex* and feudal *dominus*. Indeed, the closer we are to Tudor constructions of the expansion of royal power in practical terms, the closer we are to language that suggests the sharing through gift and exchange that is the heart of the theory of an older, patrimonial kingship.

In saying this I am not maintaining that the English monarchy remained a fully feudal monarchy into the late seventeenth or even the eighteenth century, though it is useful to recall the fuss made in 1642 about feudal dues and tenures and standing armies under William. What I am arguing is that we find in events and their traces, in documents and in contemporary interpretations, a view of things in which the state and nation had not yet been defined or cohered in a way fitting the ideas undergirding various modernist interpretations of the 1530s and its aftermath. Too much focus on sovereignty to characterize the changes in the 1530s obscures the actual operations of the government in relation to the society it ruled and is more a convenience of textbooks than a reflection of Tudor realities.[83]

NOTES

1 H. J. Laski, *The Foundations of Sovereignty and Other Essays*, New Haven, Conn., Yale University Press, 1931, p. 314.
2 This is the thesis propounded in major works by G. R. Elton: *The Tudor Revolution in Government*, Cambridge, Cambridge University Press, 1953; *England under the Tudors*, London, Methuen, 1955; *Reform and Reformation: England, 1509–1558*, Cambridge, Mass., Harvard University Press, 1977; *The Parliament of England, 1559–1581*, Cambridge, Cambridge University Press, 1986. For a full analysis of Elton's theses see A. J. Slavin, 'G. R. Elton and his era: thirty years on', *Albion*, 1983, vol. 15, pp. 207–29, and 'G. R. Elton: Reform and Reformation', *The History Teacher*, forthcoming. The footnotes in these articles give full reference to the literature.
3 J. Hurstfield, 'Was There a Tudor despotism after all?' *TRHS*, 5th ser., 1967, vol. 17, pp. 83–108; L. Stone, 'The political programme of Thomas Cromwell', *BIHR*, 1951, vol. 24, pp. 1–17; R. B. Manning, 'Violence and social conflict in mid-Tudor rebellions', *JBS*, 1977, vol. 16, pp. 18–40. A. Fletcher and J. Stevenson (eds), *Order and Disorder in Early Modern England*, Cambridge, Cambridge University Press, 1985.
4 F. H. Hinsley, *Sovereignty*, Cambridge, Cambridge University Press, 1986, chs 1–3. T. F. Mayer, 'Thomas Starkey's aristocratic reform program', *History of Political Thought*, 1986, vol. 7, pp. 439–61. See his forthcoming 'On the road to 1534: the occupation of Tournai and Henry VIII's theory of sovereignty', in D. Hoak (ed.) *Tudor Political Culture: Ideas, Images, Action*, Cambridge, Cambridge University Press, 1992. Slavin, 1983, op. cit., pp. 218–29. C. Coleman and D. Starkey (eds) *Revolution Reassessed: Revisions in the History of Tudor Government and Administration*, Oxford, Clarendon Press, 1986, pp. 1–86.
5 See Note 22 for the works of Weber and Durkheim. For analyses of their theories see the following: A. Giddens, *Politics and Sociology in the Thought of Max Weber*, New York, Macmillan, 1972; D. Kaesler, *Einführung in das Studiums Max Weber*, Munich, Oscar Beck Verlag, 1979; W. J. Mommsen, *The Political and Social Theory of Max Weber*, Chicago, Ill., University of

Chicago Press, 1989; S. N. Eisenstadt, *Revolution and the Transformation of Societies*, New York, Free Press, 1979; Eisenstadt, *Tradition, Change, and Modernity*, Englewood Cliffs, NJ, Prentice-Hall, 1966; J. Duvignaud, *Durkheim: sa vie et son oeuvre*, Paris, Hachette, 1965; R. A. Nisbet, *Emile Durkheim*, Englewood Cliffs, NJ, Prentice-Hall, 1965; and G. Davy, 'Emile Durkheim,' *Revue française de sociologie*, 1960, vol. 1, pp. 3–24.

6 See Neal Wood, Chapter 5 in this volume, especially pp. 153–4.

7 For the text (24 Henry VIII, c. 12), G. R. Elton, *The Tudor Constitution*, Cambride, Cambridge University Press, 1982, pp. 353–8, and the analysis in 'The Evolution of a reformation statute', *EHR*, 1949, vol. 64, pp. 174–97. J. A. Guy, *Tudor England*, Oxford, Oxford University Press, 1988, pp. 132–5, modifies Elton's position, though dismissing as 'legal fiction' the specific language in the Act grounding it in traditional legislation touching papal provisions and *praemunire*. On the ideas behind the Act see G. Nicholson, 'The Act of Appeals and the English Reformation', in C. Cross, D. Loades and J. J. Scarisbrick (eds) *Law and Government under the Tudors: Essays Presented to Sir Geoffrey Elton*, Cambridge, Cambridge University Press, 1989, and Z. N. Brooke, *The English Church and the Papacy*, 2nd edn, Cambridge, Cambridge University Press, 1989. For Tudor uses of the past, see D. R. Woolf, Chapter 1 in this volume.

8 Elton, 1982, op. cit., p. 341. For a Weberian analysis of 'irrationality' as a feature of English law, see D. Sugarman, *In the Spirit of Max Weber: Legal Modernity and 'The Peculiarities of the English'*, Madison, Wis., Institute for Legal Studies. On dualism, the status of the church courts and jurisdictional competition, see J. A. Guy, *Christopher St. German on Chancery and Statute*, London, Selden Society, 1986; S. Lander, 'Church courts and the Reformation in the diocese of Chichester, 1500–1558', in C. Haigh (ed.) *The English Reformation Revisited*, Cambridge, Cambridge University Press, 1987, and *The Reign of Elizabeth*, Athens, Ga, University of Georgia Press, 1984, pp. 125–46, 169–220; R. O'Day and F. Heal (eds) *Continuity and Change*, Leicester, Leicester University Press, 1976, pp. 191–214, 239–58; and R. H. Helmholz, *Roman Canon Law in Reformation England*, Cambridge, Cambridge University Press, 1990. Matrimonial law is a good example of the competition of jurisdictions. Canon law described the rules of marriage, common law decided questions of property, and equity dealt with such matters as trusts: see L. Stone, *Road to Divorce: England 1530–1987*, Oxford, Oxford University Press, 1991.

9 W. Nicholson (ed.) *Edmund Grindal, Remains*, Cambridge, PS, 1843, pp. 376–90.

10 G. R. Elton, *Reform and Renewal*, Cambridge, Cambridge University Press, 1973, pp. 9–157; T. F. Mayer, *Thomas Starkey and the Commonweal*, Cambridge, Cambridge University Press, 1989, pp. 139–246. See also Paul A. Fideler and Ben Lowe, Chapters 7 and 4 in this volume.

11 Compare Elton, 1977, op. cit., pp. 126–229 and Guy, 1986, op. cit., pp. 19–56.

12 Guy, 1988, op. cit., p. 352.

13 Ibid., pp. 111, 129, 370–2. Guy developed the theme more fully in comparing common law and caesaro-papist theories of the royal supremacy, in A. G. Fox and J. A. Guy (eds) *Reassessing the Henrician Age*, Oxford, Basil Blackwell, 1986, pp. 151–78. See also G. Nicholson, 'The nature and function of historical argument in the Henrician Reformation', unpublished PhD dissertation, Cambridge University, 1977.

14 A presentation copy of Parker's treatise *De antiquitate ecclesiae Britannicae*

survives: BL, pressmark C. 24 b. 7. For St German's advocacy of parliamentary sovereignty see J. A. Guy, 'Law, lawyers and the English Reformation', *History Today*, 1985, vol. 35, pp. 16–22, and Fox and Guy, 1986, op. cit., pp. 208–20.

15 PRO, SP 2/L, fos 203–4, shows Cromwell's revisions of the text of the 'Supplication'; Guy, 1986, op. cit., pp. 21–34 and 81–98.

16 H. de Bracton, *De legibus et consuetudinibus angliae*, G. E. Woodbine (ed.), S. B. Thorne (trans.), 4 vols, Cambridge, Mass., Harvard University Press, 1968–77; see I, bk 1, ch. 8. Compare Guy, 1988, op. cit., pp. 371–2.

17 E. Surtz and V. Murphy (eds) *The Divorce Tracts of Henry VIII*, Angers, *Moreana*, 1988, and G. Bedouelle and P. Le Gal (eds) *Le 'Divorce' du roi Henry VIII: Études et documents*, Geneva, Librairie Droz, 1987. A. J. Slavin, 'Defining the Divorce', *SCJ*, 1989, vol. 20, pp. 105–11. Guy, 1988, op. cit., pp. 370–7. On the actual character of Constantine's legislative powers, see H. F. Jolowicz, *Historical Introduction to the Study of Roman Law*, Cambridge, Cambridge University Press, 1954.

18 G. R. Elton, 'Taxation for war and peace in early Tudor England', in J. M. Winter (ed.) *War and Economic Development*, Cambridge, Cambridge University Press, 1973; G. L. Harriss, 'Thomas Cromwell's "new principles" of taxation', *EHR*, 1978, vol. 93, pp. 721–38; S. G. Ellis, 'Thomas Cromwell and Ireland', *JH*, 1980, vol. 23, pp. 497–519; A. J. Slavin, *Politics and Profit*, Cambridge, Cambridge University Press, 1966, chs 5 and 6, on claims to suzerainty in Scotland. On allegiance see Slavin, 'Craw v. Ramsey', in S. B. Baxter (ed.) *England's Rise to Greatness*, Berkeley, Calif., University of California Press, 1983.

19 A. Giddens, *Capitalism and Modern Social Theory*, Cambridge, Cambridge University Press, 1971, pp. 65–184.

20 M. Mauss, *The Gift: Forms and Functions of Exchange*, New York, Free Press, 1954; *Sociologie et anthropologie*, Paris, Presses universitaires de France, 1950; A. Moret and G. Davy, *From Tribe to Empire*, New York, Knopf, 1929; and F. Barley, *Stratagems and Spoils*, New York, Free Press, 1967. The segmentary nature of European states is argued fully by B. Guenée, *States and Rulers in Medieval Europe*, J. Vale (trans.), Oxford, Basil Blackwell, 1985; S. N. Eisenstadt, *Traditional Patrimonialism and Modern Neo-Patrimonialism*, Los Angeles, Calif., Sage Research Papers, 1973; and G. Roth, 'Personal rulership, patrimonialism, and empire-building in new states', in Eisenstadt (ed.) *Political Sociology*, New York, Basic Books.

21 M. J. Herskovits, *Man and his Works*, New York, Knopf, 1970, pp. 542–60; J. L. Byock, *Medieval Iceland: Society, Sagas and Power*, Berkeley, Calif., University of California Press, 1988; and E. Searle, *Predatory Kinship and the Creation of Norman Power*, Berkeley, Calif., University of California Press, 1988.

22 M. Weber, *Economy and Society*, 2 vols, G. Roth and C. Wittich (eds and trans), Berkeley, Calif., University of California Press, 1978; *The Protestant Ethic and the Spirit of Capitalism* T. Parsons (trans.), London, Counterpoint Books, 1985; *The Theory of Social and Economic Organization*, A. M. Henderson and T. Parsons (trans.), New York, Free Press, 1964; *On Charisma and Institution Building*, S. N. Eisenstadt (trans.), Chicago, Ill., University of Chicago Press, 1968; *Gesammelte Aufsaetze zur Religionssoziologie*, 3 vols, Tübingen, Mohr-Siebeck, 1920–1; *Gesammelte Aufsaetze zur Soziologie und Sozialpolitik*, Tübingen, Mohr-Siebeck, 1924; E. Durkheim, *On Politics and the State*, A. Giddens (ed.), W. D. Halls (trans.), Stanford, Calif., Stanford University

Press, 1986; and *The Elementary Forms of the Religious Life*, J. W. Swain (trans.), New York, Free Press, 1954.

23 The quoted phrase is in Sugarman, op. cit., p. 2. On the theory of 'irrationality' and legal rationalization in modernization, see H. Berman, *Law and Revolution: The Formation of the Legal Tradition*, Cambridge, Mass., Harvard University Press, 1983; W. J. Mommsen, 'Personal conduct and social change', in S. Whimster and S. Lash (eds) *Max Weber, Rationality and Modernity*, London, Longman, 1987; and D. Little, *Religion, Order, and Law*, Chicago, Ill., University of Chicago Press, 1984, pp. 226–37.

24 Little, op. cit., is a noteworthy exception. Weber defined patrimonialism in 1964, op. cit., p. 347, and *General Economic History*, F. H. Knight (trans.), New York, Macmillan, 1961, pp. 255–6.

25 See the language of 24 Henry VIII, c. 12; also J. N. King, *Tudor Royal Iconography*, Princeton, NJ, Princeton University Press, 1989, pp. 1–115.

26 On the importance of regalian rights, crown estates, attainder, resumptions and traditional methods of finance, see M. Howell, *Regalian Right in Medieval England*, London, Athlone Press, 1962, pp. 201–10; B. P. Wolffe, *The Royal Demesne in English History*, London, Allen & Unwin, 1971; J. R. Lander, *Crown and Nobility, 1450–1509*, London, Edward Arnold, 1976; and M. Hicks, 'Attainder, resumption and coercion, 1461–1529', *Parliamentary History*, 1984, vol. 3, pp. 15–31.

27 See generally Coleman and Starkey, op. cit., and Fox and Guy, op. cit.

28 G. W. Bernard, *War, Taxation, and Rebellion in Early Tudor England*, New York, St Martin's Press, 1986; R. Woods, 'The amicable grant', unpublished PhD dissertation, UCLA, 1974.

29 M. Weber, *Grundriss der Sozialökonomik, Abteilung III; Wirtschaft und Gesellschaft*, Tübingen, Mohr-Siebeck, 1925, pp. 130, 746. P. Ricoeur, *Lectures on Ideology and Utopia*, New York, Columbia University Press, 1986, pp. 181–215.

30 Little, op. cit., pp. 1–32, with specific application to England in the Reformation era.

31 A. J. Slavin, *The Precarious Balance*, New York, Knopf, 1973, chs 4 and 5. On the 'points of contact' model of G. R. Elton see *Studies in Tudor and Stuart Government and Politics*, 3 vols, Cambridge, Cambridge University Press, 1974–83, III, pp. 3–57.

32 Weber, 1964, op. cit., pp. 124–52; 'Social psychology of the world religions', in H. H. Gerth and C. W. Mills (eds and trans) *From Max Weber*, New York, Basic Books, 1958.

33 Weber, 1985, op. cit., p. 130; also 1964, op. cit., p. 347; Eisenstadt, 1979, op. cit., pp. 52–172; M. Mann, *The Sources of Social Power*, Cambridge, Cambridge University Press, 1986, pp. 416–500; and R. Bendix, *Kings and People*, Berkeley, Calif., University of California Press, 1978, pp. 21–61, 176–217 and 273–320, for England especially.

34 Slavin, 1983, op. cit., pp. 221–9; ' "'Tis far off, and rather like a dream": common weal, common woe, and commonwealth', *Explorations in Renaissance Culture*, 1988, vol. 14, pp. 1–28.

35 S. L. Clark, *Civil Peace and Sacred Order*, Oxford, Oxford University Press, 1989, for general theory; S. R. L. Collins, *From Divine Cosmos to Sovereign State*, Oxford, Oxford University Press, 1989, for application to England.

36 E. G. Riegler, 'Printing, protestantism, and politics', unpublished PhD dissertation, UCLA, 1978. C. Levin, *Propaganda in the English Reformation*, Lewis-

ton, NY, Edwin Mellen Press, 1988; A. G. Fox, *Thomas More, History and Providence*, New Haven, Conn., Yale University Press, 1982, pp. 111–27.

37 M. E. James, *Society, Politics and Culture: Studies in Early Modern England*, Cambridge, Cambridge University Press, 1986, pp. 1–16.

38 *L & P*, V, 898. PRO, SP 1/99, fo. 234 and 1/87, fo. 106v, both lists in Cromwell's hand, indicating opponents and supporters, respectively, of government Bills, but not division lists. On the demands for a parliament in the north, SP 1/112, fo. 119.

39 Mayer, op. cit., pp. 106–39. P. J. Holmes, 'The last Tudor Great Councils', *HJ*, 1990, vol. 33, pp. 1–22.

40 M. L. Bush, 'Enhancement and importunate changes: an analysis of the tax complaints of October, 1536', *Albion*, 1990, vol. 22, pp. 403–19.

41 Guy, 1988, op. cit., pp. 143–9; M. L. Bush, 'The Lisle–Seymour land disputes', *HJ*, 1966, vol. 9, pp. 255–74; M. E. James, *Change and Continuity in the Tudor North*, York, Borthwick Institute, 1965; H. Miller, 'Henry VIII's unwritten will: grants of lands and honours', in E. W. Ives, R. J. Knecht and J. J. Scarisbrick (eds) *Wealth and Power in Tudor England*, London, Athlone Press, 1978, pp. 87–105; M. Robertson, 'Profit and purpose in the development of Thomas Cromwell's landed estates', *JBS*, 1990, vol. 25, pp. 317–46; R. B. Smith, *Land and Politics in the England of Henry VIII*, London, Athlone Press, 1971; and F. Heal, *Of Prelates and Princes: A Study of the Economic and Social Position of the Tudor Episcopate*, Cambridge, Cambridge University Press, 1980.

42 London, Heralds' College, Shrewsbury MS. A. fos 253 and 255. *L & P*, 20, i, 129, 381 and 1,046; 20, ii, 945. *APC, 1542–1547*, p. 284.

43 R. P. Cust, *The Forced Loans and English Politics, 1626–1628*, Oxford, Oxford University Press, 1987. Slavin, 1983, op. cit., pp. 40–3.

44 Bernard, op. cit., pp. 96–135.

45 Mayer, 1989, op. cit., pp. 124–30 and 173–5; A. Kreider, *English Chantries: The Road to the Dissolution*, Cambridge, Cambridge University Press, 1979.

46 On plundering and policy, see *APC*, II, pp. 193–5 and BL, Stowe MS 141, fo. 63. N. L. Jones, *Faith by Statute*, London, Royal Historical Society, 1982, pp. 160–8; F. Heal, 'The bishops and the Act of Exchange of 1559', *HJ*, 1974, vol. 17, pp. 227–46; and R. H. Pogson, 'Renewal and reform in Mary Tudor's church: a question of money', *JEccH*, 1974, vol. 25, pp. 249–65.

47 J. J. Scarisbrick, *The Reformation of the English People*, Oxford, Basil Blackwell, 1984, chs 2, 5 and 6; R. Whiting, '"For the health of my soul": prayers for the dead in the Tudor south-west', *Southern History*, 1983, vol. 5, pp. 68–74.

48 N. L. Jones, 'Religion and politics in Tudor England', *JBS*, 1989, vol. 28, pp. 70–4; C. Haigh, 'The English reformation: a premature birth, a difficult labor, and a sickly child', *HJ*, 1990, vol. 33, pp. 449–59; A. J. Slavin, 'Upstairs, downstairs: or the roots of reformation', *HLQ*, 1986, vol. 49, pp. 243–60.

49 On Wriothesley's activities, see *L & P*, 13, ii, 133, 134, 257, 303, 317, 430 and 442. SP, 8, p. 51. BL, Arundel MS 97, fo. 34v. *L & P*, 14, i, 1073, and ii, 401 and 542. Rome, Vatican, Archivio segreto, Armaria 40/30, fo. 339. For the 'Boston pardons' see A. J. Slavin, 'The Gutenberg galaxy and the Tudor revolution', in G. P. Tyson and S. Waggonheim (eds) *Print and Culture in the Renaissance*, Dover, Del., Delaware University Press, 1986, pp. 90–109.

50 Kreider, op. cit., pp. 93–164.

51 J. Block, 'Religious non-conformity and social conflict', *Albion*, 1981, vol. 13, pp. 331–46; C. S. L. Davies, 'The pilgrimage of grace reconsidered, *P & P*,

1968, vol. 41, pp. 54–76; S. G. Ellis, 'The Kildare rebellion and the early Henrician reformation', *HJ*, 1976, vol. 19, pp. 807–30; C. Haigh, *Reformation and Resistance in Tudor Lancashire*, Cambridge, Cambridge University Press, 1975; M. E. James, 'Obedience and dissent in Henrician England: the Lincolnshire rebellion, 1536', *P & P*, vol. 48, pp. 3–78; and G. Redworth, 'A study in the formation of policy: the genesis and evolution of the Act of Six Articles,' *JEccH*, 1986, vol. 37, pp. 42–67.

52 C. Geertz, *The Interpretation of Culture*, New York, Basic Books, 1973, pp. 87–125 and 214–18; Little, op. cit., pp. 3–31; S. N. Eisenstadt, *Paradigms and Crises*, New York, Wiley, 1976; Weber, 1968, op. cit., pp. ix–lxi.

53 G. R. Elton, *Policy and Police: The Enforcement of the English Reformation in the Reign of Henry VIII*, Cambridge, Cambridge University Press, 1972; K. V. Thomas, *Religion and the Decline of Magic*, New York, Scribner, 1971; J. K. van Patten, 'Magic, prophecy and the law of treason in reformation England', *American Journal of Legal History*, 1983, vol. 27, pp. 1–32; and S. N. Eisenstadt, 'Some observations on the dynamics of tradition', *Comparative Studies in Society and History*, 1969, vol. 2, pp. 451–75.

54 W. Ullmann, *Principles of Government and Politics in the Middle Ages*, London, Methuen, 1961, pp. 29–192; R. Koebner, *Empire*, Cambridge, Cambridge University Press, 1966, pp. 1–77.

55 Murphy, op. cit., 'Introduction', pp. i–xliv.

56 R. Whiting, 'Abominable idols: images and image breaking under Henry VIII', *JEccH*, 1982, vol. 33, pp. 30–47.

57 H. Miller, *Henry VIII and the English Nobility*, Oxford, Basil Blackwell, 1986, emphasizes the reaction against the king's treatment of the nobility; also M. E. James, *Society, Politics and Culture*, Cambridge,. Cambridge University Press, 1986.

58 L. Stone, *The Crisis of the Aristocracy, 1558–1641*, Oxford, Oxford University Press, 1965. M. E. James, *Family, Lineage and Civil Society, 1500–1640*, Oxford, Oxford University Press, 1974; and J. A. Bossy, *The English Catholic Community, 1570–1850*, London, Longman, 1975.

59 S. M. Harrison, *The Pilgrimage of Grace in the Lake Counties*, London, Royal Historical Society, 1981; N. Williams, 'The risings in Norfolk in 1569 and 1570', *Norfolk Archaeology*, 1961, vol. 32, pp. 73–81.

60 A. J. Slavin, 1973, op. cit., pp. 1–46, and *The Tudor Age and Beyond*, Melbourne, R. E. Krieger, 1987, pp. 189–208, for surveys of these incongruities and the relevant bibliography; also R. Schofield, 'The geographical distribution of wealth in England, 1334–1649', *EcHR*, 1965, vol. 18, pp. 483–510, is fundamental.

61 O. E. Williamson, *Markets and Hierarchies*, New York, Free Press, 1975; H. Turk and S. R. Simpson, *Institutions and Social Exchange*, Indianapolis, Ind., Bobbs-Merrill, 1971; R. Brenner, 'The social basis of English commercial expansion', *Journal of Economic History*, 1972, vol. 32, pp. 117–52, and 'Agrarian class structures and economic development in pre-industrial Europe', *P & P*, 1982, no. 97, pp. 17–113; P. Clark and P. Slack (eds) *Crisis and Order in English Towns, 1500–1700*, London, Routledge & Kegan Paul, 1972; M. K. McIntosh, *The Royal Manor at Havering-at-Bowe, 1500–1620*, Cambridge, Cambridge University Press, 1991; and R. O'Day and F. Heal (eds) *Princes and Paupers in the English Church*, Leicester, Leicester University Press, 1981.

62 D. H. Sacks, *The Widening Gate: Bristol and the Atlantic Economy, 1450–1700*, Berkeley, Calif., University of California Press, 1991; S. Rappaport, *Worlds within Worlds: Structures of Social Life in Sixteenth Century London*, Cam-

bridge, Cambridge University Press, 1989; M. E. James, 1986, op. cit., pp. 16–48; and C. Pythian-Adams, 'Ceremony and citizen', in Clark and Slack, op. cit., pp. 57–85.

63 PRO, SP 1/106, fo. 183, for Norfolk's comment; Slavin, 1973, op. cit., p. 337, for Burghley's lists; D. MacCulloch, *Suffolk and the Tudors*, Oxford, Oxford University Press, 1986; J. A. Youings, 'The southwest rebellions of 1549', *Southern History*, vol. i, pp. 99–122; and C. E. Moreton, 'The Walsingham conspiracy, 1537', *BIHR*, 1990, vol. 63, pp. 29–43.

64 James, 1986, op. cit., pp. 91–176 and 188–308, also 1974, op. cit., pp. 19–137.

65 J. M. W. Bean, *The Estates of the Percy Family, 1416–1537*, Oxford, Oxford University Press, 1958; B. Harris, *Edward Stafford, Third Earl of Buckingham*, Stanford, Calif., Stanford University Press, 1986, pp. 104–80; L. Stone, *Family and Fortune: Studies in Aristocratic Finance in the Sixteenth and Seventeenth Centuries*, Oxford, Clarendon Press, 1973, pp. 164–259; Miller, op. cit., pp. 164–259.

66 S. K. Walker, 'Lordship and lawlessness in the Palatinate of Lancaster, 1370–1400', *JBS*, 1989, vol. 28, pp. 325–48; S. L. Waugh, 'Patronage, war and society in medieval England', *JBS*, 1990, vol. 29, pp. 386–92; C. Carpenter, 'Law, justice and landowners in late medieval England', *Law and History Review*, 1983, vol. i, pp. 205–37; and J. G. Bellamy, *Bastard Feudalism and the Law*, London, St Martin's Press, 1989.

67 P. Slack (ed.) *Rebellion, Popular Protest and the Social Order in Early Modern England*, Cambridge, Cambridge University Press, 1984. S. M. Harrison, op. cit., passim; L. Stone, 'Patriarchy and paternalism in Tudor England', *JBS*, 1974, vol. 13, pp. 19–33; R. Horrox, *Richard III: A Study of Service*, Cambridge, Cambridge University Press, 1989; C. Richmond, *The Paston Family in the Fifteenth Century: The First Phase*, Cambridge, Cambridge University Press, 1991; and M. A. Hicks, 'The 1468 Statute of Livery', *BIHR*, 1991, vol. 64, pp. 14–28.

68 G. W. Bernard, *The Power of the Early Tudor Nobility*, Brighton, Harvester, 1985; D. Loades, *The Tudor Court*, Totowa, NJ, Barnes & Noble, 1987, pp. 133–84; James, 1986, op. cit., pp. 148–75, 188–270; D. Starkey (ed.) *The English Court: From the Wars of the Roses to the Civil War*, London, Longman, 1987, pp. 1–71; K. B. McFarlane, *The Nobility of Later Medieval England*, Oxford, Oxford University Press, 1983; K. Mertes, *The English Noble Household, 1200–1600: Good Governance and Politic Rule*, Oxford, Oxford University Press, 1988; and M. A. Hicks, 'Dynastic change and northern society: the career of the fourth earl of Northumberland', *Northern History*, 1978, vol. 14, pp. 65–87.

69 E. W. Ives, 'The genesis of the statute of uses, EHR, 1967, vol. 82, pp. 673ff; James, 1986, op. cit., pp. 225–37.

70 Ibid., pp. 3–10; K. B. McFarlane, *England in the Fifteenth Century: Collected Essays*, London, Oxford University Press, 1987, pp. 87–119; M. L. Bush, 'The problem of the far north', *Northern History*, 1971, vol. 6, pp. 40–6; and R. Chartier, *Cultural History*, Ithaca, NY, Cornell University Press, 1988, pp. 71–94.

71 R. H. Fritze, 'Faith and faction: religious change, national politics, and the development of local factionalism in Hampshire, 1485–1570', unpublished PhD dissertation, Cambridge University, 1981; G. R. Elton, 'Politics and the Pilgrimage of Grace', *Studies*, vol. III, pp. 183–215; A. J. Slavin, 'Cromwell, Cranmer, Lord Lisle, and the Calais Sacramentarians', *Albion*, 1977, vol. 9, pp.

316–36; and R. Warnicke, *The Rise and Fall of Anne Boleyn*, Cambridge, Cambridge University Press, 1989.

72 James, 1986, op. cit., pp. 13–15.

73 R. Tittler, 'The emergence of urban policy, 1536–1558', in Loach and Tittler, op. cit.; Sacks, op. cit., stresses this point repeatedly. See also his 'For the "re-edification of townes": the rebuilding statutes of Henry VIII', *Albion*, 1991, vol. 22, pp. 591–606.

74 J. Hurstfield, *The Queen's Wards*, London, Jonathan Cape, 1958; Slavin, *Politics and Profit*, Cambridge, Cambridge University Press, 1966, pp. 168–212; D. Cressy, *Literacy and the Social Order*, Cambridge, Cambridge University Press, 1980; J. J. Scarisbrick, op. cit., chs 3–5, for ritual objects; B. Harris, 'Women and politics in early Tudor England', *HJ*, 1990, vol. 32, pp. 259–81, and 'Property, power, and personal relations: elite mothers and sons in Yorkist and early Tudor England', *Signs*, 1990, vol. 15, pp. 606–32; also D. Willan, 'Women in the public sphere in early modern England: the case of the urban poor', *SCJ*, 1988, vol. 19, pp. 559–75 and 'Guildswomen in the City of York', *The Historian*, 1984, vol. 46, pp. 204–18.

75 D. Starkey, 'The King's Privy Chamber, 1485–1547', unpublished PhD dissertation, Cambridge University, 1973; D. Starkey (ed.) *The English Court*, London, Longman, 1987, especially the chapters by Starkey, D. A. L. Morgan, John Murphy and Pam Wright. D. Starkey, 'Court and government', in Coleman and Starkey, op. cit.; and D. Hoak, 'The King's Privy Chamber, 1547–1553', in D. J. Guth and J. W. McKenna (eds) *Tudor Rule and Revolution*, Cambridge, Cambridge University Press, 1982.

76 H. Miller, op. cit., pp. 102–31; J. Loach, 'Parliament, a "new air?"', in Coleman and Starkey, op. cit.

77 S. E. Lehmberg, *The Reformation Parliament, 1529–1536*, Cambridge, Cambridge University Press, 1970, pp. 36–63, and *The Later Parliaments of Henry VIII, 1536–1547*, Cambridge, Cambridge University Press, 1977; M. A. R. Graves, *The House of Lords in the Parliaments of Edward VI and Mary I*, Cambridge, Cambridge University Press, 1981, pp. 32–119.

78 MacCulloch, op. cit.; A. H. Smith, *County and Court: Government and Politics in Norfolk, 1558–1603*, Oxford, Clarendon Press, 1974. See the works on towns previously cited, by Brenner, Tittler, Sacks, Clark and Slack.

79 T. F. Mayer, 'Reform and revision in the history of the state of Henrician England', *JBS*, 1988, vol. 27, pp. 190–7; S. Adams, 'England under the Tudors', *HJ*, 1990, vol. 33, pp. 677–83; D. Starkey, 'Tudor government and the facts', *HJ*, 1988, vol. 31, pp. 921–32; J. A. Guy, 'The Tudor commonwealth: revising Thomas Cromwell', *HJ*, 1980, vol. 23, pp. 681–7; N. L. Jones, 'Religion and politics in Tudor England', *JBS*, 1989, vol. 28, pp. 70–5. The responses to his critics of Sir Geoffrey Elton are fully cited in Slavin, 1983, op. cit., and *The History Teacher* (forthcoming).

80 B. Levack, 'Law and ideology: the civil laws and theory of absolutism in Elizabethan and Jacobean England', in H. Dubrow and R. Strier (eds) *The Historical Renaissance: New Essays on Tudor and Stuart Literature and Culture*, Chicago, Ill., University of Chicago Press, 1988.

81 For Husee's description of Henry receiving gifts, while Brian Tuke made a list of them, see PRO, SP 1/128, fo. 29 (3 January 1538).

82 M. Robertson, 'Thomas Cromwell's servants: the ministerial household in early Tudor government and society', unpublished PhD thesis, UCLA, 1975. Slavin, 1966, op. cit., pp. 30–68.

83 T. Elyot, *The Book Named the Governor*, S. E. Lehmberg (ed.), London,

Dent, 1962, p. 165: 'Know that the name of sovereign ruler . . . standeth not by words only but principally by act and example'. Guy, 1988, op. cit., p. 355, recognizes that the Tudor state's cohesion depended on not attempting to rule from the centre; see also S. G. Ellis, 'England in the Tudor state', *HJ*, 1983, vol. 26, pp. 201–12.

9

Critical bibliographical essay

This chapter contains nine sections. The first is a general overview of the essential literature for the study of Tudor political thought, and it is followed by topical sections for each of this volume's eight chapters. Since the collection represents as many historiographical approaches as contributors, readers should consult specific sections of this chapter for appropriate methodological sources.

TUDOR POLITICAL THOUGHT

Overlooked for too long, the history of sixteenth-century, and particularly Tudor, political thought is only recently beginning to be revived. A number of older background studies still have much to recommend them to the discerning user, however. J. W. Allen, *A History of Political Thought in the Sixteenth Century*, London, Methuen, 1977 (orig. 1928), is prone to over generalization, but many of its interpretations remain arresting. A. O. Lovejoy, *The Great Chain of Being: A Study of the History of an Idea*, Cambridge, Mass., Harvard University Press, 1957, creaking in its method, is nevertheless a classic that should be read by every student. As much can be said also for E. M. W. Tillyard, *Elizabethan World Picture*, London, Chatto & Windus, 1963. F. L. Baumer, *The Early Tudor Theory of Kingship*, New Haven, Conn., Yale University Press, 1940, a classic in its day, still warrants attention for several technical points. S. B. Chrimes, *English Constitutional Ideas in the Fifteenth Century*, Cambridge, Cambridge University Press, 1936, a work primarily of legal rather than strictly constitutional history, rests on wide reading, especially the little-known Year Books. C. Morris, *Political Thought in England: Tyndale to Hooker*, Oxford, Oxford University Press, 1953, maintained that there was little political, as distinct from social, thought in Tudor England. W. G. Zeeveld, *Foundations of Tudor Policy*, Cambridge, Mass., Harvard University Press, 1948, insisted that intellectual and literary historians must make use of manuscripts and acknowledge both human ties and continental experience in explaining English ideas. W. H. Greenleaf, *Order, Empiricism and*

254

Politics: Two Traditions of English Political Thought 1500–1700, New York, Oxford University Press, 1964, presents an overly schematic treatment of tension between 'established' and 'innovative' theories. A. B. Ferguson's work on chivalry's stubborn decline and the practical focus of the 'London Reformers' continues to be valuable. See his *The Indian Summer of English Chivalry*, Durham, NC, Duke University Press, 1960; *The Chivalric Tradition in Renaissance England*, Washington, DC, Folger Shakespeare Library, 1986; and *The Articulate Citizen and the English Renaissance*, Durham, NC, Duke University Press, 1965.

The importance of humanism, both Christian and Italianate, is crucial in understanding Tudor political thought. F. Caspari, *Humanism and the Social Order in Tudor England*, Chicago, Ill., University of Chicago Press, 1954, was an important beginning, but assumed too readily the direct influence of humanist ideas. Ferguson, 1965, op. cit., should be consulted for the contention he posits between humanist and Protestant ideas. G. M. Logan, *The Meaning of More's Utopia*, Princeton, NJ, Princeton University Press, 1983, may not appreciate More's irony but is insightful on his critique of humanism. S. E. Lehmberg provided a basic article, 'English humanists, the Reformation and the problem of counsel', *Archiv für Reformationsgeschichte*, 1961, vol. 52, pp. 74–90. J. K. McConica, *English Humanists and Reformation Politics under Henry VIII and Edward VI*, Oxford, Clarendon Press, 1965, argues strongly for the vitality of English humanism after More. J. A. Guy, *The Public Career of Sir Thomas More*, New Haven, Conn., Yale University Press, 1980, is the basic work for More as a common lawyer and useful in deciphering his political ideas. See also his *Christopher St. German on Chancery and Statute*, Selden Society, supplemental series, 1985, vol. 6, now basic to the assessment of St German's thought. J. A. Guy and A. Fox offer a stimulating set of essays, many of them on the history of political thought, in *Reassessing the Henrician Age: Humanism, Politics and Reform 1500–1550*, Oxford, Basil Blackwell, 1986. M. Dowling, *Humanism in the Reign of Henry VIII*, London, Croom Helm, 1986, is a useful compendium, especially strong on patronage and the role of women. M. Todd, *Christian Humanism and the Puritan Social Order*, Cambridge, Cambridge University Press, 1987, is impressively researched but pushes 'continuity' of 'Catholic' humanist thought to the point of implausibility.

The reorienting impact of the Reformation on Tudor thought, church and government is explored in A. B. Dickens's indispensable studies: *The English Reformation*, London, Batsford, 1964 and *Thomas Cromwell and the English Reformation*, London, English Universities Press, 1969. Sir Geoffrey Elton's contributions to the understanding of Henrician and Tudor statecraft, especially the role of the Reformation and Thomas Cromwell in all this, are ubiquitous in his prolific output. Most basic are: 'Reform by statute: Thomas Starkey's *Dialogue* and Thomas Cromwell's policy', *Proceedings of the British Academy*, 1968, vol. 54, pp. 165–88; *Reform and Renewal: Thomas Cromwell and the Common Weal*, Cambridge, Cambridge University Press, 1973; 'The political creed of Thomas Cromwell', in *Studies in Tudor and Stuart Politics and Government*, 3 vols, Cambridge, Cambridge University Press, 1974–83, vol. II, pp. 215–35; and *Reform and Reformation, England 1509–1558*, Cambridge, Mass., Harvard University Press, 1977.

The dialogic, contextualist and interdisciplinary inclinations of the 'new historicism' have both built on and challenged most of the work mentioned above. It reveals the often contradictory currents of Tudor political thought and the dilemmas these presented for individual commitments and persona crafting. S. J. Greenblatt's protean *Renaissance Self-Fashioning from More to Shakespeare*, Chicago, Ill., University of Chicago Press, 1980, synthesized this new agenda of questions and methods. A. Fox, *Politics and Literature in the Reigns of Henry VII and Henry VIII*, Oxford, Basil Blackwell, 1989, is a path-breaking study of neglected early Tudor literature in its political context. T. F. Mayer, *Thomas Starkey and the Commonweal*, Cambridge, Cambridge University Press, 1989, an intellectual and biographical study in this new mode, finds a Starkey more Italianate humanist (and evangelical) and less influential at Court than Elton's.

For medieval origins and continental contexts of Tudor political thought see Q. Skinner's lucid survey of large and small thinkers from Dante to Bodin, *The Foundations of Modern Political Thought*, 2 vols, Cambridge, Cambridge University Press, 1978. Skinner attempts to show the emergence of the 'state' (in contrast to the 'ruler') as the basis of government. B. Tierney's masterful conclusions in *Church Law and Constitutional Thought in the Middle Ages*, London, Variorum Reprints, 1979, deserves to be more widely known among historians of Tudor political thought; see also his ' "Divided sovereignty" at Constance: a problem of medieval and early modern political theory', *Annuarium Historiae Conciliorum*, 1975, vol. 7, pp. 238–56. A. J. Carlyle and R. W. Carlyle, *A History of Medieval Political Theory in the West*, 6 vols, Edinburgh, W. Blackwood, 1909–36, is still useful; it contains some good judgements and provides long extracts from inaccessible texts. A. Pagden (ed.) *The Languages of Political Theory in Early Modern Europe*, Cambridge, Cambridge University Press, 1987, offers a polyglot collection of essays; among the best may be Q. Skinner, 'Sir Thomas More's *Utopia* and the language of Renaissance humanism' (pp. 123–57) and N. Rubinstein, 'The history of the word *politicus* in early-modern Europe' (pp. 41–56). Very important for a European perspective is Rubinstein's 'Political theories in the renaissance', in *The Renaissance: Essays in Interpretation*, London, Methuen, 1982, pp. 153–200. J. Seigel's emphasis on the rhetorical side of humanism deserves more attention; see his *Rhetoric and Philosophy in Renaissance*

Humanism: The Union of Eloquence and Wisdom, Petrarch to Valla, Princeton, NJ, Princeton University Press, 1968.

Two 'primers' on the current state of historiography of political thought are J. G. A. Pocock, *Virtue, Commerce, and History*, Cambridge, Cambridge University Press, 1985, especially 'Introduction: the state of the art', and Q. Skinner, 'Meaning in the history of ideas', *History and Theory*, 1969, vol. 8, pp. 3–53. Pocock makes the case for the 'historicity' of political thought and the need to decipher its 'languages'. Skinner insists on the use of linguistic contextualism to delimit possible authorial intentions. Other Skinner articles and responses from critics are assembled in J. Tully (ed.) *Meaning and Context: Quentin Skinner and his Critics*, Princeton, NJ, Princeton University Press, 1988. D. Harlan, 'Intellectual history and the return of literature', *AHR*, 1989, vol. 94, pp. 581–609, challenges Skinner's contextualism and stresses the self-conscious determination of writers and readers to revive ageless issues that demand reinterpretation. See also in this regard C. Condren, *The Status and Appraisal of Classic Texts: An Essay on Political Theory, its Inheritance and the History of Ideas*, Princeton, NJ, Princeton University Press, 1985, an important attempt to bring more clarity of approach to intellectual history. Also of value are D. R. Kelley, 'Horizons of intellectual history: retrospect, circumspect, prospect', *JHI*, 1987, vol. 48, pp. 143–69, and A. Lockyer, ' "Traditions" as context in the history of political thought', *Political Studies*, 1979, vol. 27, pp. 201–17. On any short list of the most provocative essays on method in intellectual history more generally are several in D. LaCapra and S. L. Kaplan (eds) *Modern European Intellectual History: Reappraisals and New Perspectives*, Ithaca, NY, Cornell University Press, 1982, and D. LaCapra, *Rethinking Intellectual History: Texts, Contexts, Language*, Ithaca, NY, Cornell University Press, 1983. LaCapra's 'Rethinking intellectual history and reading texts', 1982, pp. 47–85; 1983, pp. 23–71, is one of the most approachable reflections on the intersections between historical and literary method.

THE POWER OF THE PAST

Among general works on Tudor and early Stuart historical thought see especially: F. J. Levy, *Tudor Historical Thought*, San Marino, Calif., Huntington Library, 1967; H. Baker, *The Race of Time*, Toronto, University of Toronto Press, 1967; and M. McKisack, *Medieval History in the Tudor Age*, Oxford, Clarendon Press, 1971. For the late Tudor and early Stuart period, see F. S. Fussner, *The Historical Revolution: English Historical Writing and Thought 1580–1640*, London, Routledge & Kegan Paul, 1962, which suffers from anachronistic categories and an over-rigid thesis. Better, though it still veers toward teleology, is A. B. Ferguson, *Clio Unbound: Perception of the Social and Cultural Past in Renaissance England*,

Durham, NC, Duke University Press, 1979. R. Warnicke's useful book *William Lambarde, Elizabethan Antiquary*, London, Phillimore, 1973, will soon have to be revised in the light of research by J. D. Alsop. K. Thomas, *The Perception of the Past in Early Modern England*, London, Creighton Trust, 1983, is a remarkable distillation of popular attitudes which invites full-scale research into the historical *culture* of the period, as opposed to further investigations into the formal historical literature, even when broadly conceived as in Ferguson. In this regard, see D. Cressy, *Bonfires and Bells: National Memory and the Protestant Calendar in Elizabethan and Stuart England*, Berkeley, Calif., University of California Press, 1989.

For the past as political prophecy, the best work remains K. Thomas, *Religion and the Decline of Magic*, Harmondsworth, Penguin, 1973. Prophecy also receives some attention from B. S. Capp, *Astrology and the Popular Press: English Almanacs 1500–1800*, London, Faber & Faber, 1981. G. R. Elton, *Policy and Police: The Enforcement of the Reformation in the Age of Thomas Cromwell*, Cambridge, Cambridge University Press, 1972, deals with the attack on Becket; on the saints and other visual representations of the past see especially M. Aston, *England's Iconoclasts*, I: *Laws against Images*, Oxford, Clarendon Press, 1988. The employment of scholars to 'rewrite' the past at the beginning of the Reformation is dealt with in G. D. Nicholson, 'The Act of Appeals and the English Reformation', in C. Cross, D. Loades and J. J. Scarisbrick (eds) *Law and Government under the Tudors: Essays Presented to Sir Geoffrey Elton*, Cambridge, Cambridge University Press, 1988, pp. 19–30. A. Fox, *Politics and Literature in the Reigns of Henry VII and Henry VIII*, Oxford, Basil Blackwell, 1989, contains essays on history, propaganda and polemic, and the impact of early Tudor political drama.

The role of British (and particularly Arthurian) mythology in Tudor history writing could profit from renewed investigation. Sir T. Kendrick, *British Antiquity*, London, Methuen, 1950, remains in most ways the best account of the legends. S. Anglo, *Spectacle, Pageantry and Early Tudor Policy*, Oxford, Clarendon Press, 1969, convincingly demonstrates that 1485 marked no striking departure in the deliberate use of British mythology and genealogy to support the royal line.

The revising and re-revising of attitudes to particular historical figures, most notably Richard III, Richard II and above all King John, continues. For Richard III, the reader is directed to the excellent introduction to the text in *The History of King Richard III, The Complete Works of St Thomas More*, vol. IV, R. Sylvester (ed.), New Haven, Conn., Yale University Press, 1976; see also C. Levin, *Propaganda in the English Reformation: Heroic and Villainous Images of King John*, Lewiston, NY, Edwin Mellen Press, 1988. The latter should be read together with the Introduction by A. R. Braunmuller to the new *Oxford Shakespeare* edition of *King John*, Oxford, Oxford University Press, 1989.

John Nichols's now very old collections of Elizabethan and Jacobean progresses combine the advantage of assembling much material in a single set of volumes with the disadvantages of pre-Victorian editing. Many mythohistorical references can be gleaned from the continuing *Records of Early English Drama* project in Toronto, which presents civic, Court and select private records of the costs and staging of progresses, hock-tide celebrations, and mayoral processions. Among modern authorities, Anglo, op. cit., is indispensable for the early Tudor spectacles and can be supplemented by G. Kipling, *The Triumph of Honour: Burgundian Origins of the Elizabethan Renaissance*, Leiden, Leiden University Press for the Sir Thomas Brown Institute, 1977. For the later Tudors, see D. Bergeron, *English Civic Pageantry, 1558–1642*, London, Edward Arnold, 1971, and A. Young, *Tudor and Jacobean Tournaments*, New York, Sheridan House, 1987. The chivalric ethos, so much a part of the early Tudor and later Elizabethan court, is well studied by A. B. Ferguson, *The Indian Summer of English Chivalry*, Durham, NC, Duke University Press, 1960.

Treatments of Tudor and early Stuart history plays are too numerous to be listed here. Among older works dealing specifically with the political implications of Shakespeare's plays, L. B. Campbell, *Shakespeare's Histories: Mirrors of Elizabethan Policy*, San Marino, Calif., Huntington Library, 1947, and E. M. W. Tillyard, *Shakespeare's History Plays*, London, Chatto & Windus, 1944, remain well worth reading. The non-Shakespearean drama is covered by I. Ribner, *The English History Play in the Age of Shakespeare*, Princeton, NJ, Princeton University Press, 1957. Innovative work in this area by new historicist critics, such as M. Butler, J. Dollimore, J. Limon and others cited in the chapter notes, and by F. J. Levy and other literary-minded historians, is appearing with greater regularity.

NURSERY OF RESISTANCE

The study of resistance is increasingly (if not always consciously) indebted to the work of Michel Foucault. See especially *The History of Sexuality*, R. Hurley (trans.), vol. 1, and *Discipline and Punish*, A. M. Sheridan (trans.), both New York, Random House, 1978 and 1979. Although ultimately frustrating, perhaps by design, Foucault, *The Archaeology of Knowledge*, A. M. Sheridan Smith (trans.), New York, Pantheon, 1972, ought to be required reading for historians. For one of the best explications of Foucault's thought, see A. Megill, *Prophets of Extremity: Nietzsche, Heidegger, Foucault, Derrida*, Berkeley, Calif., University of California Press, 1985, ch. 6.

P. Zagorin, *Ways of Lying: Dissimulation, Persecution and Conformity in Early Modern Europe*, Cambridge, Mass., Harvard University Press, 1990, should be equally fundamental for the study of resistance. It both usefully summarizes earlier debates and constructs a wide-ranging new problem. Of the vast literature on dissimulation see also C. Ginzburg, *Il Nicodemismo: Simulazione e dissimulazione religiosa nell'Europa del '500*, Turin, Einaudi, 1970, together with C. M. N. Eire, 'Calvin and Nicodemism: a reappraisal', *SCJ*, 1979, vol. 10, pp. 45–70; A. Biondi, 'La giustificazione della simulazione nel Cinquecento', in *Eresia e Riforma nell'Italia del Cinquecento*, Florence, Sansoni, 1974, pp. 7–68, and J. Kristoff, 'Michelangelo as Nicodemus: *The Florence Pietà*', *SCJ*, 1989, vol. 20, pp. 163–82.

Courtier poetry like Flaminio's has come to be read as in part a means of resistance. This analysis owes much to D. Javitch, *Poetry and Courtliness*, New York, Columbia University Press, 1978, which distinguishes a humanist and a courtier strand in literary evasion, perhaps a little too sharply. D. Robin demonstrates how one such courtier poet used his verse as both covert and overt resistance in *Filelfo in Milan*, Princeton, NJ, Princeton University Press, 1991. Such readings have become a staple trope of new historicist criticism. F. Whigham, *Ambition and Privilege: The Social Tropes of Elizabethan Courtesy Theory*, Berkeley, Calif., University of California Press, 1984, argues the importance of 'ordinary' courtier behaviour. By casting his net much wider than usual, A. Fox, *History and Literature in the Reigns of Henry VII and Henry VIII*, Oxford, Basil Blackwell, 1989, contributes to a similar end. His book contributes much to our understanding of the political dimensions of literature, even if there is much room for argument with Fox's intuitive approach and particular interpretations.

On the related problem of 'serious playing' (*serio ludere*) see now W. M. Gordon, *Humanist Play and Belief: The Seriocomic Art of Desiderius Erasmus*, Toronto, University of Toronto Press, 1990. For the universal trope of *vita activa–vita contemplativa*, which figures centrally in 'gardening' and many other kinds of resistance by withdrawal, see B. Vickers, 'Leisure and idleness in the Renaissance: the ambivalence of *otium*', *Renaissance Studies*, 1990, vol. 4, no. 1, pp. 1–37, and no. 2, pp. 107–54, and for the arcadian myth so important to Flaminio and many other resisters, H. Levin, *The Myth of the Golden Age in the Renaissance*, Bloomington, Ind., Indiana University Press, 1969. For the garden as an alternative reality see the work of D. Coffin, *Gardens and Gardening in Papal Rome*, Princeton, NJ, Princeton University Press, 1991, and of his student C. Lazzaro, *The Italian Renaissance Garden*, New Haven, Conn., Yale University Press, 1990. C. Frugoni, *A Distant City: Images of Urban Experience in the Medieval World*, W. McCuaig (trans.), Princeton, NJ, Princeton University Press, 1991, treats its urban foil.

For the Renaissance in Rome, the ambience of many of Pole's satellites, see J. F. D'Amico, *Renaissance Humanism in Papal Rome: Humanists and Churchmen on the Eve of the Reformation*, Baltimore, Md, Johns Hopkins University Press, 1983, and C. Stinger, *The Renaissance in Rome*, Bloomington, Ind., Indiana University Press, 1985. For Venice, see the works cited in the notes for a start.

Literary *personae* have been proven to be a major site of resistance, especially by R. A. Lanham, *The Motives of Eloquence: Literary Rhetoric in the Renaissance*, New Haven, Conn., Yale University Press, 1976, and S. J. Greenblatt, *Renaissance Self-fashioning, from More to Shakespeare*, Chicago, Ill., University of Chicago Press, 1980. Lanham takes a rhetorical approach and Greenblatt a 'serious' one. Drawing on psychoanalytic and anthropological theorists, Greenblatt's book is one of the most important origins of an entire school of literary interpretation, 'new historicism'. If Greenblatt's approach now seems a little too dependent on unexamined residual categories (above all, history), and too much inclined to ignore the surface for the depths, it still reoriented many debates about both Tudor literature and history. For a mediating interpretation, coming a little closer to Lanham, see R. C. Elliott, *The Literary Persona*, Chicago, Ill., University of Chicago Press, 1982, which also surveys the historical roots of the controversy. In a class by itself between the serious and the rhetorical camps is J. Crewe's successful balancing act in his excellent *Trials of Authorship. Anterior Forms and Poetic Reconstruction from Wyatt to Shakespeare*, Berkeley, Calif., University of California Press, 1990.

P. S. Donaldson developed a similar approach to the subject of this chapter in 'Machiavelli and Antichrist: prophetic typology in Reginald Pole's *De unitate* and *Apologia ad Carolum quintum*', in *Machiavelli and Mystery of State*, New York, Cambridge University Press, 1989, pp. 1–36. Donaldson's essay works better as literary analysis than as history or psychology, but it reopens a debate about Thomas Cromwell and Pole through which virtually the whole of both careers and consequently much of the politics and political thought of the first half of the century can be viewed. For a cautious attempt to employ Greenblatt's theory and Donaldson's insights, see T. F. Mayer, 'A mission worse than death: Reginald Pole and the Parisian theologians', *EHR*, 1988, vol. 103, pp. 870–91.

Historians have not yet had much success studying resisting selves with either literary or psychological methods. See most recently S. L. Collins, *From Divine Cosmos to Sovereign State: An Intellectual History of Consciousness and the Idea of Order in Renaissance England*, New York, Oxford University Press, 1989, a methodologically diffuse effort to trace the history of 'the self' in the English Renaissance, further crippled by insufficient support in the sources. C. Taylor, *Sources of the Self: The Making of the Modern Identity*, Cambridge, Mass., Harvard University Press, 1989, is the work of a philosopher and deals more carefully with some of the same problems as Collins, but it has limited relevance to this period, which it probably reads anachronistically.

Part of the problem in dealing with questions of identity and of resistance lies in the difficulties rhetoric poses to most historians. The work of W. Ong, one of the most important historians of early modern rhetoric, J. Seigel, and R. Hariman (for method, if not content) demonstrate the gain from paying a good deal more careful attention to Tudor rhetoric. W. Ong, especially *Orality and Literacy: The Technologizing of the Word*, London, Methuen, 1982, is indispensable. J. D. Seigel, *Rhetoric and Philosophy in Renaissance Humanism: The Union of Eloquence and Wisdom, Petrarch to Valla*, Princeton, NJ, Princeton University Press, 1968; R. Hariman, 'Decorum, power and the courtly style', *Quarterly Journal of Speech*, 1992, vol. 78, no. 2, pp. 149–72; 'Completing Machiavelli', *Journal of the History of Ideas*, 1989, vol. 50, pp. 3–29; and 'Political style in Cicero's letters to Atticus', *Rhetorica*, 1989, vol. 7, pp. 145–58, should also be consulted.

One of the favourite forms of humanist rhetoric, and one of the best modes of resistance, is the dialogue. See K. J. Wilson, *Incomplete Fictions: The Formation of English Renaissance Dialogue*, Washington, DC, Catholic University of America Press, 1985. Wilson's discussion can make heavy sledding and is frustratingly incomplete, but still must be consulted along with the pioneering counter-argument of Roger Deakins, 'The Tudor prose dialogue: genre and anti-genre', *Studies in English Literature, 1500–1800*, 1980, vol. 20, pp. 5–23. Deakins is thoroughly familiar with the range of Tudor dialogues. There is also a very large literature on dialogue in various European countries.

SIR THOMAS ELYOT AND THE PROBLEM OF COUNSEL

The foremost obstacle confronting those interested in further study of Sir Thomas Elyot is a paucity of reliable critical editions. H. H. S. Croft's cumbersome two-volume edition of *The Boke named the Governour*, London, C. K. Paul, 1880, identifies many classical and contemporary allusions together with the major passages deleted in later editions, but its notation of variants is not comprehensive and the now sorely out-of-date commentary seldom includes references to Elyot's other writings. E. J. Howard published a limited number of page-for-page reprints of two of Elyot's works, *The Defence of Good Women* and *Of the Knowledge Which Maketh a Wise Man*, both Oxford, Ohio, Anchor Press, 1940 and 1946; each has an index and a full list of variants but no further critical apparatus. L. Gottesman's edition of *Four Political Treatises by Sir Thomas Elyot*, Gainesville, Fla, Scholars' Facsimiles and Reprints, 1967, contains facsimiles of *The Doctrinal of Princes* (2nd edn), *Pasquil the Playne*, *The Banquette of Sapience* and *The Image of Governance*; the *Doctrinal* text is erroneously presented as the first edition, and the 'Table' to the *Image* has been silently transposed from the front of the text to its conclusion. The final revised form of *The Castel of Helthe*, 1541 quarto, *STC*[2] 7644 is also available in facsimile, Delmar, Scholars' Facsimiles and Reprints,

1936, as is the 1538 edition of Elyot's *Dictionary*, Menston, Scolar Press, 1970.

The best published biography of Elyot, despite some infirmities of age, remains S. Lehmberg, *Sir Thomas Elyot: Tudor Humanist*, Austin, Tex., University of Texas Press, 1960. P. Hogrefe, *The Life and Times of Sir Thomas Elyot, Englishman*, Ames, Ia., Iowa State University Press, 1967, challenges some of Lehmberg's views and often adds greater detail, if not always insight. K. J. Wilson's edition of 'The letters of Sir Thomas Elyot', *Studies in Philology*, 1976, vol. 73, provides convenient access to the texts of Elyot's dozen surviving letters and all his English prologues, but is not wholly reliable in its dating of his correspondence. For a corrective chronology of Elyot's letters, publications, and public career, see the Appendix to F. W. Conrad's unpublished dissertation, 'A preservative against tyranny: the political theology of Sir Thomas Elyot', Baltimore, Md, Johns Hopkins University, 1988. Of the published studies on Elyot, J. M. Major, *Sir Thomas Elyot and Renaissance Humanism*, Lincoln, Nebr., University of Nebraska Press, 1964, is still helpful, although it seriously exaggerates Elyot's reliance on Plato. A more recent and provoking treatment is A. Fox, 'Sir Thomas Elyot and the humanist dilemma', in A. Fox and J. Guy (eds), *Reassessing the Henrician Age: Humanism, Politics and Reform 1500–1550*, Oxford, Basil Blackwell, 1986, pp. 52–73, which presents an interpretation of *Pasquil the Playne* different from the one argued in this chapter. Fox rightly continues to call attention to the personal dimension of Elyot's dialogue but undervalues both its political significance and literary artistry.

Because Elyot interpreted his own political role and that of his fellow inferior English governors in terms of the *amici principis* of imperial Rome and the *philoi* of Hellenistic monarchs, appreciation of his political thought inescapably requires considerable knowledge of the literature and history of antiquity. Unfortunately, there is no substitute for familiarity with individual texts, especially the Latin and Greek literature of imperial Rome, e.g. the imperial *vitae* of the *Scriptores Historiae Augustae* and the moral essays of Plutarch. Although written for classicists, J. A. Crook, *Consilium Principis: Imperial Councils and Counsellors from Augustus to Diocletian*, Cambridge, Cambridge University Press, 1965, serves as a useful guide to the relevant sources. Tudor Englishmen's knowledge of imperial Roman history was not strictly limited by the extent of their classical reading, however. The Spanish humanist Antonio de Guevara's 1529 biography of the exemplary emperor Marcus Aurelius, for instance, was one of the most popular books of the century; it was translated into English initially by Lord Berners, *STC²* 12436 sqq., and later by Sir Thomas North, *STC²* 12426 sqq. Elyot's exemplary biography, *The Image of Governance Compiled of the Actes of Alexander Seuerus*, London, in off. T. Berthcleti [*sic*], 1541 *STC* 7664, is consciously modelled upon de Guevara's earlier 'mirror for governors'. The first edition of North's translation, entitled *The Dial of Princes*, is available in facsimile, *The English Experience*, 1968, no. 50, and deserves to be as well known as his later translation of Plutarch's *Lives*. Interpretative contexts for the writings of Elyot and de Guevara are supplied by Q. Skinner, *The Foundations of Modern Political Thought*, 2 vols, Cambridge, Cambridge University Press, 1978, and J. A. Fernandez-Santamaria, *The State, War and Peace: Spanish Political Thought in the Renaissance 1516–1559*, Cambridge, Cambridge University Press, 1977.

The emphasis on friendly counsel in Elyot's writings is only one facet of a much broader Tudor friendship. L. J. Mills, *One Soul in Bodies Twain: Friendship in Tudor Literature and Stuart Drama*, Bloomington, Ind., Principia Press, 1937, chronicles comprehensively English literary treatments of the topic from Aelred of Rievaulx to James Shirley but often leaves room for further analysis. G. F. Lytle's able essay, 'Friendship and patronage in renaissance Europe', in F. W. Kent and P. Simons (eds) *Patronage, Art, and Society in Renaissance Italy*, Oxford, Oxford University Press, 1987, pp. 47–61, provides continental contexts for early Tudor ideas about friendship; and Chapter 2 of L. B. Smith, *Treason in Tudor England: Politics and Paranoia*, Princeton, NJ, Princeton University Press, 1986, contains a valuable discussion of Tudor and early Stuart attitudes. M. James, 'English politics and the concept of honour 1485–1642', in *Society, Politics and Culture: Studies in Early Modern England*, Cambridge, Cambridge University Press, 1989, pp. 308–415, anticipates Smith in holding that much of the Tudor concern with friendship is a response to weakening traditional ties of lordship.

PEACE DISCOURSE AND MID-TUDOR FOREIGN POLICY

Tudor intellectual historians have neglected the role of peace in English society by largely accepting a priori an enduring and vital role for the just war, the consequence of which has been an egregious inattention to the literature of peace. As a result, very little research has been attempted on the growing awareness of peace in late medieval and early modern English discourse, much less its place in the political languages of the day. R. P. Adams made a preliminary study nearly half a century ago, 'Pre-renaissance courtly propaganda for peace in English literature', *Papers of the Michigan Academy*, [1946]–1948, vol. 32, pp. 431–46, which eventually led to a broader, more exhaustive work, *The Better Part of Valor: More, Erasmus, Colet, and Vives on Humanism, War, and Peace, 1496–1535*, Seattle, Wash., University of Washington Press, 1962. Adams's contributions are significant for their opening up of such a vital topic, but his singular concentration on humanism limited the parameters of inquiry, and he is not really concerned with linguistic analysis. C. M. C. Crowder, 'Peace and justice around 1400: a sketch', in J. G. Rowe (ed.) *Aspects of*

Late Medieval Government: Essays Presented to J. R. Lander, Toronto, University of Toronto Press, 1986, pp. 53–81, while going further in focusing on the connotations of peace, still is only providing a 'sketch' and·a rather particularized one at that (Bishop Stafford's speech to Parliament in 1433). A number of other historical works should be consulted, for example J. R. Hale, *War and Society in Renaissance Europe, 1450–1620*, Baltimore, Md, Johns Hopkins University Press, 1985, and a collection of pertinent articles, *Renaissance War Studies*, London, Hambledon Press, 1983; C. S. L. Davies, 'The English people and war in the early sixteenth century', in A. C. Duke and C. A. Tamse (eds) *War and Society, Britain and the Netherlands*, vol. VII, The Hague, Martinus Nijhoff, 1977, pp. 1–18; C. T. Allmand, *The Hundred Years War*, Cambridge, Cambridge University Press, 1988; J. Barnie, *War in Medieval English Society: Social Values and the Hundred Years War, 1337–99*, London, Weidenfeld & Nicolson, 1974; and M. Vale, *War and Chivalry: Warfare and Aristocratic Culture in England, France, and Burgundy at the End of the Middle Ages*, Athens, Ga, University of Georgia Press, 1981. Collectively they draw a more expanded context for the military histories of the period, and the roles of literature and ideology are given a place in the overall treatment of warfare. These efforts have contributed to a better understanding of the political and even social forces that led to and operated in times of war, but they have almost entirely neglected the ideational character of peace.

The 'return of literature' in early modern historiography has helped to clarify the place of ideas in both personal life and policy. New approaches to important language paradigms such as humanism and Protestant evangelism can assist historians who seek to fathom the extent to which ideology impinged on behaviour. General studies on the meaning of language include W. J. Ong, *The Presence of the Word: Some Prolegomena for Cultural and Religious History*, New Haven, Conn., Yale University Press, 1967; his more recent *Orality and Literacy: The Technologizing of the Word*, London, Methuen, 1982; W. L. Chafe, *Meaning and the Structure of Language*, Chicago, University of Chicago Press, 1970; and E. L. Eisenstein, *The Printing Revolution in Early Modern Europe*, Cambridge, Cambridge University Press, 1983, especially chs 3 and 6. A useful introduction to the study of discourses in history is J. G. A. Pocock, 'The concept of a language and the *métier d'historien*: some considerations on practice', in A. Pagden (ed.) *The Languages of Political Theory in Early-Modern Europe*, Cambridge, Cambridge University Press, 1987, pp. 19–38. The late medieval relationships between literature and politics, including war, are discussed in J. Coleman, *Medieval Readers and Writers, 1350–1400*, New York, Columbia University Press, 1981, and V. J. Scattergood, *Politics and Poetry in the Fifteenth Century*, London, Blandford Press, 1971.

'Erasmian' pacifism, which informed much of the early modern humanist position on war and peace, has yet to be given its due treatment. Nevertheless J. K. Tracy, *The Politics of Erasmus: A Pacifist Intellectual and his Political Milieu*, Toronto, University of Toronto Press, 1978; P. C. Dust, *Three Renaissance Pacifists: Essays in the Theories of Erasmus, More and Vives*, New York, Peter Lang, 1987; J. A. Fernandez, 'Erasmus on the just war', *JHI*, 1973, vol. 34, pp. 209–26; and J. A. Fernandez-Santamaria, *The State, War and Peace in Spanish Political Thought in the Renaissance, 1516–1559*, Cambridge, Cambridge University Press, 1977, are worth while. The last work, however, especially suffers from the author's inability to separate distinct concepts like the just war, from the magistrate's right to punish lawbreakers, which in this case is used to prove Erasmus' hypocritical or inconsistent pacifism. For the related topic of English humanist rejection of chivalric values and its effect on the decline of the martial spirit, see A. B. Ferguson, *The Chivalric Tradition in Renaissance England*, Washington, DC, Folger Shakespeare Library, 1986.

On the just war traditions, the works of J. T. Johnson, especially *Ideology, Reason, and the Limitation of War: Religious and Secular Concepts, 1200–1740*, Princeton, NJ, Princeton University Press, 1975, and *The Quest for Peace: Three Moral Traditions in Western Cultural History*, Princeton, NJ, Princeton University Press, 1987, are without equal. While one may disagree with Johnson's broad definition of a pacifist (any believer in peace, including Dante) or his insistence on a vibrant *jus ad bellum* tradition throughout western history, his delineation of the questions investigated and of the varieties of just war theory are difficult to challenge. F. Russell, *The Just War in the Middle Ages*, Cambridge, Cambridge University Press, 1975, offers a thorough historical survey of positions taken from ancient times to the Renaissance. See also J. M. Wallace-Hadrill, 'War and peace in the earlier Middle Ages', *TRHS*, 5th ser., 1975, vol. 25, pp. 157–74; R. A. Markus, 'Saint Augustine's views on the "just war" ', in W. J. Sheils (ed.) *The Church and War, Studies in Church History*, vol. 20, London, Basil· Blackwell, 1983; J. D. Tooke, *The Just War in Aquinas and Grotius*, London, Society for Promoting Christian Knowledge, 1965; and L. Walters, 'The just war and the crusade: antithesis or analogies?', *The Monist*, 1973, vol. 57, pp. 584–94.

A number of years ago G. R. Owst published two books on medieval preaching and religious literature which have yet to be rivalled, *Literature and the Pulpit in Medieval England*, 2nd edn, Oxford, Basil Blackwell, 1961, and *Preaching in Medieval England*, Cambridge, Cambridge University Press, 1926, which detail the opinions expressed by clergy on the vital issues of war and peace, among other things. A similar synthesis of Protestant or evangelical thought, taking into account sermons, liturgies and commentaries, has yet to be written. B. Lowe, 'War and the commonwealth in mid-Tudor England', *SCJ*, 1990, vol. 21, pp. 171–91, is a preliminary attempt to delineate some English views of war within the context of Protestant reform aspirations. In D. D. Smeeton, *Lollard Themes in the Reformation Theology of William Tyndale*, Kirksville, Mo., Sixteenth Century Journal Publishers, 1986, we find the only investigation of an English reformer's views on peace, here solely in the context of Tyndale's possible connection with Lollard pacifism. Several works provide some insights into continental Protestant views: W. Balke, *Calvin and the Anabaptist Radicals*, W. Heynen (trans.), Grand Rapids, Mich., William B. Eerdmans, 1981; H. J. Hillerbrand, 'Martin Luther and the bull *Exsurge Domine*', *Theological Studies*, 1969, vol. 30, pp. 108–12; W. F. Bense, 'Paris theologians on war and peace, 1521–1529', *Church History*, 1972, vol. 41, pp. 168–85; and R. Bainton, *Christian Attitudes Toward War and Peace: A Historical Survey and Critical Re-evaluation*, New York, Abingdon Press, 1960.

Finally, on the practice of war and government decision-making, which necessarily took into account the rewards and benefits of peace, there are several efforts to help us see better the relationship between practical politics and ideology (especially in the 1540s), including D. L. Potter, 'Foreign policy in the age of the Reformation: French involvement in the Schmalkaldic War, 1544–1547', *HJ*, 1977, vol. 20, pp. 524–44; S. Gunn, 'The French wars of Henry VIII', in J. Black (ed.) *The Origins of War in Early Modern Europe*, Edinburgh, John Donald, 1987, pp. 28–51; D. Hoak, *The King's Council in the Reign of Edward VI*, Cambridge, Cambridge University Press, 1976; M. L. Bush, *The Government Policy of Protector Somerset*, Montreal, McGill-Queen's University Press, 1975; J. J. Goring, 'Social change and military decline in mid-Tudor England', *History*, 1975, vol. 60, pp. 185–97; and P. S. Crowson, *Tudor Foreign Policy*, New York, St Martin's Press, 1973. Concerning the particular statesmen involved in making policy, besides Bush on Somerset, for Gardiner, G. Redworth, *In Defence of the Church Catholic: The Life of Stephen Gardiner*, Oxford, Basil Blackwell, 1990, has supplemented J. A. Muller, *Stephen Gardiner and the Tudor Reaction*, New York, Macmillan, 1926, repr. Octagon Books, 1970, although the latter still provides the greater depth; and for Paget, S. R. Gammon, *Statesman and Schemer: William, First Lord Paget, Tudor Minister*, Hamden, Conn., Archon Books, 1973, treats the councillor's foreign service competently. Also of particular interest is S. Anglo, *Spectacle, Pageantry and Early Tudor Policy*, Oxford, Clarendon Press, 1969, which describes the peace motif in Court pageants and festivals. Of a theoretical nature, D. R. Kelley, 'Ideas of resistance before Elizabeth', in H. Dubrow and R. Strier (eds) *The Historical Renaissance: New Essays on Tudor and Stuart Literature and Culture*, Chicago, Ill., University of Chicago Press, 1988, pp. 48–76, is most important for its attempt to assess the impact of the Reformation on language and the subsequent redefinition of concepts such as tradition, law, liberty and authority.

SIR THOMAS SMITH AND POLITICAL ECONOMY

Since the early 1960s the life and thought of Sir Thomas Smith have become better known through the scholarship of M. Dewar's carefully researched biography, *Sir Thomas Smith: A Tudor Intellectual in Office*, London, Athlone Press, 1964 and her up-to-date editions of both his major works (see Note 1 of Chapter 5). Thanks to Dewar, it now seems certain that Smith, and not John Hales, wrote *A Discourse of the Commonweal of this Realm of England* (1549). The confusion over its authorship has meant that readers search in vain for a mention of Smith in standard histories of economic thought in which the *Discourse* is usually cited and discussed. Of these commentaries, E. F. Heckscher's classic *Mercantilism*, M. Shapiro (trans.), London, Allen & Unwin, 1934, is one of the most illuminating. The few remarks in T. Hutchinson, *Before Adam Smith: The Emergence of Political Economy, 1662–1776*, Oxford, Basil Blackwell, 1988, place Smith in some historical perspective, as does also D. McNally, *Political Economy and the Rise of Capitalism: A Reinterpretation*, Berkeley, Calif., University of California, 1988. R. H. Tawney and E. Power (eds) *Tudor Economic Documents: Being Select Documents Illustrating the Economic and Social History of Tudor England*, 3 vols, New York, Longmans, Green, 1924, is an invaluable collection.

A. B. Ferguson, *The Articulate Citizen and the English Renaissance*, Durham, NC, Duke University Press, 1965, assesses Smith within the Tudor reform milieu. Guides to Smith's Renaissance contemporaries are Q. Skinner, *The Foundations of Modern Political Thought*, 2 vols, Cambridge, Cambridge University Press, 1978 and in abbreviated form his 'Political philosophy', in C. B. Schmitt (gen. ed.), Q. Skinner and E. Kessler (eds) *The Cambridge History of Renaissance Philosophy*, Cambridge, Cambridge University Press, 1988. See also Q. Skinner, 'The state', in T. Ball, J. Farr and R. L. Hanson (eds) *Political Innovation and Conceptual Change*, Cambridge, Cambridge University Press, 1989. Helpful on these matters are N. Wood, *Cicero's Social and Political Thought*, Berkeley, Calif., University of California Press, 1988, and 'Cicero and the political thought of the early English renaissance', *Modern Language Quarterly*, 1990, vol. 51, pp. 185–207.

Smith's social and political thought, of course, is also firmly embedded in Tudor practice. To be understood and appreciated, therefore, his views must be set in the context of Tudor statecraft. The best introductions to this are J. Guy, *Tudor England*, Oxford, Oxford University Press, 1988, imbued with the most recent scholarship, and G. R. Elton's still valuable *England under the Tudors*, 2nd edn, London, Methuen, 1974. Other broadly conceived volumes deserving attention are C. S. L. Davies, *Peace, Print and Protestantism 1450–1558*, London, Hart-Davis MacGibbon, 1984; P. Williams, *The Tudor Regime*, Oxford, Clarendon Press, 1979; and particularly for social history, J. Youing, *Sixteenth Century England*, London, Allen Lane, 1984.

Because Smith's *Discourse* is the most significant English economic analysis of the century and in view of this chapter's contention that he is the founder of modern political economy and even a 'theorist' of early capitalism, the emergence of capitalism (initially agricultural) in England is fundamental to any appreciation of his ideas. R. H. Tawney's famous study, *The Agrarian Problem in the Sixteenth Century*, London, Longmans, Green, 1912, which launched the scholarly interest in English capitalist agriculture, should be read in the light of subsequent scholarship. A perspicacious introduction to Tudor economics and society with a longer time-span is provided by C. Hill, *Reformation to Industrial Revolution*, New York, Pantheon, 1967; McNally, op. cit., is also useful. And, indispensable for the unique early appearance of English agrarian capitalism are R. Brenner's articles in *Past and Present* and the exchanges they initiated; see this work collected in T. H. Aston and C. H. E. Philpin (eds) *The Brenner Debate: Agrarian Class Structure and Economic Development in Pre-Industrial Europe*, Cambridge, Cambridge University Press, 1985. Some of the impressive contributions to J. Thirsk (ed.) *1500–1640: The Agrarian History of England and Wales*, vol. IV, Cambridge, Cambridge University Press, 1967, are of particular value.

E. Kerridge's four books should be read for their provocative ideas and wealth of information: see *Agricultural Revolution*, London, Allen & Unwin, 1967; *Agrarian Problems in the Sixteenth Century and After*, London, Allen & Unwin, 1969; *The Farmers of Old England*, London, Allen & Unwin, 1973; and *Trade and Banking in Early Modern England*, New York, St Martin's Press, 1988. Also useful for their attention to economic conditions are D. M. Palliser, *Tudor York*, Oxford, Oxford University Press, 1979, and *The Age of Elizabeth: England Under the Later Tudors, 1547–1603*, London, Longman, 1983. Nor should one neglect the magisterial accomplishment of L. Stone, *The Crisis of the Aristocracy, 1558–1641*, Oxford, Clarendon Press, 1965. Although it deals with a later period, some of N. Wood, *John Locke and Agrarian Capitalism*, Berkeley, Calif., University of California Press, 1984, bears on the subject. Those who are not persuaded by these authors should see A. Macfarlane's two challenging books, which argue that the English have been capitalists and individualists since the thirteenth century, *The Origins of English Individualism: The Family, Property and Social Transition*, Oxford, Basil Blackwell, 1978 and *The Culture of Capitalism*, Oxford, Basil Blackwell, 1987.

WILLIAM CECIL AND ECONOMIC POLICY

The last full biography of Sir William Cecil was written by C. Read. A two-volume work, the first volume, *Mr. Secretary Cecil and Queen Elizabeth*, New York, Knopf, 1955, deals with his life until the 1570s. Read does not treat Cecil's intellectual formation in any substantive way. Slightly better, though still tangential, is W. S. Hudson, *The Cambridge Connection and the Elizabethan Settlement of 1559*, Durham, NC, Duke University Press, 1981, which deals with the Cambridge intellectual community from which Cecil came. The high politics of the 1560s are studied by W. MacCaffrey, *The Shaping of the Elizabethan Regime*, Princeton, NJ, Princeton University Press, 1964. A good introduction to the economic and social history of the decade is D. M. Palliser, *The Age of Elizabeth 1547–1603*, London, Longman, 1983.

Intellectual historians have explored the evolution of the concept of usury in Europe in detail. The longest view is taken by B. Nelson, *The Idea of Usury: From Universal Brotherhood to Universal Otherhood*, Chicago, Ill., University of Chicago Press, 1969. A Weberian sociologist, Nelson wrote an important work flawed by a lack of good historical context (for which Nelson is not to be blamed, since the historical research on usury has been spotty). The standard work on the theology of usury is J. T. Noonan, *The Scholastic Analysis of Usury*, Cambridge, Mass., Harvard University Press, 1957. T. F. Divine goes beyond usury as a problem for scholasticism in his *Interest: An Historical and Analytical Study of Economics and Modern Ethics*, Milwaukee, Wis., Marquette University Press, 1959. J. O. Appleby, *Economic Thought and Ideology in Seventeenth-Century Engand*, Princeton, NJ, Princeton University Press, 1981, an important analysis of the distinct literature of economics that emerged in the seventeenth century, gives some attention to usury in chs 3 and 4.

Nevertheless, usury in England has been studied in depth only infrequently. The most recent work is N. L. Jones, *God and the Money-lenders: Usury and Law in Early Modern England*, Oxford, Basil Blackwell, 1989. It explores the mechanics of borrowing and lending, the construction of contracts, the enforcement of the usury law, and the political and intellectual history of the problem. Jones amplifies R. H. Tawney's long introduction to his edition of Thomas Wilson's *A Discourse Upon Usury*, London, G. Bell, 1925, the source from which most general economic histories of England draw their knowledge of moneylending. One of the mysteries of English economic history is why so little research has been devoted to transaction costs in the sixteenth and seventeenth centuries. Jones surveys the legal world in which moneylenders operated, focusing especially on the Exchequer. R. Helmholtz, 'Usury and the medieval English church courts', *Speculum*, 1986, vol. 61, pp. 364–80, surveys the courts spiritual. I. P. Ellis, 'The archbishop and the usurers', *JEccH*, 1970, vol. 21, pp. 33–42, recounts the way Archbishop Sandys used the High Commission to stop usury in York. One legal historian, W. J. Jones, has written about bankruptcy in 'The foundations of English bankruptcy: statutes and commissions in the early modern period', *Transactions of the American Philosophical Society*, 1979, vol. 69, no. 3.

The connections between changing theologies and the rise of capitalism have been explored by a number of scholars since M. Weber, *The Protestant Ethic and the Spirit of Capitalism*, Talcott Parsons (trans.), New York, C. Scribner, 1948. R. H. Tawney maintained that Protestantism did encourage capitalist economic development in *Religion and the Rise of Capitalism*, New York, Harcourt, Brace, 1926; N. L. Jones, op. cit., argues for that connection as well, although on slightly different grounds. For the more general relationship between theology and law, see D. Little's excellent book, *Religion, Order and Law: A Study in Pre-Revolutionary England*, 2nd edn, Chicago, Ill., University of Chicago Press, 1984. In a similar vein, M. Todd, *Christian Humanism and the Puritan Social Order*, Cambridge, Cambridge University Press, 1987, explores the influence of humanism on Protestant concepts of social order and obligation. Both Little and Todd point to the importance of conscience as arbiter between the self and God.

It has been assumed that the impact of religious ideology on parliamentary action was the result of particular pressure groups working for religious reform. N. L. Jones surveyed those links in 'Religion in parliament', in D. M. Dean and N. L. Jones (eds) *The Parliaments of Elizabethan England*, Oxford, Basil Blackwell, 1990, pp. 117–38. For the play of different intellectual positions in parliamentary decision-making, see D. M. Dean and N. L. Jones, 'Representation, ideology and action in the Elizabethan parliaments', ibid., pp. 1–14. A provocative treatment of the way theories of divine law affected views of parliamentary representation is found in E. S. Morgan, *Inventing the People: The Rise of Popular Sovereignty in England and America*, New York, W. W. Norton, 1988, esp. pp. 1–54.

POVERTY, POLICY AND PROVIDENCE

This chapter attempts to broaden the customary view that policy development is best explained as a series of incremental, almost mechanical, responses to new demographic and economic conditions. It brings to the historiography of the Tudor Poor Law recent departures in general explanations of policy development that move beyond narrow empiricism and rely more heavily on 'social science' and even 'humanities' questions and methods. For example, Y. Dror, *Policy Making Under Adversity*, New Brunswick, NJ, Rutgers University Press, 1986, esp. chs 1 and

8, calls for greater emphasis on theory development and historical and comparative perspectives in policy studies. The inherent ideological cant in all policy and the need to distinguish among process and substance, determination and implementation, and explanation and prescription in its formulation is argued persuasively in M. Hill and G. Bramley (eds) *Analysing Social Policy*, Oxford, Basil Blackwell, 1986, Introduction. K. B. Banting, *Poverty, Politics, and Policy: Britain in the 1960s*, London, Macmillan, 1979, emphasizes the importance of 'new information, new ideas and new interpretations of old problems' in policy innovation. M. Rein discusses the role of intellectual 'frames' in the analysis of social problems and the formulation of policy: see his 'Value-critical policy analysis', in D. Callahan and B. Jennings (eds) *Ethics, the Social Sciences, and Policy Analysis*, New York, Plenum, 1983, pp. 83–111. R. E. Goodin, *Reasons for Welfare: The Political Theory of the Welfare State*, Princeton, NJ, Princeton University Press, 1988, mounts a 'residualist' ethical defence of the welfare state against more left-leaning claims for it and in the process establishes the centrality of political theory in policy design and justification.

The study of the Poor Law over long periods of time has been almost exclusively the province of social and political historians with the emphasis on the process of legislative and institutional change. Little or no attention has been directed to the role of ideas or theory in the policy's development. J. F. Pound *Poverty and Vagrancy in Tudor England*, 2nd edn, London, Longman, 1986, embodies this historiography and thus remains unsatisfactory as a complete explanation of the government's poor relief policies. Two older studies are still valuable for their treatment of the poor relief efforts undertaken in the villages and towns; see E. M. Leonard, *The Early History of English Poor Relief*, London, F. Cass, 1965 (repr. 1900), and E. M. Hampson, *The Treatment of Poverty in Cambridgeshire 1597–1834*, Cambridge, Cambridge University Press, 1934. Much the best application of 'new social history' methods to the poverty question is K. Wrightson and D. Levine, *Poverty and Piety in an English Village: Terling, 1525–1700*, New York, Academic Press, 1979: localism and an emerging complexity of social differentiation contributed to a worsening situation for the poor. More recently M. K. McIntosh, 'Local responses to the poor in late medieval and Tudor England', *Continuity and Change*, 1988, vol. 3, pp. 209–45, provides a valuable, geographically broad survey of the poor's treatment in small towns and villages from roughly 1388 to 1601. Two other recent studies also rely mostly on the conventional 'incrementalist' assumptions but point toward a more broadly gauged historiography of policy. A. L. Beier seeks to explain why the Poor Law was implemented most thoroughly after 1620 and finds that the answer cannot be found only in the expanding numbers of poor people: see 'Poverty and progress in early modern England', in A. L. Beier, D. Cannadine and J. M. Rosenheim (eds) *The First Modern Society: Essays in English History in*

Honour of Lawrence Stone, Cambridge, Cambridge University Press, 1989, pp. 201–39. P. Slack, *Poverty and Policy in Tudor and Stuart England*, London, Longman, 1988, offers a 'reappraisal of the early history of the English poor law' around three issues: Tudor definitions of poverty, their relevance to actual social and economic conditions, and England's policy accomplishments in a comparative European context.

The case for ideology in early modern thought is made in different ways by D. R. Kelley, *The Beginnings of Ideology*, Cambridge, Cambridge University Press, 1981, Prologue; Q. Skinner, *The Foundations of Modern Political Thought*, 2 vols, Cambridge, Cambridge University Press, 1978, I, Preface; and J. O. Appleby, *Economic Thought and Ideology in Seventeenth-Century England*, Princeton, NJ, Princeton University Press, 1978, ch. 1. The work of the Frankfurt School theorists, Theodor Adorno, Max Horkheimer, Herbert Marcuse and Jürgen Habermas, is often very dense and best approached initially through one of the numerous competent summaries that are available. See, for example, R. Geuss, *The Idea of a Critical Theory*, Cambridge, Cambridge University Press, 1981; M. Poster, *Critical Theory and Poststructuralism: In Search of Context*, Ithaca, NY, Cornell University Press, 1989; and Z. Tar, *The Frankfurt School: The Critical Theory of Max Horkheimer and Theodor W. Adorno*, New York, Wiley, 1977.

The attempts that have been made thus far to understand the role of political thought in the policy-making process have generally been confined to the Henrician legislative programme of the mid-1530s, the Edwardian years, the 1560s–70s and 1590s. See the Introduction, as well as the notes to Chapter 7, for the relevant historiography; only a few additional works will be mentioned here. A central question in the study of all these policy environments has been the degree to which humanism, Protestantism or maxims of political economy were shaping the perception of social problems and the formulation of policy remedies. B. Bradshaw probably offers the most circumspect thesis on the earlier part of the century in 'The Tudor commonwealth: reform and revision', *HJ*, 1979, vol. 22, pp. 455–76; he maintains that Christian humanism was most influential in the 1530s but gave way to Protestantism during the Edwardian years. Increasingly Edward's reign is being seen as a transition from the Henrician to the Elizabethan policy climate. G. R. Elton emphasizes Sir Thomas Smith's role in that process in 'Reformation and the "commonwealth-men" of Edward VI's reign', in P. Clark, A. G. R. Smith and N. Tyacke (eds) *The English Commonwealth 1547–1640*, Leicester, Leicester University Press, 1979, pp. 23–38. P. Slack, 'Social policy and the constraints of government, 1547–58', in *The Mid-Tudor Polity, c. 1540–1560*, J. Loach and R. Tittler (eds), London, Macmillan, 1980, pp. 94–115, agrees on the linkage provided by the Edwardian policy thinkers (not necessarily Smith, however), although he sees Christian humanism as an important stimulant to Edwardian reform.

Much of the emphasis in Elizabethan studies of poverty policy has been on the dimensions of and responses to vagrancy. See, for example, A. L. Beier, 'Vagrants and the social order in Elizabethan England', *P&P*, 1964, vol. 64, pp. 3–29; *Masterless Men: The Vagrancy Problem in England*, London, Methuen, 1985; and *The Problem of the Poor in Tudor and Early Stuart England*, London, Methuen, 1983. Several essays in P. Clark and P. Slack (eds) *Crisis and Order in English Towns 1500–1700*, London, Routledge & Kegan Paul, 1972, are useful on vagrancy and local poor relief. Slack suggests that Protestantism was an important influence on Elizabethan legislation in 'Poverty and social regulation in Elizabethan England', in C. Haigh (ed.) *The Reign of Elizabeth I*, Basingstoke, Macmillan, 1984, pp. 221–41. His 'Books of orders: the making of English social policy, 1577–1631', *TRHS*, 5th ser., 1980, vol. 30, pp. 1–22, clarifies the efforts of the Privy Council to achieve compliance with the government's vagrancy and poverty relief statutes.

Policy is viewed in this chapter as a complicated historical phenomenon, the result of a dialogue on some level among ideas, statecraft and social conditions. For this theory–praxis dimension in sixteenth-century policy, see L. Stone, 'State control in sixteenth-century England', *EHR*, 1947, vol. 17, p. 110; and Slack, 1980, op. cit., pp. 114–15. Suggestive for understanding the unfolding of policy discourses is J. G. A. Pocock's point that the historicity of political thought results from tension between *langue*, a 'language's' established usage, and *parole*, a speech act reflecting new conditions; see 'Introduction: the state of the art', in Pocock, *Virtue, Commerce, and History*, Cambridge, Cambridge University Press, 1985.

A useful introduction to classical and Christian conceptual vocabularies of philanthropy, poverty and charity, some of which were recapitulated in the sixteenth century, is A. R. Hands, *Charities and Social Aid in Greece and Rome*, London, Thames & Hudson, 1968. Shaky as its monetary estimates have become, W. K. Jordan, *Philanthropy in England 1480–1660*, London, Allen & Unwin, 1959, and its two companion volumes, must still be used in parallel to the study of public poor relief. B. Tierney, *Medieval Poor Law*, Berkeley, Calif., University of California Press, 1959, is essential for the medieval church's teachings on poverty and charity and for the canon law prologue to Tudor parish-centred legislation on poor relief.

For continental comparisons to perceptions of poverty and policy developments in early modern England, see N. Z. Davis, 'Poor relief and heresy: the case of Lyon', *Studies in Medieval and Renaissance History*, 1986, vol. 5, pp. 217–75; K. Norberg, *Rich and Poor in Grenoble, 1600–1814*, Berkeley, Calif., University of California Press, 1985; B. B. Davis, 'Poverty and poor relief in sixteenth-century Toulouse', *Historical*

Reflections/Réflexions Historiques, 1991, vol. 17, pp. 267–96; B. Pullan, *Rich and Poor in Renaissance Venice*, Cambridge, Mass., Harvard University Press, 1971; J. E. Olson, *Calvin and Social Welfare: Deacons and the Bourse Française*, Selinsgrove, Pa, Susquehanna University Press, 1989; and H. J. Grimm, 'Luther's contributions to sixteenth-century organization of poor relief', *Archiv für Reformationsgeschichte*, 1970, vol. 61, pp. 222–34.

THE TUDOR STATE, REFORMATION AND CHANGE

An array of important studies provides theoretical and comparative contexts for the examination in Chapter 8 of the unsuitability of a 'modernist' theory of state to the facts and events of Tudor government and its search for alternative vocabularies of interpretation.

A good introduction to elite landed groups is J. Powis, *Aristocracy*, Oxford, Basil Blackwell, 1984. On power rooted in the law of real property see J. R. Pennock and J. W. Chapman, *Property*, a special issue of *Nomos*, 1980, vol. 22. For the importance of theory in Tudor political understanding, consult R. Eccleshall, *Order and Reason in Politics: Theories of Absolute and Limited Monarchy in Early Modern England*, Oxford, Oxford University Press, 1978, and F. L. Baumer, *The Early Tudor Theory of Kingship*, New Haven, Conn., Yale University Press, 1940. The classic work on political theology, which does shed light on Tudor thought, is E. W. Kantorowicz, *The King's Two Bodies: A Study of Medieval Political Theory*, Princeton, NJ, Princeton University Press, 1957; see also its extension, M. Axton, *The Queen's Two Bodies: Drama and the Elizabethan Succession*, London, Royal Historical Society, 1980. R. A. Nisbet, *Social Change and History*, Oxford, Oxford University Press, 1969, examines the metaphor of 'development' in understanding change. Weber grasped the implication for 'progress' in the concept; see R. Bendix and G. Roth, *Scholarship and Partisanship: Essays on Max Weber*, Berkeley, Calif., University of California Press, 1971, and also A. Giddens, *Politics and Sociology in the Thought of Max Weber*, London, Methuen, 1974. M. J. Mommsen, *The Age of Bureaucracy: Perspectives on the Political Thought of Max Weber*, New York, Harper & Row, 1974, is fundamental.

The notion that in sixteenth-century England a modern sovereign state came into being incorporates Victorian metaphors of progress and derives from their consolidation in A. F. Pollard, *Factors in Modern History*, London, Constable, 1907. The Introduction and Chapter 8's notes provide a basic guide to the theses of G. R. Elton and the works of revisionists, but it is essential to go beyond his major books to the dozens of articles, essays and reviews in Elton's collection, *Studies in Tudor and Stuart Politics and Government*, 3 vols, Cambridge, Cambridge University Press, 1974–1983. The place of evolutionary metaphors in his work is examined by A. J. Slavin, 'Telling the story: G. R. Elton and the Tudor age', *SCJ*,

1990, vol. 21, pp. 151–9. See also B. L. Beer, 'G. R. Elton: Tudor champion', in *Recent Historians of Great Britain: Essays on the post-1945 Generation*, Ames, Ia, Iowa State University Press, 1990, pp. 12–35. J. Guy, *Tudor England*, Oxford, Oxford University Press, 1988, is the most comprehensive synthesis of the Tudor years based on revisionist historiography.

It is clear that the 'modernists' join to the triumph of the royally inspired Reformation the consolidation of the sovereign nation state, on the lines of Pollard's argument. J. H. Hexter, 'Factors in modern history', in *Reappraisals in History*, Evanston, Ill., Northwestern University Press, 1961, subjected this conjunction to criticism. He argued, as Chapter 8 does from a different angle, that excessive focus on the state blurs perspective on a whole series of essential polarities: Court–country, town–hinterland, power–legitimacy, *gubernaculum–jurisdictio*, realm–province and dynasty-region. By a curious irony, this same blurring is native to the neo-Marxist theory of the strong 'core states' (e.g. England and France) shaped in the sixteenth century against the backdrop of the 'time of troubles' in the fifteenth. See I. Wallerstein, *The Modern World System*, New York, Academic Press, 1974, pp. 132–63, 224–99. He stresses the resolution of the 'feudal crisis' by bureaucratization, monopoly of violence, creation of legitimacy and homogenization of the subject people in the nation.

This chapter seeks to demonstrate that none of these was in fact an achievement of the Tudor monarchy. Whether European states fit the model is also now more than doubtful. The question was surveyed in A. J. Slavin (ed.) *The 'New Monarchies' and Representative Assemblies*, Boston, Mass., D. C. Heath, 1964; in the years since then there have been advances in our understanding of theories of absolutism and the actual politics of the centralizing states. See especially Q. Skinner, *The Foundations of Modern Political Thought*, 2 vols, Cambridge, Cambridge University Press, 1978, which may be read with profit in conjunction with Q. Skinner (ed.) *The Return of Grand Theory to the Human Sciences*, Cambridge, Cambridge University Press, 1985. See also P. Zagorin, *Rebels and Rulers, 1500–1640*, 2 vols, Cambridge, Cambridge University Press, 1982, for England; a comparative perspective is offered in C. Tilly (ed.) *The Formation of National States in Western Europe*, Princeton, NJ, Princeton University Press, 1975.

If it is objected that large comparative studies are deficient from the point of view of archival study and documentary positivism, I refer readers to the close studies based on the most scrupulous documentary work in single states which tend to support the conclusions in this chapter for England. For example, see G. Strauss, *Law, Resistance, and the State: The Opposition to Roman Law in Reformation Germany*, Princeton, NJ, Princeton University Press, 1986; J. R. Major, *Representative Institutions in Renaissance France, 1421–1559*, Madison, Wis., University of Wisconsin

Press, 1960; J. H. Salmon, *Society in Crisis: France in the Sixteenth Century*, New York, Oxford University Press, 1975; K. B. Neuschel, *Word of Honor: Interpreting Noble Culture*, Ithaca, NY, Cornell University Press, 1989; and B. B. Diefendorf, *Paris City Councillors in the Sixteenth Century: The Politics of Patrimony*, Princeton, NJ, Princeton University Press, 1983. These studies demonstrate opposition to the absolutist tendencies of Roman law, the vitality of provincial parliaments, the ability of the nobility to maintain multiple centres of power, loyalty and patronage in the face of a centralizing monarchy, and even more remarkably, that the elite Paris magistrates, eager for ennoblement, and under the very eye of the monarchy, maintained ideas of hierarchy without surrendering to the claims of the monarchy itself.

Nor do Austinian ideas of the modern sovereign state square well with the evidence. Because events and meaning never run together, interpretation intervenes, and the next step should be to integrate into documentary studies such frameworks of understanding as may be found in B. Jessop, *Social Order, Reform, and Revolution*, New York, Macmillan, 1972, or L. Kramnick, 'Reflections on revolution: definition and explanation in recent scholarship', *History and Theory*, 1972, vol. 2, pp. 26–63, and M. J. Mommsen, *Max Weber: Gesellschaft, Politik, und Geschichte*, Frankfurt am Main, Suhrkampf, 1972.

Index

classical 13, 109, 113, 212; Italian 4,
  54; Tudor 75
humanitarianism 13, 109
Hundred Years War 13, 22, 108–9, 110,
  129, 130

ideology 7, 8, 12, 19
idiota 63
individualism 158–9, 161
inflation 142, 149–51, 170, 207
intellectual biography 4
intentionality 7, 14, 178; *see also* human
  agency
interest, common 156; self- or private
  145–6, 156, 161, 172
interest rates *see* usury
Ipswich 208
Ireland 227
Isham, John 171
Isocrates 88

James, M. E. 240
James I (king of England; James VI of
  Scotland) 28, 35–6, 38, 39, 243–4
Jewel, John (bishop) 174, 180
John (king of England) 236
Johnson, Samuel 14
Jones, Norman L. 13
Jones, Whitney R. D. 5
Jonson, Ben, *Discoveries* 75; *Sejanus his
  Fall* 26
Jordan, W. K. 5
just war 13, 112
justification 209

Katharine of Aragon (queen of
  England) 31, 55, 93
Kelley, Donald R. 194
Kett's Rebellion 26, 30, 142, 206, 215
Knolles, Richard 34
Kuhn, Thomas 8

labourers 172
LaCapra, Dominick 10–11
Lake, Peter 6, 212
Lampsonius, Dominic 53
Lampridio, Benedetto 66
Langland, William 196, 205
Lanham, Richard A. 9–10, 67–8
Laslett, Peter 6, 7
Latimer, Hugh 5, 205
law 147

Leo X (pope) 50
Leonico, Niccolò 54
Lever, Thomas 205
levies, arbitrary: Henry VIII 232;
  Charles I and II 232–3
Levy, F. J. 10
'Libell of Englische Policye' 5, 111, 152
Lilly, William 25
Lipsius, Justus 37
literary historicism 10
Loach, Jennifer 3
Locke, John 162; *Two Treatises* 7
locus amoenus 52
Logan, George 197–8
Lollards, Lollardy 196, 205, 233
London 31, 208
Longland, John (bishop) 98, 99
Longolius, Christophorus 53, 54
Lovelace, Sergeant 189
Lowe, Ben 13
Lupset, Thomas 5, 52, 55
Lupton, Thomas 176
Luther, Martin 179, 183–4; poor relief
  plan for Leisnech 200
Lutheranism 13, 199–201
Lydgate, John 108, 111, 122
Lyly, John 36

Machiavelli, Niccolò 23, 65, 84, 128,
  140, 147, 149, 157, 160
McConica, James K. 4
magistrates *see* counsellors
Maitland, Frederic 155
Malynes, Gerrard de 154
Mantova, Marco 58, 65–6
Margaret (queen of England) 27
Margaret of Parma 170–1
Marius Maximus 77, 82
Marshall, William 215; poor relief plan
  202
Marsiglio of Padua 2
Marlowe, Christopher, *Edward II* 37,
  90
Marx, Karl 10, 162
Mary (Stuart; queen of Scotland) 36
Mary I (queen of England) 25, 30, 32,
  33, 36, 233
Mauss, Marcel 228
Mayer, T. F. 4, 12, 204
Mela, Pomponius 144
Menander 187
Merlin 20

Scripture on 178, 182–3; secular opposition to 188; Tübingen School on 178
utilitarianism 147–8
Utrecht, treaty of 121, 123
Unwin, George 140

vagabonds, vagrants 171, 213
Valla, Lorenzo 24
Vegetius 144
Venice 55
Vergil, Polydore 21, 37; *Anglica Historia* 22
Vida, Marco Gerolamo (bishop) 50; *Dialogues on the dignity of the republic* 50–1; *Christiad* 51
Vincent of Ferrer 23
Vitruvius 144
Vives, Juan Luis 112, 113, 115, 140, 149, 196, 208, 212; poor relief plan for Bruges 198

Waad, Armigal 170
Walsingham, Sir Francis 211
war 125
Ward, Robert 24
Warham, William (archbishop) 233
Wars of the Roses 31–2
Warwick 211
Weber, Max 9, 58, 162, 225, 228–31, 235, 244
Westminster, as center of domestic diplomacy 242

Western Rebellion 142
Whigs 1–2
White, Hayden 10
William I (king of England) 21, 37, 39
William of Ockham 2
Wilson, Thomas 4, 159, 161, 173, 174, 180, 181–2, 186
Wolsey, Thomas (cardinal; lord chancellor) 3, 4, 54, 85, 92, 98, 201, 232
Wood, Neal 13
Wooley, Sir John 182–3
Woolf, D. R. 12
workhouses 214, 215
works 199, 200–1
Wrightson, Keith 6
Wriothesley, Charles 24
Wriothesley, Sir Thomas (lord chancellor) 24, 123, 234
Wroth, Sir Robert 214
Wyatt, Sir Thomas 90
Wyatt's Rebellion 34
Wyclif, John 2, 24, 108, 110, 115, 126–7, 196, 205

York 31, 208, 211
York Minster 20
Yorkist historical tradition 22
Young, John 173, 176, 180

Zeeveld, W. Gordon 4